Contents at a Glance

C++ Recipes

A Problem-Solution Approach

Bruce Sutherland

Apress®

C++ Recipes: A Problem-Solution Approach

ISBN-13 (pbk): 978-1-4842-0158-9

ISBN-13 (electronic): 978-1-4842-0157-2

Managing Director: Welmoed Spahr
Lead Editor: Steve Anglin
Technical Reviewers: Onur Cinar, Michael Thomas, and Rohan Walia
Editorial Board: Steve Anglin, Louise Corrigan, Jonathan Gennick, Robert Hutchinson,
    Michelle Lowman, James Markham, Susan McDermott, Matthew Moodie, Jeffrey Pepper,
    Douglas Pundick, Ben Renow-Clarke, Gwenan Spearing, Steve Weiss
Coordinating Editor: Mark Powers
Copy Editor: Tiffany Taylor
Compositor: SPi Global
Indexer: SPi Global
Artist: SPi Global
Cover Designer: Anna Ishchenko

Distributed to the book trade worldwide by Springer Science+Business Media New York,
233 Spring Street, 6th Floor, New York, NY 10013. Phone 1-800-SPRINGER, fax (201) 348-4505, e-mail orders-ny@springer-sbm.com, or visit www.springeronline.com. Apress Media, LLC is a California LLC and the sole member (owner) is Springer Science + Business Media Finance Inc (SSBM Finance Inc). SSBM Finance Inc is a Delaware corporation.

For information on translations, please e-mail rights@apress.com, or visit www.apress.com.

Apress and friends of ED books may be purchased in bulk for academic, corporate, or promotional use. eBook versions and licenses are also available for most titles. For more information, reference our Special Bulk Sales–eBook Licensing web page at www.apress.com/bulk-sales.

Any source code or other supplementary material referenced by the author in this text is available to readers at www.apress.com/9781484201589. For detailed information about how to locate your book's source code, go to www.apress.com/source-code/.

Contents

About the Author

Bruce Sutherland is a video game developer working at Firemonkeys Studios in Melbourne, Australia. He is currently working on iOS and Android titles written in C++ for both platforms. Bruce has worked on *Real Racing 3, Need for Speed: No Limits, the Dead Space series*, and *The Elder Scrolls: Oblivion*, among others, in his nine-year video game development career.

About the Technical Reviewers

Onur Cinar is the author of *Android Apps with Eclipse* and *Pro Android C++ with the NDK*, and the co-author of *Android Best Practices*. He has more than 19 years of experience in the design, development, and management of large-scale, complex software projects, primarily in the mobile and telecommunication space. His expertise spans VoIP, video communication, mobile applications, grid computing, and networking technologies on diverse platforms. He has been actively working with the Android platform since its beginning. He has a B.S. in Computer Science from Drexel University in Philadelphia, PA. He is currently working at the Skype division of Microsoft as the principal development manager responsible for the Skype Qik, GroupMe, Skype for Android, and Lync for Android products.

Michael Thomas has worked in software development for more than 20 years as an individual contributor, team lead, program manager, and vice president of engineering. Michael has more than 10 years of experience working with mobile devices. His current focus is in the medical sector, using mobile devices to accelerate information transfer between patients and health care providers.

Rohan Walia is a senior software consultant with extensive experience in client/server, web-based, and enterprise application development. He is an Oracle Certified ADF Implementation Specialist and a Sun Certified Java Programmer. Rohan is responsible for designing and developing end-to-end applications consisting of various cutting-edge frameworks and utilities. His areas of expertise are Oracle ADF, Oracle WebCenter, Fusion, Spring, Hibernate, and Java/J2EE. When he's not working, Rohan loves to play tennis, hike, and travel. Rohan would like to thank his wife, Deepika Walia, for using all her experience and expertise when reviewing this book.

Acknowledgments

I'd like to thank the many people who helped me make this book become a reality. A special thank you to my wife, who continues to support me through the long hours involved in making games and writing books.

Thanks to the entire editorial team at Apress, especially Mark Powers, who had to contend with many delays while I juggled game-development and book-writing commitments.

And thank you to the technical review team, who did an excellent job of making sure the source contained in this book is as error-free and up to date as possible.

Introduction

The C++ programming language is undergoing continuous development and improvement. This effort to keep C++ on the cutting edge of language features is driven by the fact that C++ still finds an important role to play in high-performance, portable applications. Few other languages can be used on as many platforms as C++ and without having a runtime environment dependency. This is partly thanks to the nature of C++ as a compiled programming language. C++ programs are built into application binaries through a combination of processes that include compiling and linking.

Compiler choice is particularly important in today's C++ landscape, thanks to the rate at which the language is changing. Development of the C++ programming language was started by Bjarne Stoustrup in 1979, when it was called C with Classes. The language didn't see formal standardization until 1998; an updated standard was published in 2003. There was another gap of eight years until the standard was updated again with the introduction of C++11 in 2011. This version brought a considerable number of updates to the C++ programming language and is distinguished from "older" C++ with the Modern C++ moniker. A further, less significant, update to the C++ standard was introduced in late 2014, but we haven't yet begun to see compilers that support many of the features added to Modern C++.

This book introduces you to code written specifically for the C++14 standard using the Clang compiler. Clang is an open source compiler that started life as a closed source Apple project. Apple released the code to the open source community in 2007, and the compiler has been adding strengths ever since. This book explains how to install and use Clang on a computer running OS X, Windows, or Linux (Ubuntu). The examples that accompany each chapter have been compiled and tested using Clang 3.5. I chose Clang for this project because it's the compiler that provided support for the most C++14 features when I began to write this book.

The book's accompanying web site can be accessed at www.apress.com/9781484201589. You can find source code for all of the executable code listings contained in this book along with makefiles that can be used to build running programs.

CHAPTER 1

■ ■ ■

Beginning C++

The C++ programming language is a powerful low-level language that allows you to write programs that are compiled into machine instructions to be executed on a computer's processor. This makes C++ different from newer languages such as C# and Java. These languages are interpreted languages. This means they are not executed directly on the processor but instead are sent to another program that is responsible for operating the computer. Java programs are executed using the Java virtual machine (JVM), and C# programs are executed by the Common Language Runtime (CLR).

Thanks to C++ being a language that is compiled ahead of time, it still finds wide use in fields where absolute performance is paramount. The most obvious area where C++ is still the most predominantly used programming language is the video game industry. C++ allows programmers to write applications that take full advantage of the underlying system architecture. You might become familiar with phrases such as *cache coherency* while pursuing a career as a C++ programmer. There aren't many other languages that allow you to optimize your applications to suit the individual processors that your program is being designed to run on. This book introduces you to some of the pitfalls that can affect the performance of your applications at different times and shows you some techniques to tackle those issues.

Modern C++ is in a period where the language is seeing continual updates to its features. This has not always been the case. Despite being around since the early 1980s the C++ programming language was only standardized in 1998. A minor update and clarification of this standard was released in 2003 and is known as C++03. The 2003 update did not add any new features to the language however it did clarify some of the existing features that had gone overlooked. One of these was an update to the standard for the STL vector template to specify that the members of a vector should be stored contiguously in memory. The C++11 standard was released in 2011 and saw a massive update to the C++ programming language. C++ gained features for generalized type deduction system outside of templates, lambda and closure support, a built-in concurrency library and many more features. C++14 brings a smaller update to the language and generally builds upon the features already supplied by C++14. Features such as auto return type deduction from functions have been cleaned up, lambdas have been updated with new features and there are some new ways to define properly typed literal values.

This book strives to write portable, standards compliant C++14 code. At the time of writing it's possible to write C++14 code on Windows, Linux and OS X machines so long as you use a compiler that provides all of the language features. To this end, this book will use Clang as the compiler on Windows and Ubuntu and will use Xcode on OS X. The rest of this chapter focuses on the software you need to write programs in C++ before showing you how to acquire some of the more common options available for Windows, OS X, and Linux operating systems.

Recipe 1-1. Finding a Text Editor

Problem

C++ programs are constructed from lots of different source files that must be created and edited by one or more programmers. Source files are simply text files, which usually come in two different types: header files and source files. Header files are used to share information about your types and classes between different files, and source files are generally used to contain the methods and the actual executable code that makes up your program.

Solution

A text editor then becomes the first major piece of software you require to begin writing C++ programs. There are many excellent choices of text editors available on different platforms. My best two picks at the moment are the free Notepad++ for Windows and Sublime Text 2, which despite not being free is available on all major operating systems. Figure 1-1 shows a screenshot from Sublime Text 2. Vim and gvim are also very good options that are available for all three operating systems. These editors provide many powerful features and are excellent choices for someone willing to learn.

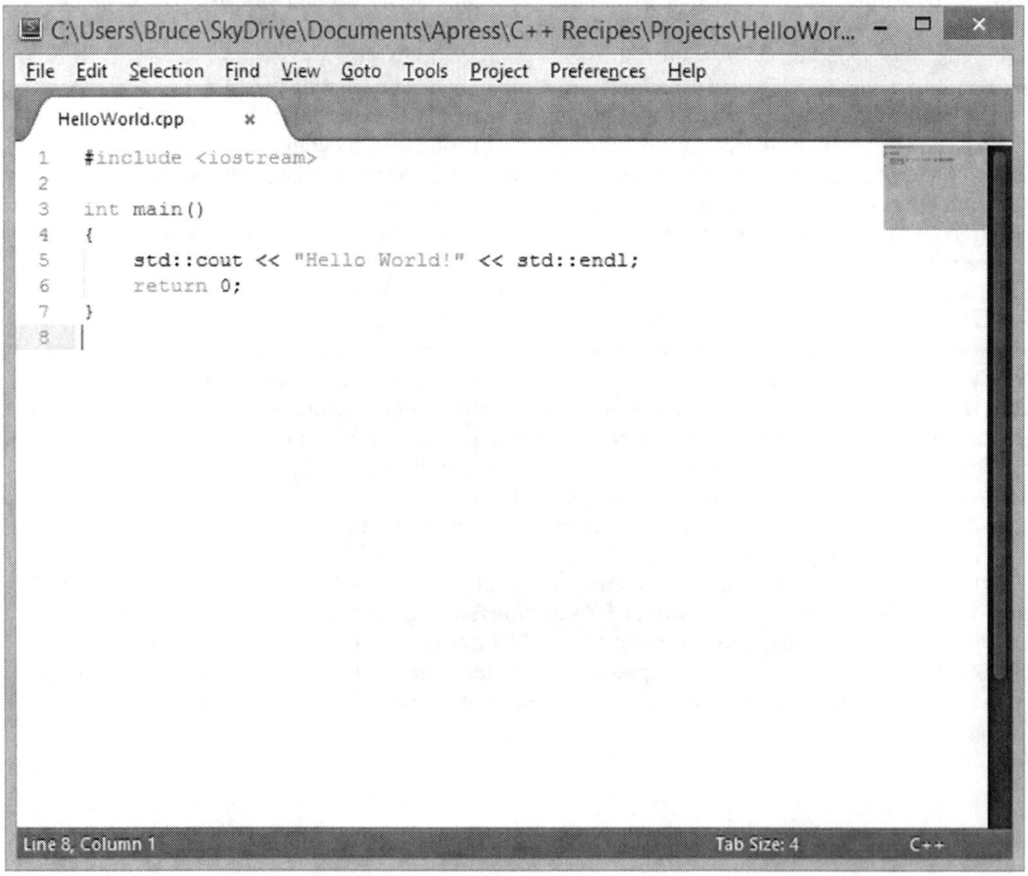

Figure 1-1. A screenshot from the Sublime Text 2 Editor

▒ **Note** Don't feel the urge to grab a text editor straight away. Some of the recipes later in this chapter cover integrated development environments (IDEs) that include all the software you need to write, build, and debug C++ applications.

Figure 1-1 shows one of the most important features of a good text editor: it should be able to highlight the different types of keywords in your source code. You can see in the simple Hello World program in Figure 1-1 that Sublime Text 2 is capable of highlighting the C++ keywords include, int, and return. It has also added different-colored highlights to the main function name and the strings <iostream> and "Hello World!". Once you have some experience writing code with your text editor of choice, you will become adept at scanning your source files to zero in on the area of code you are interested in, and syntax highlighting will be a major factor in this process.

Recipe 1-2. Installing Clang on Ubuntu

Problem

You would like to build C++ programs that support the latest C++14 language features on a computer system running Ubuntu.

Solution

The Clang compiler supports all of the latest C++14 language features and the libstdc++ library supports all of the C++14 STL features.

How It Works

The Ubuntu operating system comes configured with package repositories that allow you to install Clang without much difficulty. You can achieve this using the apt-get command in a Terminal window. Figure 1-2 shows the command that you should enter to install Clang.

Figure 1-2. An Ubuntu Terminal window showing the command needed to install Clang

To install Clang you can enter the following command on the command line sudo apt-get install clang. Running this command will cause Ubuntu to query its repositories and work out all of the dependencies needed to install Clang. You will be prompted once this process has been completed to confirm that you wish to install Clang and its dependencies. You can see this prompt in Figure 1-3.

```
⊗ ⊖ ⊡  bruce@bruce-Virtual-Machine: ~
bruce@bruce-Virtual-Machine:~$ sudo apt-get install clang
[sudo] password for bruce:
Reading package lists... Done
Building dependency tree
Reading state information... Done
The following extra packages will be installed:
  binfmt-support clang-3.5 libclang-common-3.5-dev libclang1-3.5 libffi-dev
  libobjc-4.9-dev libobjc4 libtinfo-dev llvm-3.5 llvm-3.5-dev llvm-3.5-runtime
Suggested packages:
  gnustep gnustep-devel clang-3.5-doc llvm-3.5-doc
The following NEW packages will be installed:
  binfmt-support clang clang-3.5 libclang-common-3.5-dev libclang1-3.5
  libffi-dev libobjc-4.9-dev libobjc4 libtinfo-dev llvm-3.5 llvm-3.5-dev
  llvm-3.5-runtime
0 to upgrade, 12 to newly install, 0 to remove and 208 not to upgrade.
Need to get 39.5 MB of archives.
After this operation, 196 MB of additional disk space will be used.
Do you want to continue? [Y/n] ▊
```

Figure 1-3. *The apt-get dependency confirmation prompt*

At this point you can hit enter to continue as yes is the default option. Ubuntu will then download and install all of the software needed for you to be able to install Clang on your computer. You can confirm that this has been successful by running the clang command. Figure 1-4 shows what this should look like if everything was successful.

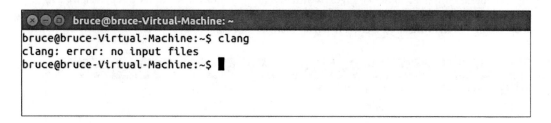

```
⊗ ⊖ ⊡  bruce@bruce-Virtual-Machine: ~
bruce@bruce-Virtual-Machine:~$ clang
clang: error: no input files
bruce@bruce-Virtual-Machine:~$ ▊
```

Figure 1-4. *A successful Clang installation in Ubuntu*

Recipe 1-3. Installing Clang on Windows

Problem

You would like to build C++14 based programs on the Windows operating system.

Solution

You can use Cygwin for Windows to install Clang and build applications.

How It Works

Cygwin provides a Unix-like command line environment for Windows computers. This is ideal for building programs using Clang as the Cygwin installed comes pre-configured with package repositories that include everything you need to install and use Clang on Windows computers.

You can get a Cygwin installer executable from the Cygwin website at http://www.cygwin.com. Be sure to download the 32bit version of the Cygwin installer as the default packages supplied by Cygwin currently only work with the 32bit environment.

Once you have downloaded the installer you should run it and click through until you are presented with the list of packages to install. At this point you want to select the Clang, make and libstdc++ packages. Figure 1-5 shows the Cygwin installer with the Clang package selected.

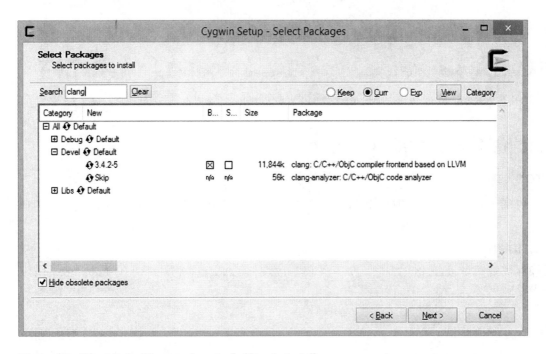

Figure 1-5. *Filtering the Clang package in the Cygwin installer*

Packages can be marked for installation in the installer by clicking on the Skip area on the line for the package. Clicking skip once moves the package version to the latest. You should select the latest packages for Clang, make and libstdc++. Once you have selected all 3 you can click Next to be taken to a window asking to confirm the installation of the dependencies needed by these three packages.

Once you have successfully downloaded and installed all of the packages that you needed to be able to run Clang you can check that it was successful by opening a Cygwin terminal and typing the clang command. You can see the result of this output in Figure 1-6.

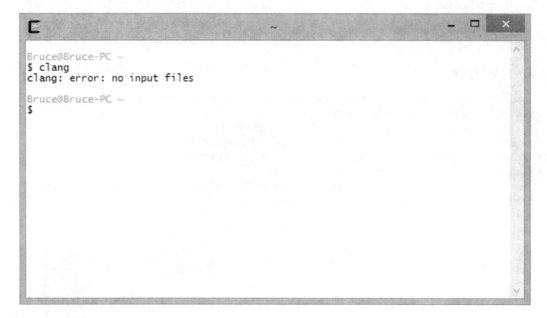

Figure 1-6. *Successfully running Clang in a Cygwin environment in Windows*

Recipe 1-4. Installing Clang on OS X

Problem

You would like to build C++14 based programs on a computer running OS X.

Solution

Apple's Xcode IDE comes with Clang as its default compiler. Installing Xcode from the OS X App Store also installs Clang.

How It Works

Install the latest version of Xcode from the App Store on your OS X computer. Once you've installed Xcode you can open a Terminal window using Spotlight and type clang to see that the compiler has been installed. Figure 1-7 shows how this should look.

```
● ● ●                  Recipe1-4 — bash — 80×24
bsutherland-macbook:Recipe1-4 bsutherlandmacbook$ clang
clang: error: no input files
bsutherland-macbook:Recipe1-4 bsutherlandmacbook$ ▉
```

Figure 1-7. *Running Clang on OS X after installing Xcode*

Recipe 1-5. Building Your First C++ Program

Problem

You would like to use your computer to generate executable applications from C++ source code that you write.

Solution

Generating executables from a C++ source file involves two steps; compiling and linking. The steps undertaken in Recipe 1-2, Recipe 1-3 or Recipe 1-4 depending on your operating system will have resulted in you having all of the software you need to build applications from C++14 source files. You are now ready to build your first C++14 program. Create a folder to contain you project and add a text file named HelloWorld. cpp. Enter the code from Listing 1-1 into the file and save.

Listing 1-1. Your first C++14 Program

```cpp
#include <iostream>

#include <string>

int main(void)
{
    using namespace std::string_literals;

    auto output = "Hello World!"s;
    std::cout << output << std::endl;

    return 0;
}
```

The code in Listing 1-1 is a C++ program that will only compile when using a C++14 compatible compiler. The Recipes 2-4 in this chapter contain instructions on how you can obtain a compiler that can be used to compile C++14 code for Windows, Ubuntu and OS X. You can build a working application once you have created a folder and the source file containing the code in Listing 1-1. You do this using a makefile. Create a file named makefile in the folder alongside your HelloWorld.cpp file. The makefile should not have a file extension which may seem a little strange to developers used to the Windows operating system however this is completely normal for Unix based operating systems such as Linux and OS X. Enter the code from Listing 1-2 into your makefile.

Listing 1-2. The makefile Needed to Build the Code in Listing 1-1

```
HelloWorld: HelloWorld.cpp
        clang++ -g -std=c++1y HelloWorld.cpp -o HelloWorld
```

■ **Note** The whitespace before the `clang++` command in Listing 1-2 is a tab. You cannot replace the tab with spaces as `make` will fail to build. Ensure that your recipes in a makefile always begin with tabs.

The text in Listing 1-2 consists of the instructions needed to build an application from your HelloWorld. cpp source file. The first word on the first line is the name of the target of the makefile. This is the name that the application executable will be given when the building process has been completed. In this case we will be building an executable named HelloWorld. This is followed by the prerequisites needed to build the program. Here you have listed HelloWorld.cpp as the only prerequisite as it is the only source file used to build the executable.

The target and prerequisites are then followed by a list of recipes that are carried out in order to build your application. In this small example you have a line that invokes the clang++ compiler to generate executable code from the HelloWorld.cpp file. The parameter passed to `clang++` using `-std=c++1y` asks Clang to build using the C++14 language standard and the `-o` switch specifies the name of the object output file generated by the compilation process.

Browse to the folder you created to store the source file and makefile using a command shell such as cmd on Windows or Terminal on Linux or OS X and type make. This will invoke the GNU make program and will automatically read and execute your makefile. This will output an executable file into the same folder that you can then run from the command line. You should be able to do this now and see that the text Hello World is output on your command line. Figure 1-8 shows what this would look like in an Ubuntu Terminal window.

```
⊗⊜⊕   bruce@bruce-Virtual-Machine: ~/Projects/C-Recipes/Recipe1-5
bruce@bruce-Virtual-Machine:~/Projects/C-Recipes/Recipe1-5$ ./HelloWorld
Hello World!
bruce@bruce-Virtual-Machine:~/Projects/C-Recipes/Recipe1-5$ █
```

Figure 1-8. The Output Generated by Runnung HelloWorld in an Ubuntu Terminal

Recipe 1-6. Debugging C++ programs using GDB in Cygwin or Linux

Problem

You are writing a C++14 program and would like to be able to debug the application from the command line.

Solution

Both Cygwin for Windows and Linux based operating systems like Ubuntu can install and use the GDB command line debugger for C++ applications.

How It Works

You can use the Cygwin installer for Windows or the Package Manager installed with your favorite Linux distribution to install the GDB debugger. This will give you a command line C++ debugger that can be used to inspect the functionality of your C++ programs. You can practice this using the source, makefile and application generated as part of Recipe 1-5. To generate debugging information for your program you should update the makefile to contain he contents of Listing 1-3 and run make to generate a debuggable executable file.

Listing 1-3. A makefile to Generate a Debuggable Program

```
HelloWorld: HelloWorld.cpp
        clang++ -g -std=c++1y HelloWorld.cpp -o HelloWorld
```

Once you have followed Recipe 1-5, updated the makefile to contain the contents of Listing 1-5 and generated an executable you can run GDB on your application by browsing to the folder on your command line and typing gdb HelloWorld. The new –g switch passed to Clang in the makefile from Listing 1-3 asks the compiler to generate additional information in the application that helps debuggers to provide you with accurate information about the program while it is executing in the debugger.

■ **Note**   You may be presented with a notice informing you that your program is already up to date if you had built previously. Simply delete the existing executable file if this occurs.

Running GDB in HelloWorld should result in your command line running GDB and providing output such as that shown in Figure 1-9.

```
⊗ ⊖ ⊕    bruce@bruce-Virtual-Machine: ~/Projects/C-Recipes/Recipe1-5
bruce@bruce-Virtual-Machine:~/Projects/C-Recipes/Recipe1-5$ gdb HelloWorld
GNU gdb (Ubuntu 7.8-1ubuntu4) 7.8.0.20141001-cvs
Copyright (C) 2014 Free Software Foundation, Inc.
License GPLv3+: GNU GPL version 3 or later <http://gnu.org/licenses/gpl.html>
This is free software: you are free to change and redistribute it.
There is NO WARRANTY, to the extent permitted by law.  Type "show copying"
and "show warranty" for details.
This GDB was configured as "x86_64-linux-gnu".
Type "show configuration" for configuration details.
For bug reporting instructions, please see:
<http://www.gnu.org/software/gdb/bugs/>.
Find the GDB manual and other documentation resources online at:
<http://www.gnu.org/software/gdb/documentation/>.
For help, type "help".
Type "apropos word" to search for commands related to "word"...
Reading symbols from HelloWorld...(no debugging symbols found)...done.
(gdb) ▋
```

Figure 1-9. *A Running Instance of GDB*

You now have a running debugger that you can use to inspect the running program while it is executing. The program has not yet begun when GDB first starts, this allows you to configure some breakpoints before you get started. To set a breakpoint you can use the break command or the b shorthand for the same command. Type break main into the GDB command prompt and hit enter. This should result in GDB echoing the command back to you along with the address of the program where the breakpoint was set and the filename and line number it detected for the function supplied. You can now type run into your window to execute the program and have GDB halt at your breakpoint. The output should resemble that shown in Figure 1-10.

CHAPTER 1 ■ BEGINNING C++

```
⊗ ⊖ ⊕    bruce@bruce-Virtual-Machine: ~/Projects/C-Recipes/Recipe1-5
bruce@bruce-Virtual-Machine:~/Projects/C-Recipes/Recipe1-5$ gdb HelloWorld
GNU gdb (Ubuntu 7.8-1ubuntu4) 7.8.0.20141001-cvs
Copyright (C) 2014 Free Software Foundation, Inc.
License GPLv3+: GNU GPL version 3 or later <http://gnu.org/licenses/gpl.html>
This is free software: you are free to change and redistribute it.
There is NO WARRANTY, to the extent permitted by law.  Type "show copying"
and "show warranty" for details.
This GDB was configured as "x86_64-linux-gnu".
Type "show configuration" for configuration details.
For bug reporting instructions, please see:
<http://www.gnu.org/software/gdb/bugs/>.
Find the GDB manual and other documentation resources online at:
<http://www.gnu.org/software/gdb/documentation/>.
For help, type "help".
Type "apropos word" to search for commands related to "word"...
Reading symbols from HelloWorld...done.
(gdb) break main
Breakpoint 1 at 0x400b3f: file HelloWorld.cpp, line 8.
(gdb) run
Starting program: /home/bruce/Projects/C-Recipes/Recipe1-5/HelloWorld

Breakpoint 1, main () at HelloWorld.cpp:8
8            auto output = "Hello World!"s;
(gdb) █
```

Figure 1-10. *The Output as Seen When GDB Halts at the Breakpoint Set in* main

At this point you have several options that allow you to continue the execution of your program. You can see a list of the most common commands below.

step

> The step command is used to step into a function that is to be called at the current line.

next

> The next command is used to step over the current line and stop on the next line of the same function.

finish

> The finish command is used to execute all of the code remaining in the current function and stop on the next line in the function that called the current function.

print <name>

> The print command followed by the name of a variable can be used to print the value of a variable in your program.

break

> The break command can be used with a line number, a function name or a source file and line number to set a breakpoint in your programs source code.

continue

> The continue command is used to resume code execution after it has been halted at a breakpoint.

until

> The until command can continue execution from a loop and stop on the first line immediately after the loop execution has finished.

info

> The info command can be used with either the locals command or the stack command to show information about the current local variables or stack state in the program.

help

> You can type help followed by any command to have GDB give you information about all of the different ways that a given command can be used.

The GDB debugger can also be run with the command -tui. This will give you a view of the source file you are currently debugging at the top of the window. You can see how this looks in Figure 1-11.

```
bruce@bruce-Virtual-Machine: ~/Projects/C-Recipes/Recipe1-5
HelloWorld.cpp
5       {
6           using namespace std::string_literals;
7
8           auto output = "Hello World!"s;
9           std::cout << output << std::endl;
10
11          return 0;
12      }
13
14
15
16
17
exec No process In:                           Line: ??    PC: ??
For bug reporting instructions, please see:
<http://www.gnu.org/software/gdb/bugs/>.
Find the GDB manual and other documentation resources online at:
<http://www.gnu.org/software/gdb/documentation/>.
For help, type "help".
Type "apropos word" to search for commands related to "word"...
Reading symbols from HelloWorld...done.
(gdb)
```

Figure 1-11. *GDB with a Source Window*

Recipe 1-7. Debugging Your C++ Programs on OS X

Problem

The OS X operating system does not provide any easy method for installing and using GDB.

Solution

Xcode comes with the LLDB debugger than can be used on the command line in-place of GDB.

How It Works

The LLDB debugger is, in essence, very similar to the GDB debugger used in Recipe 1-6. Changing between GDB and LLDB is simply a case of learning how to carry out the same simple tasks in both by using the commands provided by each to carry out the same task.

You can execute LLDB on your HelloWorld executable by browsing to the directory containing HelloWorld in Terminal and typing `lldb HelloWorld`. This will give you output that resembles that of Figure 1-12.

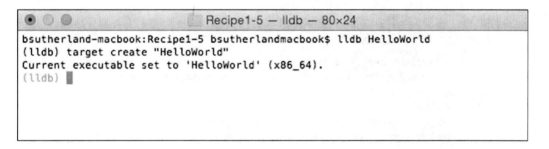

```
● ○ ○                    Recipe1-5 — lldb — 80×24
bsutherland-macbook:Recipe1-5 bsutherlandmacbook$ lldb HelloWorld
(lldb) target create "HelloWorld"
Current executable set to 'HelloWorld' (x86_64).
(lldb)
```

Figure 1-12. *The LLDB Debugger Running in an OS X Terminal*

▓ **Note** You will need to compile your program using the –g switch. Take a look at Listing 1-3 to see where this goes if you are unsure.

Once you have LLDB running as shown in Listing 1-12 you can set a breakpoint on the first line of main by typing `breakpoint set -f HelloWorld.cpp -l 8`, or `b main` as shorthand. You can use the `run` command to begin execution and have it halt at the breakpoint that you've just set. When the program stops you can use the `next` command to step over the current line and halt on the next line. You could have used the `step` command to step into a function on the current line and halt on the first line of the function. The `finish` command will step out of the current function.

You can quit LLDB by typing q and hitting enter. Restart LLDB and type `breakpoint set -f HelloWorld. cpp -l 9`. Follow this with the `run` command and LLDB should print the source around the line where the application has stopped. You can now type `print output` to see the value stored by the output variable. You can also use the `frame variable` command to see all of the local variables in the current stack frame.

These simple commands will allow you to use the LLDB debugger adequately enough while working through the samples provided along with this book. The following list can be used as a handy cheat sheet while working with LLDB.

`step`

> The `step` command is used to step into a function that is to be called at the current line.

`next`

> The `next` command is used to step over the current line and stop on the next line of the same function.

`finish`

> The `finish` command is used to execute all of the code remaining in the current function and stop on the next line in the function that called the current function.

`print <name>`

> The `print` command followed by the name of a variable can be used to print the value of a variable in your program.

`breakpoint set --name <name>`

`breakpoint set –file <name> --line <number>`

> The `breakpoint` command can be used with a line number, a function name or a source file and line number to set a breakpoint in your programs source code.

`help`

> You can type `help` followed by any command to have GDB give you information about all of the different ways that a given command can be used.

Recipe 1-8. Switching C++ Compilation Modes

Problem

You would like to be able to switch between the different C++ standards before compiling your programs.

Solution

The `std` switch is supplied by Clang so that you can specify the C++ standard to be used when compiling.

How It Works

Clang builds with the C++98 standard by default. You can use the std argument with Clang++ to tell the compiler to use a standard other than the default. Listing 1-4 shows a makefile that is configured to build a program using the C++14 standard.

Listing 1-4. Building with C++14

```
HelloWorld: HelloWorld.cpp
        clang++ -std=c++1y HelloWorld.cpp -o HelloWorld
```

The makefile in Listing 1-4 shows how you can specify that Clang should build your source file using C++14. This example was written using Clang 3.5 that uses the c++1y command to represent C++14.

Listing 1-5 shows how you can build a program using C++11.

Listing 1-5. Building with C++11

```
HelloWorld: HelloWorld.cpp
        clang++ -std=c++11 HelloWorld.cpp -o HelloWorld
```

In Listing1-5 you want to use the c++11 option with the std switch to build with C++11. Finally, Listing 1-6 shows how to configure Clang to explicitly build with C++98.

Listing 1-6. Building with C++98

```
HelloWorld: HelloWorld.cpp
        clang++ -std=c++98 HelloWorld.cpp -o HelloWorld
```

The makefile in Listing 1-6 can be used to explicitly build with C++98. You can achieve the same result by leaving out the std command altogether and Clang will build using C++98 by default.

▨ **Note**   It's not guaranteed that every compiler will use C++98 by default. Check with your compiler's documentation if you're unsure which standard is the default. You can also be adventurous with Clang and enable its experimental C++17 support using the c++1z option!

Recipe 1-9. Building with the Boost Library

Problem

You would like to write a program using the Boost library.

Solution

Boost is supplied as source code that can be included with and compiled into your application.

How It Works

Boost is a large C++ library that includes all sorts of great functionality. Coverage of the entire library is out of the scope of this book; however the string formatting library will be used. You can acquire the Boost library from the Boost website at http://www.boost.org/.

You will be able to get a compressed folder from the Boost website that contains the latest version of the Boost library. The only folder you absolutely need to be able to include basic boost functionality is the boost folder itself. I have downloaded Boost 1.55 and therefore I have created a folder inside my project folder named boost_1_55_0 and copied the boost folder into this location from the downloaded version.

15

Once you have a project folder set up with a downloaded copy of Boost you can include Boost header files into your source code. Listing 1-7 shows a program that uses the `boost::format` function.

Listing 1-7. Using boost::format

```cpp
#include <iostream>
#include "boost/format.hpp"

using namespace std;

int main()
{
    std::cout << "Enter your first name: " << std::endl;
    std::string firstName;
    std::cin >> firstName;

    std::cout << "Enter your surname: " << std::endl;
    std::string surname;
    std::cin >> surname;

    auto formattedName = str( boost::format("%1% %2%"s) % firstName % surname );
    std::cout << "You said your name is: " << formattedName << std::endl;

    return 0;
}
```

The code in Listing 1-7 shows how you can include a Boost header into a source file and how that file's functions can be used in your program.

▥ **Note**　Don't worry about how the `format` function works if it's not immediately clear, it is covered in Chapter 3.

You must also tell the compiler where to look for the Boost header files in a makefile otherwise your program will not compile. Listing 1-8 shows the contents of the makefile that can be used to build this program.

Listing 1-8. A makefile to Build with Boost

```
main: main.cpp
        clang++ -g -std=c++1y -Iboost_1_55_0 main.cpp -o main
```

The makefile in Listing 1-8 passes the –I option to Clang++. This option is used to tell Clang that you would like to include the given folder in the search paths used when including files using the `#include` directive. As you can see I have passed the boost_1_55_0 folder that I created in my project folder. This folder contains the boost folder that you can see used when including a Boost header in Listing 1-7.

▥ **Note**　If you're having trouble getting this example to work and aren't sure of where to put the Boost header files you can download the samples that accompany this book from the www.apress.com/9781484201589.

CHAPTER 2

■ ■ ■

Modern C++

Development of the C++ programming language began in 1979 as the C with Classes language. The name C++ was formally adopted in 1983 and development of the language continued throughout the 1980s and 1990s without the adoption of a formal language standard. This all changed in 1998 when the first ISO standard of the C++ programming language was adopted. There have been three updates to the standard published since that time, one in 2003, again in 2011 and the latest in 2014.

■ **Note** The standard published in 2003 was a minor update to the 1998 standard that didn't introduce much in the way of new features. For this reason, it won't be discussed in any great detail in this book.

This book is primarily going to focus on the very latest C++ programming standard, C++14. Whenever I mention the C++ programming language you can be assured that I am talking about the language as described by the current ISO standard. If I am discussing features that were introduced in 2011 then I will explicitly mention the language as C++11 and for any features that were introduced prior to 2011 I will use the name C++98.

This chapter will look at the programming features added to the language in the latest standard and with C++11. Many of the modern features of C++ were added in the C++11 standard and have been expanded with the C++14 standard therefore it is important to be able to identify the differences when working with compilers that support a standard that is not the latest.

Recipe 2-1. Initializing Variables

Problem

You would like to be able to initialize all variables in a standard manner.

Solution

Uniform initialization was introduced in C++11 and can be used to initialize a variable of any type.

How It Works

It's necessary to understand the deficiencies with variable initialization in C++98 to appreciate why uniform initialization is an important language feature in C++11. Listing 2-1 shows a program that contains a single class, MyClass.

Listing 2-1. The C++Most Vexing Parse Problem

```
class MyClass
{
private:
    int m_Member;

public:
    MyClass() = default;
    MyClass(const MyClass& rhs) = default;
};

int main()
{
    MyClass objectA;
    MyClass objectB(MyClass());
    return 0;
}
```

The code in Listing 2-1 will generate a compile error in C++ programs. The problem exists in the definition of objectB. A C++ compiler will not see this line as defining a variable named objectB of type MyClass calling a constructor that takes the object constructed by calling the MyClass constructor. This is what you might expect the compiler to see however what it actually sees is a function declaration. The compiler thinks that this line is declaring a function named objectB that returns a MyClass object and has a single, unnamed function pointer to a function that returns a MyClass object and is passed no parameters.

Compiling the program shown in Listing 2-1 causes Clang to generate the following warning:

```
main.cpp:14:20: warning: parentheses were disambiguated as a function
      declaration [-Wvexing-parse]
    MyClass objectB(MyClass());
                   ^~~~~~~~~~~
main.cpp:14:21: note: add a pair of parentheses to declare a variable
    MyClass objectB(MyClass());
                    ^
                    (         )
```

The Clang compiler has properly identified that the code entered in Listing 2-1 contains a vexing parse problem and even helpfully suggests wrapping the MyClass constructor being passed as a parameter in another pair of parentheses to solve the problem. C++11 has provided an alternative solution in uniform initialization. You can see this in Listing 2-2.

Listing 2-2. Using Uniform Initialization to Solve the Vexing Parse Problem

```
class MyClass
{
private:
    int m_Member;

public:
    MyClass() = default;
    MyClass(const MyClass& rhs) = default;
};

int main()
{
    MyClass objectA;
    MyClass objectB{MyClass{}};
    return 0;
}
```

You can see in Listing 2-2 that uniform initialization replaces parentheses with braces. This syntax change informs the compiler that you would like to use uniform initialization to initialize your variable. Uniform initialization can be used to initialize almost all types of variables.

■ **Note** The paragraph above mentions that uniform initialization can be used to initialize *almost* all variables. It can have trouble when initializing aggregates or plain old data types however you won't need to worry about those for now.

The ability to prevent narrowing conversions is another benefit of using uniform initialization. The code in Listing 2-3 will fail to compile when using uniform initialization.

Listing 2-3. Using Uniform Initialization to Prevent Narrowing Conversions

```
int main()
{
    int number{ 0 };
    char another{ 512 };

    double bigNumber{ 1.0 };
    float littleNumber{ bigNumber };

    return 0;
}
```

The compiler will throw errors when compiling the code in Listing 2-3 as there are two narrowing conversions present in the source. The first occurs when trying to define a char variable with the literal value 512. A char type can store a maximum value of 255 therefore the value 512 would be narrowed into this data type. A C++11 or newer compiler will not compile this code due to this error. The initialization of the float from a double type is also a narrowing conversion. Narrowing conversions occur when data is transferred from one type to another in where the destination type cannot store all of the values represented by the source type. Precision is lost in the case of a double being converted to a float therefore the compiler correctly will not build this code as-is. The code in Listing 2-4 uses a `static_cast` to inform the compiler that the narrowing conversions are intentional and to compile the code.

Listing 2-4. Using a static_cast to Compile Narrowing Conversions

```cpp
int main()
{
    int number{ 0 };
    char another{ static_cast<char>(512) };

    double bigNumber{ 1.0 };
    float littleNumber{ static_cast<float>(bigNumber) };

    return 0;
}
```

Recipe 2-2. Initializing Objects with Initializer Lists

Problem

You would like to construct objects from multiple objects of a given type.

Solution

Modern C++ provides initializer lists that can be used to supply many objects of the same type to a constructor.

How It Works

Initializer lists in C++11 build upon uniform initialization to allow you to initialize complex types with ease. A common example of a complex type that can be difficult to initialize with data is a vector. Listing 2-5 shows two different calls to a standard vector constructor.

Listing 2-5. Constructing vector Objects

```cpp
#include <iostream>
#include <vector>

using namespace std;

int main()
{
    using MyVector = vector<int>;

    MyVector vectorA( 1 );
    cout << vectorA.size() << " " << vectorA[0] << endl;

    MyVector vectorB( 1, 10 );
    cout << vectorB.size() << " " << vectorB[0] << endl;

    return 0;
}
```

The code in Listing 2-5 might not do what you expect at first glance. The vectorA variable will be initialized with a single int containing 0. You might expect that it would contain a single integer containing 1 but this would be incorrect. The first parameter to a vector constructor determines how many values the initial vector will be set up to store and in this case we are asking it to store a single variable. You might similarly expect vectorB to contain two values, 1 and 10 however what we have here is a vector that contains one value and that value is 10. The vectorB variable is constructed using the same constructor as vectorA however it specifies a value to use to instantiate the members of the vector rather than using the default value.

The code in Listing 2-6 uses an initializer list in conjunction with uniform initialization to construct a vector that contains two elements with the specified values.

Listing 2-6. Using Uniform Initialization to Construct a vector

```cpp
#include <iostream>
#include <vector>

using namespace std;

int main()
{
    using MyVector = vector<int>;

    MyVector vectorA( 1 );
    cout << vectorA.size() << " " << vectorA[0] << endl;

    MyVector vectorB( 1, 10 );
    cout << vectorB.size() << " " << vectorB[0] << endl;

    MyVector vectorC{ 1, 10 };
    cout << vectorC.size() << " " << vectorC[0] << endl;

    return 0;
}
```

The code in Listing 2-6 creates three different vector objects. You can see the output generated by this program in Figure 2-1.

```
😕😑🔲  bruce@bruce-Virtual-Machine: ~/Projects/C-Recipes/Recipe2-2/Listing2-6
bruce@bruce-Virtual-Machine:~/Projects/C-Recipes/Recipe2-2/Listing2-6$ ./main
1 0
1 10
2 1
bruce@bruce-Virtual-Machine:~/Projects/C-Recipes/Recipe2-2/Listing2-6$ ▮
```

Figure 2-1. *The Output Generated by Listing 2-6*

The console output shown in Figure 2-1 shows the size of each vector and the value stored in the first element of each vector. You can see that the first vector contains a single element and that its value is 0. The second vector also contains a single element however its value is 10. The third vector is constructed using uniform initialization and it contains two values and the value of its first element is 1. The value of the second element will be 10. This can cause a significant different to the behavior of your programs if you are not taking particular care to ensure that the correct type of initialization has been used with your types. The code in Listing 2-7 shows a more explicit use of the initializer_list to construct a vector.

Listing 2-7. Explicit initializer_list Usage

```
#include <iostream>
#include <vector>

using namespace std;

int main()
{
    using MyVector = vector<int>;

    MyVector vectorA( 1 );
    cout << vectorA.size() << " " << vectorA[0] << endl;

    MyVector vectorB( 1, 10 );
    cout << vectorB.size() << " " << vectorB[0] << endl;

    initializer_list<int> initList{ 1, 10 };
    MyVector vectorC(initList);
    cout << vectorC.size() << " " << vectorC[0] << endl;

    return 0;
}
```

The code in Listing 2-7 contains an explicit initializer_list that is used to construct a vector. The code in Listing 2-6 implicitly created this object when constructing a vector using uniform initialization. There's usually little need to explicitly create initializer lists like this however it's important that you understand what the compiler is doing when you write code using uniform initialization.

Recipe 2-3. Using Type Deduction

Problem

You would like to write portable code that doesn't have a high maintenance cost when changing types.

Solution

C++ provides the auto keyword that can be used to let the compiler deduce the type for a variable automatically.

How It Works

C++98 compilers had the ability to automatically deduce the type of a variable however this functionality was only available while you were writing code that used templates and you omitted the type specialization. Modern C++ has extended this type deduction support to many more scenarios. The code in Listing 2-8 shows the use of the auto keyword and the typeid method of working out the type of a variable.

Listing 2-8. Using the auto Keyword

```
#include <iostream>
#include <typeinfo>

using namespace std;

int main()
{
    auto variable = 1;
    cout << "Type of variable: " << typeid(variable).name() << endl;

    return 0;
}
```

The code in Listing 2-8 shows how to create a variable with automatically deduced type in C++. The compiler will automatically work out that you wanted to create an int variable with this code and that's the type that will be output by the program, sort of. The Clang compiler will output its internal representation of an integer type which is actually i. You can pass this output to a program named c++filt to convert this into a normal typename. Figure 2-2 shows how this can be achieved.

```
bruce@bruce-Virtual-Machine: ~/Projects/C-Recipes/Recipe2-3/Listing2-8
bruce@bruce-Virtual-Machine:~/Projects/C-Recipes/Recipe2-3/Listing2-8$ ./main |
c++filt -t
Type of variable: int
bruce@bruce-Virtual-Machine:~/Projects/C-Recipes/Recipe2-3/Listing2-8$ █
```

Figure 2-2. *Using c++filt to Produce Proper Type Output From Clang*

The c++filt program has successfully converted the Clang type i into a human readable C++ type format. The auto keyword also works with classes. Listing 2-9 shows this.

Listing 2-9. Using auto with a class

```
#include <iostream>
#include <typeinfo>

using namespace std;

class MyClass
{
};

int main()
{
    auto variable = MyClass();
    cout << "Type of variable: " << typeid(variable).name() << endl;

    return 0;
}
```

This program will print out the name MyClass as you can see in Figure 2-3.

```
bruce@bruce-Virtual-Machine: ~/Projects/C-Recipes/Recipe2-3/Listing2-9
bruce@bruce-Virtual-Machine:~/Projects/C-Recipes/Recipe2-3/Listing2-9$ ./main |
c++filt -t
Type of variable: MyClass
bruce@bruce-Virtual-Machine:~/Projects/C-Recipes/Recipe2-3/Listing2-9$ ▮
```

Figure 2-3. *Using auto with MyClass*

Unfortunately there are times where the auto keyword can produce less than desirable results. You will definitely come unstuck if you try to combine the auto keyword with uniform initialization. Listing 2-10 shows the use of the auto keyword with uniform initialization.

Listing 2-10. Using auto with Uniform Initialization

```
#include <iostream>
#include <typeinfo>

using namespace std;

class MyClass
{
};

int main()
{
    auto variable{ 1 };
    cout << "Type of variable: " << typeid(variable).name() << endl;
```

```
    auto variable2{ MyClass{} };
    cout << "Type of variable: " << typeid(variable2).name() << endl;

    return 0;
}
```

You might expect that the code in Listing 2-10 will produce a variable of type int and a variable of type MyClass however this is not the case. Figure 2-4 shows the output generated by the program.

```
bruce@bruce-Virtual-Machine: ~/Projects/C-Recipes/Recipe2-3/Listing2-10
bruce@bruce-Virtual-Machine:~/Projects/C-Recipes/Recipe2-3/Listing2-10$ ./main |
 c++filt -t
Type of variable: std::initializer_list<int>
Type of variable: std::initializer_list<MyClass>
bruce@bruce-Virtual-Machine:~/Projects/C-Recipes/Recipe2-3/Listing2-10$ █
```

Figure 2-4. *Output Generated When using auto with Uniform Initialization*

A quick look at Figure 2-4 shows the immediate problem encountered when using the auto keyword along with uniform initialization. The C++ uniform initialization feature automatically creates an initializer_list variable that contains the value of the type we want, not the type and value itself. This leads to a relatively simple piece of advice, do not use uniform initialization when defining variables using auto. I'd recommend not using auto even if the type you want is actually an initializer_list as the code is much easier to understand and much less error prone if you don't mix and match you variable initialization styles. There's a final piece of advice to bear in mind, use auto for local variables as much as possible. It's impossible to declare an auto variable and not define it therefore it's impossible to have an undefined local auto variable. You can use this piece of knowledge to cut down on one potential source of bugs in your programs.

Recipe 2-4. Using auto with Functions

Problem

You would like to create more generic functions using type deduction to increase code maintainability.

Solution

Modern C++ allows you to use type deduction for function parameters and for return types.

How It Works

C++ allows you to utilize type deduction when working with function using two methods. Types can be deduced for function parameters by creating a template function and calling that function without explicit specializers. The return type can be deduced for a function using the auto keyword in place of its return type. Listing 2-11 shows the use of auto to deduce the return type for a function.

Listing 2-11. Deducing a Function's Return Type Using auto

```cpp
#include <iostream>

using namespace std;

auto AutoFunctionFromReturn(int parameter)
{
    return parameter;
}

int main()
{
    auto value = AutoFunctionFromReturn(1);
    cout << value << endl;

    return 0;
}
```

The `AutoFunctionFromReturn` function's return type in Listing 2-11 is automatically deduced. The compiler inspects the type of the variable returned from the function and uses that to deduce the type to be returned. This all works properly because the compiler has everything it needs inside the function to be able to deduce the type. The `parameter` variable is being returned therefore the compiler can use its type as the return type for the function.

Things get a bit more complicated when you need to build with a C++11 compiler. Building Listing 2-11 using C++11 results in the following error.

```
main.cpp:5:1: error: 'auto' return without trailing return type
auto AutoFunctionFromReturn(int parameter)
```

Listing 2-12 includes a function with automatic return type deduction that works in C++11.

Listing 2-12. Return Type Deduction in C++11

```cpp
#include <iostream>

using namespace std;

auto AutoFunctionFromReturn(int parameter) -> int
{
    return parameter;
}

int main()
{
    auto value = AutoFunctionFromReturn(1);
    cout << value << endl;

    return 0;
}
```

You might be wondering why you would bother doing this when looking at the code in Listing 2-12. There's little use in deducing the return type for a function when you always specify that it will be an int and you'd be right. Return type deduction is much more useful in functions that don't have their parameter types declared in their signature. Listing 2-13 shows the type deduction in action for a template function.

Listing 2-13. Deducing return types for C++11 template functions

```
#include <iostream>

using namespace std;

template <typename T>
auto AutoFunctionFromParameter(T parameter) -> decltype(parameter)
{
    return parameter;
}

int main()
{
    auto value = AutoFunctionFromParameter(2);
    cout << value << endl;

    return 0;
}
```

Listing 2-13 shows a useful application of return type deduction. This time the function is specified as a template therefore the compiler cannot work out the return type using the parameter type. C++11 introduced the decltype keyword to compliment the auto keyword. decltype is used to tell the compiler to use the type of a given expression. The expression can be a variable name however you could also give a function here and decltype would deduce the type returned from the function.

At this point the code has come full circle. The C++11 standard allowed auto to be used on functions to deduce return type but required that the type still be specified as a trailing return type. The trailing return type can be deduced using decltype however this leads to overly verbose code. C++14 rectifies this situation by allowing auto to be used on functions without having the trailing return type even when used with templates as you can see in Listing 2-14.

Listing 2-14. Using auto to Deduce Return Type on a Template Function

```
#include <iostream>

using namespace std;

template <typename T>
auto AutoFunctionFromParameter(T parameter)
{
    return parameter;
}

int main()
{
    auto value = AutoFunctionFromParameter(2);
    cout << value << endl;

    return 0;
}
```

Recipe 2-5. Working with Compile Time Constants

Problem

You would like to optimize the runtime operation of your program using compile time constant.

Solution

C++ provides the `constexpr` keyword that can be used to guarantee that an expression can be evaluated at compile time.

How It Works

The `constexpr` keyword can be used to create variables and functions that guarantee that their evaluation can be evaluated at compile time. Your compiler will throw an error if you add any code to them that prevents compile time evaluation. Listing 2-15 shows program that uses a `constexpr` variable to define the size of an `array`.

Listing 2-15. Using `constexpr` to Define the Size of an `array`

```
#include <array>
#include <cstdint>
#include <iostream>

int main()
{
    constexpr uint32_t ARRAY_SIZE{ 5 };
    std::array<uint32_t, ARRAY_SIZE> myArray{ 1, 2, 3, 4, 5 };

    for (auto&& number : myArray)
    {
        std::cout << number << std::endl;
    }

    return 0;
}
```

The `constexpr` variable in Listing 2-15 guarantees that the value can be evaluated at compile time. This is necessary here as the size of an `array` is something that must be determined when your program is compiled. Listing 2-16 shows how you can extend this example to include a `constexpr` function.

Listing 2-16. A `constexpr` Function

```
#include <array>
#include <cstdint>
#include <iostream>

constexpr uint32_t ArraySizeFunction(int parameter)
{
    return parameter;
}
```

```
int main()
{
    constexpr uint32_t ARRAY_SIZE{ ArraySizeFunction(5) };
    std::array<uint32_t, ARRAY_SIZE> myArray{ 1, 2, 3, 4, 5 };

    for (auto&& number : myArray)
    {
        std::cout << number << std::endl;
    }

    return 0;
}
```

You can go another step further than the code in Listing 2-16 and create a class with a constexpr constructor. This is shown in Listing 2-17.

Listing 2-17. Creating constexpr class Constructors

```
#include <array>
#include <cstdint>
#include <iostream>

class MyClass
{
private:
    uint32_t m_Member;

public:
    constexpr MyClass(uint32_t parameter)
        : m_Member{parameter}
    {
    }

    constexpr uint32_t GetValue() const
    {
        return m_Member;
    }
};

int main()
{
    constexpr uint32_t ARRAY_SIZE{ MyClass{ 5 }.GetValue() };
    std::array<uint32_t, ARRAY_SIZE> myArray{ 1, 2, 3, 4, 5 };

    for (auto&& number : myArray)
    {
        std::cout << number << std::endl;
    }

    return 0;
}
```

The code in Listing 2-17 is able to create an object and call a method in a constexpr statement. This was possible because the constructor for MyClass was declared as a constexpr constructor. The code shown so far for constexpr has all been compatible with C++11 compilers. The C++14 standard has relaxed many of the restrictions that existed in C++11. C++11 constexpr statements are not permitted to do many things that normal C++ code can. Examples of these things are creating variables and using if statements. The code in Listing 2-18 shows a C++14 constexpr function that can be used to limit the maximum size of an array.

Listing 2-18. Using a C++14 constexpr Function

```
#include <array>
#include <cstdint>
#include <iostream>

constexpr uint32_t ArraySizeFunction(uint32_t parameter)
{
    uint32_t value{ parameter };
    if (value > 10 )
    {
        value = 10;
    }
    return value;
}

int main()
{
    constexpr uint32_t ARRAY_SIZE{ ArraySizeFunction(15) };
    std::array<uint32_t, ARRAY_SIZE> myArray{ 1, 2, 3, 4, 5, 6, 7, 8, 9, 10 };

    for (auto&& number : myArray)
    {
        std::cout << number << std::endl;
    }

    return 0;
}
```

The code in Listing 2-18 expands on the C++11 compatible code in Listing 2-16 to include a function that declares a variable and uses an if statement. Compiling this code with a C++11 compiler results in the following error.

```
main.cpp:7:14: warning: variable declaration in a constexpr function is a C++1y extension
[-Wc++1y-extensions]
    uint32_t value{ parameter };
            ^
main.cpp:8:5: warning: use of this statement in a constexpr function is a C++1y extension
[-Wc++1y-extensions]
    if (value > 10 )
    ^
main.cpp:17:24: error: constexpr variable 'ARRAY_SIZE' must be initialized by a constant
expression
    constexpr uint32_t ARRAY_SIZE{ ArraySizeFunction(15) };
```

Two warnings are presented to show that the constexpr function cannot be used in a constexpr context. This is not a compile error because the function can still be used in a non-constexpr context. The actual error is thrown when the function is used to initialize a constexpr variable.

Recipe 2-6. Working with Lambdas

Problem

You would like to write programs that utilize unnamed function objects.

Solution

C++ provides lambdas that can be used to create closures and can be passed around in your code.

How It Works

The lambda syntax introduced in C++11 can be a little confusing at first. Listing 2-19 shows a simple example of a program that uses a lambda to print out all of the values in an array.

Listing 2-19. Using a Lambda to Print array Values

```
#include <algorithm>
#include <array>
#include <cstdint>
#include <iostream>

int main()
{
    using MyArray = std::array<uint32_t, 5>;
    MyArray myArray{ 1, 2, 3, 4, 5 };

    std::for_each(myArray.cbegin(),
        myArray.cend(),
        [](auto&& number) {
            std::cout << number << std::endl;
        });

    return 0;
}
```

This code shows how a lambda is defined in C++ source code. The syntax for a lambda is as follows:

```
[] () {};
```

The braces represent the capture block. A lambda uses a capture block to capture existing variables to be used in the lambda. The code in Listing 2-19 does not have a need to capture any variables therefore it is empty. The parentheses represent the argument block as it does in a normal function. The lambda in Listing 2-19 has a single parameter that is of type auto&&. The std::for_each algorithm applies the given function to every element in the sequence. The function here happens to be a closure that was created by the compiler when it encountered the lambda syntax and passed it to the for_each function. There's a subtle terminology difference there that you should become familiar with. A lambda is the source code construct that defines an anonymous or unnamed function. The compiler uses this syntax to create a closure object from the lambda.

A closure can be referenced by a variable as shown in Listing 2-20.

Listing 2-20. Referencing a Closure in a Variable

```
#include <algorithm>
#include <array>
#include <cstdint>
#include <iostream>
#include <typeinfo>

int main()
{
    using MyArray = std::array<uint32_t, 5>;
    MyArray myArray{ 1, 2, 3, 4, 5 };

    auto myClosure = [](auto&& number) {
            std::cout << number << std::endl;
        };
    std::cout << typeid(myClosure).name() << std::endl;

    std::for_each(myArray.begin(),
        myArray.end(),
        myClosure);

    return 0;
}
```

The example in Listing 2-20 captures the lambda into an auto typed variable. Figure 2-5 shows the output that this generates.

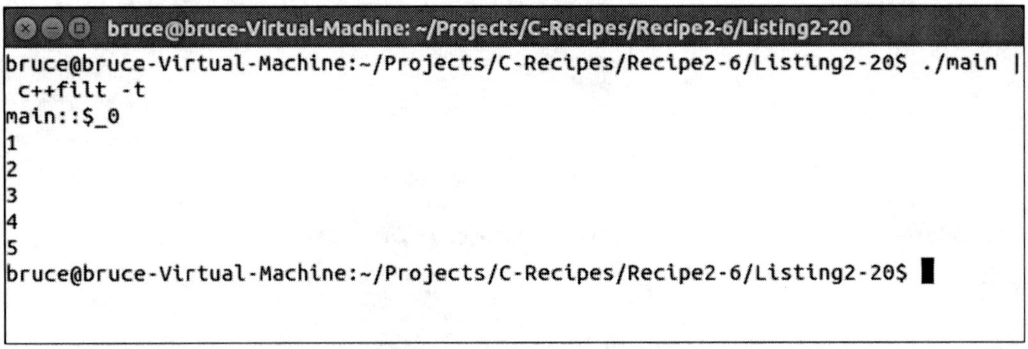

Figure 2-5. The Type Output by typeid when Passed a Closure

Figure 2-5 shows the type of the closure stored by the myClosure variable in Listing 2-20. The automatically generated type here isn't particularly useful however C++ does provide a method for passing around any type of object that can be called like a function. The function template is provided in the functional header and is part of the STL. This template takes the signature of the function that the object represents. You can see how this code looks in Listing 2-21.

Listing 2-21. Passing a Closure into a Function

```
#include <algorithm>
#include <array>
#include <cstdint>
#include <functional>
#include <iostream>
#include <typeinfo>

using MyArray = std::array<uint32_t, 5>;

void PrintArray(const std::function<void(MyArray::value_type)>& myFunction)
{
    MyArray myArray{ 1, 2, 3, 4, 5 };

    std::for_each(myArray.begin(),
        myArray.end(),
        myFunction);
}

int main()
{
    auto myClosure = [](auto&& number) {
            std::cout << number << std::endl;
        };
    std::cout << typeid(myClosure).name() << std::endl;

    PrintArray(myClosure);

    return 0;
}
```

You can now create closures and pass them around your program using the function template as shown in Listing 2-21. This allows you to add some touches to your programs that would have been much more difficult to achieve in C++98. Listing 2-22 shows a method to copy an array into a vector through a lambda using the capture block.

Listing 2-22. Using the Lambda Capture Feature

```cpp
#include <algorithm>
#include <array>
#include <cstdint>
#include <functional>
#include <iostream>
#include <typeinfo>
#include <vector>

using MyArray = std::array<uint32_t, 5>;
using MyVector = std::vector<MyArray::value_type>;

void PrintArray(const std::function<void(MyArray::value_type)>& myFunction)
{
    MyArray myArray{ 1, 2, 3, 4, 5 };

    std::for_each(myArray.begin(),
        myArray.end(),
        myFunction);
}

int main()
{
    MyVector myCopy;
    auto myClosure = [&myCopy](auto&& number) {
            std::cout << number << std::endl;
            myCopy.push_back(number);
        };
    std::cout << typeid(myClosure).name() << std::endl;

    PrintArray(myClosure);

    std::cout << std::endl << "My Copy: " << std::endl;
    std::for_each(myCopy.cbegin(),
        myCopy.cend(),
        [](auto&& number){
            std::cout << number << std::endl;
        });

    return 0;
}
```

The code in Listing 2-22 contains a use of the lambda capture to store a reference to the object myCopy in the closure. This object can then be used inside the lambda and has each member of the array pushed onto it. The main function ends by printing all of the values stored by myCopy to show that the closure was sharing the same vector as main thanks to the reference capture. The capture was specified as a reference capture using the & operator. The vector would have been copied into the closure if this had been omitted and the myCopy vector in main would have remained empty.

Capturing myCopy by value rather than by reference would have led to another problem. The type the compiler creates for the lambda would no longer be a compatible argument with the parameter used to declare the function's signature. Listing 2-23 shows the lambda using capture by value to copy myCopy.

Listing 2-23. Capturing myCopy by Value

```cpp
#include <algorithm>
#include <array>
#include <cstdint>
#include <functional>
#include <iostream>
#include <typeinfo>
#include <vector>

using MyArray = std::array<uint32_t, 5>;
using MyVector = std::vector<MyArray::value_type>;

void PrintArray(const std::function<void(MyArray::value_type)>& myFunction)
{
    MyArray myArray{ 1, 2, 3, 4, 5 };

    std::for_each(myArray.begin(),
        myArray.end(),
        myFunction);
}

int main()
{
    MyVector myCopy;
    auto myClosure = [myCopy](auto&& number) {
            std::cout << number << std::endl;
            myCopy.push_back(number);
        };
    std::cout << typeid(myClosure).name() << std::endl;

    PrintArray(myClosure);

    std::cout << std::endl << "My Copy: " << std::endl;
    std::for_each(myCopy.cbegin(),
        myCopy.cend(),
        [](auto&& number){
            std::cout << number << std::endl;
        });

    return 0;
}
```

The code in Listing 2-23 won't compile and your compiler is unlikely to give you a meaningful or helpful error message. Clang provides the following error output when trying to compile this code using Cygwin on Windows.

```
$ make
clang++ -g -std=c++1y main.cpp -o main
main.cpp:26:13: error: no matching member function for call to 'push_back'
            myCopy.push_back(number);
            ~~~~~~~^~~~~~~~~
```

```
/usr/lib/gcc/i686-pc-cygwin/4.9.2/include/c++/functional:2149:27: note: in instantiation of
function template
    specialization 'main()::<anonymous class>::operator()<unsigned int>' requested here
        using _Invoke = decltype(__callable_functor(std::declval<_Functor&>()))
                        ^
/usr/lib/gcc/i686-pc-cygwin/4.9.2/include/c++/functional:2158:2: note: in instantiation of
template type alias
    '_Invoke' requested here
        using _Callable
        ^
/usr/lib/gcc/i686-pc-cygwin/4.9.2/include/c++/functional:2225:30: note: in instantiation of
template type alias
    '_Callable' requested here
            typename = _Requires<_Callable<_Functor>, void>>
                       ^
/usr/lib/gcc/i686-pc-cygwin/4.9.2/include/c++/functional:2226:2: note: in instantiation of
default argument for
    'function<<lambda at main.cpp:24:22> >' required here
        function(_Functor);
        ^~~~~~~~~
/usr/lib/gcc/i686-pc-cygwin/4.9.2/include/c++/functional:2226:2: note: while substituting
deduced template arguments
    into function template 'function' [with _Functor = <lambda at main.cpp:24:22>, $1 =
<no value>]
        function(_Functor);
        ^
/usr/lib/gcc/i686-pc-cygwin/4.9.2/include/c++/bits/stl_vector.h:913:7: note: candidate
function not viable: 'this'
    argument has type 'const MyVector' (aka 'const vector<MyArray::value_type>'), but
method is not marked const
    push_back(const value_type& __x)
    ^
/usr/lib/gcc/i686-pc-cygwin/4.9.2/include/c++/bits/stl_vector.h:931:7: note: candidate
function not viable: 'this'
    argument has type 'const MyVector' (aka 'const vector<MyArray::value_type>'), but
method is not marked const
    push_back(value_type&& __x)
    ^
main.cpp:30:5: error: no matching function for call to 'PrintArray'
    PrintArray(myClosure);
    ^~~~~~~~~~
main.cpp:12:6: note: candidate function not viable: no known conversion from '<lambda at
main.cpp:24:22>' to 'const
    std::function<void (MyArray::value_type)>' for 1st argument
void PrintArray(const std::function<void(MyArray::value_type)>& myFunction)
    ^
2 errors generated.
makefile:2: recipe for target 'main' failed
make: *** [main] Error 1
```

Given the verbose and confusing error messages output by Clang you may think that the code is very far from being in a working state however you might be surprised to learn that this can be solved with a single keyword, mutable. Listing 2-24 shows the code in a proper compiling state.

Listing 2-24. Creating a mutable Closure

```
#include <algorithm>
#include <array>
#include <cstdint>
#include <functional>
#include <iostream>
#include <typeinfo>
#include <vector>

using MyArray = std::array<uint32_t, 5>;
using MyVector = std::vector<MyArray::value_type>;

void PrintArray(const std::function<void(MyArray::value_type)>& myFunction)
{
    MyArray myArray{ 1, 2, 3, 4, 5 };

    std::for_each(myArray.begin(),
        myArray.end(),
        myFunction);
}

int main()
{
    MyVector myCopy;
    auto myClosure = [myCopy](auto&& number) mutable {
            std::cout << number << std::endl;
            myCopy.push_back(number);
        };
    std::cout << typeid(myClosure).name() << std::endl;

    PrintArray(myClosure);

    std::cout << std::endl << "My Copy: " << std::endl;
    std::for_each(myCopy.cbegin(),
        myCopy.cend(),
        [](auto&& number){
            std::cout << number << std::endl;
        });

    return 0;
}
```

Listing 2-24 contains the solution to all of the error output that you can see above. The mutable keyword is used to tell the compiler that the lambda function should generate a closure with non-const members that have been copied by value.

The closures created by the compiler when they encounter a lambda function are const by default. This causes the compiler to create a type for the closure that can no longer be implicitly converted to a standard function pointer. The resulting error messages generated by a compiler when you try to use a lambda function to generate a closure that is not a suitable type for your code can be exceptionally confusing so there is no real solution here other than to properly learn how to use lambda functions and to compile often when working to pick up when you have made a change that the compiler cannot handle.

The next problem you might encounter while trying to compile the code that you've seen so far in this Recipe is to compile with a C++11 compiler that does not support C++14. The problem here is that C++11 lambdas do not support the auto keyword as a parameter. Building Listing 2-24 with a C++11 compiler results in the following output.

```
clang++ -g -std=c++11 main.cpp -o main
main.cpp:24:31: error: 'auto' not allowed in lambda parameter
    auto myClosure = [myCopy](auto&& number) mutable {
                              ^~~~
main.cpp:30:5: error: no matching function for call to 'PrintArray'
    PrintArray(myClosure);
    ^~~~~~~~~~~
main.cpp:12:6: note: candidate function not viable: no known conversion from '<lambda at
main.cpp:24:22>' to 'const
      std::function<void (MyArray::value_type)>' for 1st argument
void PrintArray(const std::function<void(MyArray::value_type)>& myFunction)
     ^
main.cpp:35:5: error: 'auto' not allowed in lambda parameter
        [](auto&& number){
           ^~~~
In file included from main.cpp:1:
In file included from /usr/lib/gcc/i686-pc-cygwin/4.9.2/include/c++/algorithm:62:
/usr/lib/gcc/i686-pc-cygwin/4.9.2/include/c++/bits/stl_algo.h:3755:2: error: no matching
function for call to object
      of type '<lambda at main.cpp:35:2>'
        __f(*__first);
        ^~~
main.cpp:33:10: note: in instantiation of function template specialization
      'std::for_each<__gnu_cxx::__normal_iterator<const unsigned int *, std::vector<unsigned int,
      std::allocator<unsigned int> > >, <lambda at main.cpp:35:2> >' requested here
    std::for_each(myCopy.cbegin(),
         ^
main.cpp:35:2: note: candidate template ignored: couldn't infer template argument '$auto-0-0'
        [](auto&& number){
        ^
4 errors generated.
makefile:2: recipe for target 'main' failed
make: *** [main] Error 1
```

Thankfully this is a much clearer message than when trying to compile Listing 2-23 and it's reasonably clear that C++11 does not support auto type deduction for lambda function parameters. Listing 2-25 shows the code needed to build a working program that copied an array into a vector using a lambda function.

Listing 2-25. A C++11 Compatible Lambda Function

```cpp
#include <algorithm>
#include <array>
#include <cstdint>
#include <functional>
#include <iostream>
#include <typeinfo>
#include <vector>

using MyArray = std::array<uint32_t, 5>;
using MyVector = std::vector<MyArray::value_type>;

void PrintArray(const std::function<void(MyArray::value_type)>& myFunction)
{
    MyArray myArray{ 1, 2, 3, 4, 5 };

    std::for_each(myArray.begin(),
        myArray.end(),
        myFunction);
}

int main()
{
    MyVector myCopy;
    auto myClosure = [&myCopy](const MyArray::value_type& number) {
            std::cout << number << std::endl;
            myCopy.push_back(number);
        };
    std::cout << typeid(myClosure).name() << std::endl;

    PrintArray(myClosure);

    std::cout << std::endl << "My Copy: " << std::endl;
    std::for_each(myCopy.cbegin(),
        myCopy.cend(),
        [](const MyVector::value_type& number){
            std::cout << number << std::endl;
        });

    return 0;
}
```

The code in Listing 2-25 will work just fine with a C++11 compiler but it does result in lambda functions that are slightly less portable between different types. The lambda function used to print the values from myCopy can now only be used with the type defined by MyVector::value_type whereas the C++14 version could have been reused with any type that could be passed as input to cout.

It goes without saying that none of this code will compile with a C++98 compiler as C++98 does not support lambda functions.

Recipe 2-7. Working with Time

Problem

You would like to write portable programs that are aware of the current time or their execution time.

Solution

Modern C++ provides STL templates and classes that provide portable time handling capabilities.

How It Works

Getting the Current Date and Time

C++11 provides access to different real-time clocks in a given computer system. The implementation of each clock may be different depending on the computer system that you are running on itself however the general intent of each clock will remain the same. You can use the system_clock to query the current time from a system wide real time clock. This means that you can use this type of clock to get the current date and time for a computer whilst your program is running. Listing 2-26 shows how this can be achieved.

Listing 2-26. Getting the Current Date and Time

```
#include <ctime>
#include <chrono>
#include <iostream>

using namespace std;
using namespace chrono;

int main()
{
    auto currentTimePoint = system_clock::now();
    auto currentTime = system_clock::to_time_t( currentTimePoint );
    auto timeText = ctime( &currentTime );

    cout << timeText << endl;

    return 0;
}
```

The program in Listing 2-26 shows how to retrieve the current time from system_clock. You do this using the system_clock::now method. The object returned from now is a time_point that contains a representation of time offset from some epoch. The epoch is a reference time that the system uses to offset all other times. You will not have to worry about the epoch by using the same clock for all of your time work. However you will have to be aware that a time from one computer may not be transferrable directly to another if the systems use different epochs for their time.

The time_point structure cannot be printed out directly and there is no method to convert it to a string however the class does provide a method to convert the time_point object into a time_t object. The time_t type is an old C type that can be converted to a string representation using the ctime function. You can see the result of running this program in Figure 2-6.

```
⊗ ⊖ ⊡   bruce@bruce-Virtual-Machine: ~/Projects/C-Recipes/Recipe2-7/Listing2-26
bruce@bruce-Virtual-Machine:~/Projects/C-Recipes/Recipe2-7/Listing2-26$ ./main
Mon Apr  6 13:15:40 2015

bruce@bruce-Virtual-Machine:~/Projects/C-Recipes/Recipe2-7/Listing2-26$ █
```

Figure 2-6. *The Current Time Printed to the Terminal*

Comparing Times

You can also use the STL time capabilities to compare one time to another. Listing 2-27 shows how you can compare a time to another.

Listing 2-27. Comparing Times

```cpp
#include <ctime>
#include <chrono>
#include <iostream>
#include <thread>

using namespace std;
using namespace chrono;
using namespace literals;

int main()
{
    auto startTimePoint = system_clock::now();

    this_thread::sleep_for(5s);

    auto endTimePoint = system_clock::now();

    auto timeTaken = duration_cast<milliseconds>(endTimePoint - startTimePoint);

    cout << "Time Taken: " << timeTaken.count() << endl;

    return 0;
}
```

Listing 2-27 shows that you can call the now method on a clock multiple times and retrieve different values. The program gets a time into the startTimePoint variable then calls the sleep_for method on the current execution thread. This call causes the program to go to sleep for 5 seconds and calls the system_clock::now method again after it resumes. At this point you have two time_point objects that can be used to subtract one from the other. The duration_cast can then be used to turn the result of the subtraction into a concrete time with a given type of duration. The valid duration types are hours, minutes, seconds, milliseconds, microseconds and nanoseconds. The count method is then used on the duration object to get the actual number of milliseconds that elapsed between calls to now.

> ■ **Note** The code in Listing 2-27 uses a C++14 standard user-defined literal. The 5s passed to sleep for defines a literal of 5 seconds. There are also literals defined for h (hours), min (minutes), s (seconds), ms (milliseconds), us (microseconds) and ns (nanoseconds). These literals can all be applied to an integer literal to inform the compiler that you would like to create a literal of a duration object with the given type of time. Applying s to a character literal such as "A String"s tells the compiler to create a literal of type std::string. These literals are defined in the std::literals namespace and are a C++14 only feature, meaning that they cannot be used in C++11 or C++98 code.

Figure 2-7 shows the output generated when this program is run.

```
bruce@bruce-Virtual-Machine: ~/Projects/C-Recipes/Recipe2-7/Listing2-27
bruce@bruce-Virtual-Machine:~/Projects/C-Recipes/Recipe2-7/Listing2-27$ ./main
Time Taken: 5002
bruce@bruce-Virtual-Machine:~/Projects/C-Recipes/Recipe2-7/Listing2-27$ ./main
Time Taken: 5001
bruce@bruce-Virtual-Machine:~/Projects/C-Recipes/Recipe2-7/Listing2-27$ ./main
Time Taken: 5002
bruce@bruce-Virtual-Machine:~/Projects/C-Recipes/Recipe2-7/Listing2-27$ ./main
Time Taken: 5003
bruce@bruce-Virtual-Machine:~/Projects/C-Recipes/Recipe2-7/Listing2-27$ ▋
```

Figure 2-7. *Output from Several Runs of Listing 2-27*

Figure 2-7 shows that the sleep_for method isn't 100% accurate however it is reasonably close to 5000ms with each run. You can now see how you can use the now method to compare two time_points and it's not much more of a stretch to imagine that you can create an if statement that only executes once a certain amount of time has passed.

Recipe 2-8. Understanding lvalue and rvalue References

Problem

C++ contains a distinction between an lvalue reference and an rvalue reference. You need to be able to understand these concepts to write optimal C++ programs.

Solution

Modern C++ contains two different reference operators, & (lvalue) and && (rvalue). These work hand-in-hand with move semantics to reduce the time spent copying objects in your programs.

How It Works

Move semantics are one of the headline features of the modern C++ programming language. Their usefulness is being significantly overplayed and programmers new to modern C++ programming may be tempted to jump head first into the shiny new feature and actually make their programs worse due to a lack of understanding as to when and why to use an rvalue reference over a lvalue reference.

To put it simply, an rvalue reference should be used to move construct or move assign objects in place of copy operations where appropriate. Move semantics should not be used to replace passing parameters to methods by const reference. A move operation could be faster than a copy, in the worst case it can be slower than a copy and it will always be slower than passing by const reference. This recipe will show you the difference between an lvalue reference, an rvalue reference, the copy and move class constructors and operators and show some performance issues related to each.

The code in Listing 2-28 shows the implementation for a simple class that uses a static counter value to keep track of the number of objects in memory at any given time.

Listing 2-28. A Class that Counts the Number of Instances

```
#include <iostream>

using namespace std;

class MyClass
{
private:
    static int s_Counter;

    int* m_Member{ &s_Counter };

public:
    MyClass()
    {
        ++(*m_Member);
    }

    ~MyClass()
    {
        --(*m_Member);
        m_Member = nullptr;
    }

    int GetValue() const
    {
        return *m_Member;
    }
};
```

```
int MyClass::s_Counter{ 0 };

int main()
{
    auto object1 = MyClass();
    cout << object1.GetValue() << endl;

    {
        auto object2 = MyClass();
        cout << object2.GetValue() << endl;
    }

    auto object3 = MyClass();
    cout << object3.GetValue() << endl;

    return 0;
}
```

The s_Counter static member in Listing 2-28 counts the number of active instances of the class that exist in memory at any given time. This is achieved by initializing the static to 0 and pre-incrementing the value in the MyClass constructor through the member integer pointer. The s_Counter value is also decremented in ~MyClass to ensure that the number never grows out of control. The need for an unconventional setup will become clear when you see the move constructor in action. The output generated by this program is shown in Figure 2-8.

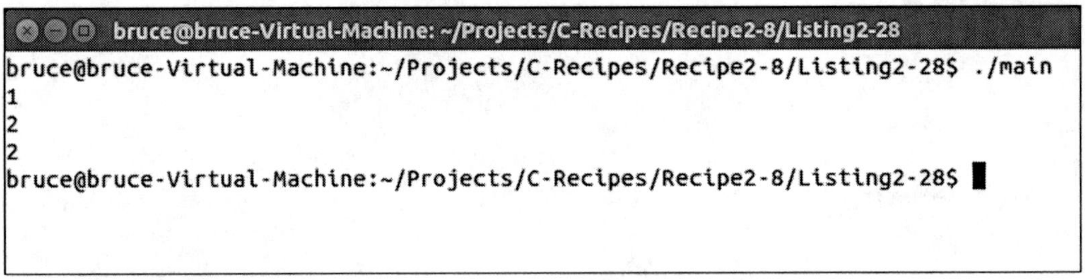

Figure 2-8. *The s_Counter variable in action*

You can now extend MyClass to contain a copy constructor and determine the impact this has on the number of objects in memory at any given time. Listing 2-29 shows a program that includes a MyClass copy constructor.

Listing 2-29. Copying MyClass

```
#include <iostream>

using namespace std;

class MyClass
{
private:
    static int s_Counter;

    int* m_Member{ &s_Counter };
```

CHAPTER 2 ▨ MODERN C++

```cpp
public:
    MyClass()
    {
        ++(*m_Member);
        cout << "Constructing: " << GetValue() << endl;
    }

    ~MyClass()
    {
        --(*m_Member);
        m_Member = nullptr;

        cout << "Destructing: " << s_Counter << endl;
    }

    MyClass(const MyClass& rhs)
        : m_Member{ rhs.m_Member }
    {
        ++(*m_Member);
        cout << "Copying: " << GetValue() << endl;
    }

    int GetValue() const
    {
        return *m_Member;
    }
};

int MyClass::s_Counter{ 0 };

MyClass CopyMyClass(MyClass parameter)
{
    return parameter;
}

int main()
{
    auto object1 = MyClass();

    {
        auto object2 = MyClass();
    }

    auto object3 = MyClass();
    auto object4 = CopyMyClass(object3);

    return 0;
}
```

The code in Listing 2-29 has added a copy constructor and a function to copy object3 into object4. This has the impact of needing two copies, one to copy object3 into parameter and one to copy parameter into object4. Figure 2-9 shows that the two copy operations have occurred and that there are also two subsequent destructors called to destroy these objects.

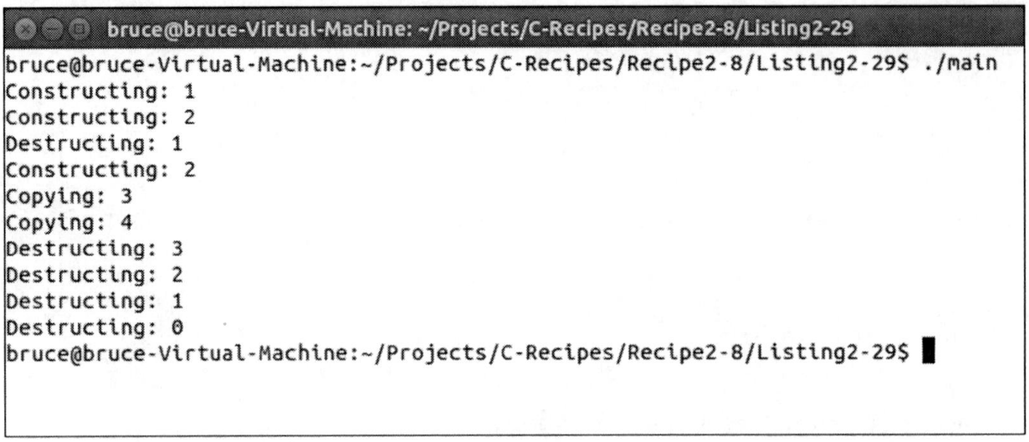

Figure 2-9. *Copy Constructors in Action*

Move constructors can be utilized to cut down on the complexity of a copy constructor. There will be just as many objects in flight however you can safely shallow copy an object in a move constructor thanks to the rvalue reference type that they are passed. A rvalue reference is a guarantee from the compiler that the object referenced by the variable was a temporary object. This means that you are free to cannibalize the object so that you can implement a copy operation faster than if the pre-existing state was needed to be preserved. Listing 2-30 shows how to add a move constructor to MyClass.

Listing 2-30. Adding a Move Constructor to MyClass

```cpp
#include <iostream>

using namespace std;

class MyClass
{
private:
    static int s_Counter;

    int* m_Member{ &s_Counter };

public:
    MyClass()
    {
        ++(*m_Member);
        cout << "Constructing: " << GetValue() << endl;
    }
```

```
    ~MyClass()
    {
        if (m_Member)
        {
            --(*m_Member);
            m_Member = nullptr;

            cout << "Destructing: " << s_Counter << endl;
        }
        else
        {
            cout << "Destroying a moved-from instance" << endl;
        }
    }

    MyClass(const MyClass& rhs)
        : m_Member{ rhs.m_Member }
    {
        ++(*m_Member);
        cout << "Copying: " << GetValue() << endl;
    }

    MyClass(MyClass&& rhs)
        : m_Member{ rhs.m_Member }
    {
        cout << hex << showbase;
        cout << "Moving: " << &rhs << " to " << this << endl;
        cout << noshowbase << dec;
        rhs.m_Member = nullptr;
    }
    int GetValue() const
    {
        return *m_Member;
    }
};

int MyClass::s_Counter{ 0 };

MyClass CopyMyClass(MyClass parameter)
{
    return parameter;
}

int main()
{
    auto object1 = MyClass();

    {
        auto object2 = MyClass();
    }

    auto object3 = MyClass();
    auto object4 = CopyMyClass(object3);

    return 0;
}
```

The code in Listing 2-30 adds a move constructor to MyClass. This has an immediate impact on the running code. You can see that the move constructor is being invoked in Figure 2-10.

```
bruce@bruce-Virtual-Machine:~/Projects/C-Recipes/Recipe2-8/Listing2-30$ ./main
Constructing: 1
Constructing: 2
Destructing: 1
Constructing: 2
Copying: 3
Moving: 0x7ffffcab4b20 to 0x7ffffcab4b28
Destroying a moved-from instance
Destructing: 2
Destructing: 1
Destructing: 0
bruce@bruce-Virtual-Machine:~/Projects/C-Recipes/Recipe2-8/Listing2-30$ █
```

Figure 2-10. *Using a Move Constructor*

The compiler has realized that the state of parameter in Listing 2-30 does not need to be maintained after the return statement has ended. This means that the code can invoke a move constructor to create object4. This creates a scenario for a possible optimization in your code. This example is trivial and therefore there may be minimal performance and memory benefits. If the class was more complicated then you would save the memory needed to have both objects in memory at the same time and the time taken to copy from one object to the other. The performance benefits of this can be seen in Listing 2-31.

Listing 2-31. Comparing Copy Constructors with Move Constructors

```cpp
#include <chrono>
#include <iostream>
#include <string>
#include <vector>

using namespace std;
using namespace chrono;
using namespace literals;

class MyClass
{
private:
    vector<string> m_String{
        "This is a pretty long string that"
        " must be copy constructed into"
        " copyConstructed!"s
    };

    int m_Value{ 1 };
```

```cpp
public:
    MyClass() = default;
    MyClass(const MyClass& rhs) = default;
    MyClass(MyClass&& rhs) = default;

    int GetValue() const
    {
        return m_Value;
    }
};

int main()
{
    using MyVector = vector<MyClass>;
    constexpr unsigned int ITERATIONS{ 1000000U };

    MyVector copyConstructed(ITERATIONS);
    int value{ 0 };

    auto copyStartTime = high_resolution_clock::now();
    for (unsigned int i=0; i < ITERATIONS; ++i)
    {
        MyClass myClass;
        copyConstructed.push_back(myClass);
        value = myClass.GetValue();
    }
    auto copyEndTime = high_resolution_clock::now();

    MyVector moveConstructed(ITERATIONS);

    auto moveStartTime = high_resolution_clock::now();
    for (unsigned int i=0; i < ITERATIONS; ++i)
    {
        MyClass myClass;
        moveConstructed.push_back(move(myClass));
        value = myClass.GetValue();
    }
    auto moveEndTime = high_resolution_clock::now();

    cout << value << endl;

    auto copyDuration =
        duration_cast<milliseconds>(copyEndTime - copyStartTime);
    cout << "Copy lasted: " << copyDuration.count() << "ms" << endl;

    auto moveDuration =
        duration_cast<milliseconds>(moveEndTime - moveStartTime);
    cout << "Move lasted: " << moveDuration.count() << "ms" << endl;

    return 0;
}
```

The code in Listing 2-31 makes use of the `default` keyword to inform the compiler that we would like to use the default constructor, copy constructor and move constructor for this class. This is valid here because there is no manual memory management or behavior needed by `MyClass`. We simple want to construct, copy or move the members `m_String` and `m_Value`. The `m_Value` variable is used to try to prevent the compiler from over-optimizing our example and producing unexpected results. You can see that the move constructor is faster in this instance than the copy constructor in Figure 2-11.

```
bruce@bruce-Virtual-Machine: ~/Projects/C-Recipes/Recipe2-8/Listing2-31
bruce@bruce-Virtual-Machine:~/Projects/C-Recipes/Recipe2-8/Listing2-31$ ./main
1
Copy lasted: 429ms
Move lasted: 368ms
bruce@bruce-Virtual-Machine:~/Projects/C-Recipes/Recipe2-8/Listing2-31$ ./main
1
Copy lasted: 438ms
Move lasted: 333ms
bruce@bruce-Virtual-Machine:~/Projects/C-Recipes/Recipe2-8/Listing2-31$ ./main
1
Copy lasted: 471ms
Move lasted: 357ms
bruce@bruce-Virtual-Machine:~/Projects/C-Recipes/Recipe2-8/Listing2-31$
```

Figure 2-11. *Showing a Move Constructor can be Faster than a Copy Constructor*

Recipe 2-9. Using Managed Pointers

Problem

You would like to automate the task of managing memory in your C++ programs.

Solution

Modern C++ provides the capability to automatically manage dynamically allocated memory.

How It Works

Using unique_ptr

C++ provides three smart pointer types that can be used to automatically manage the lifetime of dynamically allocated objects. Listing 2-32 shows the use of a `unique_ptr`.

Listing 2-32. Using unique_ptr

```cpp
#include <iostream>
#include <memory>

using namespace std;

class MyClass
{
private:
    int m_Value{ 10 };

public:
    MyClass()
    {
        cout << "Constructing!" << endl;
    }

    ~MyClass()
    {
        cout << "Destructing!" << endl;
    }

    int GetValue() const
    {
        return m_Value;
    }
};

int main()
{
    unique_ptr<MyClass> uniquePointer{ make_unique<MyClass>() };
    cout << uniquePointer->GetValue() << endl;

    return 0;
}
```

The code in Listing 3-32 manages to create and destroy a dynamically allocated object without ever using new or delete. The make_unique template handles calling new and the unique_ptr object handles calling delete when the unique_ptr instance goes out of scope. Unfortunately the make_unique template is a C++14 feature and does not exist in C++11. The code in Listing 2-33 shows how you can rectify this.

Listing 2-33. Creating Your Own make_unique

```cpp
#include <iostream>
#include <memory>

using namespace std;

#if __cplusplus > 200400L && __cplusplus < 201200L

template <typename T, typename... Args>
```

```cpp
unique_ptr<T> make_unique(Args... args)
{
    return unique_ptr<T>{ new T(args...) };
}

#endif

class MyClass
{
private:
    string m_Name;
    int m_Value;

public:
    MyClass(const string& name, int value)
        : m_Name{ name }
        , m_Value{ value }
    {
        cout << "Constructing!" << endl;
    }

    ~MyClass()
    {
        cout << "Destructing!" << endl;
    }

    const string& GetName() const
    {
        return m_Name;
    }

    int GetValue() const
    {
        return m_Value;
    }
};

int main()
{
    unique_ptr<MyClass> uniquePointer{
        make_unique<MyClass>("MyClass", 10) };

    cout << uniquePointer->GetName() << endl;
    cout << uniquePointer->GetValue() << endl;

    return 0;
}
```

The code in Listing 2-33 uses another C++11 feature to create a make_unique template. The template is a variadic template and it can take as many arguments as you wish to pass to it. This is proven in the call to make unique where a string and an int are passed through to the MyClass constructor. The __cplusplus preprocessor symbol is used to detect the version of C++ that the compiler is using to build. You may need to ensure that this is working properly with the compiler that you are using as not all compilers implement this correctly. This code will build in C++11 using the user supplied make_unique template and will compile in C++14 using the standard supplied make_unique template.

Unique pointers are exactly as you expect, they are unique and therefore your code cannot have more than a single instance of a unique_ptr pointing to the same object at the same time. It achieves this by preventing copy operations on unqiue_ptr instances. A unique_ptr can be moved however and this allows you to pass a unique_ptr around in your program. Listing 2-34 shows how you can use move semantics to pass a unqiue_ptr around your program.

Listing 2-34. Moving a unqiue_ptr

```cpp
#include <iostream>
#include <memory>

using namespace std;

class MyClass
{
private:
    string m_Name;
    int m_Value;

public:
    MyClass(const string& name, int value)
        : m_Name{ name }
        , m_Value{ value }
    {
        cout << "Constructing!" << endl;
    }

    ~MyClass()
    {
        cout << "Destructing!" << endl;
    }

    const string& GetName() const
    {
        return m_Name;
    }

    int GetValue() const
    {
        return m_Value;
    }
};
```

```
using MyUniquePtr = unique_ptr<MyClass>;

auto PassUniquePtr(MyUniquePtr ptr)
{
    cout << "In Function Name: " << ptr->GetName() << endl;
    return ptr;
}

int main()
{
    auto uniquePointer = make_unique<MyClass>("MyClass", 10);

    auto newUniquePointer = PassUniquePtr(move(uniquePointer));

    if (uniquePointer)
    {
        cout << "First Object Name: " << uniquePointer->GetName() << endl;
    }

    cout << "Second Object Name: " << newUniquePointer->GetName() << endl;

    return 0;
}
```

The code in Listing 2-34 moves a unique_ptr instance into a function. That instance is then moved back out of the function into a second unique_ptr object. There's no reason why the same unique_ptr couldn't have been used in main other than to show that the original instance is not valid after it has been moved from. This is evident in the if call to check if the pointer is valid as this will fail when the code is executed. The unique_ptr can be used in this manner and the object pointed to by the instance will be deleted once it goes out of scope without having been moved from. The output from this program is shown in Figure 2-12.

```
● ● ●   bruce@bruce-Virtual-Machine: ~/Projects/C-Recipes/Recipe2-9/Listing2-34
bruce@bruce-Virtual-Machine:~/Projects/C-Recipes/Recipe2-9/Listing2-34$ ./main
Constructing!
In Function Name: MyClass
Second Object Name: MyClass
Destructing!
bruce@bruce-Virtual-Machine:~/Projects/C-Recipes/Recipe2-9/Listing2-34$ ▮
```

Figure 2-12. *Valid unique_ptr Instances Moved Through a Function*

Using shared_ptr Instances

Where a unique_ptr can give you sole ownership over a single object that you can move around in a single pointer instance, a shared_ptr can give you shared ownership over a single object. This works by having a shared_ptr storing an internal reference count along with the pointer to the object and only deleting the object once all of the values have gone out of scope. Listing 2-35 shows the use of a shared_ptr.

Listing 2-35. Using a shared_ptr

```cpp
#include <iostream>
#include <memory>

using namespace std;

class MyClass
{
private:
    string m_Name;
    int m_Value;

public:
    MyClass(const string& name, int value)
        : m_Name{ name }
        , m_Value{ value }
    {
        cout << "Constructing!" << endl;
    }

    ~MyClass()
    {
        cout << "Destructing!" << endl;
    }

    const string& GetName() const
    {
        return m_Name;
    }

    int GetValue() const
    {
        return m_Value;
    }
};

using MySharedPtr = shared_ptr<MyClass>;

auto PassSharedPtr(MySharedPtr ptr)
{
    cout << "In Function Name: " << ptr->GetName() << endl;
    return ptr;
}

int main()
{
    auto sharedPointer = make_shared<MyClass>("MyClass", 10);

    {
        auto newSharedPointer = PassSharedPtr(sharedPointer);
        if (sharedPointer)
```

```
        {
                cout << "First Object Name: " << sharedPointer->GetName() << endl;
        }

        cout << "Second Object Name: " << newSharedPointer->GetName() << endl;
    }

    return 0;
}
```

The shared_ptr in Listing 2-35 has a different to the unique_ptr that you have seen before. A shared_ptr can be copied through your program and you can have multiple pointers pointing to the same object. This can be seen in Figure 2-13 where the output from the First Object Name statement can be seen.

```
● ● ●  bruce@bruce-Virtual-Machine: ~/Projects/C-Recipes/Recipe2-9/Listing2-35
bruce@bruce-Virtual-Machine:~/Projects/C-Recipes/Recipe2-9/Listing2-35$ ./main
Constructing!
In Function Name: MyClass
First Object Name: MyClass
Second Object Name: MyClass
Destructing!
bruce@bruce-Virtual-Machine:~/Projects/C-Recipes/Recipe2-9/Listing2-35$ █
```

Figure 2-13. *Using a shared_ptr*

Using a weak_ptr

Modern C++ also allows you to hold weak references to smart pointers. This allows you to get a reference to a pointer to a shared object temporarily while you need it for as long as the shared object exists. Listing 2-36 shows how you can achieve this using a weak_ptr.

Listing 2-36. Using a weak_ptr

```
#include <iostream>
#include <memory>

using namespace std;

class MyClass
{
private:
    string m_Name;
    int m_Value;
```

```cpp
public:
    MyClass(const string& name, int value)
        : m_Name{ name }
        , m_Value{ value }
    {
        cout << "Constructing!" << endl;
    }

    ~MyClass()
    {
        cout << "Destructing!" << endl;
    }

    const string& GetName() const
    {
        return m_Name;
    }

    int GetValue() const
    {
        return m_Value;
    }
};

using MySharedPtr = shared_ptr<MyClass>;
using MyWeakPtr = weak_ptr<MyClass>;

auto PassSharedPtr(MySharedPtr ptr)
{
    cout << "In Function Name: " << ptr->GetName() << endl;
    return ptr;
}

int main()
{
    MyWeakPtr weakPtr;
    {
        auto sharedPointer = make_shared<MyClass>("MyClass", 10);
        weakPtr = sharedPointer;

        {
            auto newSharedPointer = PassSharedPtr(sharedPointer);
            if (sharedPointer)
            {
                cout << "First Object Name: " << sharedPointer->GetName() << endl;
            }

            cout << "Second Object Name: " << newSharedPointer->GetName() << endl;
```

```
        auto sharedFromWeak1 = weakPtr.lock();
        if (sharedFromWeak1)
        {
            cout << "Name From Weak1: " << sharedFromWeak1->GetName() << endl;
        }
    }
}

auto sharedFromWeak2 = weakPtr.lock();
if (!sharedFromWeak2)
{
    cout << "Shared Pointer Out Of Scope!" << endl;
}

return 0;
}
```

You can see in Listing 2-36 that a weak_ptr can be assigned a shared_ptr however you cannot access the shared object directly through the weak pointer. Instead a weak pointer supplies a lock method. The lock method returns a shared_ptr instance pointing to the object that you are referencing. This shared_ptr holds the object alive for the entirety of its scope if it ends up being the last object pointing to the object. The lock method always returns a shared_ptr however the shared_ptr returned by lock will fail an if test if the object no longer exists. You can see this at the end of the main function where lock is called after the object has been deleted. Figure 2-14 shows that the weak_ptr cannot get a valid shared_ptr after this has occurred.

```
● ● ●  bruce@bruce-Virtual-Machine: ~/Projects/C-Recipes/Recipe2-9/Listing2-36
bruce@bruce-Virtual-Machine:~/Projects/C-Recipes/Recipe2-9/Listing2-36$ ./main
Constructing!
In Function Name: MyClass
First Object Name: MyClass
Second Object Name: MyClass
Name From Weak1: MyClass
Destructing!
Shared Pointer Out Of Scope!
bruce@bruce-Virtual-Machine:~/Projects/C-Recipes/Recipe2-9/Listing2-36$ ▮
```

Figure 2-14. A weak_ptr Failing to lock a Deleted Object

■ ■ ■

CHAPTER 3

Working with Text

Working with text will be one of the most regular tasks a C++ programmer will have to deal with. You are likely to need to read in user input, write out messages to the user or writing logging functionality for other programmers to more easily debug running programs. Unfortunately working with text is not an easy or straight-forward task. All too often programmers rush into the job and make fundamental errors with their text handling which become major issues later into their projects. The worst of these is not properly accounting for localized versions of text strings. Working with English character sets is generally easy as all English characters and punctuation fit into the ASCII character set. This is convenient as every character needed to represent the English language can fit into a single 8-bit char variable. Things become unstuck as soon as you are required to support foreign languages with your programs. Every character which you need to support will no longer fit into a single 8-bit value. C++ can handle non-English languages in a number of ways which I will cover in this chapter.

Recipe 3-1. Representing Strings in Code Using Literals

Problem

It's is often useful to supply output text when debugging programs. To do this C++ allows you to embed strings directly into your code.

Solution

C++ programs have a concept known as a string table and all string literals in your program are included in the program's executable.

How It Works

A standard C++ string literal is easy to work with. Listing 3-1 shows code which creates a string literal.

Listing 3-1. A string literal

```
#include <iostream>
#include <string>

using namespace std;

namespace
{
    const std::string STRING{ "This is a string"s };
}

int main()
{
    cout << STRING << endl;

    return 0;
}
```

The string literal in this example is the sentence which is included inside the quote marks and followed by the letter s. The compiler will create a table of strings during compilation and place them all together. You can see this string inside the exe file created from the source in Figure 3-1.

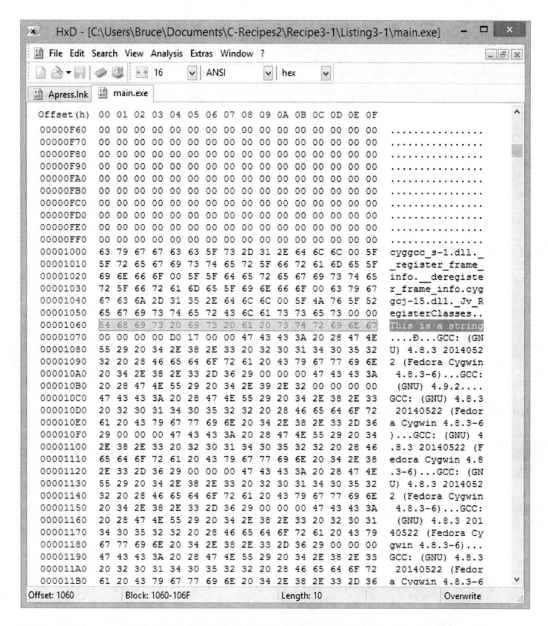

Figure 3-1. *A screenshot from HxD showing the string literal embedded into an executable*

You can use string literals to initialize STL string objects. The compiler will find all of the strings in your program and use the address from the string table to initialize your string. You can see this in Listing 3-1 where the pointer STRING is initialized using the string literal, in effect this code is actually telling the compiler to add the literal to the string table and get the address of this specific string from the table to pass it to the string constructor.

The string literal in Listing 3-1 is a C++14 style string literal. Older style string literals must be used with care as they come with a few caveats. The first is that you should never try to alter the contents of a string literal. Consider the code in Listing 3-2.

Listing 3-2. Editing a string literal

```
#include <iostream>

using namespace std;

namespace
{
    const char* const STRING{ "This is a string" };
    char* EDIT_STRING{ "Attempt to Edit" };
}

int main()
{
    cout << STRING << endl;

    cout << EDIT_STRING << endl;
    EDIT_STRING[0] = 'a';
    cout << EDIT_STRING << endl;

    return 0;
}
```

Listing 3-2 adds a new string literal which is assigned to a non-const pointer. The `main` function also has code which tries to edit the first character in the string to be a lower case a. This code will compile without error, however you should receive a warning from a C++11/C++14 compiler, as it is perfectly valid to attempt to alter strings using the array operator. However it is a runtime exception to try to alter data contained within string literals. Trying to run this program results in the error shown in Figure 3-2.

```
bruce@bruce-Virtual-Machine: ~/Projects/C-Recipes/Recipe3-1/Listing3-2
bruce@bruce-Virtual-Machine:~/Projects/C-Recipes/Recipe3-1/Listing3-2$ ./main
This is a string
Attempt to Edit
Segmentation fault (core dumped)
bruce@bruce-Virtual-Machine:~/Projects/C-Recipes/Recipe3-1/Listing3-2$ █
```

Figure 3-2. *Runtime error generated when attempting to alter string literals*

You can catch these errors at compile time rather than runtime by following a very simple piece of advice. Always assign old-style string literals to variables of type `const char* const`. You can use the makefile from Listing 3-3 if you want to enforce this in a very straight forward fashion.

Listing 3-3. Compiling with warnings as errors

```
main: main.cpp
    clang++ -Werror -std=c++1y main.cpp -o main
```

Compiling your program with the makefile in Listing 3-3 will ensure that the compiler fails to build your application with non-const string literals. An example of the output you can expect can be seen in Figure 3-3.

```
bruce@bruce-Virtual-Machine: ~/Projects/C-Recipes/Recipe3-1/Listing3-3
bruce@bruce-Virtual-Machine:~/Projects/C-Recipes/Recipe3-1/Listing3-3$ make
clang++ -Werror -std=c++1y main.cpp -o main
main.cpp:8:24: error: ISO C++11 does not allow conversion from string literal to
      'char *' [-Werror,-Wwritable-strings]
   char* EDIT_STRING{ "Attempt to Edit" };

1 error generated.
makefile:2: recipe for target 'main' failed
make: *** [main] Error 1
bruce@bruce-Virtual-Machine:~/Projects/C-Recipes/Recipe3-1/Listing3-3$ █
```

Figure 3-3. *Error Output When Compiling with –Werror and Writiable String Literals*

The second problem caused by string literals is that they increase the size of your program. In a digital world, reducing the download size of your programs is a key target to help increase the number of installs of your software. Removing unnecessary string literals is one thing you can do to reduce the size of your executable. Listing 3-4 shows how this can be achieved using the preprocessor.

Listing 3-4. Removing debug string literals from builds

```cpp
#include <iostream>
#include <string>

using namespace std;

#define DEBUG_STRING_LITERALS !NDEBUG

namespace
{
#if DEBUG_STRING_LITERALS
    using StringLiteral = string;
#endif

    StringLiteral STRING{ "This is a String!"s };
}

int main()
{
    cout << STRING << endl;

    return 0;
}
```

Listing 3-4 creates a preprocessor symbol DEBUG_STRING_LITERALS using the NDEBUG symbol. The NDEBUG preprocessor symbol stands for not debug and therefore we can use it to determine whether we would like to have debug string literals included in our program or not. The definition of the type alias StringLiteral is then wrapped in a #if...#endif block which ensures that StringLiteral only exists when building debug builds. The NDEBUG symbol is commonly used in IDEs when building release builds of your program. As the samples that accompany this book are built using make you will have to manually define this in your makefile. An example makefile is shown in Listing 3-5.

Listing 3-5. A makefile that Defines NDEBUG

```
main: main.cpp
        clang++ -D NDEBUG -O2 -Werror -std=c++1y main.cpp -o main
```

At that point you will also need to wrap any code which creates or uses any variables of the StringLiteral type. You should see a problem at this point, using this define means that you cannot have any string literals in your program. A better solution is shown in Listing 3-6.

Listing 3-6. Separating debug and non-debug string literals

```
#include <iostream>
#include <string>

using namespace std;

#define DEBUG_STRING_LITERALS !NDEBUG

namespace
{
#if DEBUG_STRING_LITERALS
    using DebugStringLiteral = string;
#endif

#if DEBUG_STRING_LITERALS
    DebugStringLiteral STRING{ "This is a String!"s };
#endif
}

int main()
{
#if DEBUG_STRING_LITERALS
    cout << STRING << endl;
#endif

    return 0;
}
```

Using the debug literals for diagnostic code, as in Listing 3-6, that the end user should never see allows you to remove strings and code and in turn reduces the size of your executable and increases execution speed.

Recipe 3-2. Localizing User Facing Text

Problem

You never know when you might need to support a language other than your own native tongue. Ensure that any strings the user can see come from a localized source.

Solution

Build a string manager class which returns strings from a self-created table and only ever reference strings using IDs.

How It Works

You could legitimately code your entire project by communicating with the user using strings that you define in your source as string literals. This has a few major drawbacks. First is that it's difficult to switch out languages on the fly. Today it's very likely that your software will be distributed via the internet. It's exceptionally unlikely that your program will not be used by people who speak a different language to yourself. On large development teams there is a possibility that people on the development team have a different first language. Building the ability to localize text into your programs from the beginning will save you many headaches further down the track. This is achieved by loading in the string data for your program from a file. You can then include multiple different languages in your data by writing your strings in your native tongue and having friends or a translation service translate the strings into other languages for you.

You will need to create a class to handle the localized string content for your game. Listing 3-7 shows the class definition for the Localization Manager.

Listing 3-7. The Localization Manager

```
#pragma once

#include <array>
#include <cinttypes>
#include <string>
#include <unordered_map>

namespace Localization
{
    using StringID = int32_t;

    enum class Languages
    {
        EN_US,
        EN_GB,
        Number
    };

    const StringID STRING_COLOR{ 0 };

    class Manager
    {
    private:
        using Strings = std::unordered_map<StringID, std::string>;
        using StringPacks =
            std::array<Strings, static_cast<size_t>(Languages::Number)>;

        StringPacks m_StringPacks;
        Strings* m_CurrentStringPack{ nullptr };

        uint32_t m_LanguageIndex;
```

```
public:
    Manager();

    void SetLanguage(Languages language);

    std::string GetString(StringID stringId) const;
};
}
```

There are a number of things being done in the Listing 3-7. The first aspect of the source to pay attention to is the namespace. You'll find it easier to manage your code if you keep different classes in namespaces that have names which make sense. For the localization module I've used the name Localization. This will help make it clear in your code when you are using classes and objects from this module.

There is a type alias being created to act as an identifier for different strings. Once again a type alias is useful here as you may decide to change the type of your string ids at some point in the future. There is an enum class which determines the languages the Localization Manager supports. The StringID STRING_COLOR is defined as being 0. This is the only StringID in this example as it is all we need to illustrate how the Localization Manager operates.

The Manager itself defines some private type aliases to make the code clear. There is an alias defined to allow us to create an unordered_map of StringID to std::string pairs and another that allows the creation of an array of these string maps. There is also a variable declared to instantiate an array of string maps as well as a pointer to the current string map in use. The class has a constructor and two other methods, SetLanguage and GetString. Listing 3-8 shows the source for the constructor.

Listing 3-8. Localization::Manager Constructor

```
Manager::Manager()
{
    static const uint32_t INDEX_EN_US{ static_cast<uint32_t>(Languages::EN_US) };
    m_StringPacks[INDEX_EN_US][STRING_COLOR] = "COLOR"s;

    static const uint32_t INDEX_EN_GB{ static_cast<uint32_t>(Languages::EN_GB) };
    m_StringPacks[INDEX_EN_GB][STRING_COLOR] = "COLOUR"s;

    SetLanguage(Languages::EN_US);
}
```

This basic constructor is initializing two string maps, one for the US English language and one for British English. You can see the different spellings of the word color being passed into each map. The last line of the source sets the default language to US English. The SetLanguage method is shown in Listing 3-9.

Listing 3-9. Localization::Manager::SetLanguage

```
void Manager::SetLanguage(Languages language)
{
    m_CurrentStringPack = &(m_StringPacks[static_cast<uint32_t>(language)]);
}
```

This method is straight forward. It simply sets the `m_CurrentStringPack` variable to store the address of the string map for the selected language. You must `static_cast` the enum type variable as C++'s STL array will not allow you to use an index which is not a numeric type. You can see the `static_cast` in action converting the language parameter to a `uint32_t`.

The last method in the `Manager` class is the `GetString` method which you can see in Listing 3-10.

Listing 3-10. Localization::Manager::GetString

```
std::string Manager::GetString(StringID stringId) const
{
    stringstream resultStream;
    resultStream << "!!!"s;
    resultStream << stringId;
    resultStream << "!!!"s;
    string result{ resultStream.str() };

    auto iter = m_CurrentStringPack->find(stringId);
    if (iter != m_CurrentStringPack->end())
    {
        result = iter->second;
    }

    return result;
}
```

The `GetString` method begins by building a default string to return from the function. This will allow you to print out any missing string ids in your program to help with localization testing efforts. The `unordered_map::find` method is then used to search for the string id in the map. You know if the `find` call was successful if it returns a valid `iterator`. It will return the end `iterator` if the search fails to find a match. The `if` statement is checking to see whether the string id was found in the map. If it was found the string for the given id is stored in the `result` variable and passed back to the method caller.

▪ **Note**   You could make the default missing string happen only for non-final builds. This would save the execution cost of building this string on your end user's computers. They should hopefully never see missing strings in their programs.

Listing 3-11 lists an updated `main` function which shows how this `Manager` can be used in your code.

Listing 3-11. Using the `Localization::Manager` class

```
#include <iostream>
#include "LocalizationManager.h"

using namespace std;

int main()
{
    Localization::Manager localizationManager;
    string color{ localizationManager.GetString(Localization::STRING_COLOR) };
    cout << "EN_US Localized string: " << color.c_str() << endl;
```

```
    localizationManager.SetLanguage(Localization::Languages::EN_GB);
    color = localizationManager.GetString(Localization::STRING_COLOR);
    cout << "EN_GB Localized string: " << color.c_str() << endl;

    color = localizationManager.GetString(1);
    cout << color.c_str() << endl;

    return 0;
}
```

The main function now creates an instance of the Localization::Manager class. You can see an example of how to retrieve a string from the manager and use it to output using cout. The language is then switched to British English and the string is retrieved and printed a second time. For completeness sake the last example shows what happens when you request a string id which does not exist. Figure 3-4 contains the output from the program.

```
😑 😑 😑   bruce@bruce-Virtual-Machine: ~/Projects/C-Recipes/Recipe3-2/Listing3-7
bruce@bruce-Virtual-Machine:~/Projects/C-Recipes/Recipe3-2/Listing3-7$ ./main
EN_US Localized string: COLOR
EN_GB Localized string: COLOUR
!!!1!!!
bruce@bruce-Virtual-Machine:~/Projects/C-Recipes/Recipe3-2/Listing3-7$ ▉
```

Figure 3-4. *The output from the Localization Manager's strings*

This figure shows output as you would expect. The US English spelling of color appears first, followed by the British English spelling and finally the missing id is output with triple exclamation points at the beginning and end. This should help to have missing string identifiers stand out in your program.

Recipe 3-3. Reading Strings from a File

Problem

Embedding user facing text in your source code makes future text updates and localization difficult to manage.

Solution

You can load your localized string data from a data file.

How It Works

I'm going to show you how to load string data into your program from a Comma Separated Values (.csv) file. Before you can load such a file you will need to create one. Figure 3-5 shows the data I entered into Excel for export as a .csv file.

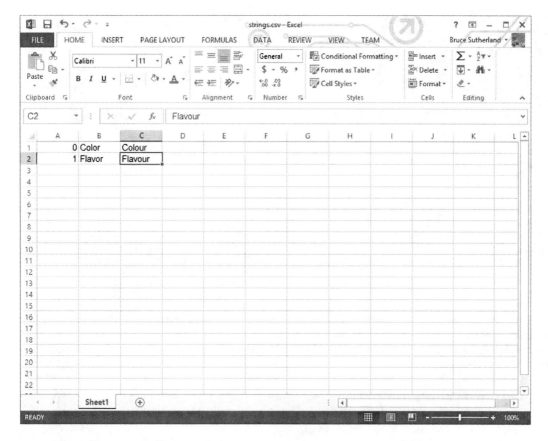

Figure 3-5. *The strings.csv file in Excel 2013*

I have used Excel to create a very basic .csv file. You can see the Color and Colour values I used in the last section as well as the US and UK spellings of flavor. Figure 3-6 shows how this file appears in a basic text editor.

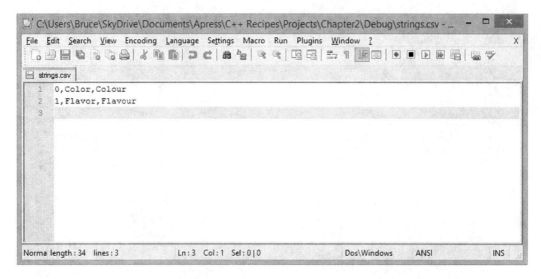

Figure 3-6. *The strings.csv file open in Notepad++*

Each row from the Excel document has been placed into its own line in the csv file and each column has been separated by a comma. This is from where the csv derives its name. Now that we have a csv file we can load the data in the Localization::Manager's constructor. Listing 3-12 contains code which can be used to load and parse the string csv file.

Listing 3-12. Loading strings from a csv

```
Manager::Manager()
{
    ifstream csvStringFile{ "strings.csv"s };

    assert(csvStringFile);
    if (csvStringFile)
    {
        while (!csvStringFile.eof())
        {
            string line;
            getline(csvStringFile, line);

            if (line.size() > 0)
            {
                // Create a stringstream for the line
                stringstream lineStream{ line };

                // Use the line stream to read in the string id
                string stringIdText;
                getline(lineStream, stringIdText, ',');

                stringstream idStream{ stringIdText };
                uint32_t stringId;
                idStream >> stringId;
```

```
            // Loop over the line and read in each string
            uint32_t languageId = 0;
            string stringText;
            while (getline(lineStream, stringText, ','))
            {
                m_StringPacks[languageId++][stringId] = stringText;
            }
        }
    }
}

    SetLanguage(Languages::EN_US);
}
```

The code to read in the strings.csv file isn't overly complicated. The first step is to open the file for reading and the code achieves this using an ifstream object. The ifstream class is provided by C++ to read data in from files and provides methods to achieve this. The first method we use is the overloaded pointer operator. This is called when we use assert or if to determine whether the file passed into the ifstream was valid and was opened. This is followed by a while loop which will run until the end of file or eof method returns true. This is ideal because we do not wish to stop reading data until all of our strings are loaded.

The ifstream class provides a getline method which can be used with C-style string arrays. It's generally better and less error prone to use std::string rather than raw C strings so in Listing 3-12 you can see a use of the std::getline method which takes a reference to any type of stream. The first use of getline retrieves a whole line of text from the csv file into a std::string object. This line contains data about a single string starting with its id, followed by each of the localized versions of the text.

The std::getline method has a very useful third parameter. By default the method retrieves text from a file until it reaches a newline character however we can pass in a different character as a third parameter and the function will stop gathering text when this character is encountered. Listing 3-11 makes use of this feature by passing in a comma as the delimiter. This allows us to pull out the values from each of the cells in the Excel document.

The getline function requires a stream object to be passed to it however the line was read into a std::string. You can see that this problem is solved by creating a stringstream object and passing the line variable to the constructor. Once the stringstream has been created the getline method is used to retrieve the string id using a stringstream object.

■ **Note** C++ provides several methods to convert strings into values. These include stoi to convert to integers and stof to convert to floats as well as others. These are all defined in the string header file. You'll also find a function there named to_string which can be used to convert several different types into a string. These aren't always supplied by the implementation of the STL that you may be using. The version of libstdc++ currently available in Cygwin for example does not provide these functions therefore the code samples have not used them.

After the method has retrieved the id it loops over the rest of the line and reads out the string data for each language. This relies on the Languages enum class definition having the languages in the same order as the columns in the csv file.

Recipe 3-4. Reading the Data from an XML File

Problem

Whilst CSV files are a very simple format and great for some applications they have a major flaw; separating strings by comma means that you cannot use commas in your string data because the loading code would interpret those as the end of the string. If this happens the code can crash as it tries to read in too many strings and overrun the array.

Solution

Save the string file as an XML document and use a parser to load the data.

How It Works

The RapidXML library is an open source XML solution which can be used with your C++ applications. It is supplied as a header file which can be included into any source file you need to have XML handling capabilities. You can download the latest version of RapidXML from the following location http://rapidxml.sourceforge.net/. I saved my Excel document using the XML Spreadsheet 2003 file type. The code shown in this section is capable of loading this type of XML file. Listing 3-13 shows the entire file which contains our string data.

Listing 3-13. The XML Spreadsheet file

```
<?xml version="1.0"?>
<?mso-application progid="Excel.Sheet"?>
<Workbook xmlns="urn:schemas-microsoft-com:office:spreadsheet"
 xmlns:o="urn:schemas-microsoft-com:office:office"
 xmlns:x="urn:schemas-microsoft-com:office:excel"
 xmlns:ss="urn:schemas-microsoft-com:office:spreadsheet"
 xmlns:html="http://www.w3.org/TR/REC-html40">
<DocumentProperties xmlns="urn:schemas-microsoft-com:office:office">
 272103_1_EnBruce Sutherland</Author>
 <LastAuthor>Bruce</LastAuthor>
 <Created>2014-06-13T06:29:44Z</Created>
 <Version>15.00</Version>
</DocumentProperties>
<OfficeDocumentSettings xmlns="urn:schemas-microsoft-com:office:office">
 <AllowPNG/>
</OfficeDocumentSettings>
<ExcelWorkbook xmlns="urn:schemas-microsoft-com:office:excel">
 <WindowHeight>12450</WindowHeight>
 <WindowWidth>28800</WindowWidth>
 <WindowTopX>0</WindowTopX>
 <WindowTopY>0</WindowTopY>
 <ProtectStructure>False</ProtectStructure>
 <ProtectWindows>False</ProtectWindows>
</ExcelWorkbook>
```

```
<Styles>
 <Style ss:ID="Default" ss:Name="Normal">
  <Alignment ss:Vertical="Bottom"/>
  <Borders/>
  <Font ss:FontName="Calibri" x:Family="Swiss" ss:Size="11" ss:Color="#000000"/>
  <Interior/>
  <NumberFormat/>
  <Protection/>
 </Style>
</Styles>
<Worksheet ss:Name="strings">
 <Table ss:ExpandedColumnCount="3" ss:ExpandedRowCount="2" x:FullColumns="1"
  x:FullRows="1" ss:DefaultColumnWidth="54" ss:DefaultRowHeight="14.25">
  <Row>
   <Cell><Data ss:Type="Number">0</Data></Cell>
   <Cell><Data ss:Type="String">Color</Data></Cell>
   <Cell><Data ss:Type="String">Colour</Data></Cell>
  </Row>
  <Row>
   <Cell><Data ss:Type="Number">1</Data></Cell>
   <Cell><Data ss:Type="String">Flavor</Data></Cell>
   <Cell><Data ss:Type="String">Flavour</Data></Cell>
  </Row>
 </Table>
 <WorksheetOptions xmlns="urn:schemas-microsoft-com:office:excel">
  <PageSetup>
   <Header x:Margin="0.3"/>
   <Footer x:Margin="0.3"/>
   <PageMargins x:Bottom="0.75" x:Left="0.7" x:Right="0.7" x:Top="0.75"/>
  </PageSetup>
  <Selected/>
  <ProtectObjects>False</ProtectObjects>
  <ProtectScenarios>False</ProtectScenarios>
 </WorksheetOptions>
</Worksheet>
</Workbook>
```

You might be able to tell from this file listing that our parsing code is going to be required to ignore an awful lot of data. From the document root we will access the string data through the Workbook node then the Worksheet, Table, Row, Cell and finally Data nodes.

▓ **Note** This XML data format is very verbose and a bit heavy on unnecessary data. You would be better served by writing your own lightweight exporter using Excel's Visual Basic for Applications macro support but that topic is out with the scope of this book.

Listing 3-14 covers the code necessary to use RapidXML to load your string data.

Listing 3-14. Using RapidXML to load the strings

```
Manager::Manager()
{
    ifstream xmlStringFile{ "strings.xml"s };
    xmlStringFile.seekg(0, ios::end);
    uint32_t size{ static_cast<uint32_t>(xmlStringFile.tellg()) + 1 };
    char* buffer{ new char[size]{} };
    xmlStringFile.seekg(0, ios::beg);
    xmlStringFile.read(buffer, size);
    xmlStringFile.close();

    rapidxml::xml_document<> document;
    document.parse<0>(buffer);

    rapidxml::xml_node<>* workbook{ document.first_node("Workbook") };
    if (workbook != nullptr)
    {
        rapidxml::xml_node<>* worksheet{ workbook->first_node("Worksheet") };
        if (worksheet != nullptr)
        {
            rapidxml::xml_node<>* table{ worksheet->first_node("Table") };
            if (table != nullptr)
            {
                rapidxml::xml_node<>* row{ table->first_node("Row") };
                while (row != nullptr)
                {
                    uint32_t stringId{ UINT32_MAX };

                    rapidxml::xml_node<>* cell{ row->first_node("Cell") };
                    if (cell != nullptr)
                    {
                        rapidxml::xml_node<>* data{ cell->first_node("Data") };
                        if (data != nullptr)
                        {
                            stringId = static_cast<uint32_t>(atoi(data->value()));
                        }
                    }

                    if (stringId != UINT32_MAX)
                    {
                        uint32_t languageIndex{ 0 };

                        cell = cell->next_sibling("Cell");
                        while (cell != nullptr)
                        {
                            rapidxml::xml_node<>* data = cell->first_node("Data");
                            if (data != nullptr)
                            {
                                m_StringPacks[languageIndex++][stringId] = data->value();
                            }
```

```
                        cell = cell->next_sibling("Cell");
                }
        }

        row = row->next_sibling("Row");
    }
  }
 }
}
```

This listing has a lot going on so I will break it down section by section. The first step involves using the following code to load the entire contents of the XML file into memory.

```
ifstream xmlStringFile{ "strings.xml"s };
xmlStringFile.seekg(0, ios::end);
uint32_t size{ static_cast<uint32_t>(xmlStringFile.tellg()) + 1 };
char* buffer{ new char[size]{} };
xmlStringFile.seekg(0, ios::beg);
xmlStringFile.read(buffer, size);
xmlStringFile.close();
```

You need the entire file to be stored in a memory buffer which is null terminated and this is why the file is opened using ifstream and then seekg is used to move to the end of the stream. Once at the end the tellg method can be used to work out how big the file is. There is a 1 added to the value from tellg to ensure that there is enough memory allocated to allow for a null terminating character as RapidXML requires. Dynamic memory allocation is used to create the buffer in memory and memset clears the entire buffer to contain zeroes. The seekg method is used to move the file stream location to the beginning of the file before read is used to obtain the entire contents of the file into the allocated buffer. The last step is to close the file stream as soon as the code is finished with the file.

These two lines are responsible for initializing the XML data structure from the contents of the file.

```
rapidxml::xml_document<> document;
document.parse<0>(buffer);
```

This code creates an XML document object which contains a parse method. The 0 passed as a template parameter can be used to set different flags on the parser but this example has no need for any of these. Now that the code has created a parsed representation of the XML document it can begin to access the nodes it contains. The next few lines retrieve pointers to the Workbook, Worksheet, Table and Row nodes.

```
rapidxml::xml_node<>* workbook{ document.first_node("Workbook") };
if (workbook != nullptr)
{
    rapidxml::xml_node<>* worksheet{ workbook->first_node("Worksheet") };
    if (worksheet != nullptr)
    {
        rapidxml::xml_node<>* table{ worksheet->first_node("Table") };
        if (table != nullptr)
        {
            rapidxml::xml_node<>* row{ table->first_node("Row") };
            while (row != nullptr)
            {
```

These lines are all straight forward. There is only a single Workbook, Worksheet and Table in a simple Excel XML document so we can simply ask each node for its first child of that name. Once the code gets to the row elements there is a while loop. This will allow us to go over each line from the spreadsheet and load our strings into the appropriate maps. The entire row while loop is as follows.

```cpp
rapidxml::xml_node<>* row{ table->first_node("Row") };
while (row != nullptr)
{
    uint32_t stringId{ UINT32_MAX };

    rapidxml::xml_node<>* cell{ row->first_node("Cell") };
    if (cell != nullptr)
    {
        rapidxml::xml_node<>* data{ cell->first_node("Data") };
        if (data != nullptr)
        {
            stringId = static_cast<uint32_t>(atoi(data->value()));
        }
    }

    if (stringId != UINT32_MAX)
    {
        uint32_t languageIndex{ 0 };

        cell = cell->next_sibling("Cell");
        while (cell != nullptr)
        {
            rapidxml::xml_node<>* data = cell->first_node("Data");
            if (data != nullptr)
            {
                m_StringPacks[languageIndex++][stringId] = data->value();
            }

            cell = cell->next_sibling("Cell");
        }
    }

    row = row->next_sibling("Row");
}
```

The while loop starts by getting the stringId from the first Cell and Data nodes. The atoi function is used to turn the C-style string into an integer that must be cast to an unsigned int. The following if checks whether a valid string id was obtained, if it was then the code enters another while loop. This loop grabs each string from the subsequent Cell and Data nodes and places them into the correct map. It does this by setting the language index to 0 initially and post-incrementing the index after each string is entered. This, again, requires that the localized strings be entered into the spreadsheet in the correct order.

That is all you need to be able to load string data in from XML files. You should be able to come up with a better way to generate these files which don't consume so much data. You might also reach a point where having all of your text loaded consumes too much system RAM. At that point you should consider splitting each language into a separate file and only loading the languages when you need them. It will be unlikely for a user to need every translated language which you choose to support.

Recipe 3-5. Inserting Runtime Data into Strings

Problem

Occasionally you will be required to enter runtime data such as numbers or the user's name into your strings. While C++ supports the older C functions for formatting C-style strings these do not work with STL's string class.

Solution

The boost library provides extensive library support for C++ which includes methods and function for formatting data held in STL strings.

How It Works

To begin you should add a new row to your spreadsheet with the following data; 2, %1% %2%, %2% %1%. You should place each element that comes after a comma in a new cell. Listing 3-15 has updated the main function to utilize this new string.

Listing 3-15. Using `boost::format`

```cpp
#include <iostream>
#include "LocalizationManager.h"
#include "boost/format.hpp"

using namespace std;

int main()
{
    Localization::Manager localizationManager;
    std::string color{ localizationManager.GetString(Localization::STRING_COLOR) };
    std::cout << "EN_US Localized string: " << color.c_str() << std::endl;

    std::string flavor{ localizationManager.GetString(Localization::STRING_FLAVOR) };
    std::cout << "EN_US Localized string: " << flavor.c_str() << std::endl;

    localizationManager.SetLanguage(Localization::Languages::EN_GB);
    color = localizationManager.GetString(Localization::STRING_COLOR);
    std::cout << "EN_GB Localized string: " << color.c_str() << std::endl;

    flavor = localizationManager.GetString(Localization::STRING_FLAVOR);
    std::cout << "EN_GB Localized string: " << flavor.c_str() << std::endl;

    color = localizationManager.GetString(3);
    std::cout << color.c_str() << std::endl;

    std::cout << "Enter your first name: " << std::endl;
    std::string firstName;
    std::cin >> firstName;
```

```
std::cout << "Enter your surname: " << std::endl;
std::string surname;
std::cin >> surname;

localizationManager.SetLanguage(Localization::Languages::EN_US);
std::string formattedName{ localizationManager.GetString(Localization::STRING_NAME) };
formattedName = str( boost::format(formattedName) % firstName % surname );
std::cout << "You said your name is: " << formattedName << std::endl;

localizationManager.SetLanguage(Localization::Languages::EN_GB);
formattedName = localizationManager.GetString(Localization::STRING_NAME);
formattedName = str(boost::format(formattedName) % firstName % surname);
std::cout << "You said your name is: " << formattedName << std::endl;

return 0;
}
```

You can see that the additions to main added in Listing 3-15 ask the user to enter their own name. The call to cin will stall program execution until the user has entered their first name then surname. Once the program has stored the user's name it changes the language to EN_US and gets the string from the Localization Manager. The next line uses the boost::format function to replace the symbols in the string with the firstName and surname values. Our new string contained the symbols %1% and %2%. This is used to decide which variables are replaced into the string. The call to format is followed by a % operator then the firstName string. Because firstName is the first parameter passed to the % operator it will replace the %1% in our string. Similarly the surname will be used to replace the %2% because it is the second parameter passed using %.

This all works because the format function is setting up an object which is returned from the format function. This object is then passed to its % operator which stores the value in firstName. This first call to operator % returns a reference to the boost format object which is passed to the second call to the operator %. The symbols in the source string aren't actually resolved until the format object is passed into the str function. Boost declares the str function in the global namespace therefore it does not need a namespace scope operator. The str method takes the format object and constructs a new string with the parameters replaced into the appropriate positions. When you entered the source strings into the spreadsheet the EN_GB string had the names switched. You can see the results of the code in Figure 3-7.

```
●●● bruce@bruce-Virtual-Machine: ~/Projects/C-Recipes/Recipe3-5/Listing3-15
bruce@bruce-Virtual-Machine:~/Projects/C-Recipes/Recipe3-5/Listing3-15$ ./main
EN_US Localized string: Color
EN_US Localized string: Flavor
EN_GB Localized string: Colour
EN_GB Localized string: Flavour
!!!3!!!
Enter your first name:
Bruce
Enter your surname:
Sutherland
You said your name is: Bruce Sutherland
You said your name is: Sutherland Bruce
bruce@bruce-Virtual-Machine:~/Projects/C-Recipes/Recipe3-5/Listing3-15$ ▮
```

Figure 3-7. *The output from boost::format*

You can use boost::format to replace all sorts of data into strings. Unfortunately boost does not follow the same conventions as the standard C printf functions therefore you will be required to use different strings to standard C programs. A full list of the formatting options provided by boost can be found at http://www.boost.org/doc/libs/1_55_0/libs/format/doc/format.html.

The makefile needed to include the boost/format.hpp header in your program is relatively straight forward. You can see it in Listing 3-16.

Listing 3-16. Including the Boost Library

```
main: main.cpp LocalizationManager.cpp
        clang++ -g -std=c++1y -Iboost_1_55_0 main.cpp LocalizationManager.cpp -o main
```

You can see from this makefile that I was using the 1.55 version of the Boost library and that I placed the folder in the same folder as my makefile. The convention for including Boost headers is to name the Boost folder in the include directive therefore the –I switch in the clang++ command simply tells the compiler to look inside the boost_1_55_0 folder. The boost folder sits inside this folder.

CHAPTER 4

■ ■ ■

Working with Numbers

Computers are designed and built to crunch numbers. The programs you write will take advantage of the computational power of computers to provide experiences to users that are completely dependent on your ability to understand and utilize the tools provided by C++ to manipulate numbers. C++ provides support for different types of numbers, this support includes whole numbers and real numbers as well as multiple different ways of storing and representing these.

The C++ integer types will be used to store whole numbers and the floating point types will be used to store real numbers with decimal points. There are different tradeoffs and considerations to be taken into account when using each type of number in C++ and this chapter will introduce you to different challenges and scenarios where each type is appropriate. You'll also see an older technique named fixed point arithmetic that can use integer types to approximate floating point types.

Recipe 4-1. Using the Integer Types in C++

Problem

You need to represent whole numbers in your program but are unsure of the limitations and capabilities of the different integer types.

Solution

Learning about the different integer types supported by C++ will allow you to use the correct type for the task at hand.

How It Works

Working with the int Type

C++ provides an exact representation of the different integer types supported by modern processors. All of the integer types behave in exactly the same way however they may contain more or less data than each other. Listing 4-1 shows how to define an integer variable in C++.

Listing 4-1. Defining an integer

```cpp
int main(int argc, char* argv[])
{
    int wholeNumber{ 64 };
    return 0;
}
```

As you can see an integer is defined using the int type in C++. The int type in C++ can be used in conjunction with standard arithmetic operators that allow you to add, subtract, multiply, divide and take the modulus. Listing 4-2 uses these operator to initialize additional integer variables.

Listing 4-2. Initializing integerss using opertors

```cpp
#include <iostream>

using namespace std;

int main(int argc, char* argv[])
{
    int wholeNumber1{ 64 };
    cout << "wholeNumber1 equals " << wholeNumber1 << endl;

    int wholeNumber2{ wholeNumber1 + 32 };
    cout << "wholeNumber2 equals " << wholeNumber2 << endl;

    int wholeNumber3{ wholeNumber2 - wholeNumber1 };
    cout << "wholeNumber3 equals " << wholeNumber3 << endl;

    int wholeNumber4{ wholeNumber2 * wholeNumber1 };
    cout << "wholeNumber4 equals " << wholeNumber4 << endl;

    int wholeNumber5{ wholeNumber4 / wholeNumber1 };
    cout << "wholeNumber5 equals " << wholeNumber5 << endl;

    int wholeNumber6{ wholeNumber4 % wholeNumber1 };
    cout << "wholeNumber6 equals " << wholeNumber6 << endl;

    return 0;
}
```

The code in Listing 4-2 contains lines that use operators to initialize additional integers. The operators can be used in a number of ways. You can see that the operators can have either literal values such as 32 or other variables on either side. Figure 4-1 shows the output from this program.

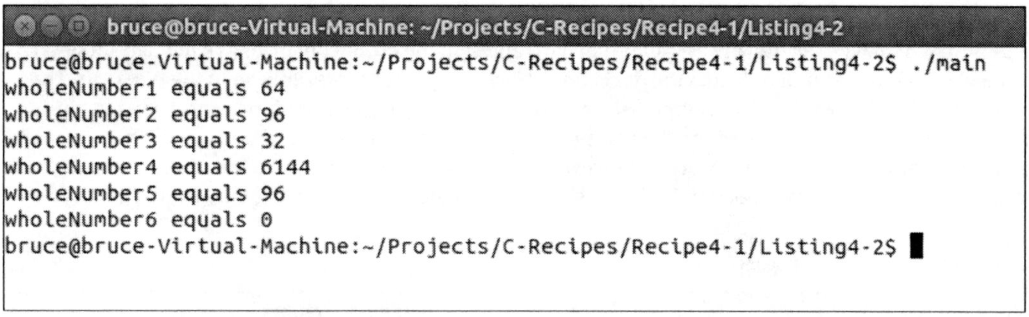

Figure 4-1. *The output from running the code in Listing 4-2*

The output from Listing 4-2 is shown in Figure 4-1. The following list explains how the values shown in the output ends up in each variable.

- The variable wholeNumber1 was initialized with the value of 64 and therefore the output is 64.

- The literal 32 is added to the value of wholeNumber1 and stored in wholeNumber2 therefore the output in 96.

- The next line outputs 32 as the code has subtracted wholeNumber2 from wholeNumber1. The effect of this is that we have managed to store the literal value from the initialization of wholeNumber2 in the variable wholeNumber3.

- The value of wholeNumber4 is output as 6144 which is the result of 64*96.

- The program prints the value of 96 for wholeNumber5 as it is the result of dividing 6144 by 64 or the value of wholeNumber4 divided by the value of wholeNumber1.

- The value of wholeNumber6 is output as 32. The modulo operator returns the remainder from a division. In this case the remainder of 96/64 is 32 therefore the modulo operator has returned 32.

Working with Different Types of Integers

The C++ programming language provides support for different types of integers. Table 4-1 shows the different types of integers and their properties.

Table 4-1. *The C++ integer types*

Type Name	Number of Bytes	Minimum Value	Maximum Value
char	1	-128	127
short	2	-32,768	32,767
int	4	-2,147,483,648	2,147,483,647
long	4	-2,147,483,648	2,147,483,647
long long	8	-9,223,372,036,854,775,808	9,223,372,036,854,775,807

Table 4-1 lists the five main types that C++ supplies to work with whole numbers. The problem C++ presents is that these types are not always guaranteed to represent the number of bytes as shown in Table 4-1. This is because the C++ standard leaves the decision of how many bytes represents up to the platform. The situation isn't entirely the fault of C++. Processor manufacturers may choose to represent integers using different numbers of bytes and therefore the compiler writers for those platforms are free to alter the types to suit their processor by the standard. You can however write code that guarantees the number of bytes in your integers by using the cinttypes header. Table 4-2 shows the different integers available through cinttypes.

Table 4-2. *The cinttypes integers*

Type Name	Number of Bytes	Minimum Value	Maximum Value
int8_t	1	-128	127
int16_t	2	-32,768	32,767
int32_t	4	-2,147,483,648	2,147,483,647
int64_t	8	-9,223,372,036,854,775,808	9,223,372,036,854,775,807

The types supplied by cinttypes contain the number of bits that they represent. Given that there are 8 bits in a byte you can see the relationship by the type and the number of bytes in Table 4-2. Listing 4-3 uses the same operators as Listing 4-2 but is updated to use the int32_t type in place of int.

Listing 4-3. Using the int32_t type with operators

```
#include <iostream>
#include <cinttypes>

using namespace std;

int main(int argc, char* argv[])
{
    int32_t whole32BitNumber1{ 64 };
    cout << "whole32BitNumber1 equals " << whole32BitNumber1 << endl;

    int32_t whole32BitNumber2{ whole32BitNumber1 + 32 };
    cout << "whole32BitNumber2 equals " << whole32BitNumber2 << endl;

    int32_t whole32BitNumber3{ whole32BitNumber2 - whole32BitNumber1 };
    cout << "whole32BitNumber3 equals " << whole32BitNumber3 << endl;

    int32_t whole32BitNumber4{ whole32BitNumber2 * whole32BitNumber1 };
    cout << "whole32BitNumber4 equals " << whole32BitNumber4 << endl;

    int32_t whole32BitNumber5{ whole32BitNumber4 / whole32BitNumber1 };
    cout << "whole32BitNumber5 equals " << whole32BitNumber5 << endl;

    int whole32BitNumber6{ whole32BitNumber2 % whole32BitNumber1 };
    cout << "whole32BitNumber6 equals " << whole32BitNumber6 << endl;

    return 0;
}
```

The output resulting from this code is similar to that of Figure 4-1 as you can see in Figure 4-2.

```
bruce@bruce-Virtual-Machine: ~/Projects/C-Recipes/Recipe4-1/Listing4-3
bruce@bruce-Virtual-Machine:~/Projects/C-Recipes/Recipe4-1/Listing4-3$ ./main
whole32BitNumber1 equals 64
whole32BitNumber2 equals 96
whole32BitNumber3 equals 32
whole32BitNumber4 equals 6144
whole32BitNumber5 equals 96
whole32BitNumber6 equals 32
bruce@bruce-Virtual-Machine:~/Projects/C-Recipes/Recipe4-1/Listing4-3$ ▮
```

Figure 4-2. The output when using the int32_t and code from Listing 4-2

Working with Unsigned Integers

Each of the types shown in Table 4-1 and Table 4-2 have unsigned counterparts. Using an *unsigned* version of the type means that you will no longer have access to negative numbers however you will have a much longer range of positive numbers represented by the same number of bytes. You can see the C++ standard unsigned types in Table 4-3.

Table 4-3. C++'s built-in unsigned types

Type Name	Number of Bytes	Minimum Value	Maximum Value
unsigned char	1	0	255
unsigned short	2	0	65,535
unsigned int	4	0	4,294,967,295
unsigned long	4	0	4,294,967,295
unsigned long long	8	0	18,446,744,073,709,551,615

The unsigned numbers store the same range of numbers as their signed counterparts. Both a signed char and an unsigned char can store 256 unique values. The signed char stores values from -128 to 127 while the unsigned version stores the 256 values from 0 to 255. The built-in unsigned types suffer from the same problem as the signed types, they may not represent the same number of bytes on different platforms. C++'s cinttypes header file provides unsigned types that guarantee their size. Table 4-4 documents these types.

Table 4-4. The cintypes header file's unsigned ineteger types

Type Name	Number of Bytes	Minimum Value	Maximum Value
uint8_t	1	0	255
uint16_t	2	0	65,535
uint32_t	4	0	4,294,967,295
uint64_t	8	0	18,446,744,073,709,551,615

Recipe 4-2. Making Decisions with Relational Operators

Problem

You are writing a program and must make a decision based on the result of a comparison between two values.

Solution

C++ provides relational operators that return true or false based on the comparison being calculated.

How It Works

C++ provides four major relational operators. These are:

- The equality operator

- The inequality operator

- The greater-than operator

- The less-than operator

These operators allow you to quickly compare two values and determine whether the result is true or false. The result of a true or false comparison can be stored in the bool type provided by C++. A bool can only represent either true or false.

The Equality Operator

Listing 4-4 shows the equality operator in use.

Listing 4-4. The C++ equality operator

```
#include <iostream>

using namespace std;

int main(int argc, char* argv[])
{
    int32_t equal1{ 10 };
    int32_t equal2{ 10 };
    bool isEqual = equal1 == equal2;
    cout << "Are the numbers equal? " << isEqual << endl;

    int32_t notEqual1{ 10 };
    int32_t notEqual2{ 100 };
    bool isNotEqual = notEqual1 == notEqual2;
    cout << "Are the numbers equal? " << isNotEqual << endl;

    return 0;
}
```

The code in Listing 4-4 generates the output shown in Figure 4-3.

```
bruce@bruce-Virtual-Machine: ~/Projects/C-Recipes/Recipe4-2/Listing4-4
bruce@bruce-Virtual-Machine:~/Projects/C-Recipes/Recipe4-2/Listing4-4$ ./main
Are the numbers equal? 1
Are the numbers equal? 0
bruce@bruce-Virtual-Machine:~/Projects/C-Recipes/Recipe4-2/Listing4-4$ ▉
```

Figure 4-3. *Output from the relational equality operator*

The equality operator will set a bool variable's value to true (represented by 1 in the output) in the event of the values on both sides of the operator being the same. This is the case where Listing 4-4 compares equal1 to equal2. The result of the operator is false when the values on both sides are different as when the code compares notEqual1 to notEqual2.

The Inequality Operator

The inequality operator is used to determine when numbers are not equal. Listing 4-5 shows the inequality operator in use.

Listing 4-5. The Inequality Operator

```
#include <iostream>

using namespace std;

int main(int argc, char* argv[])
{
    int32_t equal1{ 10 };
    int32_t equal2{ 10 };
    bool isEqual = equal1 != equal2;
    cout << "Are the numbers not equal? " << isEqual << endl;

    int32_t notEqual1{ 10 };
    int32_t notEqual2{ 100 };
    bool isNotEqual = notEqual1 != notEqual2;
    cout << "Are the numbers not equal? " << isNotEqual << endl;

    return 0;
}
```

The output generated by Listing 4-5 is shown in Figure 4-4.

```
● ● ⊙   bruce@bruce-Virtual-Machine: ~/Projects/C-Recipes/Recipe4-2/Listing4-5
bruce@bruce-Virtual-Machine:~/Projects/C-Recipes/Recipe4-2/Listing4-5$ ./main
Are the numbers not equal? 0
Are the numbers not equal? 1
bruce@bruce-Virtual-Machine:~/Projects/C-Recipes/Recipe4-2/Listing4-5$ ▮
```

Figure 4-4. *The output from Listing 4-5 showing the results of the inequality operator*

You can see from Listing 4-5 and Figure 4-4 that the inequality operator will return true when the values are not equal and false when the values are equal.

The Greater-than Operator

The greater-than operator can tell you whether the number on the left is greater-than the number on the right. Listing 4-6 shows this in action.

Listing 4-6. The greater-than operator

```cpp
#include <iostream>

using namespace std;

int main(int argc, char* argv[])
{
    int32_t greaterThan1{ 10 };
    int32_t greaterThan2{ 1 };
    bool isGreaterThan = greaterThan1 > greaterThan2;
    cout << "Is the left greater than the right? " << isGreaterThan << endl;

    int32_t notGreaterThan1{ 10 };
    int32_t notGreaterThan2{ 100 };
    bool isNotGreaterThan = notGreaterThan1 > notGreaterThan2;
    cout << "Is the left greater than the right? " << isNotGreaterThan << endl;

    return 0;
}
```

The greater-than operator sets the value of a bool to be either true or false. The result will be true when the number on the left is greater than the number on the right and false when the number on the right is greater than that on the left. Figure 4-5 shows the output generated by Listing 4-6.

```
bruce@bruce-Virtual-Machine: ~/Projects/C-Recipes/Recipe4-2/Listing4-6
bruce@bruce-Virtual-Machine:~/Projects/C-Recipes/Recipe4-2/Listing4-6$ ./main
Is the left greater than the right? 1
Is the left greater than the right? 0
bruce@bruce-Virtual-Machine:~/Projects/C-Recipes/Recipe4-2/Listing4-6$ 
```

Figure 4-5. *The output generated by Listing 4-6*

The Less-than Operator

The less-than operator produces the opposite result of the greater than operator. The less-than operator returns true when the number of the left is less than that on the right. Listing 4-7 shows the operator in use.

Listing 4-7. The Less-than operator

```cpp
#include <iostream>

using namespace std;

int main(int argc, char* argv[])
{
    int32_t lessThan1{ 1 };
    int32_t lessThan2{ 10 };
    bool isLessThan = lessThan1 < lessThan2;
    cout << "Is the left less than the right? " << isLessThan << endl;

    int32_t notLessThan1{ 100 };
    int32_t notLessThan2{ 10 };
    bool isNotLessThan = notLessThan1 < notLessThan2;
    cout << "Is the left less than the right? " << isNotLessThan << endl;

    return 0;
}
```

Figure 4-6 shows the results when the code in Listing 4-7 is executed.

```
bruce@bruce-Virtual-Machine: ~/Projects/C-Recipes/Recipe4-2/Listing4-7
bruce@bruce-Virtual-Machine:~/Projects/C-Recipes/Recipe4-2/Listing4-7$ ./main
Is the left less than the right? 1
Is the left less than the right? 0
bruce@bruce-Virtual-Machine:~/Projects/C-Recipes/Recipe4-2/Listing4-7$ 
```

Figure 4-6. *The output generated when the less-than operator is used in Listing 4-7*

Recipe 4-3. Chaining Decisions with Logical Operators

Problem

Sometimes your code will require that multiple conditions are satisfied in order to set a Boolean value to true.

Solution

C++ provides logical operators that allow the chaining of relational statements.

How It Works

C++ provides two logical operators that allow the chaining of multiple relational statements. These are:

- The && (and) Operator
- The || (or) Operator

The && Operator

The && operator is used when you would like to determine that two different relational operators are both true. Listing 4-8 shows the && operator in use.

Listing 4-8. The Logical && Operator

```
#include <iostream>

using namespace std;

int main(int argc, char* argv[])
{
    bool isTrue { (10 == 10) && (12 == 12) };
    cout << "True? " << isTrue << endl;

    bool isFalse = isTrue && (1 == 2);
    cout << "True? " << isFalse << endl;

    return 0;
}
```

The value of isTrue is set to true because both of the relational operations result in a true value. The value of isFalse is set to false because both of the relational statements do not result in a true statement. The output of these operations can be seen in Figure 4-7.

```
● ● ●   bruce@bruce-Virtual-Machine: ~/Projects/C-Recipes/Recipe4-3/Listing4-8
bruce@bruce-Virtual-Machine:~/Projects/C-Recipes/Recipe4-3/Listing4-8$ ./main
True? 1
True? 0
bruce@bruce-Virtual-Machine:~/Projects/C-Recipes/Recipe4-3/Listing4-8$ █
```

Figure 4-7. *The Logical && Operator output generated by Listing 4-8*

The Logical || Operator

The logical || operator is used to determine when either or both of the statements used are true. Listing 4-9 contains code that tests the results of the || operator.

Listing 4-9. The Logical || Operator

```cpp
#include <iostream>

using namespace std;

int main(int argc, char* argv[])
{
    bool isTrue { (1 == 1) || (0 == 1) };
    cout << "True? " << isTrue << endl;

    isTrue = (0 == 1) || (1 == 1);
    cout << "True? " << isTrue << endl;

    isTrue = (1 == 1) || (1 == 1);
    cout << "True? " << isTrue << endl;

    isTrue = (0 == 1) || (1 == 0);
    cout << "True? " << isTrue << endl;

    return 0;
}
```

The resulting output generated by this code can be seen in Figure 4-8.

```
● ● ●   bruce@bruce-Virtual-Machine: ~/Projects/C-Recipes/Recipe4-3/Listing4-9
bruce@bruce-Virtual-Machine:~/Projects/C-Recipes/Recipe4-3/Listing4-9$ ./main
True? 1
True? 1
True? 1
True? 0
bruce@bruce-Virtual-Machine:~/Projects/C-Recipes/Recipe4-3/Listing4-9$ █
```

Figure 4-8. *The output generated when using logical || operators*

Listing 4-9 proves that the logical || operator will return true whenever either or both of the relational operations are also true. When both are false the || operator will also return false.

■ **Note**   There is a commonly used optimization when using logical operators. Execution will end as soon as the operator is satisfied. This means that a || operator will not evaluate the second term when the first is true and the && operator will not evaluate the second term when the first is false. Be wary of this when calling functions in the right side statement that have secondary effects outside of their Boolean return value.

Recipe 4-4. Using Hexadecimal Values

Problem

You are working with code that contains hexadecimal value and you need to understand how they work.

Solution

C++ allows the use of hexadecimal values in code and programmers routinely use hex values when writing out binary representation of numbers.

How It Works

Computer processors use a binary representation to store numbers in memory and used binary instructions to test and modify these values. Due to its low level nature, C++ provides bitwise operators that can operate on the bits in variables exactly as a processor would. A bit of information can either be a 1 or a 0. We can construct higher numbers by using chains of bits. A single bit can represent the digits 1 or 0. Two bits however can represent 0, 1, 2 or 3. This can be achieved because two bits can represent four unique signals; 00, 01, 10 and 11. The C++ int8_t data type is made up of 8 bits. The data in Table 4-5 shows how these different bits are represented numerically.

Table 4-5. *The numerical values of bits in an 8bit variable*

128	64	32	16	8	4	2	1
1	0	0	0	1	0	0	1

A uint8_t variable that stored the value represented by Table 4-5 would contain the number 137. In fact, an 8bit variable can store 256 individual values. You can work out the number of values a variable can store by raising the number 2 to the power of the number of bits i.e. 2^8 is 256.

■ **Note** Negative numbers are represented in signed types using the same number of bits as unsigned types. In Table 4-4, a signed value would lose the position at 128 to become a sign bit. You can convert a positive number to a negative using the Two's Complement of the number. To do this you flip all of the bits and add 1. For a two bit number 1 you would have the binary representation 01. To get the Two's Complement, and therefore the negative, firstly flip the bits to 10 then add 1 ending with 11. In an 8 bit value you'd follow the same process. 00000001 becomes 11111110 and adding 1 results in 11111111. No matter than number of bits in a variable, -1 is always represented in Two's Complement by all bits being turned on, this is a useful fact to remember.

Writing bits out in their entirety quickly gets out of hand when dealing with 16, 32 and 64 bit numbers. Programmers tend to write binary representations in a *hexadecimal* format instead. Hex numbers are represented by the values 0-9 and, A, B, C, D, E and F. The values A-F represent the numbers 10 through 15. It takes 4 bits to represent the 16 hexadecimal values therefore we can now represent the bit pattern in Table 4-5 using the hexadecimal 0x89 where the 9 represents the lower 4 bits (8+1 is 9) and the 8 represents the higher 4 bits.

Listing 4-10 shows how you can use hexadecimal literals in your code and use cout to print them to the console.

Listing 4-10. Using Hexadecimal Literal Values

```
#include <iostream>

using namespace std;

int main(int argc, char* argv[])
{
    uint32_t hexValue{ 0x89 };
    cout << "Decimal: " << hexValue << endl;
    cout << hex << "Hexadecimal: " << hexValue << endl;
    cout << showbase << hex << "Hexadecimal (with base): " << hexValue << endl;

    return 0;
}
```

Hexadecimal literals in C++ are proceeded by 0x. This lets the compiler know that you intend for it to interpret the number in hex and not decimal. Figure 4-9 shows the effect of the different output flags used with cout in Listing 4-10.

```
bruce@bruce-Virtual-Machine: ~/Projects/C-Recipes/Recipe4-4/Listing4-10
bruce@bruce-Virtual-Machine:~/Projects/C-Recipes/Recipe4-4/Listing4-10$ ./main
Decimal: 137
Hexadecimal: 89
Hexadecimal (with base): 0x89
bruce@bruce-Virtual-Machine:~/Projects/C-Recipes/Recipe4-4/Listing4-10$ █
```

Figure 4-9. Printing out hexadecimal values

The cout stream by default prints the decimal representation of integer variables. You must pass flags to cout to alter this behavior. The hex flag informs cout that it should print the number in hexadecimal however this does not automatically prepend the 0x base. If you wish your output to have the base on your hexadecimal numbers (and you usually will so that other users don't read the value as decimal 89 instead of 137) you can use the showbase flag which will make cout add the 0x to your hex values.

Listing 4-10 stores the value of 0x89 in a 32bit integer type but the representation still only has an 8 bit value. The other 6 bits are implicitly 0. The proper 32bit representation of 137 would actually be 0x00000089.

■ **Note**   While it's acceptable to drop the 0s when they are implied however it is also common practice to print all 8 hex values out when a 32bit number is intended. This is more important when representing negative numbers such as -1. When using an int32_t 0xF would represent 16 or 0x0000000F where -1 would be 0xFFFFFFFF. Be sure you're setting the value you really wanted when using hexadecimal values.

Recipe 4-5. Bit Twiddling with Binary Operators

Problem

You are developing an application where you would like to pack data into as small a format as possible.

Solution

You can use bitwise operators to set and test individual bits on a variable.

How It Works

C++ provides the following bitwise operators:

- The & (bitwise and) operator
- The | (bitwise or) operator
- The ^ (exclusive or) operator
- The << (left shift) operator
- The >> (right shift) operator
- The ~ (One's Complement) operator

The & (Bitwise And) Operator

The bitwise & operator returns a value that has all of the bits that were set in both the left and right sides of the operator. Listing 4-11 shows an example of this in action.

Listing 4-11. The & operator

```
#include <iostream>

using namespace std;

int main(int argc, char* argv[])
{
    uint32_t bits{ 0x00011000 };
    cout << showbase << hex;
    cout << "Result of 0x00011000 & 0x00011000: "  << (bits & bits) << endl;
    cout << "Result of 0x00011000 & 0x11100111: "  << (bits & ~bits) << endl;

    return 0;
}
```

Listing 4-11 makes use of both the & and ~ operators. The fest use of & will result in the value 0x00011000 being output to the console. The second use of & is used in conjunction with ~. The ~ operator flips all of the bits therefore the output from this use of & will be 0. You can see this in Figure 4-10.

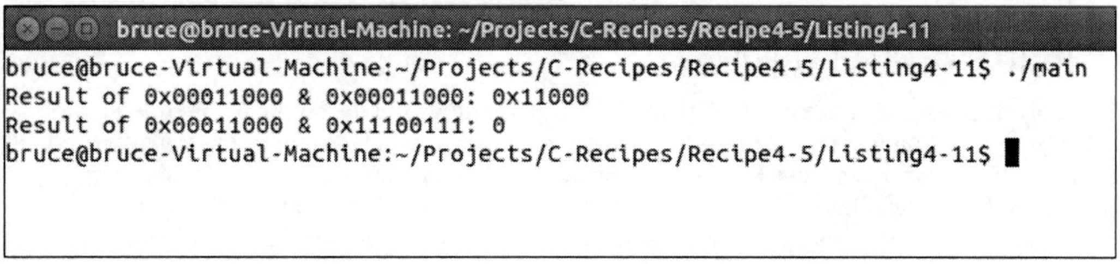

Figure 4-10. The output resulting from Listing 4-11

The | (Bitwise Or) Operator

The bitwise or operator returns a value that contains all of the set bits from the left and right side of the operator. This is true whether either or both of the values are set. The only time a 0 will be placed into a bit is when both the left and right side of the operator does not have that position set. Listing 4-12 shows the | operator in use.

Listing 4-12. The | Operator

```
#include <iostream>

using namespace std;

int main(int argc, char* argv[])
{
    uint32_t leftBits{ 0x00011000 };
    uint32_t rightBits{ 0x00010100 };
    cout << showbase << hex;
    cout << "Result of 0x00011000 | 0x00010100: " << (leftBits | rightBits) << endl;
    cout << "Result of 0x00011000 & 0x11100111: " << (leftBits | ~leftBits) << endl;

    return 0;
}
```

The first use of | will result in the value 0x00011100 and the second will result in 0xFFFFFFFF. You can see that this is true in Figure 4-11.

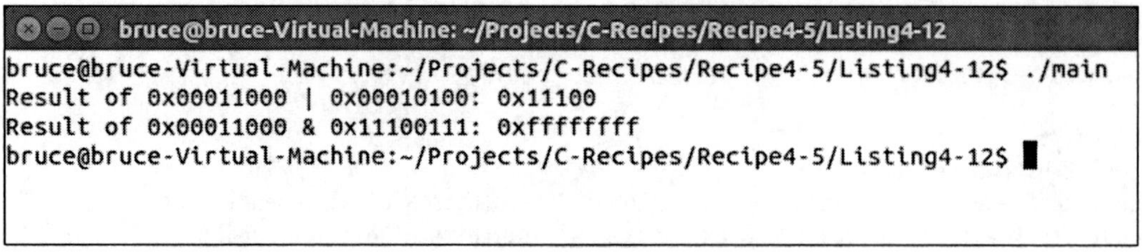

Figure 4-11. *The output generated by Listing 4-12*

The values stored in leftBits and rightBits share a single bit position that is set to 1. There are two positions where one has a bit set and the other doesn't. All three of these bits are set in the resulting value. The second use demonstrates that all bits are set so long as the bit position is set in one of the two places. The distinction between the two is important when you look at the results of the next operator.

The ^ (Exclusive Or) Operator

This operator will produce a single bit of difference between its output and the output of the | operator shown in Figure 4-11. This is because the exclusive or operator only sets the resulting bit to true when either the left or the right bit is set, not when both are set and not when neither are set. The first | operator in Listing 4-12 resulted in the value 0x00011100 being stored as the result. The ^ operator will result in 0x00001100 being stored when using the same values. Listing 4-13 shows the code for this scenario.

Listing 4-13. The ^ operator

```cpp
#include <iostream>

using namespace std;

int main(int argc, char* argv[])
{
    uint32_t leftBits{ 0x00011000 };
    uint32_t rightBits{ 0x00010100 };
    cout << showbase << hex;
    cout << "Result of 0x00011000 ^ 0x00010100: " << (leftBits ^ rightBits) << endl;
    cout << "Result of 0x00011000 ^ 0x11100111: " << (leftBits ^ ~leftBits) << endl;

    return 0;
}
```

The evidence of the different output produced can be seen in Figure 4-12.

```
bruce@bruce-Virtual-Machine: ~/Projects/C-Recipes/Recipe4-5/Listing4-13
bruce@bruce-Virtual-Machine:~/Projects/C-Recipes/Recipe4-5/Listing4-13$ ./main
Result of 0x00011000 ^ 0x00010100: 0x1100
Result of 0x00011000 ^ 0x11100111: 0xffffffff
bruce@bruce-Virtual-Machine:~/Projects/C-Recipes/Recipe4-5/Listing4-13$ ▊
```

Figure 4-12. *The output generated by the ^ operator in Listing 4-13*

The << and >> Operators

The left shift and right shift operators are handy tools that allow you to pack smaller sets of data into larger variables. Listing 4-14 shows code that shifts a value from the lower 16 bits of a uint32_t into the upper 16 bits.

Listing 4-14. Using the << operator

```cpp
#include <iostream>

using namespace std;

int main(int argc, char* argv[])
{
    const uint32_t maskBits{ 16 };
    uint32_t leftShifted{ 0x00001010 << maskBits };
    cout << showbase << hex;
    cout << "Left shifted: " << leftShifted << endl;

    return 0;
}
```

This code results in the value 0x10100000 being stored in the variable leftShifted. This has freed up the lower 16 bits which you can now use to store another 16 bit value. Listing 4-15 uses the |= and & operators to do just that.

■ **Note**   Each of the bitwise operators have an assignment variant for use in statements such as that in Listing 4-15.

Listing 4-15. Using a mask to pack values into a variable

```cpp
#include <iostream>

using namespace std;

int main(int argc, char* argv[])
{
    const uint32_t maskBits{ 16 };
    uint32_t leftShifted{ 0x00001010 << maskBits };
    cout << showbase << hex;
    cout << "Left shifted: " << leftShifted << endl;

    uint32_t lowerMask{ 0x0000FFFF };
    leftShifted |= (0x11110110 & lowerMask);
    cout << "Packed left shifted: " << leftShifted << endl;

    return 0;
}
```

This code now sees two separate 16 bit values being packed into a single 32 bit variable. The value packed into the lower 16 bits has all of its upper 16 bits *masked* out using the & operator in conjunction with a mask value, in this case 0x0000FFFF. This ensures that the |= operator leaves the values in the upper 16 bits unchanged by virtue of the fact that the value being or'd in won't have any of those upper bits set. You can see this is true in Figure 4-13.

```
bruce@bruce-Virtual-Machine: ~/Projects/C-Recipes/Recipe4-5/Listing4-15
bruce@bruce-Virtual-Machine:~/Projects/C-Recipes/Recipe4-5/Listing4-15$ ./main
Left shifted: 0x10100000
Packed left shifted: 0x10100110
bruce@bruce-Virtual-Machine:~/Projects/C-Recipes/Recipe4-5/Listing4-15$ 
```

Figure 4-13. *The results of masking values into integers using bitwise operators*

The final two lines of output in Figure 4-13 are the result of operations to unmask the values from the lower and upper sections of the variable. You can see how this was achieved in Listing 4-16.

Listing 4-16. Unmasking packed data

```cpp
#include <iostream>

using namespace std;

int main(int argc, char* argv[])
{
    const uint32_t maskBits{ 16 };
    uint32_t leftShifted{ 0x00001010 << maskBits };
    cout << showbase << hex;
    cout << "Left shifted: " << leftShifted << endl;
```

```
    uint32_t lowerMask{ 0x0000FFFF };
    leftShifted |= (0x11110110 & lowerMask);
    cout << "Packed left shifted: " << leftShifted << endl;

    uint32_t lowerValue{ (leftShifted & lowerMask) };
    cout << "Lower value unmasked: " << lowerValue << endl;

    uint32_t upperValue{ (leftShifted >> maskBits) };
    cout << "Upper value unmasked: " << upperValue << endl;

    return 0;
}
```

The & operator and the >> operator are used in Listing 4-16 to retrieve the two distinct values from our packed variable. Unfortunately this code has an issue that has yet to be uncovered. Listing 4-17 provides an example of the issue.

Listing 4-17. Shifting and narrowing conversions

```
#include <iostream>

using namespace std;

int main(int argc, char* argv[])
{
    const uint32_t maskBits{ 16 };
    uint32_t narrowingBits{ 0x00008000 << maskBits };

    return 0;
}
```

The code in Listing 4-17 would fail to compile. You will receive an error that a narrowing conversion was going to take place and your compiler will prevent you from building your executable until the problem code is fixed. The problem here is that the value 0x00008000 has the 16th bit set and once it is shifted 16 bits to the right the 32nd bit would be set. This would cause the value to become a negative number under normal circumstances. At this stage you have two different options in your arsenal to deal with the situation.

■ **Note**   Those of you who have used C++ before may have noticed that the samples are not using the = operator to initialize variables, such as uint32_t maskBits = 16; Instead I'm using *uniform initialization* that was introduced in C++11. Uniform initialization is the form of initialization using the {} operator as seen in these examples. The major benefit of uniform initialization is the protection from narrowing conversions that I've just described.

Listing 4-18 shows how you can use an unsigned literal to tell the compiler the value should be unsigned.

Listing 4-18. Using unsigned literals

```
#include <iostream>

using namespace std;

int main(int argc, char* argv[])
{
    const uint32_t maskBits{ 16 };
    uint32_t leftShifted{ 0x00008080u << maskBits };
    cout << showbase << hex;
    cout << "Left shifted: " << leftShifted << endl;

    uint32_t lowerMask{ 0x0000FFFF };
    leftShifted |= (0x11110110 & lowerMask);
    cout << "Packed left shifted: " << leftShifted << endl;

    uint32_t lowerValue{ (leftShifted & lowerMask) };
    cout << "Lower value unmasked: " << lowerValue << endl;

    uint32_t upperValue{ (leftShifted >> maskBits) };
    cout << "Upper value unmasked: " << upperValue << endl;

    return 0;
}
```

Adding a u to the end of a numeric literal causes the compiler to evaluate that literal as an unsigned value. Another option would have been to use signed values instead. However this introduces a new consideration. When right shifting signed values the sign bit is placed into the new values coming in from the right. The following things can occur:

- 0x10100000 >> 16 becomes 0x00001010

- 0x80800000 >> 16 becomes 0xFFFF8080

Listing 4-19 and Figure 4-14 show code and output that proves the negative sign bit propagation.

Listing 4-19. Right shifting negative values

```
#include <iostream>

using namespace std;

int main(int argc, char* argv[])
{
    const uint32_t maskBits{ 16 };
    int32_t leftShifted{ 0x00008080 << maskBits };
    cout << showbase << hex;
    cout << "Left shifted: " << leftShifted << endl;
```

```
    int32_t lowerMask{ 0x0000FFFF };
    leftShifted |= (0x11110110 & lowerMask);
    cout << "Packed left shifted: " << leftShifted << endl;

    int32_t rightShifted{ (leftShifted >> maskBits) };
    cout << "Right shifted: " << rightShifted << endl;
    cout << "Unmasked right shifted: " << (rightShifted & lowerMask) << endl;

    return 0;
}
```

You can see the new code need two extract the upper masked value in the bold lines in Listing 4-19. A shift alone is no longer suitable when using signed integers. Figure 4-14 shows the output proving this point.

```
bruce@bruce-Virtual-Machine: ~/Projects/C-Recipes/Recipe4-5/Listing4-19
bruce@bruce-Virtual-Machine:~/Projects/C-Recipes/Recipe4-5/Listing4-19$ ./main
Left shifted: 0x80800000
Packed left shifted: 0x80800110
Right shifted: 0xffff8080
Unmasked right shifted: 0x8080
bruce@bruce-Virtual-Machine:~/Projects/C-Recipes/Recipe4-5/Listing4-19$ ▮
```

Figure 4-14. *Output showing the sign bit propagation after a right shift*

As you can see, I've had to shift the variable to the right and mask out the upper bits in order to retrieve the original value from the upper part of the variable. After our shift the value contained the decimal value -32,640 (0xFFFF8080) but the value we expected was actually 32,896 (0x00008080). 0x00008080 was retrieved by using the & operator (0xFFFF8080 | 0x0000FFFF = 0x00008080).

CHAPTER 5

■ ■ ■

Classes

Classes are the language feature that sets C++ apart from the C programming language. The addition of classes to C++ allows it to be used for programs designed using the object-oriented programming (OOP) paradigm. OOP quickly became the main software engineering practice used worldwide to build complex applications. You can find class support in most leading languages today, including Java, C#, and Objective-C.

Recipe 5-1. Defining a Class

Problem

Your program design calls for objects, and you need to be able to define classes in your programs.

Solution

C++ provides the class keyword and syntax for creating class definitions.

How It Works

The class keyword is used in C++ to create class definitions. This keyword is followed by the class name and then the body of the class. Listing 5-1 shows a class definition.

Listing 5-1. A Class Definition

```
class Vehicle
{

};
```

The Vehicle class definition in Listing 5-1 tells the compiler that it should recognize the word Vehicle as a type. This means code can now create variables of type Vehicle. Listing 5-2 shows this in action.

Listing 5-2. Creating a Vehicle Variable

```cpp
class Vehicle
{

};

int main(int argc, char* argv[])
{
    Vehicle myVehicle;
    return 0;
}
```

Creating a variable like this results in your program creating an *object*. In the common terminology used when working with classes, the class definition itself is referred to as the *class*. Variables of the class are referred to as *objects*, so you can have multiple objects of the same class. The process of creating an object from a class is referred to as *instantiating* a class.

Recipe 5-2. Adding Data to a Class

Problem

You would like to be able to store data in your classes.

Solution

C++ allows classes to contain variables. Each object gets its own unique variable and can store its own values.

How It Works

C++ has the concept of a *member variable*: a variable that exists in the class definition. Each instantiated object from the class definition gets its own copy of the variable. Listing 5-3 shows a class that contains a single member variable.

Listing 5-3. The Vehicle Class with a Member Variable

```cpp
#include <cinttypes>

class Vehicle
{
public:
    uint32_t m_NumberOfWheels;
};
```

The Vehicle class contains a single uint32_t variable to store the number of wheels the vehicle has. Listing 5-4 shows how you can set this value and print it.

Listing 5-4. Accessing Member Variables

```cpp
#include <cinttypes>
#include <iostream>

using namespace std;

class Vehicle
{
public:
    uint32_t m_NumberOfWheels;
};

int main(int argc, char* argv[])
{
    Vehicle myCar;
    myCar.m_NumberOfWheels = 4;

    cout << "Number of wheels: " << myCar.m_NumberOfWheels << endl;

    return 0;
}
```

Listing 5-4 shows that you can use the dot (.) operator to access member variables on an object. This operator is used twice in the code: once to set the value of m_NumberOfWheels to 4 and once to retrieve the value to print it. Listing 5-5 adds another instance of the class to show that different objects can store different values in their members.

Listing 5-5. Adding a Second Object

```cpp
#include <cinttypes>
#include <iostream>

using namespace std;

class Vehicle
{
public:
    uint32_t m_NumberOfWheels;
};

int main(int argc, char* argv[])
{
    Vehicle myCar;
    myCar.m_NumberOfWheels = 4;

    cout << "Number of wheels: " << myCar.m_NumberOfWheels << endl;

    Vehicle myMotorcycle;
    myMotorcycle.m_NumberOfWheels = 2;

    cout << "Number of wheels: " << myMotorcycle.m_NumberOfWheels << endl;

    return 0;
}
```

105

Listing 5-5 adds a second object and names it myMotorcycle. This instance of the class has its m_NumberOfWheels variable set to 2. You can see the different output values in Figure 5-1.

```
bruce@bruce-Virtual-Machine: ~/Projects/C-Recipes/Recipe5-2/Listing5-5
bruce@bruce-Virtual-Machine:~/Projects/C-Recipes/Recipe5-2/Listing5-5$ ./main
Number of wheels: 4
Number of wheels: 2
bruce@bruce-Virtual-Machine:~/Projects/C-Recipes/Recipe5-2/Listing5-5$ ▮
```

Figure 5-1. *The output generated by Listing 5-5*

Recipe 5-3. Adding Methods

Problem

You need to be able to carry out repeatable tasks on a class.

Solution

C++ allows programmers to add functions to classes. These functions are known as *member methods* and have access to class member variables.

How It Works

You can add a member method to a class simply by adding a function to that class. Any function you add can then use the member variables that belong to the class. Listing 5-6 shows two member methods in action.

Listing 5-6. Adding Member Methods to a Class

```cpp
#include <cinttypes>

class Vehicle
{
public:
    uint32_t m_NumberOfWheels;

    void SetNumberOfWheels(uint32_t numberOfWheels)
    {
        m_NumberOfWheels = numberOfWheels;
    }

    uint32_t GetNumberOfWheels()
    {
        return m_NumberOfWheels;
    }
};
```

The Vehicle class shown in Listing 5-6 contains two member methods: SetNumberOfWheels takes a parameter that is used to set the member m_NumberOfWheels, and GetNumberOfWheels retrieves the value of m_NumberOfWheels. Listing 5-7 uses these methods.

Listing 5-7. Using the Member Methods from the Vehicle Class

```cpp
#include <cinttypes>
#include <iostream>

using namespace std;

class Vehicle
{
private:
    uint32_t m_NumberOfWheels;

public:
    void SetNumberOfWheels(uint32_t numberOfWheels)
    {
        m_NumberOfWheels = numberOfWheels;
    }

    uint32_t GetNumberOfWheels()
    {
        return m_NumberOfWheels;
    }
};

int main(int argc, char* argv[])
{
    Vehicle myCar;
    myCar.SetNumberOfWheels(4);

    cout << "Number of wheels: " << myCar.GetNumberOfWheels() << endl;

    Vehicle myMotorcycle;
    myMotorcycle.SetNumberOfWheels(2);

    cout << "Number of wheels: " << myMotorcycle.GetNumberOfWheels() << endl;

    return 0;
}
```

The member methods are used to alter and retrieve the value of the m_NumberOfWheels member variable in Listing 5-7. The output generated by this code is shown in Figure 5-2.

```
bruce@bruce-Virtual-Machine: ~/Projects/C-Recipes/Recipe5-3/Listing5-7
bruce@bruce-Virtual-Machine:~/Projects/C-Recipes/Recipe5-3/Listing5-7$ ./main
Number of wheels: 4
Number of wheels: 2
bruce@bruce-Virtual-Machine:~/Projects/C-Recipes/Recipe5-3/Listing5-7$
```

Figure 5-2. *The output generated by the code in Listing 5-7*

Recipe 5-4. Using Access Modifiers

Problem

Exposing all member variables to calling code can lead to several problems including high coupling and higher maintenance costs.

Solution

Use the C++ access modifiers to utilize encapsulation and hide class implementations from calling code.

How It Works

C++ provides access modifiers that allow you to control whether code can access internal member variables and methods. Listing 5-8 shows how you can use the private access modifier to restrict access to a variable and the public access specifier to provide methods that access the member indirectly.

Listing 5-8. Using the public and private Access Modifiers

```cpp
#include <cinttypes>

class Vehicle
{
private:
    uint32_t m_NumberOfWheels;

public:
    void SetNumberOfWheels(uint32_t numberOfWheels)
    {
        m_NumberOfWheels = numberOfWheels;
    }

    uint32_t GetNumberOfWheels()
    {
        return m_NumberOfWheels;
    }
};
```

To use an access modifier, insert the keyword into your class, followed by a colon. Once invoked, the access modifier is applied to all member variables and methods that follow until another access modifier is specified. In Listing 5-8, this means the m_NumberOfWheels variable is private and the SetNumberOfWheels and GetNumberOfWheels member methods are public.

If you tried to access m_NumberOfWheels directly in calling code, your compiler would give you an access error. Instead, you have to access the variable through the member methods. Listing 5-9 shows a working sample with a private member variable.

Listing 5-9. Using Access Modifiers

```
#include <cinttypes>
#include <iostream>

using namespace std;

class Vehicle
{
private:
    uint32_t m_NumberOfWheels;

public:
    void SetNumberOfWheels(uint32_t numberOfWheels)
    {
        m_NumberOfWheels = numberOfWheels;
    }

    uint32_t GetNumberOfWheels()
    {
        return m_NumberOfWheels;
    }
};

int main(int argc, char* argv[])
{
    Vehicle myCar;
    // myCar.m_NumberOfWheels = 4; -Access error
    myCar.SetNumberOfWheels(4);

    cout << "Number of wheels: " << myCar.GetNumberOfWheels() << endl;

    Vehicle myMotorcycle;
    myMotorcycle.SetNumberOfWheels(2);

    cout << "Number of wheels: " << myMotorcycle.GetNumberOfWheels() << endl;

    return 0;
}
```

You can see the error that the compiler generates by uncommenting the bold line in Listing 5-9. Encapsulating data in this manner allows you to alter the implementation at a later time without affecting the rest of your code. Listing 5-10 updates the code from Listing 5-9 to use a completely different method of working out the number of wheels on a vehicle.

Listing 5-10. Altering the Vehicle Class Implementation

```cpp
#include <vector>
#include <cinttypes>
#include <iostream>

using namespace std;

class Wheel
{

};

class Vehicle
{
private:
    using Wheels = vector<Wheel>;
    Wheels m_Wheels;

public:
    void SetNumberOfWheels(uint32_t numberOfWheels)
    {
        m_Wheels.clear();
        for (uint32_t i = 0; i < numberOfWheels; ++i)
        {
            m_Wheels.push_back({});
        }
    }

    uint32_t GetNumberOfWheels()
    {
        return m_Wheels.size();
    }
};

int main(int argc, char* argv[])
{
    Vehicle myCar;
    myCar.SetNumberOfWheels(4);

    cout << "Number of wheels: " << myCar.GetNumberOfWheels() << endl;

    Vehicle myMotorcycle;
    myMotorcycle.SetNumberOfWheels(2);

    cout << "Number of wheels: " << myMotorcycle.GetNumberOfWheels() << endl;

    return 0;
}
```

Comparing the Vehicle class from Listing 5-9 and that in Listing 5-10 reveals that the implementations of SetNumberOfWheels and GetNumberOfWheels are completely different. The class in Listing 5-10 doesn't store the value in a uint32_t member; instead, it stores a vector of Wheel objects. The SetNumberOfWheels method adds a new instance of Wheel to the vector for the number supplied as its numberOfWheels parameter. The GetNumberOfWheels method returns the size of the vector. The main function in both listings is identical, as is the output generated by executing the code.

Recipe 5-5. Initializing Class Member Variables

Problem

Uninitialized variables can cause undefined program behavior.

Solution

C++ classes can initialize their member variables at instantiation and provide constructor methods for user-supplied values.

How It Works

Uniform Initialization

Classes in C++ can use uniform initialization to provide default values to class members when they're instantiated. Uniform initialization allows you to use a common syntax when initializing built-in types or objects created from your classes. C++ uses the curly-braces syntax to support this form of initialization. Listing 5-11 shows a class with a member variable initialized in this way.

Listing 5-11. Initializing a Class Member Variable

```
#include <cinttypes>

class Vehicle
{
private:
    uint32_t m_NumberOfWheels{};

public:
    uint32 GetNumberOfWheels()
    {
        return m_NumberOfWheels;
    }
};
```

In Listing 5-11, the class's m_NumberOfWheels member is initialized using uniform initialization. This is achieved using the curly braces after the name. No value is supplied to the initializer, which causes the compiler to initialize the value to 0. Listing 5-12 shows this class used in context.

Listing 5-12. Using the Vehicle Class

```cpp
#include <cinttypes>
#include <iostream>

using namespace std;

class Vehicle
{
private:
    uint32_t m_NumberOfWheels{};

public:
    uint32_t GetNumberOfWheels()
    {
        return m_NumberOfWheels;
    }
};

int main(int argc, char* argv[])
{
    Vehicle myCar;
    cout << "Number of wheels: " << myCar.GetNumberOfWheels() << endl;

    Vehicle myMotorcycle;
    cout << "Number of wheels: " << myMotorcycle.GetNumberOfWheels() << endl;

    return 0;
}
```

Figure 5-3 shows the output generated by this code.

```
😮➖◻ bruce@bruce-Virtual-Machine: ~/Projects/C-Recipes/Recipe5-5/Listing5-12
bruce@bruce-Virtual-Machine:~/Projects/C-Recipes/Recipe5-5/Listing5-12$ ./main
Number of wheels: 0
Number of wheels: 0
bruce@bruce-Virtual-Machine:~/Projects/C-Recipes/Recipe5-5/Listing5-12$ █
```

Figure 5-3. *The output generated by the code in Listing 5-12.*

Figure 5-3 shows output with a 0 for each class. This is an improvement on code that doesn't initialize the data, as shown in Figure 5-4.

```
bruce@bruce-Virtual-Machine: ~/Projects/C-Recipes/Recipe5-5/Listing5-12
bruce@bruce-Virtual-Machine:~/Projects/C-Recipes/Recipe5-5/Listing5-12$ ./main
Number of wheels: 4196331
Number of wheels: 4196800
bruce@bruce-Virtual-Machine:~/Projects/C-Recipes/Recipe5-5/Listing5-12$ ▮
```

Figure 5-4. *The output generated by a program that doesn't initialize its member variables*

Using Constructors

Figure 5-3 represents a better situation than Figure 5-4, but neither is ideal. You'd really like the myCar and myMotorcycle objects in Listing 5-12 to print different values. Listing 5-13 adds a constructor so that you can specify the number of wheels when instantiating classes.

Listing 5-13. Adding a Constructor to a Class

```cpp
#include <cinttypes>
#include <iostream>

using namespace std;

class Vehicle
{
private:
    uint32_t m_NumberOfWheels{};

public:
    Vehicle(uint32_t numberOfWheels)
        : m_NumberOfWheels{ numberOfWheels }
    {

    }

    uint32_t GetNumberOfWheels()
    {
        return m_NumberOfWheels;
    }
};

int main(int argc, char* argv[])
{
    Vehicle myCar{ 4 };
    cout << "Number of wheels: " << myCar.GetNumberOfWheels() << endl;

    Vehicle myMotorcycle{ 2 };
    cout << "Number of wheels: " << myMotorcycle.GetNumberOfWheels() << endl;

    return 0;
}
```

Listing 5-13 adds the ability to initialize the number of wheels on a Vehicle at the time of instantiation. It does this by adding a constructor to the Vehicle class that takes the number of wheels as a parameter. The use of a constructor lets you rely on a function call to occur at the time of object creation. This function is used to ensure that all the member variables your class contains have been properly initialized. Uninitialized data is a very common cause of unexpected program behavior such as crashes.

The myCar and myMotorcycle objects are instantiated with different values for their number of wheels. Unfortunately, adding a constructor to the class means you can no longer construct default versions of this class; you must always supply a value for the number of wheels in Listing 5-13. Listing 5-14 overcomes this limitation by adding an explicit default operator to the class.

Listing 5-14. Default Constructors

```cpp
#include <cinttypes>
#include <iostream>

using namespace std;

class Vehicle
{
private:
    uint32_t m_NumberOfWheels{};

public:
    Vehicle() = default;

    Vehicle(uint32_t numberOfWheels)
        : m_NumberOfWheels{ numberOfWheels }
    {

    }

    uint32_t GetNumberOfWheels()
    {
        return m_NumberOfWheels;
    }
};

int main(int argc, char* argv[])
{
    Vehicle myCar{ 4 };
    cout << "Number of wheels: " << myCar.GetNumberOfWheels() << endl;

    Vehicle myMotorcycle{ 2 };
    cout << "Number of wheels: " << myMotorcycle.GetNumberOfWheels() << endl;

    Vehicle noWheels;
    cout << "Number of wheels: " << noWheels.GetNumberOfWheels() << endl;

    return 0;
}
```

The Vehicle class in Listing 5-14 contains an explicit default constructor. The default keyword is used along with an equals operator to inform the compiler that you want to add a default constructor to this class. Thanks to the uniform initialization of the m_NumberOfWheels variable, you can create an instance of the class noWheels that contains 0 in the m_NumberOfWheels variable. Figure 5-5 shows the output generated by this code.

```
● ● ●  bruce@bruce-Virtual-Machine: ~/Projects/C-Recipes/Recipe5-5/Listing5-14
bruce@bruce-Virtual-Machine:~/Projects/C-Recipes/Recipe5-5/Listing5-14$ ./main
Number of wheels: 4
Number of wheels: 2
Number of wheels: 0
bruce@bruce-Virtual-Machine:~/Projects/C-Recipes/Recipe5-5/Listing5-14$ ▮
```

Figure 5-5. *The output generated by Listing 5-14, showing the 0 in the noWheels class*

Recipe 5-6. Cleaning Up Classes

Problem

Some classes require their members to be cleaned up when an object is being destroyed.

Solution

C++ provides for destructors to be added to classes that allow code to be executed when a class is being destroyed.

How It Works

You can add a special destructor method to your classes in C++ using the ~ syntax. Listing 5-15 shows how to achieve this.

Listing 5-15. Adding a Destructor to a Class

```cpp
#include <cinttypes>
#include <string>

using namespace std;

class Vehicle
{
private:
    string m_Name;
    uint32_t m_NumberOfWheels{};

public:
    Vehicle() = default;
```

```
    Vehicle(string name, uint32_t numberOfWheels)
        : m_Name{ name }
        , m_NumberOfWheels{ numberOfWheels }
    {

    }

    ~Vehicle()
    {
        cout << m_Name << " is being destroyed!" << endl;
    }

    uint32_t GetNumberOfWheels()
    {
        return m_NumberOfWheels;
    }
};
```

The Vehicle class in Listing 5-15 contains a destructor. This destructor simply prints out the name of the object being destroyed. The constructor can be initialized with the name of an object, and the default constructor of Vehicle calls the default constructor of the string class automatically. Listing 5-16 shows how this class can be used in practice.

Listing 5-16. Using Classes with Destructors

```
#include <cinttypes>
#include <iostream>
#include <string>

using namespace std;

class Vehicle
{
private:
    string m_Name;
    uint32_t m_NumberOfWheels{};

public:
    Vehicle() = default;

    Vehicle(string name, uint32_t numberOfWheels)
        : m_Name{ name }
        , m_NumberOfWheels{ numberOfWheels }
    {

    }

    ~Vehicle()
    {
        cout << m_Name << " is being destroyed!" << endl;
    }
```

```cpp
        uint32_t GetNumberOfWheels()
        {
            return m_NumberOfWheels;
        }
};

int main(int argc, char* argv[])
{
    Vehicle myCar{ "myCar", 4 };
    cout << "Number of wheels: " << myCar.GetNumberOfWheels() << endl;

    Vehicle myMotorcycle{ "myMotorcycle", 2 };
    cout << "Number of wheels: " << myMotorcycle.GetNumberOfWheels() << endl;

    Vehicle noWheels;
    cout << "Number of wheels: " << noWheels.GetNumberOfWheels() << endl;

    return 0;
}
```

As you can see from the main function in Listing 5-16, you don't have to add any special code to call a class destructor. Destructors are called automatically when objects go *out of scope*. In this case, the calls to the destructors of the Vehicle objects occur after the return. Figure 5-6 shows the output from this program to prove the destructor code is executed.

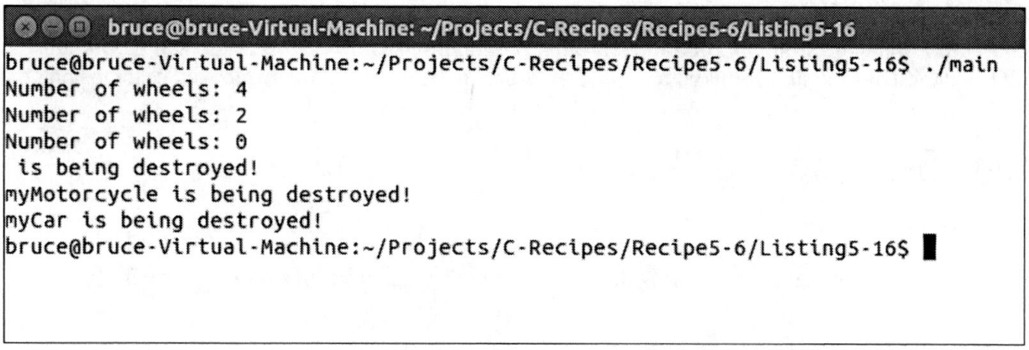

Figure 5-6. *The output generated by Listing 5-16, showing that destructors have been executed*

It's important to pay attention to the order in which these destructors are called. The Vehicle objects are destroyed in an order that's the reverse of that in which they were created. This is important if you have resources that rely on being created and destroyed in the correct order.

The compiler implicitly creates a default destructor if you don't define your own. You can also explicitly define a destructor using the code shown in Listing 5-17.

Listing 5-17. Explicitly Defining a Destructor

```
#include <cinttypes>

class Vehicle
{
private:
        uint32_t m_NumberOfWheels{};

public:
        Vehicle() = default;

        Vehicle(uint32_t numberOfWheels)
                : m_NumberOfWheels{ numberOfWheels }
        {

        }

        ~Vehicle() = default;

        uint32_t GetNumberOfWheels()
        {
                return m_NumberOfWheels;
        }
};
```

It's considered good practice to always be explicit with your default constructor and destructors. Doing so removes any ambiguity from the code and lets other programmers know that you were happy with the default behavior. The omission of this code could lead others to believe that you overlooked its inclusion.

Recipe 5-7. Copying Classes
Problem
You would like to ensure that you're copying data from one object to another in a proper manner.

Solution
C++ provides the copy constructor and assignment operator that you can use to add code to your class that is executed when a copy takes place.

How It Works
You can copy objects in C++ in a number of scenarios. An object is copied when you pass it into the constructor of another object of the same type. An object is also copied when you assign one object to another. Passing an object into a function or method by value also results in a copy operation taking place.

Implicit and Default Copy Constructors and Assignment Operators

C++ classes support these operations through the copy constructor and assignment operator. Listing 5-18 shows the default versions of these methods being invoked in the main method.

Listing 5-18. Using the Copy Constructor and Assignment Operator

```cpp
#include <cinttypes>
#include <iostream>
#include <string>

using namespace std;

class Vehicle
{
private:
    string m_Name;
    uint32_t m_NumberOfWheels{};

public:
    Vehicle() = default;

    Vehicle(string name, uint32_t numberOfWheels)
        : m_Name{ name }
        , m_NumberOfWheels{ numberOfWheels }
    {

    }

    ~Vehicle()
    {
        cout << m_Name << " at " << this << " is being destroyed!" << endl;
    }

    uint32_t GetNumberOfWheels()
    {
        return m_NumberOfWheels;
    }
};

int main(int argc, char* argv[])
{
    Vehicle myCar{ "myCar", 4 };
    cout << "Number of wheels: " << myCar.GetNumberOfWheels() << endl;

    Vehicle myMotorcycle{ "myMotorcycle", 2 };
    cout << "Number of wheels: " << myMotorcycle.GetNumberOfWheels() << endl;

    Vehicle myCopiedCar{ myCar };
    cout << "Number of wheels: " << myCopiedCar.GetNumberOfWheels() << endl;
```

119

```
    Vehicle mySecondCopy;
    mySecondCopy = myCopiedCar;
    cout << "Number of wheels: " << mySecondCopy.GetNumberOfWheels() << endl;

    return 0;
}
```

The `myCopiedCar` variable is constructed using a copy constructor. This is achieved by passing another object of the same type into `myCopiedCar`'s brace initializer. The `mySecondCopy` variable is constructed using the default constructor. Thus the object is initialized with an empty name and 0 as the number of wheels. The code then assigns to `mySecondCopy` using `myCopiedCar`. You can see the results of these operations in Figure 5-7.

```
● ● ●   bruce@bruce-Virtual-Machine: ~/Projects/C-Recipes/Recipe5-7/Listing5-18
bruce@bruce-Virtual-Machine:~/Projects/C-Recipes/Recipe5-7/Listing5-18$ ./main
Number of wheels: 4
Number of wheels: 2
Number of wheels: 4
Number of wheels: 4
myCar at 0x7fff2fb37480 is being destroyed!
myCar at 0x7fff2fb37490 is being destroyed!
myMotorcycle at 0x7fff2fb374b0 is being destroyed!
myCar at 0x7fff2fb374e0 is being destroyed!
bruce@bruce-Virtual-Machine:~/Projects/C-Recipes/Recipe5-7/Listing5-18$ ▮
```

Figure 5-7. *The output generated by Listing 5-18*

As expected, you have three objects named `myCar`, each of which has four wheels. You can see the distinct objects when the destructor prints the address in memory where each object resides.

Explicit Copy Constructors and Assignment Operators

The code in Listing 5-18 takes advantage of the implicit copy constructor and assignment operator. The C++ compiler automatically adds these functions to your classes when it encounters code that will use them. Listing 5-19 shows how you can create these functions explicitly.

Listing 5-19. Explicitly Creating the Copy Constructor and Assignment Operator

```
#include <cinttypes>
#include <iostream>
#include <string>

using namespace std;

class Vehicle
{
private:
    string m_Name;
    uint32_t m_NumberOfWheels{};
```

```
public:
    Vehicle() = default;

    Vehicle(string name, uint32_t numberOfWheels)
        : m_Name{ name }
        , m_NumberOfWheels{ numberOfWheels }
    {

    }

    ~Vehicle()
    {
        cout << m_Name << " at " << this << " is being destroyed!" << endl;
    }

    Vehicle(const Vehicle& other) = default;
    Vehicle& operator=(const Vehicle& other) = default;

    uint32_t GetNumberOfWheels()
    {
        return m_NumberOfWheels;
    }
};
```

The signature for a copy constructor resembles that of a normal constructor. It's a method with no return type; however, the copy constructor takes a constant reference to an object of the same type as a parameter. The assignment operator uses operator overloading to overload the = arithmetic operator for the class when the right side of the statement is another object of the same type, as in someVehicle = someOtherVehicle. The default keyword comes in useful again to allow you to communicate with other programmers that you're happy with the default operations.

Disallowing Copy and Assignment

Sometimes you'll create classes in which you absolutely don't want copy constructors and assignment operators to be used. C++ provides the delete keyword for these cases. Listing 5-20 shows how this is implemented.

Listing 5-20. Disallowing Copy and Assignment

```
#include <cinttypes>
#include <iostream>
#include <string>

using namespace std;

class Vehicle
{
private:
    string m_Name;
    uint32_t m_NumberOfWheels{};
```

```cpp
public:
    Vehicle() = default;

    Vehicle(string name, uint32_t numberOfWheels)
        : m_Name{ name }
        , m_NumberOfWheels{ numberOfWheels }
    {

    }

    ~Vehicle()
    {
        cout << m_Name << " at " << this << " is being destroyed!" << endl;
    }

    Vehicle(const Vehicle& other) = delete;
    Vehicle& operator=(const Vehicle& other) = delete;

    uint32_t GetNumberOfWheels()
    {
        return m_NumberOfWheels;
    }
};

int main(int argc, char* argv[])
{
    Vehicle myCar{ "myCar", 4 };
    cout << "Number of wheels: " << myCar.GetNumberOfWheels() << endl;

    Vehicle myMotorcycle{ "myMotorcycle", 2 };
    cout << "Number of wheels: " << myMotorcycle.GetNumberOfWheels() << endl;

    Vehicle myCopiedCar{ myCar };
    cout << "Number of wheels: " << myCopiedCar.GetNumberOfWheels() << endl;

    Vehicle mySecondCopy;
    mySecondCopy = myCopiedCar;
    cout << "Number of wheels: " << mySecondCopy.GetNumberOfWheels() << endl;

    return 0;
}
```

The delete keyword is used in place of default to inform the compiler that you don't wish the copy and assignment operations to be available to a class. The code in the main function will no longer compile and operate.

Custom Copy Constructors and Assignment Operators

In addition to using the default versions of these operations, it's possible to supply your own versions. This is done by using the same signatures for the methods in your class definition but providing a method body in place of the default assignment.

More often than not in modern C++, the places you'll overload these operators are limited; but it's important to be aware of the one place where you absolutely want to do so. The default copy and assignment operations carry out a *shallow copy*. They call the assignment operator on each member of an object and assign the value from the class passed in. There are occasions when you have a class that manually manages a resource, such as memory, and a shallow copy ends up with a pointer in both classes pointing to the same address in memory. If that memory is freed in the class's destructor, you're left in a situation where one object is pointing to memory that has been freed by another. In this case, your program is likely to crash or exhibit other strange behavior. Listing 5-21 shows an example in which this could occur.

Listing 5-21. Shallow-Copying a C-Style String Member

```
#include <cinttypes>
#include <cstring>
#include <iostream>

using namespace std;

class Vehicle
{
private:
    char* m_Name{};
    uint32_t m_NumberOfWheels{};

public:
    Vehicle() = default;

    Vehicle(const char* name, uint32_t numberOfWheels)
        : m_NumberOfWheels{ numberOfWheels }
    {
        const uint32_t length = strlen(name) + 1; // Add space for null terminator
        m_Name = new char[length]{};
        strcpy(m_Name, name);
    }

    ~Vehicle()
    {
        delete m_Name;
        m_Name = nullptr;
    }

    Vehicle(const Vehicle& other) = default;
    Vehicle& operator=(const Vehicle& other) = default;

    char* GetName()
    {
        return m_Name;
    }
```

```
    uint32_t GetNumberOfWheels()
    {
        return m_NumberOfWheels;
    }
};

int main(int argc, char* argv[])
{
    Vehicle myAssignedCar;

    {
        Vehicle myCar{ "myCar", 4 };
        cout << "Vehicle name: " << myCar.GetName() << endl;

        myAssignedCar = myCar;
        cout << "Vehicle name: " << myAssignedCar.GetName() << endl;
    }

    cout << "Vehicle name: " << myAssignedCar.GetName() << endl;

    return 0;
}
```

■ **Note**   The code in Listing 5-21 is purposefully constructed to create a situation that would be better solved by using a STL string class. This code is simply intended to be an easy-to-understand example of how things can go wrong.

The main function in Listing 5-21 creates two instances of the Vehicle class. The second is created in a block. This block causes the myCar object to be destructed when the block ends and the object goes out of scope. This is a problem because the last line of the block invokes the assignment operator and does a shallow copy of the class members. After this takes place, the myCar and myAssignedCar objects point to the same memory address in their m_Name variables. This memory is released in the destructor for myCar before the code tries to print the name of myAssignedCar. You can see the result of this error in Figure 5-8.

```
😣⊜⊚  bruce@bruce-Virtual-Machine: ~/Projects/C-Recipes/Recipe5-7/Listing5-21
bruce@bruce-Virtual-Machine:~/Projects/C-Recipes/Recipe5-7/Listing5-21$ ./main
Vehicle name: myCar
Vehicle name: myCar
Vehicle name:
*** Error in `./main': double free or corruption (fasttop): 0x00000000021c2010 *
**
Aborted (core dumped)
bruce@bruce-Virtual-Machine:~/Projects/C-Recipes/Recipe5-7/Listing5-21$ ▊
```

Figure 5-8.   *Output showing the error from shallow-copying an object before it's destroyed*

Figure 5-8 proves that the shallow copy results in a dangerous situation for the code. The memory pointed to by the m_Name variable in myAssignedCar is no longer valid as soon as the myCar variable has been destroyed. Listing 5-22 solves this problem by providing a copy constructor and an assignment operator that carry out a deep copy of the class.

Listing 5-22. Carrying Out a Deep Copy

```cpp
#include <cinttypes>
#include <cstring>
#include <iostream>

using namespace std;

class Vehicle
{
private:
    char* m_Name{};
    uint32_t m_NumberOfWheels{};

public:
    Vehicle() = default;

    Vehicle(const char* name, uint32_t numberOfWheels)
        : m_NumberOfWheels{ numberOfWheels }
    {
        const uint32_t length = strlen(name) + 1; // Add space for null terminator
        m_Name = new char[length]{};
        strcpy(m_Name, name);
    }

    ~Vehicle()
    {
        delete m_Name;
        m_Name = nullptr;
    }

    Vehicle(const Vehicle& other)
    {
        const uint32_t length = strlen(other.m_Name) + 1; // Add space for null terminator
        m_Name = new char[length]{};
        strcpy(m_Name, other.m_Name);

        m_NumberOfWheels = other.m_NumberOfWheels;
    }

    Vehicle& operator=(const Vehicle& other)
    {
        if (m_Name != nullptr)
        {
            delete m_Name;
        }
```

```
        const uint32_t length = strlen(other.m_Name) + 1; // Add space for null terminator
        m_Name = new char[length]{};
        strcpy(m_Name, other.m_Name);

        m_NumberOfWheels = other.m_NumberOfWheels;

        return *this;
    }

    char* GetName()
    {
        return m_Name;
    }

    uint32_t GetNumberOfWheels()
    {
        return m_NumberOfWheels;
    }
};

int main(int argc, char* argv[])
{
    Vehicle myAssignedCar;

    {
        Vehicle myCar{ "myCar", 4 };
        cout << "Vehicle name: " << myCar.GetName() << endl;

        myAssignedCar = myCar;
        cout << "Vehicle name: " << myAssignedCar.GetName() << endl;
    }

    cout << "Vehicle name: " << myAssignedCar.GetName() << endl;

    return 0;
}
```

This time, the code provides methods to be carried out when a copy or assignment takes place. The copy constructor is invoked when a new object is created by copying an old object, so you never need to worry about deleting the old data. The assignment operator, on the other hand, can't guarantee that the existing class didn't already exist. You can see the implications of this in the assignment operator when it's responsibly deleting the memory allocated for the existing m_Name variable. The result of these deep copies can be seen in Figure 5-9.

```
⊗ ⊜ ⊜    bruce@bruce-Virtual-Machine: ~/Projects/C-Recipes/Recipe5-7/Listing5-22
bruce@bruce-Virtual-Machine:~/Projects/C-Recipes/Recipe5-7/Listing5-22$ ./main
Vehicle name: myCar
Vehicle name: myCar
Vehicle name: myCar
bruce@bruce-Virtual-Machine:~/Projects/C-Recipes/Recipe5-7/Listing5-22$ ▮
```

Figure 5-9. *The result of using a deep copy*

The output is now correct, thanks to the use of a deep copy. This gives the myAssignedCar variable its own copy of the name string rather than simply having its pointer assigned the same address as the myCar class. The proper solution to solving the problem in this case is to use an STL string in place of the C-style string, but the example will be valid if you ever have to write classes that may end up pointed to the same dynamically allocated memory or stack memory in the future.

Recipe 5-8. Optimizing Code with Move Semantics

Problem

Your code is running slowly, and you think the problem is caused by copying temporary objects.

Solution

C++ provides support for move semantics in the form of a move constructor and a move assignment operator.

How It Works

The code shown in Listing 5-23 performs a deep copy of an object to avoid the scenario where a different object is left pointing at an invalid memory address.

Listing 5-23. Using Deep Copy to Avoid Invalid Pointers

```
#include <cinttypes>
#include <cstring>
#include <iostream>

using namespace std;

class Vehicle
{
private:
    char* m_Name{};
    uint32_t m_NumberOfWheels{};

public:
    Vehicle() = default;
```

```cpp
    Vehicle(const char* name, uint32_t numberOfWheels)
        : m_NumberOfWheels{ numberOfWheels }
    {
        const uint32_t length = strlen(name) + 1; // Add space for null terminator
        m_Name = new char[length]{};
        strcpy(m_Name, name);
    }

    ~Vehicle()
    {
        delete m_Name;
        m_Name = nullptr;
    }

    Vehicle(const Vehicle& other)
    {
        const uint32_t length = strlen(other.m_Name) + 1; // Add space for null terminator
        m_Name = new char[length]{};
        strcpy(m_Name, other.m_Name);

        m_NumberOfWheels = other.m_NumberOfWheels;
    }

    Vehicle& operator=(const Vehicle& other)
    {
        if (m_Name != nullptr)
        {
            delete m_Name;
        }

        const uint32_t length = strlen(other.m_Name) + 1; // Add space for null terminator
        m_Name = new char[length]{};
        strcpy(m_Name, other.m_Name);

        m_NumberOfWheels = other.m_NumberOfWheels;

        return *this;
    }

    char* GetName()
    {
        return m_Name;
    }

    uint32_t GetNumberOfWheels()
    {
        return m_NumberOfWheels;
    }
};
```

```
int main(int argc, char* argv[])
{
    Vehicle myAssignedCar;

    {
        Vehicle myCar{ "myCar", 4 };
        cout << "Vehicle name: " << myCar.GetName() << endl;

        myAssignedCar = myCar;
        cout << "Vehicle name: " << myAssignedCar.GetName() << endl;
    }

    cout << "Vehicle name: " << myAssignedCar.GetName() << endl;

    return 0;
}
```

This is the correct solution when you know that two objects may live a considerable time but one may be destroyed before the other, which would likely result in a crash. Sometimes, however, you know that the object you're copying from is about to destroyed. C++ allows you to optimize such situations using move semantics. Listing 5-24 adds a move constructor and a move assignment operator to the class and uses the move function to invoke them.

Listing 5-24. The Move Constructor and Move Assignment Operator

```
#include <cinttypes>
#include <cstring>
#include <iostream>

using namespace std;

class Vehicle
{
private:
    char* m_Name{};
    uint32_t m_NumberOfWheels{};

public:
    Vehicle() = default;

    Vehicle(const char* name, uint32_t numberOfWheels)
        : m_NumberOfWheels{ numberOfWheels }
    {
        const uint32_t length = strlen(name) + 1; // Add space for null terminator
        m_Name = new char[length]{};
        strcpy(m_Name, name);
    }
```

```cpp
    ~Vehicle()
    {
        if (m_Name != nullptr)
        {
            delete m_Name;
            m_Name = nullptr;
        }
    }

    Vehicle(const Vehicle& other)
    {
        const uint32_t length = strlen(other.m_Name) + 1; // Add space for null terminator
        m_Name = new char[length]{};
        strcpy(m_Name, other.m_Name);

        m_NumberOfWheels = other.m_NumberOfWheels;
    }

    Vehicle& operator=(const Vehicle& other)
    {
        if (m_Name != nullptr)
        {
            delete m_Name;
        }

        const uint32_t length = strlen(other.m_Name) + 1; // Add space for null terminator
        m_Name = new char[length]{};
        strcpy(m_Name, other.m_Name);

        m_NumberOfWheels = other.m_NumberOfWheels;

        return *this;
    }

    Vehicle(Vehicle&& other)
    {
        m_Name = other.m_Name;
        other.m_Name = nullptr;

        m_NumberOfWheels = other.m_NumberOfWheels;
    }

    Vehicle& operator=(Vehicle&& other)
    {
        if (m_Name != nullptr)
        {
            delete m_Name;
        }
```

```
            m_Name = other.m_Name;
            other.m_Name = nullptr;

            m_NumberOfWheels = other.m_NumberOfWheels;

            return *this;
        }

    char* GetName()
    {
        return m_Name;
    }

    uint32_t GetNumberOfWheels()
    {
        return m_NumberOfWheels;
    }
};

int main(int argc, char* argv[])
{
    Vehicle myAssignedCar;

    {
        Vehicle myCar{ "myCar", 4 };
        cout << "Vehicle name: " << myCar.GetName() << endl;

        myAssignedCar = move(myCar);
        //cout << "Vehicle name: " << myCar.GetName() << endl;
        cout << "Vehicle name: " << myAssignedCar.GetName() << endl;
    }

    cout << "Vehicle name: " << myAssignedCar.GetName() << endl;

    return 0;
}
```

Move semantics work by providing class methods that take rvalue references as parameters. These rvalue references are denoted by using the double ampersand operator on the parameter type. You can invoke the move operations using the move function; you can see this in action in the main function. The move function can be used here because you know that myCar is about to be destroyed. The move assignment operator is invoked, and the pointer address is shallow-copied to myAssignedCar. The move assignment operator releases the memory that the object may already have been using for m_Name. Importantly, it then copies the address from other before setting other.m_Name to nullptr. Setting the other object's pointer to nullptr prevents that object from deleting the memory in its destructor. In this case, the code is able to move the value of m_Name from other to this without having to allocate more memory and deep-copy the values from one to the other. The end result is that you can no longer use the value of m_Name stored by myCar—the commented-out line in Listing 5-24's main function would result in a crash.

CHAPTER 6

Inheritance

C++ allows you to build complex software applications in a number of ways. One of the most common is the object-oriented programming (OOP) paradigm. Classes in C++ are used to provide a blueprint for objects that contain your data and the operations that can be carried out on that data.

Inheritance takes this a step further by letting you construct complex hierarchies of classes. The C++ language provides various different features you can use to organize your code in a logical manner.

Recipe 6-1. Inheriting from a Class

Problem

You're writing a program that has a natural is-a relationship between objects and would like to reduce code duplication.

Solution

Inheriting a class from a parent class allows you to add your code to the parent and share it between multiple derived types.

How It Works

In C++, you can inherit one class from another. The inheriting class gains all the properties of the base class. Listing 6-1 shows an example of two classes that inherit from a shared parent.

Listing 6-1. Class Inheritance

```
#include <cinttypes>
#include <iostream>

using namespace std;

class Vehicle
{
private:
    uint32_t m_NumberOfWheels{};
```

```cpp
public:
    Vehicle(uint32_t numberOfWheels)
        : m_NumberOfWheels{ numberOfWheels }
    {

    }

    uint32_t GetNumberOfWheels() const
    {
        return m_NumberOfWheels;
    }
};

class Car : public Vehicle
{
public:
    Car()
        : Vehicle(4)
    {

    }
};

class Motorcycle : public Vehicle
{
public:
    Motorcycle()
        : Vehicle(2)
    {

    }
};

int main(int argc, char* argv[])
{
    Car myCar{};
    cout << "A car has " << myCar.GetNumberOfWheels() << " wheels." << endl;

    Motorcycle myMotorcycle;
    cout << "A motorcycle has " << myMotorcycle.GetNumberOfWheels() << " wheels." << endl;

    return 0;
}
```

The Vehicle class contains a member variable to store the number of wheels the vehicle has. This value is initialized to 0 by default or is set in the constructor. Vehicle is followed by another class named Car. The Car class contains only a constructor that is used to call the constructor for Vehicle. The Car constructor passes the number 4 into the Vehicle constructor and therefore sets m_NumberOfWheels to 4.

The Motorcycle class also contains only a constructor, but it passes 2 to the Vehicle constructor. Because both Car and Motorcycle inherit from the Vehicle class, they both inherit its properties. They both contain a variable to hold the number of wheels, and they will both have a method to retrieve the number of wheels. You can see this in the main function, where GetNumberOfWheels is called on both the myCar object and the myMotorcycle object. Figure 6-1 shows the output generated by this code.

```
●  ●  ●    bruce@bruce-Virtual-Machine: ~/Projects/C-Recipes/Recipe6-1/Listing6-1
bruce@bruce-Virtual-Machine:~/Projects/C-Recipes/Recipe6-1/Listing6-1$ ./main
A car has 4 wheels.
A motorcycle has 2 wheels.
bruce@bruce-Virtual-Machine:~/Projects/C-Recipes/Recipe6-1/Listing6-1$ ▉
```

Figure 6-1. *Output generated by the code in Listing 6-1*

The Car class and the Motorcycle class both inherit the properties of Vehicle and both set the appropriate number of wheels in their constructor.

Recipe 6-2. Controlling Access to Member Variables and Methods in Derived Classes

Problem

Your derived class needs to be able to access the fields in its parent.

Solution

C++ access modifiers have an effect on the way variables can be accessed in derived classes. Using the correct access modifier is essential in properly constructing a class hierarchy.

How It Works

The public Access Specifier

The public access specifier grants public access to a variable or method in a class. This applies equally to member variables and methods. You can see this clearly in Listing 6-2.

Listing 6-2. The public Access Specifier

```cpp
#include <cinttypes>
#include <iostream>

using namespace std;

class Vehicle
{
public:
    uint32_t m_NumberOfWheels{};

    Vehicle() = default;
};

class Car : public Vehicle
{
public:
    Car()
    {
        m_NumberOfWheels = 4;
    }
};

class Motorcycle : public Vehicle
{
public:
    Motorcycle()
    {
        m_NumberOfWheels = 2;
    }
};

int main(int argc, char* argv[])
{
    Car myCar{};
    cout << "A car has " << myCar.m_NumberOfWheels << " wheels." << endl;
    myCar.m_NumberOfWheels = 3;
    cout << "A car has " << myCar.m_NumberOfWheels << " wheels." << endl;

    Motorcycle myMotorcycle;
    cout << "A motorcycle has " << myMotorcycle.m_NumberOfWheels << " wheels." << endl;
    myMotorcycle.m_NumberOfWheels = 3;
    cout << "A motorcycle has " << myMotorcycle.m_NumberOfWheels << " wheels." << endl;

    return 0;
}
```

Any variables with public access can be accessed by a derived class. Both the Car constructor and the Motorcycle constructor take advantage of this and set the number of wheels they have appropriately. The downside is that other code can also access the public member variables. You can see this in the main function, where the m_NumberOfWheels is read and assigned to both the myCar object and the myMotorcycle object. Figure 6-2 shows the output generated by this code.

```
bruce@bruce-Virtual-Machine: ~/Projects/C-Recipes/Recipe6-2/Listing6-2
bruce@bruce-Virtual-Machine:~/Projects/C-Recipes/Recipe6-2/Listing6-2$ ./main
A car has 4 wheels.
A car has 3 wheels.
A motorcycle has 2 wheels.
A motorcycle has 3 wheels.
bruce@bruce-Virtual-Machine:~/Projects/C-Recipes/Recipe6-2/Listing6-2$
```

Figure 6-2. *The output generated by Listing 6-2*

The private Access Specifier

Instead of making variables public, you can make them private and provide public accessors to them.
Listing 6-3 shows the use of a private member variable.

Listing 6-3. The private Access Specifier

```cpp
#include <cinttypes>
#include <iostream>

using namespace std;

class Vehicle
{
private:
    uint32_t m_NumberOfWheels{};

public:
    Vehicle(uint32_t numberOfWheels)
        : m_NumberOfWheels{ numberOfWheels }
    {

    }

    uint32_t GetNumberOfWheels() const
    {
        return m_NumberOfWheels;
    }
};

class Car : public Vehicle
{
public:
    Car()
        : Vehicle(4)
    {

    }
};
```

137

```
class Motorcycle : public Vehicle
{
public:
    Motorcycle()
        : Vehicle(2)
    {

    }
};

int main(int argc, char* argv[])
{
    Car myCar{};
    cout << "A car has " << myCar.GetNumberOfWheels() << " wheels." << endl;

    Motorcycle myMotorcycle;
    cout << "A motorcycle has " << myMotorcycle.GetNumberOfWheels() << " wheels." << endl;

    return 0;
}
```

Listing 6-3 shows the use of the private access specifier with the m_NumberOfWheels variable. The Car and Motorcycle classes can no longer access the m_NumberOfWheels variable directly; therefore, the Vehicle class provides a method to initialize the variable through its constructor. This makes the classes a little harder to work with but adds the benefit of not allowing any external code direct access to the member variable. You ca see this in the main function, where the code must get the number of wheels through the GetNumberOfWheels accessor method.

The protected Access Specifier

The protected access specifier allows for a mix of public and private access specifiers. It acts like a public specifier for classes that derive from the current class, and it acts like a private specifier for external code. Listing 6-4 shows this behavior.

Listing 6-4. The protected Access Specifier

```
#include <cinttypes>
#include <iostream>

using namespace std;

class Vehicle
{
protected:
    uint32_t m_NumberOfWheels{};

public:
    Vehicle() = default;
```

```
    uint32_t GetNumberOfWheels() const
    {
        return m_NumberOfWheels;
    }
};

class Car : public Vehicle
{
public:
    Car()
    {
        m_NumberOfWheels = 4;
    }
};

class Motorcycle : public Vehicle
{
public:
    Motorcycle()
    {
        m_NumberOfWheels = 2;
    }
};

int main(int argc, char* argv[])
{
    Car myCar{};
    cout << "A car has " << myCar.GetNumberOfWheels() << " wheels." << endl;

    Motorcycle myMotorcycle;
    cout << "A motorcycle has " << myMotorcycle.GetNumberOfWheels() << " wheels." << endl;

    return 0;
}
```

Listing 6-4 shows that both Car and Motorcycle can access the m_NumberOfWheels variable directly from their parent class, Vehicle. Both classes set the m_NumberOfWheels variable in their constructors. The calling code in the main function doesn't have access to this variable and therefore has to call the GetNumberOfWheels method to be able to print this value.

Recipe 6-3. Hiding Methods in Derived Classes

Problem

You have a derived class that needs behavior in a method that is different than the behavior provided by the parent class.

Solution

C++ allows you to hide methods in parent classes by defining a method with the same signature in the derived class.

How It Works

You can hide a method in a parent class by defining a method with exactly the same signature in the base class. This example shows how derived classes can use explicit method hiding to provide functionality that differs from the parent class's. This is a key concept to understand when you're using inheritance, because it's the primary method employed to differentiate hierarchies of class types.

Listing 6-5 contains a Vehicle class, a Car class, and a Motorcycle class. The Vehicle class defines a method named GetNumberOfWheels that returns 0. The same method is defined in the Car class and the Motorcycle class; these versions of the method return 4 and 2, respectively.

Listing 6-5. Hiding Methods

```cpp
#include <cinttypes>
#include <iostream>

using namespace std;

class Vehicle
{
public:
    Vehicle() = default;

    uint32_t GetNumberOfWheels() const
    {
        return 0;
    }
};

class Car : public Vehicle
{
public:
    Car() = default;

    uint32_t GetNumberOfWheels() const
    {
        return 4;
    }
};

class Motorcycle : public Vehicle
{
public:
    Motorcycle() = default;
```

```
    uint32_t GetNumberOfWheels() const
    {
        return 2;
    }
};

int main(int argc, char* argv[])
{
    Vehicle myVehicle{};
    cout << "A vehicle has " << myVehicle.GetNumberOfWheels() << " wheels." << endl;

    Car myCar{};
    cout << "A car has " << myCar.GetNumberOfWheels() << " wheels." << endl;

    Motorcycle myMotorcycle;
    cout << "A motorcycle has " << myMotorcycle.GetNumberOfWheels() << " wheels." << endl;

    return 0;
}
```

The main function in Listing 6-5 calls the three different versions of GetNumberOfWheels and returns the appropriate value for each. You can see the output generated by this code in Figure 6-3.

```
● ● ◉    bruce@bruce-Virtual-Machine: ~/Projects/C-Recipes/Recipe6-3/Listing6-5
bruce@bruce-Virtual-Machine:~/Projects/C-Recipes/Recipe6-3/Listing6-5$ ./main
A car has 4 wheels.
A motorcycle has 2 wheels.
bruce@bruce-Virtual-Machine:~/Projects/C-Recipes/Recipe6-3/Listing6-5$ ▌
```

Figure 6-3. The output generated by executing the code in Listing 6-5

Accessing these methods directly through objects or pointers to these class types results in the correct output.

■ **Note**   Method hiding doesn't work properly when you're using polymorphism. Accessing a derived class through a pointer to a base class results in the method on the base class being called. This is very rarely the behavior you want. See Recipe 8-5 for the proper solution when using polymorphism.

Recipe 6-4. Using Polymorphic Base Classes
Problem

You would like to write generic code that works with pointers to base classes and that still calls the proper methods in derived classes.

Solution

The virtual keyword allows you to create methods that can be overridden by derived classes.

How It Works

The virtual keyword tells the C++ compiler that you would like a class to contain a virtual method table (v-table). A v-table contains lookups for methods that allows the correct method to be called for a given type even if the object is being accessed through a pointer to one of its parent classes. Listing 6-6 shows a class hierarchy that uses the virtual keyword to specify that a method should be included in the class's v-table.

Listing 6-6. Creating a Virtual Method

```cpp
#include <cinttypes>

class Vehicle
{
public:
    Vehicle() = default;

    virtual uint32_t GetNumberOfWheels() const
    {
        return 2;
    }
};

class Car : public Vehicle
{
public:
    Car() = default;

    uint32_t GetNumberOfWheels() const override
    {
        return 4;
    }
};

class Motorcycle : public Vehicle
{
public:
    Motorcycle() = default;
};
```

The Car and Motorcycle classes in Listing 6-6 derive from the Vehicle class. The GetNumberOfWheels method in the Vehicle class is listed as a virtual method. This causes any calls to that method through a pointer to be called through the v-table. Listing 6-7 shows a full example with a main function that accesses objects through a Vehicle pointer.

Listing 6-7. Accessing Virtual Methods through a Base Pointer

```cpp
#include <cinttypes>
#include <iostream>

using namespace std;

class Vehicle
{
public:
    Vehicle() = default;

    virtual uint32_t GetNumberOfWheels() const
    {
        return 2;
    }
};

class Car : public Vehicle
{
public:
    Car() = default;

    uint32_t GetNumberOfWheels() const override
    {
        return 4;
    }
};

class Motorcycle : public Vehicle
{
public:
    Motorcycle() = default;
};

int main(int argc, char* argv[])
{
    Vehicle* pVehicle{};

    Vehicle myVehicle{};
    pVehicle = &myVehicle;
    cout << "A vehicle has " << pVehicle->GetNumberOfWheels() << " wheels." << endl;

    Car myCar{};
    pVehicle = &myCar;
    cout << "A car has " << pVehicle->GetNumberOfWheels() << " wheels." << endl;

    Motorcycle myMotorcycle;
    pVehicle = &myMotorcycle;
    cout << "A motorcycle has " << pVehicle->GetNumberOfWheels() << " wheels." << endl;

    return 0;
}
```

The main function defines a pointer to a Vehicle object on its first line. This pointer is then used in each of the cout statements to access the GetNumberOfWheels method for the current object. The Vehicle and Motorcycle objects have the address of the Vehicle::GetNumberOfWheels method in their v-tables; therefore, both return 2 for their number of wheels.

The Car class overrides the GetNumberOfWheels method. This causes Car to replace the address for Vehicle::GetNumberOfWheels in the lookup table with the address of Car::GetNumberOfWheels. As a result, when the same Vehicle pointer is assigned the address of myCar and subsequently calls GetNumberOfWheels, it calls the method defined in the Car class and not that defined in the Vehicle class. Figure 6-4 shows the output generated by the code in Listing 6-7, where you can see that this is the case.

```
bruce@bruce-Virtual-Machine: ~/Projects/C-Recipes/Recipe6-4/Listing6-7
bruce@bruce-Virtual-Machine:~/Projects/C-Recipes/Recipe6-4/Listing6-7$ ./main
A vehicle has 2 wheels.
A car has 4 wheels.
A motorcycle has 2 wheels.
bruce@bruce-Virtual-Machine:~/Projects/C-Recipes/Recipe6-4/Listing6-7$
```

Figure 6-4. *The output generated by executing the code in Listing 6-7*

The override keyword is used at the end of the GetNumberOfWheels method's signature in the Car class. This keyword is a hint to the compiler that you expect this method to override a virtual method in the parent class. The compiler will throw an error if you enter the signature incorrectly or if the signature of the method you're overriding is changed later. This feature is very useful, and I recommend that you use it (although the override keyword itself is optional).

Recipe 6-5. Preventing Method Overrides

Problem

You have a method that you don't wish to be overridden by deriving classes.

Solution

You can use the final keyword to prevent classes from overriding a method.

How It Works

The final keyword informs the compiler that you don't want a virtual method to be overridden by a deriving class. Listing 6-8 shows an example of using the final keyword.

Listing 6-8. Using the final Keyword

```cpp
#include <cinttypes>
#include <iostream>

using namespace std;

class Vehicle
{
public:
    Vehicle() = default;

    virtual uint32_t GetNumberOfWheels() const final
    {
        return 2;
    }
};

class Car : public Vehicle
{
public:
    Car() = default;

    uint32_t GetNumberOfWheels() const override
    {
        return 4;
    }
};

class Motorcycle : public Vehicle
{
public:
    Motorcycle() = default;
};

int main(int argc, char* argv[])
{
    Vehicle* pVehicle{};

    Vehicle myVehicle{};
    pVehicle = &myVehicle;
    cout << "A vehicle has " << pVehicle->GetNumberOfWheels() << " wheels." << endl;

    Car myCar{};
    pVehicle = &myCar;
    cout << "A car has " << pVehicle->GetNumberOfWheels() << " wheels." << endl;

    Motorcycle myMotorcycle;
    pVehicle = &myMotorcycle;
    cout << "A motorcycle has " << pVehicle->GetNumberOfWheels() << " wheels." << endl;

    return 0;
}
```

The GetNumberOfWheels method in the Vehicle class uses the final keyword to prevent derived classes from trying to override it. This causes the code in Listing 6-8 to fail to compile, because the Car class attempts to override GetNumberOfWheels. You can comment out this method to get the code to compile.

The final keyword can also stop further overrides of a method in a longer chain. Listing 6-9 shows how this is possible.

Listing 6-9. Preventing Overrides in an Inheritance Hierarchy

```
#include <cinttypes>

class Vehicle
{
public:
    Vehicle() = default;

    virtual uint32_t GetNumberOfWheels() const
    {
        return 2;
    }
};

class Car : public Vehicle
{
public:
    Car() = default;

    uint32_t GetNumberOfWheels() const final
    {
        return 4;
    }
};

class Ferrari : public Car
{
public:
    Ferrari() = default;

    uint32_t GetNumberOfWheels() const override
    {
        return 5;
    }
};
```

Vehicle defines a virtual method named GetNumberOfWheels that returns the value 2. Car overrides this method to return 4 (this example ignores the fact that not all cars have four wheels) and declares that the method is final. No other classes deriving from Car are allowed to override the same method. This makes sense for the application if the requirements only require support for four-wheeled cars. The compiler will throw an error when it reaches any class that derives from Car or derives from any other class that has Car in its hierarchy and that tries to override the GetNumberOfWheels method.

Recipe 6-6. Creating Interfaces

Problem

You have a base class method that should not define any behavior but should simply be overridden by deriving classes.

Solution

You can create pure virtual methods in C++ that don't define a method body.

How It Works

You can define pure virtual methods in C++ by adding = 0 to the end of the method signature. Listing 6-10 shows an example.

Listing 6-10. Creating Pure Virtual Methods

```cpp
#include <cinttypes>
#include <iostream>

using namespace std;

class Vehicle
{
public:
    Vehicle() = default;

    virtual uint32_t GetNumberOfWheels() const = 0;
};

class Car : public Vehicle
{
public:
    Car() = default;

    uint32_t GetNumberOfWheels() const override
    {
        return 4;
    }
};

class Motorcycle : public Vehicle
{
public:
    Motorcycle() = default;
```

```
        uint32_t GetNumberOfWheels() const override
        {
            return 2;
        }
};

int main(int argc, char* argv[])
{
    Vehicle* pVehicle{};

    Car myCar{};
    pVehicle = &myCar;
    cout << "A car has " << pVehicle->GetNumberOfWheels() << " wheels." << endl;

    Motorcycle myMotorcycle;
    pVehicle = &myMotorcycle;
    cout << "A motorcycle has " << pVehicle->GetNumberOfWheels() << " wheels." << endl;

    return 0;
}
```

The Vehicle class defines GetNumberOfWheels as a pure virtual method. This has the effect of ensuring that an object of type Vehicle can never be created. The compiler doesn't allow this because it doesn't have a method to call for GetNumberOfWheels. Car and Motorcycle both override this method and can be instantiated. You can see this occur in the main function. Figure 6-5 shows that the methods return the correct values for Car and Motorcycle.

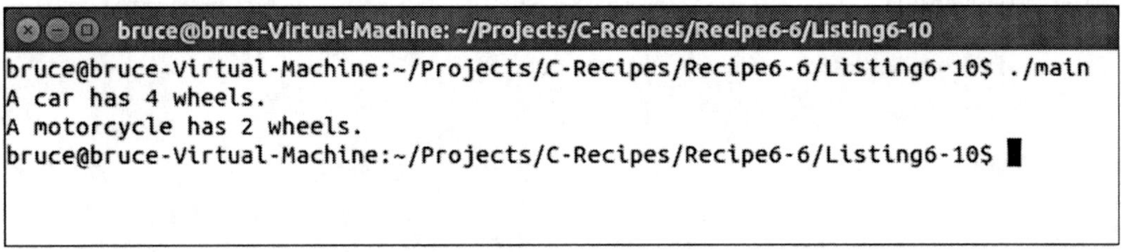

Figure 6-5. *The output generated by executing the code in Listing 6-10*

A class that contains a pure virtual method is known as an *interface*. If a class inherits from an interface and you wish to be able to instantiate that class, you must override any pure virtual methods in the parent. It's possible to derive from an interface and not override these methods, but that derived class can then only be used as an interface to further derived classes.

Recipe 6-7. Multiple Inheritance

Problem

You have a class that you wish to derive from more than one parent.

Solution

C++ supports multiple inheritance.

How It Works

You can derive a class from multiple parents in C++ using a comma-separated list of parent classes. Listing 6-11 shows how this can be achieved.

Listing 6-11. Multiple Inheritance

```cpp
#include <cinttypes>
#include <iostream>

using namespace std;

class Printable
{
public:
    virtual void Print() = 0;
};

class Vehicle
{
public:
    Vehicle() = default;

    virtual uint32_t GetNumberOfWheels() const = 0;
};

class Car
    : public Vehicle
    , public Printable
{
public:
    Car() = default;

    uint32_t GetNumberOfWheels() const override
    {
        return 4;
    }

    void Print() override
    {
        cout << "A car has " << GetNumberOfWheels() << " wheels." << endl;
    }
};
```

```cpp
class Motorcycle
    : public Vehicle
    , public Printable
{
public:
    Motorcycle() = default;

    uint32_t GetNumberOfWheels() const override
    {
        return 2;
    }

    void Print() override
    {
        cout << "A motorcycle has " << GetNumberOfWheels() << " wheels." << endl;
    }
};

int main(int argc, char* argv[])
{
    Printable* pPrintable{};

    Car myCar{};
    pPrintable = &myCar;
    pPrintable->Print();

    Motorcycle myMotorcycle;
    pPrintable = &myMotorcycle;
    pPrintable->Print();

    return 0;
}
```

The Car and Motorcycle classes both derive from multiple parents. These classes are now both Vehicles and Printables. You can see the interplay between the two parents in the overridden Print methods. These methods both call the overridden GetNumberOfWheels method in Car and Motorcycle. The main function accesses the overridden Print methods through a pointer to a Printable object, using polymorphism to call the correct Print method and also the correct GetNumberOfWheels method in Print. Figure 6-6 shows that the output from the program is correct.

```
bruce@bruce-Virtual-Machine: ~/Projects/C-Recipes/Recipe6-7/Listing6-11
bruce@bruce-Virtual-Machine:~/Projects/C-Recipes/Recipe6-7/Listing6-11$ ./main
A car has 4 wheels.
A motorcycle has 2 wheels.
bruce@bruce-Virtual-Machine:~/Projects/C-Recipes/Recipe6-7/Listing6-11$ ▊
```

Figure 6-6. Output showing that multiple inheritance works with polymorphism

■ ■ ■

CHAPTER 7

The STL Containers

The Standard Template Library (STL) consists of a standard set of functionality that implementers are required to support. Creating a standard ensures that code can be used interchangeably on different platforms and operating systems as long as the supplied implementations conform to that standard. A large part of the standard defines a set of containers that can be used to store data structures. This chapter looks at different scenarios where each of the STL containers prove useful.

■ **Note** The string container was covered in Chapter 3.

Recipe 7-1. Storing a Fixed Number of Objects

Problem

You have a requirement to store a fixed number of objects in your program.

Solution

C++ provides built in arrays that can be used for this purpose however the STL array provides a more flexible interface comparable to other STL containers.

How It Works

C++ has support for built-in arrays that have existed since the formation of the language. If you have programmed in C or C++ before these will be familiar to you. Listing 7-1 shows a standard C-style array.

Listing 7-1. A C-style array

```
#include <cinttypes>
#include <iostream>

using namespace std;

int main(int argc, char* argv[])
{
    const uint32_t numberOfElements{ 5 };
    int32_t normalArray[numberOfElements]{ 10, 65, 3000, 2, 49 };

    for (uint32_t i{ 0 }; i < numberOfElements; ++i)
    {
        cout << normalArray[i] << endl;
    }

    return 0;
}
```

This code shows the use of a C-style array in C++. The array contains 5 integers and the main function has a for loop that is used to iterate the array and print out the values at each position. It's also possible to use a range based for loop to iterate a C-style array. Listing 7-2 shows how this is done.

Listing 7-2. Using a range based for loop with a C-style array

```
#include <cinttypes>
#include <iostream>

using namespace std;

int main(int argc, char* argv[])
{
    const uint32_t numberOfElements{ 5 };
    int32_t normalArray[numberOfElements]{ 10, 65, 3000, 2, 49 };

    for (auto&& number : normalArray)
    {
        cout << number << endl;
    }

    return 0;
}
```

The main function in Listing 7-2 takes advantage of a range based for loop to iterate the array. This is a useful construct to use when you have no need for the value of the index of the array.

■ **Note** The range based for loop in Listing 7-2 uses syntax that looks like a rvalue reference. This isn't the case. Head to Chapter 2 if you're not sure how this code works or of the difference between a lvalue and a rvalue.

C-style arrays are useful in many circumstances however modern C++ also provides another version of arrays that can be used with the STL iterators and algorithms. Listing 7-3 shows how to define an STL array.

Listing 7-3. Using a STL array

```
#include <array>
#include <cinttypes>
#include <iostream>

int main(int argc, char* argv[])
{
    const uint32_t numberOfElements{ 5 };
    std::array<int32_t, numberOfElements> stlArray{ 10, 65, 3000, 2, 49 };

    for (uint32_t i = 0; i < numberOfElements; ++i)
    {
        std::cout << stlArray[i] << std::endl;
    }

    for (auto&& number : stlArray)
    {
        std::cout << number << std::endl;
    }

    return 0;
}
```

Listing 7-3 shows that a STL `array` is defined by passing the type stored in the `array` and the number of elements it contains into the type template. Once the `array` has been defined it can be used interchangeably with a normal C-style array. This is because the range based for loop can iterate both types of array and because the STL array defines an array operator overload that allows elements to be accessed using [ ].

▓ **Note**   The major advantage to using the STL array container over C-style arrays is that it allows access to STL iterators and algorithms, both of which are covered in Chapter 8.

Arrays store their objects in a contiguous block of memory. This means that the address of each array element lies next to each other in memory. This makes them very efficient for iteration on modern processors. An array will generally result in excellent cache coherency and as a result cause fewer stalls as the processor reads from RAM into a local cache. Arrays are excellent choices for algorithms where performance is paramount and a fixed number of objects is needed.

Recipe 7-2. Storing a Growing Number of Objects

Problem

Sometimes you will not know at compile time how many objects you need to store in your array.

Solution

The STL provides the vector template that allows for dynamically growing arrays.

How It Works

The vector works in a very similar way to array. Listing 7-4 shows the definition of a vector and two styles of for loop.

Listing 7-4. Using STL vector

```cpp
#include <cinttypes>
#include <iostream>
#include <vector>

using namespace std;

int main(int argc, char* argv[])
{
    vector<int32_t> stlVector{ 10, 65, 3000, 2, 49 };

    for (uint32_t i = 0; i < stlVector.size(); ++i)
    {
        std::cout << stlVector[i] << std::endl;
    }

    for (auto&& number : stlVector)
    {
        std::cout << number << endl;
    }

    return 0;
}
```

The major different between the definition of a vector and an array is the lack of a size. As a vector is resizable setting a limit on the number of elements it can contain makes little sense. This manifests itself in the traditional for loop in the main function. You can see that the loop end condition checks for completion by comparing the index against the value returned from the size method. In this case size will return 5 as the vector contains 5 elements.

Listing 7-5 lets you see that a vector can be resized at runtime unlike an array.

Listing 7-5. Resizing a vector

```
#include <cinttypes>
#include <iostream>
#include <vector>

using namespace std;

int main(int argc, char* argv[])
{
    vector<int32_t> stlVector{ 10, 65, 3000, 2, 49 };

    cout << "The size is: " << stlVector.size() << endl;

    stlVector.emplace_back( 50 );

    cout << "The size is: " << stlVector.size() << endl;

    for (auto&& number : stlVector)
    {
        std::cout << number << endl;
    }

    return 0;
}
```

The resulting output from Listing 7-5 is shown in Figure 7-1.

```
bruce@bruce-Virtual-Machine: ~/Projects/C-Recipes/Recipe7-2/Listing7-5
bruce@bruce-Virtual-Machine:~/Projects/C-Recipes/Recipe7-2/Listing7-5$ ./main
The size is: 5
The size is: 6
10
65
3000
2
49
50
bruce@bruce-Virtual-Machine:~/Projects/C-Recipes/Recipe7-2/Listing7-5$
```

Figure 7-1. *The output generated by Listing 7-5 showing a growing vector*

Figure 7-1 shows that the vector has grown from size 5 to size 6 after the call to emplace_back. The range based for loop prints out all the values stored in the vector. You can see that emplace_back has added the value to the end of the vector.

The way a vector resizes is implementation defined which means that it's up to the vendor creating the library you are using. All implementations operate by using a similar method. They generally tend to allocate memory for a new array internally that includes the current size of the vector as well as a variable number of empty slots for new values. Listing 7-6 contains code that uses the capacity method to determine how many elements the vector is capable of storing before it will resize.

Listing 7-6. A resizing vector

```cpp
#include <cinttypes>
#include <iostream>
#include <vector>

using namespace std;

int main(int argc, char* argv[])
{
    vector<int32_t> stlVector
    {
        1,
        2,
        3,
        4,
        5,
        6,
        7,
        8,
        9,
        10,
        11,
        12,
        13,
        14,
        15,
        16
    };

    cout << "The size is: " << stlVector.size() << endl;
    cout << "The capacity is: " << stlVector.capacity() << endl;

    stlVector.emplace_back(17);

    cout << "The size is: " << stlVector.size() << endl;
    cout << "The capacity is: " << stlVector.capacity() << endl;

    for (auto&& number : stlVector)
    {
        std::cout << number << std::endl;
    }

    return 0;
}
```

The code in Listing 7-6 creates a vector that contains 16 elements. Figure 7-2 shows the affect adding a new element has on the capacity of the vector.

```
● ● ◯    bruce@bruce-Virtual-Machine: ~/Projects/C-Recipes/Recipe7-2/Listing7-6
bruce@bruce-Virtual-Machine:~/Projects/C-Recipes/Recipe7-2/Listing7-6$ ./main
The size is: 16
The capacity is: 16
The size is: 17
The capacity is: 32
1
2
3
4
5
6
7
8
9
10
11
12
13
14
15
16
17
bruce@bruce-Virtual-Machine:~/Projects/C-Recipes/Recipe7-2/Listing7-6$ ▌
```

Figure 7-2. *Output showing the increased capacity of a* vector *when using Microsoft Visual Studio 2013 STL*

Figure 7-2 shows that adding a value to a vector does not result in an increase in size of one element. Microsoft have decided that their implementation of the STL will increase the capacity of the vector by 50%. Adding a new element to a vector of size 16 adds capacity for 8 new elements when a single new element is added.

It's also possible to add elements into a vector at places other than the end. Listing 7-7 shows how the emplace method can be used for this purpose.

Listing 7-7. Adding elements to arbitrary points in a vector

```cpp
#include <cinttypes>
#include <iostream>
#include <vector>

using namespace std;

int main(int argc, char* argv[])
{
    vector<int32_t> stlVector
    {
        1,
        2,
```

```
        3,
        4,
        5
    };

    auto iterator = stlVector.begin() + 2;
    stlVector.emplace(iterator, 6);

    for (auto&& number : stlVector)
    {
        std::cout << number << std::endl;
    }

    return 0;
}
```

Listing 7-7 uses an iterator to place the value 6 into the 3rd position of the vector. This operation increases the capacity of the vector if necessary and shifts all elements after the position one place to the right. Figure 7-3 shows the output from this operation.

```
● ● ●    bruce@bruce-Virtual-Machine: ~/Projects/C-Recipes/Recipe7-2/Listing7-7
bruce@bruce-Virtual-Machine:~/Projects/C-Recipes/Recipe7-2/Listing7-7$ ./main
1
2
6
3
4
5
bruce@bruce-Virtual-Machine:~/Projects/C-Recipes/Recipe7-2/Listing7-7$ ▮
```

Figure 7-3. *The output from Listing 7-7 showing the element inserted into the 3rd position in the* vector

It is also possible to remove elements from a vector. Listing 7-8 shows code that removes each element of the vector using an iterator to the last element.

Listing 7-8. Removing elements from a vector

```
#include <cinttypes>
#include <iostream>
#include <vector>

using namespace std;

int main(int argc, char* argv[])
{
    vector<int32_t> stlVector
    {
        1,
        2,
```

```
            3,
            4,
            5,
            6,
            7,
            8,
            9,
            10,
            11,
            12,
            13,
            14,
            15,
            16
};

cout << "The size is: " << stlVector.size() << endl;
cout << "The capacity is: " << stlVector.capacity() << endl << endl;

for (auto&& number : stlVector)
{
    std::cout << number << ", ";
}

while (stlVector.size() > 0)
{
    auto iterator = stlVector.end() - 1;
    stlVector.erase(iterator);
}

cout << endl << endl << "The size is: " << stlVector.size() << endl;
cout << "The capacity is: " << stlVector.capacity() << endl << endl;

for (auto&& number : stlVector)
{
    std::cout << number << ", ";
}

std::cout << std::endl;

return 0;
}
```

The while loop in the main function of Listing 7-8 erases each element from the vector one by one. This will change the size of the vector but not the capacity. Listing 7-9 adds code to reduce the capacity of the vector.

Listing 7-9. Reducing the capacity of a vector

```cpp
#include <cinttypes>
#include <iostream>
#include <vector>

using namespace std;

int main(int argc, char* argv[])
{
    vector<int32_t> stlVector
    {
        1,
        2,
        3,
        4,
        5,
        6,
        7,
        8,
        9,
        10,
        11,
        12,
        13,
        14,
        15,
        16
    };

    while (stlVector.size() > 0)
    {
        auto iterator = stlVector.end() - 1;
        stlVector.erase(iterator);

        if ((stlVector.size() * 2) == stlVector.capacity())
        {
            stlVector.shrink_to_fit();
        }

        cout << "The size is: " << stlVector.size() << endl;
        cout << "The capacity is: " << stlVector.capacity() << endl << endl;
    }

    return 0;
}
```

As the while loop removes elements it also checks for when the size of the vector reaches half of the capacity. When this condition is met the shrink_to_fit method is called. Figure 7-4 shows the effect shrink_to_fit has on the capacity of the vector.

```
bruce@bruce-Virtual-Machine: ~/Projects/C-Recipes/Recipe7-2/Listing7-9
bruce@bruce-Virtual-Machine:~/Projects/C-Recipes/Recipe7-2/Listing7-9$ ./main
The size is: 15
The capacity is: 16
The size is: 14
The capacity is: 16
The size is: 13
The capacity is: 16
The size is: 12
The capacity is: 16
The size is: 11
The capacity is: 16
The size is: 10
The capacity is: 16
The size is: 9
The capacity is: 16
The size is: 8
The capacity is: 8
The size is: 7
The capacity is: 8
The size is: 6
The capacity is: 8
The size is: 5
The capacity is: 8
The size is: 4
The capacity is: 4
The size is: 3
The capacity is: 4
The size is: 2
The capacity is: 2
The size is: 1
The capacity is: 1
The size is: 0
The capacity is: 1
bruce@bruce-Virtual-Machine:~/Projects/C-Recipes/Recipe7-2/Listing7-9$
```

Figure 7-4. *The effect of shrink_to_fit on a vector's capacity*

Resizing a vector, either up or down, comes with a performance cost. New memory has to be allocated and the elements in the internal array have to be transferred from one to another. Two things are recommended in this scenario:

- Work out the maximum number of elements that can be added to the vector at runtime and use the reserve method to allocate the requisite amount of memory required only once.

- Determine if you can avoid using a vector altogether and use an array to create a pool of objects. This can be achieved by reusing elements in the array using a scheme such as a least recently used algorithm.

Recipe 7-3. Storing a Set of Elements that Is Constantly Altered

Problem

You have a set of data where you will be constantly entering and removing elements from arbitrary positions.

Solution

The STL provides two containers that offer efficient insertion and deletion from the middle of the container. These are the `list` and `forward_list` containers.

How It Works

The `array` and `vector` containers store elements in contiguous memory. This provides for fast iteration over the set as they play into the strengths of the modern CPU architectures. The array container cannot be added to or removed from at runtime, elements can simply be altered. The `vector` container can have elements added and removed but this requires a new memory allocation and the transfer of all elements from the old memory block to the new memory block.

The `list` containers on the other hand do not store elements in contiguous blocks of memory. Instead each element in the list is stored in an independent node that contains a pointer to the next and last element in the list. This allows bi-directional traversal in the `list` container. A `forward_list` only stores a pointer to the next element, not the last, and can therefore only be traversed front to back. Adding and removing elements from a list becomes a trivial exercise in updating the pointers that reference the next and last nodes in the list structure.

This non-contiguous storage results in a performance penalty when traversing the list. The CPU cache cannot always pre-load the next element in the list therefore these structures should be avoided for sets of data that are regularly traversed. Their advantage comes from the rapid insertion and deletion of nodes. Listing 7-10 shows a `list` container in use.

Listing 7-10. Using a list

```
#include <cinttypes>
#include <iostream>
#include <list>

using namespace std;

int main(int argv, char* argc[])
{
    list<int32_t> myList{ 1, 2, 3, 4, 5 };

    myList.emplace_front(6);
    myList.emplace_back(7);
```

```
    auto forwardIter = myList.begin();
    ++forwardIter;
    ++forwardIter;
    myList.emplace(forwardIter, 9);

    auto reverseIter = myList.end();
    --reverseIter;
    --reverseIter;
    --reverseIter;
    myList.emplace(reverseIter, 8);

    for (auto&& number : myList)
    {
        cout << number << endl;
    }

    return 0;
}
```

The list container used in the main function of Listing 7-10 allows for forward and backward traversal from the iterators returned from begin or end. Figure 7-5 contains the output generated by traversing the list where you can see the arbitrary order of the added elements.

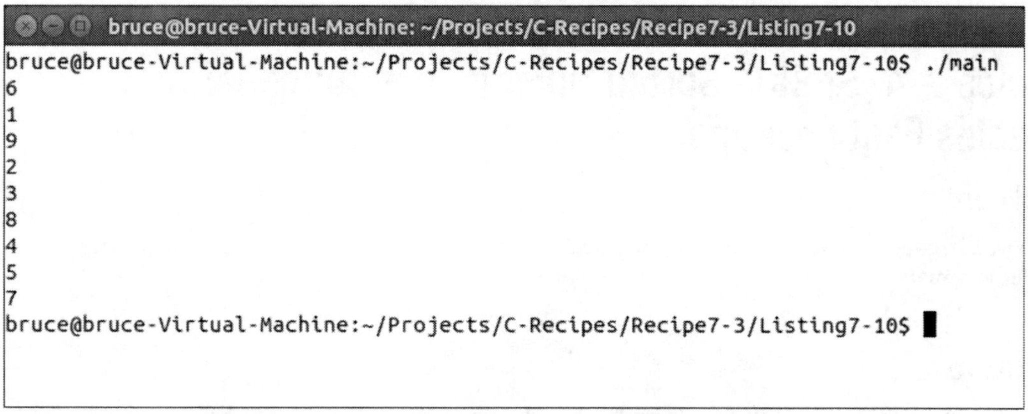

Figure 7-5. *The output when traversing the* list *container in Listing 7-10*

Listing 7-11 shows similar code with a forward_list

Listing 7-11. Using a forward_list

```
#include <cinttypes>
#include <forward_list>
#include <iostream>

using namespace std;
```

163

```
int main(int argv, char* argc[])
{
    forward_list<int32_t> myList{ 1, 2, 3, 4, 5 };

    myList.emplace_front(6);

    auto forwardIter = myList.begin();
    ++forwardIter;
    ++forwardIter;
    myList.emplace_after(forwardIter, 9);

    for (auto&& number : myList)
    {
        cout << number << endl;
    }

    return 0;
}
```

There are a few differences in Listing 7-11 when compared to Listing 7-10. A forward_list does not contain the methods emplace or emplace_back. It does contain emplace_front and also emplace_after which allow you to add elements to the beginning of the forward_list or after a specific position in the forward_list.

Recipe 7-4. Storing Sorted Objects in a Container that Enables Fast Lookups

Problem

You have a large collection of objects that you would like to be ordered and frequently have to look up to find specific information.

Solution

The STL provides the **set** and **map** containers that can automatically sort their objects and provide very fast search characteristics.

How It Works

The set and map containers are associative containers. This means that they associate their data elements with a key. In the case of a set the key is the object or value itself and for a map they key is a value supplied along with an object or value.

These containers are implemented using binary search trees and this is why they offer automatic sorting and fast search characteristics. Binary search trees operate by comparing keys for objects. If an object's key is less than that of the current node then it is added to the left, if it is greater it goes to the right or vice versa.

> **Note** In fact you can provide a function to both containers that allows you to specify the sort order for yourself.

Listing 7-12 shows the creation of a **set** that orders its elements from smallest to largest.

Listing 7-12. Using a set

```
#include <cinttypes>
#include <iostream>
#include <set>
#include <string>

using namespace std;

class SetObject
{
private:
    string m_Name;
    int32_t m_Key{};

public:
    SetObject(int32_t key, const string& name)
        : m_Name{ name }
        , m_Key{ key }
    {

    }

    SetObject(int32_t key)
        : SetObject(key, "")
    {

    }

    const string& GetName() const
    {
        return m_Name;
    }

    int32_t GetKey() const
    {
        return m_Key;
    }

    bool operator<(const SetObject& other) const
    {
        return m_Key < other.m_Key;
    }
```

```cpp
        bool operator>(const SetObject& other) const
        {
            return m_Key > other.m_Key;
        }
};

int main(int argv, char* argc[])
{
    set<SetObject> mySet
    {
        { 6, "Six" },
        { 3, "Three" },
        { 4, "Four" },
        { 1, "One" },
        { 2, "Two" }
    };

    for (auto&& number : mySet)
    {
        cout << number.GetName() << endl;
    }

    auto iter = mySet.find(3);
    if (iter != mySet.end())
    {
        cout << "Found: " << iter->GetName() << endl;
    }

    return 0;
}
```

The set defined in the main function of Listing 7-12 is initialized with five SetObject instances. Each of these instances stores an integer key and a string representation of that key. By default a **set** is initialized to order the elements it contains from lowest to highest. You can see this proven in Figure 7-6.

```
● ● ●    bruce@bruce-Virtual-Machine: ~/Projects/C-Recipes/Recipe7-4/Listing7-12
bruce@bruce-Virtual-Machine:~/Projects/C-Recipes/Recipe7-4/Listing7-12$ ./main
One
Two
Three
Four
Six
Found: Three
bruce@bruce-Virtual-Machine:~/Projects/C-Recipes/Recipe7-4/Listing7-12$ ▮
```

Figure 7-6. The output generated by the code in Listing 7-12

The ordering of class objects was achieved using operator overloading. The SetObject class overloads the < and > operators and this enables the class to be used with these operators. When adding a new element the **set** will call a comparison function that determines the order the elements should appear in the set. The **default case** calls for the use of the < operator on the elements. As you can see the SetObject class compares the m_Key variables in the operators to determine the order in which they should be stored.

Listing 7-13 shows how you can alter the default set to order the elements from highest to lowest.

Listing 7-13. Ordering elements in a set from highest to lowest

```
#include <cinttypes>
#include <functional>
#include <iostream>
#include <set>
#include <string>

using namespace std;

class SetObject
{
private:
    string m_Name;
    int32_t m_Key{};

public:
    SetObject(int32_t key, const string& name)
        : m_Name{ name }
        , m_Key{ key }
    {

    }

    SetObject(int32_t key)
        : SetObject(key, "")
    {
    }

    const string& GetName() const
    {
        return m_Name;
    }

    int32_t GetKey() const
    {
        return m_Key;
    }

    bool operator<(const SetObject& other) const
    {
        return m_Key < other.m_Key;
    }
```

```cpp
    bool operator>(const SetObject& other) const
    {
        return m_Key > other.m_Key;
    }
};

using namespace std;

int main(int argv, char* argc[])
{
    set<SetObject, greater<SetObject>> mySet
    {
        { 6, "Six" },
        { 3, "Three" },
        { 4, "Four" },
        { 1, "One" },
        { 2, "Two" }
    };

    for (auto&& number : mySet)
    {
        cout << number.GetName() << endl;
    }

    auto iter = mySet.find(3);
    if (iter != mySet.end())
    {
        cout << "Found: " << iter->GetName() << endl;
    }

    return 0;
}
```

The only difference between Listing 7-12 and Listing 7-13 is the addition of a second template parameter to set. Listing 7-13 supplies the greater template from the *functional* header. This template will create a method from a function that can call the > operator on two SetObject instances. You can imagine that the default set had an implied less parameter:

```cpp
set<SetObject, less<SetObject>>
```

Figure 7-7 shows the resulting output from a set with elements ordered from highest to lowest.

```
bruce@bruce-Virtual-Machine: ~/Projects/C-Recipes/Recipe7-4/Listing7-13
bruce@bruce-Virtual-Machine:~/Projects/C-Recipes/Recipe7-4/Listing7-13$ ./main
Six
Four
Three
Two
One
Found: Three
bruce@bruce-Virtual-Machine:~/Projects/C-Recipes/Recipe7-4/Listing7-13$
```

Figure 7-7. *The set ordered from highest to lowest using greater*

Listing 7-14 shows how you can add elements to a set after initialization.

Listing 7-14. Adding elements to a set

```
#include <cinttypes>
#include <functional>
#include <iostream>
#include <set>
#include <string>

using namespace std;

class SetObject
{
private:
    string m_Name;
    int32_t m_Key{};

public:
    SetObject(int32_t key, const string& name)
        : m_Name{ name }
        , m_Key{ key }
    {

    }

    SetObject(int32_t key)
        : SetObject(key, "")
    {

    }

    const string& GetName() const
    {
        return m_Name;
    }

    int32_t GetKey() const
    {
        return m_Key;
    }

    bool operator<(const SetObject& other) const
    {
        return m_Key < other.m_Key;
    }

    bool operator>(const SetObject& other) const
    {
        return m_Key > other.m_Key;
    }
};
```

169

```
int main(int argv, char* argc[])
{
    set<SetObject, greater<SetObject>> mySet
    {
        { 6, "Six" },
        { 3, "Three" },
        { 4, "Four" },
        { 1, "One" },
        { 2, "Two" }
    };

    for (auto&& number : mySet)
    {
        cout << number.GetName() << endl;
    }

    cout << endl;

    mySet.emplace(SetObject( 5, "Five" ));

    for (auto&& number : mySet)
    {
        cout << number.GetName() << endl;
    }

    cout << endl;

    auto iter = mySet.find(3);
    if (iter != mySet.end())
    {
        cout << "Found: " << iter->GetName() << endl;
    }

    return 0;
}
```

The emplace method can be used to add new elements to a set as in Listing 7-14. Figure 7-8 shows that the new element was inserted into the set in the correct position given the greater ordering.

```
● ● ●   bruce@bruce-Virtual-Machine: ~/Projects/C-Recipes/Recipe7-4/Listing7-14
bruce@bruce-Virtual-Machine:~/Projects/C-Recipes/Recipe7-4/Listing7-14$ ./main
Six
Four
Three
Two
One

Six
Five
Four
Three
Two
One

Found: Three
bruce@bruce-Virtual-Machine:~/Projects/C-Recipes/Recipe7-4/Listing7-14$ ▮
```

Figure 7-8. *Shows a new element has been added to the* set *in the correct position*

The map container is very similar to the set container except for the fact that the key is stored independently of the object value. Listing 7-15 shows code to create a map container.

Listing 7-15. Creating a map

```cpp
#include <cinttypes>
#include <functional>
#include <iostream>
#include <map>
#include <string>

using namespace std;

class MapObject
{
private:
    string m_Name;

public:
    MapObject(const string& name)
        : m_Name{ name }
    {

    }

    const string& GetName() const
    {
        return m_Name;
    }
};
```

171

```cpp
int main(int argv, char* argc[])
{
    map<int32_t, MapObject, greater<int32_t>> myMap
    {
        pair<int32_t, MapObject>(6, MapObject("Six")),
        pair<int32_t, MapObject>(3, MapObject("Three")),
        pair<int32_t, MapObject>(4, MapObject("Four")),
        pair<int32_t, MapObject>(1, MapObject("One")),
        pair<int32_t, MapObject>(2, MapObject("Two"))
    };

    for (auto&& number : myMap)
    {
        cout << number.second.GetName() << endl;
    }

    cout << endl;

    myMap.emplace(pair<int32_t, MapObject>(5, MapObject("Five")));

    for (auto&& number : myMap)
    {
        cout << number.second.GetName() << endl;
    }

    cout << endl;

    auto iter = myMap.find(3);
    if (iter != myMap.end())
    {
        cout << "Found: " << iter->second.GetName() << endl;
    }

    return 0;
}
```

Listing 7-15 achieves exactly the same result as the code in Listing 7-14 using a map in place of a set. The MapObject class does not contain a key nor does it contain any overloaded operators to compare the objects instantiated using this class. That's because the key for a **map** is stored independently of the data. Elements are added to a map using the pair template and each pair associates a key value to an object.

The code for a map is more verbose than for that of a set however the objects contained can be less complex. A map is a good candidate over a set when the key is not related to the rest of the data in the class. Objects that have a natural order and are already comparable are good candidates for storing in a set.

The iterator to a **map** is also a **pair**. The **MapObject** it contains can be retrieved using the **second** field on the **iterator** while first stores the key value. Iterting over a **map** or a **set** is a slow operation as the elements are not contained in contiguous memory. The benefit of associative containers is mostly their fast lookups while the ordering is a secondary benefit that should only be used sparingly for performance reasons.

Recipe 7-5. Storing Unsorted Elements in a Container for Very Fast Lookups

Problem

You have a set of data that does not need to be sorted but will be used for frequent lookups and data retrieval.

Solution

The STL provides the unordered_set and unordered_map containers for this purpose.

How It Works

The unordered_set and unordered_map containers are implemented as hash maps. A hash map provides for constant time insertion, removal and searching of objects. Constant time means that the operations will take the same length of time regardless of how many elements are in the container.

As the unordered_set and unordered_map containers are hash maps they rely on a hashing function being supplied that can convert your data into a numeric value. Listing 7-16 shows how you can create a set to store user defined classes that can be hashed and compared.

Listing 7-16. Using an unordered_set

```
#include <cinttypes>
#include <functional>
#include <iostream>
#include <string>
#include <unordered_set>

using namespace std;

class SetObject;

namespace std
{
    template <>
    class hash<SetObject>
    {
    public:
        template <typename... Args>
        size_t operator()(Args&&... setObject) const
        {
            return hash<string>()((forward<Args...>(setObject...)).GetName());
        }
    };
}

class SetObject
{
private:
    string m_Name;
    size_t m_Hash{};
```

```cpp
public:
    SetObject(const string& name)
        : m_Name{ name }
        , m_Hash{ hash<SetObject>()(*this) }
    {

    }

    const string& GetName() const
    {
        return m_Name;
    }

    const size_t& GetHash() const
    {
        return m_Hash;
    }

    bool operator==(const SetObject& other) const
    {
        return m_Hash == other.m_Hash;
    }
};

int main(int argv, char* argc[])
{
    unordered_set<SetObject> mySet;
    mySet.emplace("Five");
    mySet.emplace("Three");
    mySet.emplace("Four");
    mySet.emplace("One");
    mySet.emplace("Two");

    cout << showbase << hex;

    for (auto&& number : mySet)
    {
        cout << number.GetName() << " - " << number.GetHash() << endl;
    }

    auto iter = mySet.find({ "Three" });
    if (iter != mySet.end())
    {
        cout << "Found: " << iter->GetName() << " with hash: " << iter->GetHash() << endl;
    }

    return 0;
}
```

Using an unordered_set to store class objects requires some difficult to understand code. First off we have a partial specialization for the hash template. This allows us to create a function that is capable of creating a hash value for the SetObject class. This is achieved by passing a SetObject instance and calling the STL hash function for a string. The SetObject instance is passed to the () operator using a *universal reference* and the forward function to achieve *perfect forwarding*.

■ **Note**   Templates are covered in Chapter 9 and universal references are covered along with lvaues, rvalues and perfect forwarding in Chapter 2.

The SetObject class requires an overloaded == operator to function properly in an unordered_set. The code would not compile if this was missing. The m_Hash member variable is not needed, I simply included this to show you the values hash creates and how you can call the hash function for yourself. If the m_Hash variable did not exist you can compare the m_Name strings for equality. Figure 7-9 shows the resulting output generated by this code.

```
bruce@bruce-Virtual-Machine: ~/Projects/C-Recipes/Recipe7-5/Listing7-16
bruce@bruce-Virtual-Machine:~/Projects/C-Recipes/Recipe7-5/Listing7-16$ ./main
Two - 0xfbc12e62b080c09d
One - 0x4507392ecc2d4a7d
Four - 0x5a35e8b1129ec8a7
Three - 0x6431c54b8d6100a4
Five - 0xbe47095c1663fb3c
Found: Three with hash: 0x6431c54b8d6100a4
bruce@bruce-Virtual-Machine:~/Projects/C-Recipes/Recipe7-5/Listing7-16$ ▌
```

Figure 7-9. *The output generated by Listing 7-16*

An unordered_map does not come with the difficulty of creating your own hash function so long as you use a type for the key that the STL can already hash. Listing 7-17 shows an unordered_map that uses an integer as the key.

Listing 7-17. Using unordered_map

```
#include <cinttypes>
#include <iostream>
#include <string>
#include <unordered_map>

using namespace std;

class MapObject
{
private:
    string m_Name;
```

```cpp
public:
    MapObject(const string& name)
        : m_Name{ name }
    {

    }

    const string& GetName() const
    {
        return m_Name;
    }
};

int main(int argv, char* argc[])
{
    unordered_map<int32_t, MapObject> myMap;
    myMap.emplace(pair<int32_t, MapObject>(5, MapObject("Five")));
    myMap.emplace(pair<int32_t, MapObject>(3, MapObject("Three")));
    myMap.emplace(pair<int32_t, MapObject>(4, MapObject("Four")));
    myMap.emplace(pair<int32_t, MapObject>(1, MapObject("One")));
    myMap.emplace(pair<int32_t, MapObject>(2, MapObject("Two")));

    cout << showbase << hex;

    for (auto&& number : myMap)
    {
        cout << number.second.GetName() << endl;
    }

    auto iter = myMap.find(3);
    if (iter != myMap.end())
    {
        cout << "Found: " << iter->second.GetName() << endl;
    }

    return 0;
}
```

Listing 7-17 shows that the unordered_map container stores key value pairs as its elements. The first field of the pair stores the key while the second field of the pair stores the value, in this case an instance of MapObject.

■ ■ ■

CHAPTER 8

The STL Algorithms

The STL provides a set of algorithms that can be used along with the containers that it also supplies. These algorithms all work with iterators. An iterator is an abstraction mechanism that allows traversal behavior on many different STL collections. This chapter covers iterators and some of different algorithms along with their uses.

Recipe 8-1. Using an iterator to Define a Sequence within a Container

Problem

You have a STL container and would like to mark a sequence within that container that begins and ends at certain points.

Solution

The STL provides iterators that work with all containers and can be used to denote the beginning and end of a sequence within that container. The sequence can include every node in the container or it can include a subset of the nodes in the container.

How It Works

Iterators are designed to work in a similar manner to pointers. Their syntax turns out to be very similar. You can see the use of iterators in Listing 8-1.

Listing 8-1. Using an iterator with a vector

```
#include <cinttypes>
#include <iostream>
#include <vector>

using namespace std;

int main(int arcg, char* argv[])
{
    using IntVector = vector<int32_t>;
    using IntVectorIterator = IntVector::iterator;
```

```
IntVector myVector{ 0, 1, 2, 3, 4 };
for (IntVectorIterator iter = myVector.begin(); iter != myVector.end(); ++iter)
{
    cout << "The value is: " << *iter << endl;
}

return 0;
}
```

A vector of int type is created in the main function in Listing 8-1. A type alias is used to make a new type of IntVector to represent this type of collection. A second alias is used to represent the type of the iterator that is used with this collection. You can see that the iterator type is accessed through the initial vector type. This is necessary as the iterator must also operate on the same type of objects that the vector itself operates with. Including the iterator type within the vector type allows you to specify the type to operate on, in this case int32 _t, at the same time for both.

The iterator type is used to get references to the beginning and the end of the myVector collection in the for loop. The begin and end methods of a vector return iterators. A collection is said to be empty if the iterator denoting the beginning of the collection is equal to the iterator denoting the end of the collection. This is the first property that iterators share in common with pointers, they are comparable.

The iter variable in the for loop is initialized to the value returned by the vector::begin method. The for loop executes until the iter variable is equal to the iterator returned by the vector::end method. This shows that sequences of values in a collection can be represented by two iterators, one at the beginning of a sequence and one at the end of a sequence. An iterator provides an increment operator that allows the iterator to be moved to the next element in the sequence. This is how the iter variable in the for loop can be initialized to the iterator returned by begin and can be tested against end until the sequence traversal has been completed. This also happens to be another property that iterators share with pointers, an increment or decrement will move the iterator to the next or last element in a sequence.

■ **Note**   not all iterators support increment and decrement operations. You'll see some situations where that is the case in the following paragraphs.

The last operation that is important to cover with an iterator is the dereference operator. You may be familiar with these from standard pointer operations and this is the last property that iterators share with pointers. You can see from Listing 8-1 that the dereference operator is used to retrieve the value represented by the iterator. In this example the dereference is used to retrieve each iterator from the collection to be sent to the console. Figure 8-1 shows that this is the case.

```
bruce@bruce-Virtual-Machine: ~/Projects/C-Recipes/Recipe8-1/Listing8-1
bruce@bruce-Virtual-Machine:~/Projects/C-Recipes/Recipe8-1/Listing8-1$ ./main
The value is: 0
The value is: 1
The value is: 2
The value is: 3
The value is: 4
bruce@bruce-Virtual-Machine:~/Projects/C-Recipes/Recipe8-1/Listing8-1$ ▮
```

Figure 8-1. *The output from Listing 8-1 when the myVector collection is traversed*

Trying to print out the iterator without using the dereference operator would have resulted in a compilation error as the cout::<< operator does not include support for iterator types.

The code from Listing 8-1 is using a standard *forward iterator*. This type of iterator provides non-const access to each element in the container. Listing 8-2 shows the implication of this attribute.

Listing 8-2. Using non-const iterators

```
#include <cinttypes>
#include <iostream>
#include <vector>

using namespace std;

int main(int arcg, char* argv[])
{
    using IntVector = vector<int32_t>;
    using IntVectorIterator = IntVector::iterator;

    IntVector myVector(5, 0);
    int32_t value{ 0 };
    for (IntVectorIterator iter = myVector.begin(); iter != myVector.end(); ++iter)
    {
        *iter = value++;
    }

    for (IntVectorIterator iter = myVector.begin(); iter != myVector.end(); ++iter)
    {
        cout << "The value is: " << *iter << endl;
    }

    return 0;
}
```

If you were to compare Listing 8-2 to Listing 8-1 you would see that the initialization of the myVector collection is handled in a different way. Listing 8-2 initializes the vector to contain 5 copies of the value 0. A for loop then walks the vector and assigns the post-incremented value variable to each position in myVector using the iterator dereference operator. This is possible due to the non-const nature of the iterator type. If you wish to use an iterator that you know should not have write access to its value then you can use a const_iterator as shown in Listing 8-3.

Listing 8-3. Using a const_iterator

```
#include <cinttypes>
#include <iostream>
#include <vector>

using namespace std;

int main(int arcg, char* argv[])
{
    using IntVector = vector<int32_t>;
    using IntVectorIterator = IntVector::iterator;
    using ConstIntVectorIterator = IntVector::const_iterator;
```

```
    IntVector myVector(5, 0);
    int32_t value{ 0 };
    for (IntVectorIterator iter = myVector.begin(); iter != myVector.end(); ++iter)
    {
        *iter = value++;
    }

    for (ConstIntVectorIterator iter = myVector.cbegin(); iter != myVector.cend(); ++iter)
    {
        cout << "The value is: " << *iter << endl;
    }

    return 0;
}
```

Listing 8-3 uses the vector::cbegin and vector::cend methods in the second for loop to gain access to the elements of myVector without providing write access. Any attempt to assign values to a const_iterator results in a compile error being thrown when you try to build your program. The iterator and const_iterator types provided by C++ collections are both examples of *forward iterators*. That means that they both traverse the collection in the order you would suspect, from beginning to end. STL collections also supply support for the reverse_iterator and const_reverse_iterator types. These allow you to traverse your sequence backwards. Listing 8-4 shows the use of a reverse_itertor to initialize the myVector collection from highest to lowest.

Listing 8-4. Initializing myVector using a reverse_iterator

```
#include <cinttypes>
#include <iostream>
#include <vector>

using namespace std;

int main(int arcg, char* argv[])
{
    using IntVector = vector<int32_t>;

    using IntVectorIterator = IntVector::iterator;
    using ConstIntVectorIterator = IntVector::const_iterator;

    using ReverseIntVectorIterator = IntVector::reverse_iterator;
    using ConstReverseIntVectorIterator = IntVector::const_reverse_iterator;

    IntVector myVector(5, 0);
    int32_t value { 0 };
    for (ReverseIntVectorIterator iter = myVector.rbegin(); iter != myVector.rend(); ++iter)
    {
        *iter = value++;
    }
```

```
for (ConstIntVectorIterator iter = myVector.cbegin(); iter != myVector.cend(); ++iter)
{
    cout << "The value is: " << *iter << endl;
}

return 0;
}
```

Listing 8-4 shows that the reverse_iterator should be used with the rbegin and rend methods supplied by vector. Incrementing a reverse_iterator causes it to move backwards through the collection. Figure 8-2 shows that the myVector collection has stored the values in reverse order.

```
● ● ◎   bruce@bruce-Virtual-Machine: ~/Projects/C-Recipes/Recipe8-1/Listing8-4
bruce@bruce-Virtual-Machine:~/Projects/C-Recipes/Recipe8-1/Listing8-4$ ./main
The value is: 4
The value is: 3
The value is: 2
The value is: 1
The value is: 0
bruce@bruce-Virtual-Machine:~/Projects/C-Recipes/Recipe8-1/Listing8-4$ █
```

Figure 8-2. *The values from myVector in reverse order*

The output in Figure 8-2 can also be achieved using the code in Listing 8-5 which uses a const_reverse_iterator to print the values.

Listing 8-5. Using a const_reverse_iterator to print myVector in reverse

```
#include <cinttypes>
#include <iostream>
#include <vector>

using namespace std;

int main(int arcg, char* argv[])
{
    using IntVector = vector<int32_t>;

    using IntVectorIterator = IntVector::iterator;
    using ConstIntVectorIterator = IntVector::const_iterator;

    using ReverseIntVectorIterator = IntVector::reverse_iterator;
    using ConstReverseIntVectorIterator = IntVector::const_reverse_iterator;

    IntVector myVector(5, 0);
    int32_t value{ 0 };
    for (IntVectorIterator iter = myVector.begin(); iter != myVector.end(); ++iter)
    {
        *iter = value++;
    }
```

```
    for (ConstReverseIntVectorIterator iter = myVector.crbegin();
        iter != myVector.crend();
        ++iter)
    {
        cout << "The value is: " << *iter << endl;
    }

    return 0;
}
```

Listing 8-5 uses const_reverse_iterator along with the crbegin and crend methods to walk the collection from last to first and print the values in reverse order.

Iterators will play an important part in the rest of this chapter as they are used as the input to the algorithms supplied by the STL.

Recipe 8-2. Calling a Function on Every Element in a Container

Problem

You have a container and would like a simple method to call a function on every element.

Solution

The STL provides the for_each function that takes a beginning iterator, an ending iterator and a function to call on each element between the two.

How It Works

The for_each function can be passed two iterators. These iterators define the beginning point and the end point in the container that should be traversed. The 3rd parameter is a function that should be called for each element. The element itself is passed into the function. Listing 8-6 shows a use of the for_each function.

Listing 8-6. The for_each algorithm

```
#include <algorithm>
#include <cinttypes>
#include <iostream>
#include <vector>

using namespace std;

int main(int argc, char* argv[])
{
    vector<int32_t> myVector
    {
        1,
        2,
        3,
        4,
        5
    };
```

```
for_each(myVector.begin(), myVector.end(),
    [](int32_t value)
    {
        cout << value << endl;
    });

return 0;
}
```

The code in Listing 8-6 creates a vector with 5 elements, the numbers 1 through 5. The for_each function is passed the iterators returned by the begin and end methods to define the range of values that should be passed to the function supplied in parameter 3. Parameter 3 is an unnamed function or a lambda.

The square braces of the lambda denote a capture list. This list is used to allow the lambda access to variables that exist in the function where it is created. In this case we do not capture any variables from the function. The brackets then denote the parameter list. The lambda in Listing 8-1 takes an int32_t as a parameter as that is the type stored in the vector. The curly braces denote the function body just as they do with standard function bodies. Executing this code results in the output shown in Figure 8-3.

```
bruce@bruce-Virtual-Machine: ~/Projects/C-Recipes/Recipe8-2/Listing8-6
bruce@bruce-Virtual-Machine:~/Projects/C-Recipes/Recipe8-2/Listing8-6$ ./main
1
2
3
4
5
bruce@bruce-Virtual-Machine:~/Projects/C-Recipes/Recipe8-2/Listing8-6$ ▮
```

Figure 8-3. *The output generated by the for_each and lambda in Listing 8-6*

This output is generated because the for_each algorithm passes the integer from each position in myVector into the function supplied, in this case a lambda.

Recipe 8-3. Finding the Maximum and Minimum Values in a Container

Problem

Occasionally you will want to find the largest or smallest value in a container.

Solution

The STL provides algorithms that allow you to find both the largest and smallest values in a STL container. These are the min_element and max_element functions.

How It Works

Finding the Minimum Value in a Container

The min_element function operates by taking an iterator to the beginning and the end of a given sequence. It walks this sequence and finds the minimum value contained in that sequence. Listing 8-7 shows this algorithm being used.

Listing 8-7. Using the min_element algorithm

```
#include <algorithm>
#include <iostream>
#include <vector>

using namespace std;

int main(int argc, char* argv[])
{
    vector<int> myVector{ 4, 10, 6, 9, 1 };
    auto minimum = min_element(myVector.begin(), myVector.end());

    cout << "Minimum value: " << *minimum << std::endl;

    return 0;
}
```

In this case you can see that a vector is being used to store integer elements. The min_element function is passed the iterator that denotes the beginning and the end of the sequence contained by the vector. This algorithm returns an iterator to the element that contains the smallest value. I'm using auto here to avoid having to write out the entirety of the iterator's type (which would be vector<int>::iterator). It is clear that an iterator is returned when looking at the line that outputs the value. The pointer dereference operator is required to retrieve the integer value from the iterator. You can see the output generated by the code in Figure 8-4.

```
● ● ●   bruce@bruce-Virtual-Machine: ~/Projects/C-Recipes/Recipe8-3/Listing8-7
bruce@bruce-Virtual-Machine:~/Projects/C-Recipes/Recipe8-3/Listing8-7$ ./main
Minimum value: 1
bruce@bruce-Virtual-Machine:~/Projects/C-Recipes/Recipe8-3/Listing8-7$ ▮
```

Figure 8-4. *The output from Listing 8-7 showing the retrieved minimum value*

The container in Listing 8-7 shows a trivial case where the container stores integer values. This case is trivial as two int variables are already comparable using the < operator. You can use min_element with your own classes by providing an overloaded < operator in your class. You can see an example of this in Listing 8-8.

Listing 8-8. Using `min_element` in conjunction with a class that contains a `<` operator

```cpp
#include <algorithm>
#include <iostream>
#include <vector>

using namespace std;

class MyClass
{
private:
    int m_Value;

public:
    MyClass(const int value)
        : m_Value{ value }
    {

    }

    int GetValue() const
    {
        return m_Value;
    }

    bool operator <(const MyClass& other) const
    {
        return m_Value < other.m_Value;
    }
};

int main(int argc, char* argv[])
{
    vector<MyClass> myVector{ 4, 10, 6, 9, 1 };
    auto minimum = min_element(myVector.begin(), myVector.end());

    if (minimum != myVector.end())
    {
        cout << "Minimum value: " << (*minimum).GetValue() << std::endl;
    }

    return 0;
}
```

Listing 8-7 and 10-8 differ by using a vector of MyClass objects rather than a vector of integer values. The call to min_element however remains exactly the same. In this case the min_element call will walk the sequence and use the `<` operator added to the MyClass class to find the lowest value. It's also necessary to protect against hitting the end of the sequence in this case as the end element will not point to a valid object and therefore the dereference and call to GetValue will likely crash.

Another option to compare non-basic types is to provide a comparison function directly to the min_element function directly. This option is shown in Listing 8-9.

Listing 8-9. Using a separate function with min_element

```cpp
#include <algorithm>
#include <iostream>
#include <vector>

using namespace std;

class MyClass
{
private:
    int m_Value;

public:
    MyClass(const int value)
        : m_Value{ value }
    {

    }

    int GetValue() const
    {
        return m_Value;
    }
};

bool CompareMyClasses(const MyClass& left, const MyClass& right)
{
    return left.GetValue() < right.GetValue();
}

int main(int argc, char* argv[])
{
    vector<MyClass> myVector{ 4, 10, 6, 9, 1 };
    auto minimum = min_element(myVector.begin(), myVector.end(), CompareMyClasses);

    if (minimum != myVector.end())
    {
        cout << "Minimum value: " << (*minimum).GetValue() << std::endl;
    }

    return 0;
}
```

In Listing 8-9 we supply a pointer to a comparison function to the min_element function. This function is used to compare the values returned from the MyClass GetValue method. The comparison function is constructed in a very specific way and takes two parameters, both constant references to MyClass objects. The function should return true if the first parameter is evaluated as being less than the second. The names left and right are chosen to help visualize the usual look of a < operator. The call to min_element is altered to contain a third parameter, the pointer to the CompareMyClasses function. The code shown in Listings 10-8 and 10-9 both produce output that is identical to that shown in Figure 8-4.

Finding the Maximum Values in a Container

Where the min_element function can be used to find the smallest value in a sequence, the max_element function can be used to find the largest. The function can be used in exactly the same way as the min_element function as you can see in Listing 8-10.

Listing 8-10. Using max_element

```cpp
#include <algorithm>
#include <iostream>
#include <vector>

using namespace std;

class MyClass
{
private:
    int m_Value;

public:
    MyClass(const int value)
        : m_Value{ value }
    {

    }

    int GetValue() const
    {
        return m_Value;
    }

    bool operator <(const MyClass& other) const
    {
        return m_Value < other.m_Value;
    }
};

bool CompareMyClasses(const MyClass& left, const MyClass& right)
{
    return left.GetValue() < right.GetValue();
}

int main(int argc, char* argv[])
{
    vector<int> myIntVector{ 4, 10, 6, 9, 1 };
    auto intMinimum = max_element(myIntVector.begin(), myIntVector.end());
    if (intMinimum != myIntVector.end())
    {
        cout << "Maxmimum value: " << *intMinimum << std::endl << std::endl;
    }
```

```
vector<MyClass> myMyClassVector{ 4, 10, 6, 9, 1 };
auto overrideOperatorMinimum = max_element(myMyClassVector.begin(),
    myMyClassVector.end());
if (overrideOperatorMinimum != myMyClassVector.end())
{
    cout << "Maximum value: " << (*overrideOperatorMinimum).GetValue() <<
        std::endl << std::endl;
}

auto functionComparisonMinimum = max_element(myMyClassVector.begin(),
    myMyClassVector.end(),
    CompareMyClasses);
if (functionComparisonMinimum != myMyClassVector.end())
{
    cout << "Maximum value: " << (*functionComparisonMinimum).GetValue() <<
        std::endl << std::endl;
}

return 0;
}
```

Listing 8-10 shows that the max_element function can be used in place of the min_element function. It's important to realize that the max_element function still uses the < operator. It may seem that the max_element would use the > operator instead but it's just as valid to use the < operator and respond to a result of false rather than true to indicate that one value is greater than another.

Recipe 8-4. Counting Instances of a Value in a Sequence

Problem

Sometimes you may wish to know how many instances of a specific value exist in a sequence.

Solution

The STL provides an algorithm called count. This algorithm can search through a sequence of values and return the number of times a supplied value is found.

How It Works

The count function takes 3 parameters, a beginning iterator, an ending iterator and a value to find. Given these three pieces of information the algorithm will return the number of times the value is present. Listing 8-11 shows this algorithm in use.

Listing 8-11. Using the count algorithm

```
#include <algorithm>
#include <iostream>
#include <vector>

using namespace std;

int main(int argc, char* argv[])
{
    vector<int> myVector{ 3, 2, 3, 7, 3, 8, 9, 3 };
    auto number = count(myVector.begin(), myVector.end(), 3);
    cout << "The number of 3s in myVector is: " << number << endl;

    return 0;
}
```

The code in Listing 8-11 will have the count function walk the sequence and return the number of times the value 3 is encountered. You can see that the result of this operation is 4 in Figure 8-5.

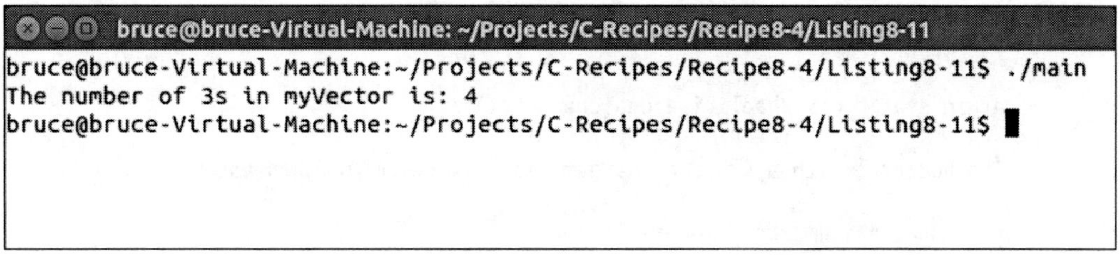

Figure 8-5. *The resulting output generated by Listing 8-11*

C++ also provides some special predicate functions that can be used in conjunction with character data and the count_if function. These include functions that can be used to count the number of upper or lower case letter and whether a character is alphanumeric, white space or punctuation. You can see all of these in action in Listing 8-12.

Listing 8-12. Using character predicates with count

```
#include <algorithm>
#include <cctype>
#include <iostream>
#include <string>

using namespace std;

int main(int argc, char* argv[])
{
    string myString{ "Bruce Sutherland!" };
```

```
    auto numberOfCapitals = count_if(
        myString.begin(),
        myString.end(),
        [](auto&& character)
        {
            return static_cast<bool>(isupper(character));
        });
    cout << "The number of capitals: " << numberOfCapitals << endl;

    auto numberOfLowerCase = count_if(
        myString.begin(),
        myString.end(),
        [](auto&& character)
        {
            return static_cast<bool>(islower(character));
        });
    cout << "The number of lower case letters: " << numberOfLowerCase << endl;

    auto numberOfAlphaNumerics = count_if(
        myString.begin(),
        myString.end(),
        [](auto&& character)
        {
            return static_cast<bool>(isalpha(character));
        });
    cout << "The number of alpha numeric characters: " << numberOfAlphaNumerics << endl;

    auto numberOfPunctuationMarks = count_if(
        myString.begin(),
        myString.end(),
        [](auto&& character)
        {
            return static_cast<bool>(ispunct(character));
        });
    cout << "The number of punctuation marks: " << numberOfPunctuationMarks << endl;

    auto numberOfWhiteSpaceCharacters = count_if(
        myString.begin(),
        myString.end(),
        [](auto&& character)
        {
            return static_cast<bool>(isspace(character));
        });
    cout << "The number of white space characters: " << numberOfWhiteSpaceCharacters << endl;

    return 0;
}
```

The predicates can be seen being passed to the count_if function using a lambda in Listing 8-12. The lambda is necessary for the count_if template to be properly satisfied that the function being supplied is a predicate returns a bool. The count_if function will return the number of times the supplied function returns true. You can see the result of the different calls to count_if in Figure 8-6.

```
● ● ●   bruce@bruce-Virtual-Machine: ~/Projects/C-Recipes/Recipe8-4/Listing8-12
bruce@bruce-Virtual-Machine:~/Projects/C-Recipes/Recipe8-4/Listing8-12$ ./main
The number of capitals: 2
The number of lower case letters: 13
The number of alpha numeric characters: 15
The number of punctuation marks: 1
The number of white space characters: 1
bruce@bruce-Virtual-Machine:~/Projects/C-Recipes/Recipe8-4/Listing8-12$ ▇
```

Figure 8-6. *The results from calling the code in Listing 8-6*

The string supplied in Listing 8-6 is fairly simple so it's easy to confirm that the character predicates are working as expected. You can cross check the results from Figure 8-6 to confirm this is the case.

Recipe 8-5. Finding Values in a Sequence

Problem

You may wish to find an iterator to the first element in a sequence that matches a specific value.

Solution

The STL provides the find function to retrieve iterators to the first element in a sequence that matches a supplied value.

How It Works

The find function can be used to retrieve an iterator to the first value that matches a value that you supply. You can use this to walk along a sequence from beginning to end. Listing 8-13 shows how you can use this along with a while loop to move along an entire sequence.

Listing 8-13. Using find

```cpp
#include <algorithm>
#include <iostream>
#include <string>

using namespace std;

int main(int argc, char* argv[])
{
    string myString{ "Bruce Sutherland" };
```

```
    auto found = find(myString.begin(), myString.end(), 'e');
    while (found != myString.end())
    {
        cout << "Found: " << *found << endl;

        found = find(found+1, myString.end(), 'e');
    }

    return 0;
}
```

The code in Listing 8-13 will print out the letter e twice as there are two of these in the string stored in the variable myString. The first call to find returns an iterator that points to the first instance of the character e in the string. The call inside the while loop then starts at the position immediately after that iterator. This causes the find function to search progressively through the supplied set of data and eventually reach the end. The while loop will terminate once this occurs. The code in Listing 8-13 generates the output shown in Figure 8-7.

```
⊗ ⊜ ⊕   bruce@bruce-Virtual-Machine: ~/Projects/C-Recipes/Recipe8-5/Listing8-13
bruce@bruce-Virtual-Machine:~/Projects/C-Recipes/Recipe8-5/Listing8-13$ ./main
Found: e
Found: e
bruce@bruce-Virtual-Machine:~/Projects/C-Recipes/Recipe8-5/Listing8-13$ ▌
```

Figure 8-7. *The output generatedby executing the code shown in Listing 8-13*

Recipe 8-6. Sorting Elements in a Sequence

Problem

Sometimes you will have data in a container that has become out of order and you wish to reorder that data.

Solution

The STL provides the sort algorithm to reorder data in a sequence.

How It Works

The sort function takes an iterator to the beginning of a sequence and an iterator to the end of a sequence. It will automatically sort the values between the iterators into an ascending numerical order. You can see code that achieves this in Listing 8-14.

Listing 8-14. Using the sort algorithm

```cpp
#include <algorithm>
#include <iostream>
#include <vector>

using namespace std;

int main(int argc, char* argv[])
{
    vector<int> myVector{ 10, 6, 4, 7, 8, 3, 9 };
    sort(myVector.begin(), myVector.end());

    for (auto&& element : myVector)
    {
        cout << element << ", ";
    }

    cout << endl;

    return 0;
}
```

The code in Listing 8-14 will reorder the values in myVector into ascending order. Figure 8-8 shows the output this code generates.

```
⊗ ⊜ ⊡   bruce@bruce-Virtual-Machine: ~/Projects/C-Recipes/Recipe8-6/Listing8-14
bruce@bruce-Virtual-Machine:~/Projects/C-Recipes/Recipe8-6/Listing8-14$ ./main
3, 4, 6, 7, 8, 9, 10,
bruce@bruce-Virtual-Machine:~/Projects/C-Recipes/Recipe8-6/Listing8-14$ ▮
```

Figure 8-8. *The myVector elements sorted into ascending order*

If you wish to sort the data into a custom order, such as descending then you must supply a predicate function to the sort algorithm. Listing 8-15 shows the use of a predicate to sort a numeric vector into descending order.

Listing 8-15. Using a predicate with sort

```cpp
#include <algorithm>
#include <iostream>
#include <vector>

using namespace std;

bool IsGreater(int left, int right)
{
    return left > right;
}
```

193

```
int main(int argc, char* argv[])
{
    vector<int> myVector{ 10, 6, 4, 7, 8, 3, 9 };
    sort(myVector.begin(), myVector.end(), IsGreater);

    for (auto&& element : myVector)
    {
        cout << element << ", ";
    }

    return 0;
}
```

The data in myVector in Listing 8-15 is the same as the data stored in Listing 8-14. The difference between the two Listings is the use of the IsGreater function in Listing 8-15. This is passed to the sort function and is used to compare the values in myVector. The standard sort function will order values from lowest to highest as you saw in Figure 8-9. Figure 8-10 shows that the code in Listing 8-15 will order the numbers from highest to lowest.

```
😵😑⊟  bruce@bruce-Virtual-Machine: ~/Projects/C-Recipes/Recipe8-6/Listing8-15
bruce@bruce-Virtual-Machine:~/Projects/C-Recipes/Recipe8-6/Listing8-15$ ./main
10, 9, 8, 7, 6, 4, 3,
bruce@bruce-Virtual-Machine:~/Projects/C-Recipes/Recipe8-6/Listing8-15$ ▉
```

Figure 8-9. *The output generated by Listing 8-15 with numbers ordered from highest to lowest*

CHAPTER 9

■ ■ ■

Templates

The STL is written using a language feature provided by C++ called *templates*. Templates provide a method you can use to write generic code that can be specialized at compile time to create concrete functions and classes of varying type. The only requirement for template code is that output can be generated for all of the types used to specialize a template in your program. This may be a little difficult to understand at this point, but it should be clearer by the time you finish this chapter.

9-1. Creating a Template Function

Problem

You would like to create a function that can be passed different types of parameters and return different types of values.

Solution

It's possible to use method overloading to supply different versions of a function for each type you wish to support, but this still limits you to functions with the types supplied. A better approach is to create a template function that that be specialized to work with any type.

How It Works

C++ includes a template compiler that can be used to turn generic function definitions into concrete functions at compile time.

Creating a Template Function

Templates allow you to write code without specifying concrete types. Code usually contains the types you wish to work with; Listing 9-1 shows a function written under these normal circumstances.

Listing 9-1. A Non-Template Function

```
#include <iostream>

using namespace std;

int Add(int a, int b)
{
    return a + b;
}

int main(int argc, char* argv[])
{
    const int number1{ 1 };
    const int number2{ 2 };
    const int result{ Add(number1, number2) };

    cout << "The result of adding" << endl;
    cout << number1 << endl;
    cout << "to" << endl;
    cout << number2 << endl;
    cout << "is" << endl;
    cout << result;

    return 0;
}
```

The Add function in Listing 9-1 is a standard C++ function. It takes two `int` parameters and returns an `int` value. You could supply a `float` version of this function by copying the function and altering every reference to `int` so that it used a `float` instead. You could then do the same for `string` and any other types you wished the function to support. The problem with this approach is that you must duplicate the function for every type, even though the body of the function remains the same. An alternative solution is to use a template function. You can see a template version of Add in Listing 9-2.

Listing 9-2. A Template Version of Add

```
template <typename T>
T Add(const T& a, const T& b)
{
    return a + b;
}
```

As you can see, the template version of Add no longer uses the concrete type `int`. Instead, the function is defined inside a template block. The `template` keyword is used to tell the compiler that the next block of code should be treated as a template. This is followed by an angled bracket section (`< >`) that defines any types the template uses. This example defines a single template type, represented by the character T. T is then used to specify the return type and the types of both parameters being passed to the function.

> ■ **Note** It's a good idea to pass parameters to template functions as `const` references. The initial implementation of `Add` passed `int` types by value, but there's no guarantee that a template won't be used by a type that would create a performance penalty when passed by value, such as a copied object.

Now that you have templatized the Add function, you can see in Listing 9-3 that the calling code in the `main` function is no different than that shown in Listing 9-1.

Listing 9-3. Calling the Template Add Function

```
#include <iostream>

using namespace std;

template <typename T>
T Add(const T& a, const T& b)
{
    return a + b;
}

int main(int argc, char* argv[])
{
    const int number1{ 1 };
    const int number2{ 2 };
    const int result{ Add(number1, number2) };

    cout << "The result of adding" << endl;
    cout << number1 << endl;
    cout << "to" << endl;
    cout << number2 << endl;
    cout << "is" << endl;
    cout << result;

    return 0;
}
```

Listing 9-3 contains a call to the Add function in exactly the same place as the code in Listing 9-1. This is possible because compilers can implicitly work out the correct type to use with a template.

Explicit vs. Implicit Template Specialization

Sometimes you want to be explicit about the types your template can use. Listing 9-4 shows an example of explicit template specialization.

Listing 9-4. Explicit and Implicit Template Specialization

```
#include <iostream>

using namespace std;

template <typename T>
T Add(const T& a, const T& b)
{
    return a + b;
}

template <typename T>
void Print(const T& value1, const T& value2, const T& result)
{
    cout << "The result of adding" << endl;
    cout << value1 << endl;
    cout << "to" << endl;
    cout << value2 << endl;
    cout << "is" << endl;
    cout << result;

    cout << endl << endl;
}

int main(int argc, char* argv[])
{
    const int number1{ 1 };
    const int number2{ 2 };
    const int intResult{ Add(number1, number2) };
    Print(number1, number2, intResult);

    const float floatResult{ Add(static_cast<float>(number1), static_cast<float>(number2))
};
    Print<float>(number1, number2, floatResult);

    return 0;
}
```

Listing 9-4 adds a template `Print` function that takes three templatized parameters. This function is called twice in the `main` function. The first time, the template type is deduced implicitly. This is possible because all three parameters passed to the function are of type `int`; therefore the compiler works out that you intended to call an `int` version of the template. The second call to `Print` is explicit. This is achieved by adding angled brackets containing the type to use (in this case, `float`) immediately after the function name. This is necessary due to the different types of variables being passed to the function. Here `number1` and `number2` are both of type `int`, but `floatResult` is of type `float`; as a result, the compiler can't deduce the correct type to use with the template. Visual Studio generated the following error when I tried to compile this code using implicit specialization:

```
error C2782: 'void Print(const T &,const T &,const T &)' : template parameter 'T' is ambiguous
```

9-2. Partially Specializing a Template

Problem

You have a template function that won't compile with a specific type.

Solution

You can create template overloads using partial template specialization.

How It Works

The body of a template function contains code that requires implicit properties from the types you use to specialize that template. Consider the code in Listing 9-5.

Listing 9-5. A Template Function

```cpp
#include <iostream>

using namespace std;

template <typename T>
T Add(const T& a, const T& b)
{
    return a + b;
}

template <typename T>
void Print(const T& value1, const T& value2, const T& result)
{
    cout << "The result of adding" << endl;
    cout << value1 << endl;
    cout << "to" << endl;
    cout << value2 << endl;
    cout << "is" << endl;
    cout << result;

    cout << endl << endl;
}

int main(int argc, char* argv[])
{
    const int number1{ 1 };
    const int number2{ 2 };
    const int intResult{ Add(number1, number2) };
    Print(number1, number2, intResult);

    return 0;
}
```

This code requires two implicit properties from the types used by the Add function and then the Print function. The Add function requires that the type used can also be used with the + operator. The Print function requires that the type used can be passed to the << operator. The main function uses these functions with int variables, so both of these conditions are met. If you were to use Add or Print with a class you created, then chances are that the compiler wouldn't be able to use that class with the + or << operator.

▩ **Note**   The "proper" solution in this case is to add overloaded + and << operators so that the original code works as expected. This example shows how you can use partial specialization to achieve the same result.

You can easily update Listing 9-5 to use a simple class, as shown in Listing 9-6.

Listing 9-6. Using Templates with Classes

```cpp
#include <iostream>

using namespace std;

class MyClass
{
private:
    int m_Value{ 0 };

public:
    MyClass() = default;

    MyClass(int value)
        : m_Value{ value }
    {

    }

    MyClass(int number1, int number2)
        : m_Value{ number1 + number2 }
    {

    }

    int GetValue() const
    {
        return m_Value;
    }
};

template <typename T>
T Add(const T& a, const T& b)
{
    return a + b;
}
```

```
template <typename T>
void Print(const T& value1, const T& value2, const T& result)
{
    cout << "The result of adding" << endl;
    cout << value1 << endl;
    cout << "to" << endl;
    cout << value2 << endl;
    cout << "is" << endl;
    cout << result;

    cout << endl << endl;
}

int main(int argc, char* argv[])
{
    const MyClass number1{ 1 };
    const MyClass number2{ 2 };
    const MyClass intResult{ Add(number1, number2) };
    Print(number1, number2, intResult);

    return 0;
}
```

The code in Listing 9-6 won't compile. Your compiler won't be able to find suitable operators that can be used with the MyClass type for + and <<. You can fix this problem by using partial template specialization, as shown in Listing 9-7.

Listing 9-7. Using Partial Template Specialization

```
#include <iostream>

using namespace std;

class MyClass
{
private:
    int m_Value{ 0 };

public:
    MyClass() = default;

    MyClass(int value)
        : m_Value{ value }
    {

    }

    MyClass(int number1, int number2)
        : m_Value{ number1 + number2 }
    {

    }
```

```
        int GetValue() const
        {
            return m_Value;
        }
};

template <typename T>
T Add(const T& a, const T& b)
{
    return a + b;
}

template <>
MyClass Add(const MyClass& myClass1, const MyClass& myClass2)
{
    return MyClass(myClass1.GetValue(), myClass2.GetValue());
}

template <typename T>
void Print(const T& value1, const T& value2, const T& result)
{
    cout << "The result of adding" << endl;
    cout << value1 << endl;
    cout << "to" << endl;
    cout << value2 << endl;
    cout << "is" << endl;
    cout << result;

    cout << endl << endl;
}

template <>
void Print(const MyClass& value1, const MyClass& value2, const MyClass& result)
{
    cout << "The result of adding" << endl;
    cout << value1.GetValue() << endl;
    cout << "to" << endl;
    cout << value2.GetValue() << endl;
    cout << "is" << endl;
    cout << result.GetValue();

    cout << endl << endl;
}

int main(int argc, char* argv[])
{
    const MyClass number1{ 1 };
    const MyClass number2{ 2 };
    const MyClass intResult{ Add(number1, number2) };
    Print(number1, number2, intResult);

    return 0;
}
```

The code in Listing 9-7 adds specialized versions of Add and Print. It does so by using an empty template-type specifier and the concrete MyClass types in the function signatures. You can see this in the Add function, where the parameters being passed are of type MyClass and the return value is of type MyClass. The partially specialized Print function also passes const references to MyClass variables. The template functions can still be used with variables such as ints and floats but now also explicitly support the MyClass type.

For the sake of completeness, Listing 9-8 shows a preferred implementation that adds support for the + and << operators and MyClass.

Listing 9-8. Adding + and << Operator Support to MyClass

```cpp
#include <iostream>

using namespace std;

class MyClass
{
    friend ostream& operator <<(ostream& os, const MyClass& myClass);

private:
    int m_Value{ 0 };

public:
    MyClass() = default;

    MyClass(int value)
        : m_Value{ value }
    {

    }

    MyClass(int number1, int number2)
        : m_Value{ number1 + number2 }
    {

    }

    MyClass operator +(const MyClass& other) const
    {
        return m_Value + other.m_Value;
    }
};

ostream& operator <<(ostream& os, const MyClass& myClass)
{
    os << myClass.m_Value;
    return os;
}
```

```
template <typename T>
T Add(const T& a, const T& b)
{
    return a + b;
}

template <typename T>
void Print(const T& value1, const T& value2, const T& result)
{
    cout << "The result of adding" << endl;
    cout << value1 << endl;
    cout << "to" << endl;
    cout << value2 << endl;
    cout << "is" << endl;
    cout << result;

    cout << endl << endl;
}

int main(int argc, char* argv[])
{
    const MyClass number1{ 1 };
    const MyClass number2{ 2 };
    const MyClass intResult{ Add(number1, number2) };
    Print(number1, number2, intResult);

    return 0;
}
```

This code adds support for the + operator to MyClass directly. A function is also specified for the << operator that works along with the ostream type. This works because cout is compatible with ostream (which stands for *output stream*). This function signature is added as a friend of MyClass so that the function can access internal data from MyClass. You could also leave the GetValue accessor and not add the operator as a friend function.

9-3. Creating Class Templates

Problem

You would like to create a class that can store variables of different types without duplicating all the code.

Solution

C++ allows for the creation of template classes that support abstract types.

How It Works

You can define a class as a template using the `template` specifier. The `template` specifier takes types and values as parameters that the compiler uses to build a specialization of the template code. Listing 9-9 shows an example that uses an abstract type and value to construct a template class.

Listing 9-9. Creating a Template Class

```cpp
#include <iostream>

using namespace std;

template <typename T, int numberOfElements>
class MyArray
{
private:
    T m_Array[numberOfElements];

public:
    MyArray()
        : m_Array{}
    {

    }

    T& operator[](const unsigned int index)
    {
        return m_Array[index];
    }
};

int main(int argc, char* argv[])
{
    const unsigned int ARRAY_SIZE{ 5 };
    MyArray<int, ARRAY_SIZE> myIntArray;
    for (unsigned int i{ 0 }; i < ARRAY_SIZE; ++i)
    {
        myIntArray[i] = i;
    }

    for (unsigned int i{ 0 }; i < ARRAY_SIZE; ++i)
    {
        cout << myIntArray[i] << endl;
    }

    cout << endl;

    MyArray<float, ARRAY_SIZE> myFloatArray;
    for (unsigned int i{ 0 }; i < ARRAY_SIZE; ++i)
    {
        myFloatArray[i] = static_cast<float>(i)+0.5f;
    }
```

```
    for (unsigned int i{ 0 }; i < ARRAY_SIZE; ++i)
    {
        cout << myFloatArray[i] << endl;
    }

    return 0;
}
```

The class MyArray creates a C-style array of type T and a number of elements. Both of these are abstract at the time you write the class and are specified at the time you use them in your code. You can now use the MyArray class to create an array of any size and containing any number of elements that can be represented by an int. You can see this in practice in the main function, where the MyArray class template is specialized to create an array of ints and an array of floats. Figure 9-1 shows the output generated when running this code: the two arrays contain different types of variables.

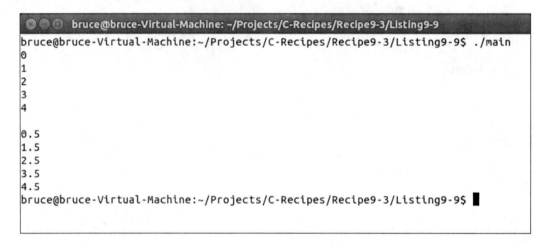

Figure 9-1. *The output generated by running the code in Listing 9-9*

▨ **Note** The creation of an array template wrapper is a simple example that shows the foundation of the std::array template supplied by the STL. The STL version supports STL iterators and algorithms and is a better choice than writing your own implementation.

9-4. Creating Singletons

Problem

You have a system, and you would like to create a single instance of it that you can access from many places in your application.

Solution

You can use a template to create a `Singleton` base class.

How It Works

The basis of the singleton is a class template. The `Singleton` class template contains a `static` pointer to an abstract type that can be used to represent any type of class you like. A byproduct of using a `static` pointer is that the instance of the class can be accessed from anywhere in your program. You should be careful not to abuse this, although it can be a useful property. Listing 9-10 shows show to create and use a `Singleton` template.

Listing 9-10. The Singleton Template

```
#include <cassert>
#include <iostream>

using namespace std;

template <typename T>
class Singleton
{
private:
    static T* m_Instance;

public:
    Singleton()
    {
        assert(m_Instance == nullptr);
        m_Instance = static_cast<T*>(this);
    }

    virtual ~Singleton()
    {
        m_Instance = nullptr;
    }

    static T& GetSingleton()
    {
        return *m_Instance;
    }

    static T* GetSingletonPtr()
    {
        return m_Instance;
    }
};

template <typename T>
T* Singleton<T>::m_Instance = nullptr;
```

```
class Manager
    : public Singleton < Manager >
{
public:
    void Print() const
    {
        cout << "Singleton Manager Successfully Printing!";
    }
};

int main(int argc, char* argv[])
{
    new Manager();
    Manager& manager{ Manager::GetSingleton() };
    manager.Print();
    delete Manager::GetSingletonPtr();

    return 0;
}
```

The Singleton class in Listing 9-10 is a template class that contains a private static pointer to the abstract type T. The Singleton constructor assigns a cast of this to the m_Instance variable. It's possible to use a static_cast in this manner because you know that the type of the object will be the type supplied to the template. The class's virtual destructor is responsible for setting m_Instance back to nullptr; there are also reference and pointer accessors to the instance.

Listing 9-10 then uses this template to create a Singleton-capable Manager class. It does so by creating a class that inherits from Singleton and passes its own type into the Singleton template parameter.

▓ **Note**   Passing the type of a class into a template from which the class derives is known as the *curiously recursive template pattern.*

The main function creates a Manager using the new keyword. The Manager isn't stored as a reference or pointer to the class. Although you could do this, it's better to simply use the accessor to the Singleton from this point. You do so by using the static function syntax with the name of the derived class. The main function creates a reference to the Manager instance by calling the Manager::GetSingleton function.

The Singleton instance is deleted by calling delete on the value returned by Manager::GetSingletonPtr. This causes ~Singleton to be called, which clears the address stored in m_Instance and releases the memory used to store the instance.

▓ **Note**   This Singleton class is based on the implementation originally written by Scott Bilas in *Game Programming Gems* (Charles River Media, 2000).

9-5. Calculating Values at Compile Time

Problem

You need to calculate complex values and would like to avoid computing them at runtime.

Solution

Template metaprogramming takes advantage of the C++ template compiler to calculate values at compile time and save runtime performance for users.

How It Works

Template metaprogramming can be a complex topic to understand. This complexity comes from the scope of the C++ template compiler's capabilities. In addition to letting you carry out generic programming by abstracting types from functions and classes, the template compiler can also compute values.

Hashing data is a common method of comparing two sets of data for equality. It works by creating a hash of the data at the time of creation and comparing the hash to the runtime version of the data. You can use this method to detect changes in executables of data files when your program is being executed. The SDBM hash is a simple-to-implement hashing function; Listing 9-11 shows a normal function implementation of the SDBM hash algorithm.

Listing 9-11. The SDBM Hash Algorithm

```cpp
#include <iostream>
#include <string>

using namespace std;

unsigned int SDBMHash(const std::string& key)
{
    unsigned int result{ 0 };

    for (unsigned int character : key)
    {
        result = character + (result << 6) + (result << 16) - result;
    }

    return result;
}

int main(int argc, char* argv[])
{
    std::string data{ "Bruce Sutherland" };
    unsigned int sdbmHash{ SDBMHash(data) };

    cout << "The hash of " << data << " is " << sdbmHash;

    return 0;
}
```

The SDBMHash function in Listing 9-11 works by iterating over the supplied data and calculating a result by manipulating each byte from the data set into a result variable. This functional version of SDBMHash is useful for creating a hash of data loaded at runtime, but here the data being supplied was known at compile time. You can optimize the execution speed of your program by replacing this function with a template metaprogram. Listing 9-12 does just that.

Listing 9-12. Replacing SDBMHash with a Template Metaprogram

```
#include <iostream>

using namespace std;

template <int stringLength>
struct SDBMCalculator
{
    constexpr static unsigned int Calculate(const char* const stringToHash, unsigned int& value)
    {
        unsigned int character{
            SDBMCalculator<stringLength - 1>::Calculate(stringToHash, value)
        };
        value = character + (value << 6) + (value << 16) - value;
        return stringToHash[stringLength - 1];
    }

    constexpr static unsigned int CalculateValue(const char* const stringToHash)
    {
        unsigned int value{};
        unsigned int character{ SDBMCalculator<stringLength>::Calculate(stringToHash, value) };
        value = character + (value << 6) + (value << 16) - value;
        return value;
    }
};

template<>
struct SDBMCalculator < 1 >
{
    constexpr static unsigned int Calculate(const char* const stringToHash, unsigned int& value)
    {
        return stringToHash[0];
    }
};

constexpr unsigned int sdbmHash{ SDBMCalculator<16>::CalculateValue("Bruce Sutherland") };

int main(int argc, char* argv[])
{
    cout << "The hash of Bruce Sutherland is " << sdbmHash << endl;

    return 0;
}
```

You can immediately see that the code in Listing 9-12 looks much more complicated than Listing 9-11. The syntax required to write template metaprograms isn't the nicest to read. The main function is now a single line of code. The hash value is stored in a constant, and no call is made to any of the template functions. You can test this by placing a breakpoint in the template functions and running a release build of your program.

The template metaprogram in Listing 9-12 works by using recursion. The length of the data to be hashed is supplied to the template parameter and can be seen when the sdbmHash variable is initialized. Here, 16 is passed to the template, which is the length of the string "Bruce Sutherland". The template compiler recognizes that it has been supplied with data that it can evaluate at compile time, and therefore it automatically calls the Calculate metaprogram function in the CalculateValue function. This recursion occurs until the terminator is hit. The terminator is the partially specialized version of Calculate that is written to be called once the length of the data to be hashed is 1. When the terminator is reached, the recursive calls begin to unwind, and the compiler eventually stores the result of the template metaprogram in the sdbmHash variable. You can see the template metaprogram in action using a debug build. The compiler won't optimize out the template metaprogram in a debug build, which allows you to test your code and step through it to see the results. Figure 9-2 shows the output from running the code in Listing 9-12.

```
bruce@bruce-Virtual-Machine: ~/Projects/C-Recipes/Recipe9-5/Listing9-12
bruce@bruce-Virtual-Machine:~/Projects/C-Recipes/Recipe9-5/Listing9-12$ ./main
The hash of Bruce Sutherland is 2561640807
bruce@bruce-Virtual-Machine:~/Projects/C-Recipes/Recipe9-5/Listing9-12$ ▊
```

Figure 9-2. *The output generated by the code in Listing 9-12, showing the SDBM hash of the string "Bruce Sutherland"*

CHAPTER 10

Memory

Memory is a fundamentally important resource in modern computers. All the data that your program operates on will at some point or other be stored into RAM to be retrieved by the processor at a later time when required to complete part of your algorithms.

Because of this, it's vitally important for a C++ programmer to understand how and when your program uses different types of memory. This chapter introduces three different memory spaces, how they can be utilized, and the potential performance impacts that each may cause on your programs.

10-1. Using Static Memory

Problem

You have an object that you would like to be able to access anywhere in your code.

Solution

Static memory can be thought of as global variables. These variables and their values can be accessed by any part of your program at any time.

How It Works

The compiler you use automatically adds memory in static memory space for any globals you create. The address of static variables can usually be found in the address space of your executable and as such can be accessed by any part of your program at any time. Listing 10-1 shows an example of an unsigned integer global variable.

Listing 10-1. An Unsigned Integer Global Variable

```
#include <iostream>

using namespace std;

unsigned int counter{ 0 };
```

```
void IncreaseCounter()
{
    counter += 10;
    cout << "counter is " << counter << endl;
}

int main(int argc, char* argv[])
{
    counter += 5;
    cout << "counter is " << counter << endl;

    IncreaseCounter();

    return 0;
}
```

The variable counter in Listing 10-1 is declared with global scope. The result is that the variable can be accessed globally in your program. You can see this in effect in the main function and in the IncreaseCounter function. Both of these functions increase the value of the same global counter variable. The result shown in Figure 10-1 confirms that this is the case.

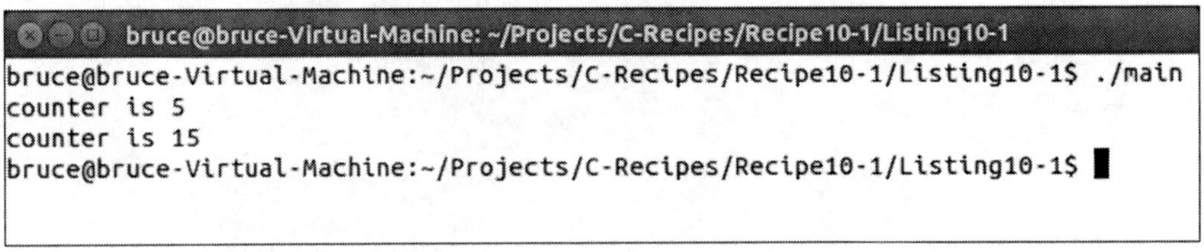

Figure 10-1. Output showing the result of changing a global variable

Global variables may be useful under certain circumstances but can cause many problems in other situations. Recipe 9-4 showed the use of a static class member variable to create a Singleton object. A static member is also a type of global variable and as such is accessible from anywhere in your program. A general problem with static variables is their order of creation. The C++ standard doesn't guarantee that static variables will be initialized in a given order. This can cause programs that use many dependent globals to run into problems and crashes as a result of an unexpected initialization order. Global variables also cause many problems in multithreaded programming because multiple threads can access the static address space at the same time with unexpected results. It's generally recommended that you keep the usage of global variables to a minimum.

10-2. Using Stack Memory

Problem

You require memory for temporary variables for doing work within functions.

Solution

A C++ program can use a growing and shrinking stack to provide temporary space for local variables.

How It Works

Because all variables in a C++ program are required to be backed by memory, temporary space is created on the fly for variables defined within functions. This is achieved using a stack. When a function is called, the compiler adds machine code that allocates enough stack space to store all the variables needed by a function.

The stack is manipulated using two registers (on x86-based CPUs) called esp and ebp. esp is the stack pointer, and ebp is the base pointer. The base pointer is used to store the address of the previous stack frame. This allows the current function to return to the correct stack when its execution is over. The esp register is used to store the current top of the stack; this allows the ebp to be updated if the current function calls another function.

The process of creating enough space on the program stack for local variables is shown in Listing 10-2.

Listing 10-2. x86 Assembly Showing the Creation of a 20-Byte Stack Frame

```
push ebp
mov ebp, esp
sub esp 20
```

The three lines of x86 Assembly language in Listing 10-2 show the basics of stack-frame creation in x86. First the push instruction is used to move the current base pointer onto the stack. The push instruction moves esp down far enough the store the value of ebp and then moves that value onto the stack. The current value of esp is then moved into ebp, moving the base pointer up to the beginning of the current stack frame. The last instruction subtracts the size of the stack frame from esp. It should be clear from this that a stack in an x86-based computer grows down toward 0.

A program then accesses each of the variables in the stack using an offset from the base pointer. You can see these three lines in the disassembly from Visual Studio shown in Figure 10-2.

```
void Function()
{
012D35B0   push          ebp
012D35B1   mov           ebp,esp
012D35B3   sub           esp,0CCh
012D35B9   push          ebx
012D35BA   push          esi
012D35BB   push          edi
012D35BC   lea           edi,[ebp-0CCh]
012D35C2   mov           ecx,33h
012D35C7   mov           eax,0CCCCCCCCh
012D35CC   rep stos      dword ptr es:[edi]
    int a{ 0 };
012D35CE   mov           dword ptr [a],0

    cout << a;
012D35D5   mov           esi,esp
012D35D7   mov           eax,dword ptr [a]
012D35DA   push          eax
012D35DB   mov           ecx,dword ptr ds:[12E00A0h]
012D35E1   call          dword ptr ds:[12E00FCh]
012D35E7   cmp           esi,esp
012D35E9   call          __RTC_CheckEsp (012D1334h)
}
```

Figure 10-2. *Disassembly from an x86 program, showing the creation of a stack frame*

Listing 10-3 shows the code from which the disassembly in Figure 10-2 is taken.

Listing 10-3. Simple Program Used to View the Disassembly

```
#include <iostream>

using namespace std;

void Function()
{
    int a{ 0 };

    cout << a;
}

int main(int argc, char* argv[])
{
    Function();

    return 0;
}
```

All the local variables that you create are allocated on the stack. Class variables' constructors are called at the point they're created, and their destructors are called when the stack is being destroyed. Listing 10-4 shows a simple program that consists of a **class** with a constructor and a destructor.

Listing 10-4. Class Variables on the Stack

```
#include <iostream>

using namespace std;

class MyClass
{
public:
    MyClass()
    {
        cout << "Constructor called!" << endl;
    }

    ~MyClass()
    {
        cout << "Destructor called!" << endl;
    }
};

int main(int argc, char* argv[])
{
    MyClass myClass;

    cout << "Function body!" << endl;

    return 0;
}
```

The constructor of the variable myClass in Listing 10-4 is called at the point of initialization. The rest of the function body is executed, and the **class** destructor is called when the variable goes out of scope. The myClass variable goes out of scope after the return statement. This happens because the local variables in the function may be needed to calculate the value returned from the function. You can see the output from Listing 10-4 in Figure 10-3.

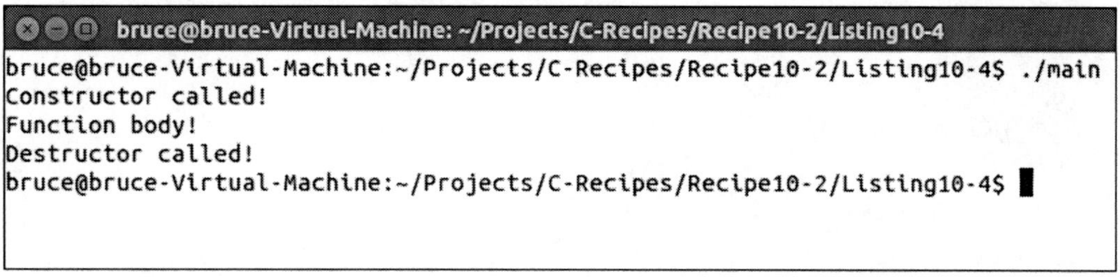

Figure 10-3. *The output from running the code in Listing 10-4*

The code in Listing 10-4 shows the creation and destruction of **class** variables in a function. It's also possible to control the creation of stack frames in C++. You do so by using curly braces to create a new scope within an existing scope. Listing 10-5 creates several different scopes, each with their own local variables.

Listing 10-5. Creating Multiple Scopes

```
#include <iostream>

using namespace std;

class MyClass
{
private:
    static int m_Count;
    int m_Instance{ -1 };

public:
    MyClass()
        : m_Instance{m_Count++}
    {
        cout << "Constructor called on " << m_Instance << endl;
    }

    ~MyClass()
    {
        cout << "Destructor called on " << m_Instance << endl;
    }
};
```

217

```
int MyClass::m_Count{ 0 };

int main(int argc, char* argv[])
{
    MyClass myClass1;

    {
        MyClass myClass2;

        {
            MyClass myClass3;
        }
    }

    return 0;
}
```

The code in Listing 10-5 shows the use of curly braces to create multiple stack frames within a single function. The class MyClass contains a static variable m_Count that is used to track the different instances. This variable is post-incremented every time a new instance is created, and the pre-incremented value is stored in m_Instance. The destructor is called on local variables each time a scope is closed. The results are shown in Figure 10-4.

```
bruce@bruce-Virtual-Machine: ~/Projects/C-Recipes/Recipe10-2/Listing10-5
bruce@bruce-Virtual-Machine:~/Projects/C-Recipes/Recipe10-2/Listing10-5$ ./main
Constructor called on 0
Constructor called on 1
Constructor called on 2
Destructor called on 2
Destructor called on 1
Destructor called on 0
bruce@bruce-Virtual-Machine:~/Projects/C-Recipes/Recipe10-2/Listing10-5$ 
```

Figure 10-4. Output showing the destruction order of objects with multiple scopes

10-3. Using Heap Memory

Problem

You need to create a large pool of memory that outlives a single local scope.

Solution

C++ provides the new and delete operators that allow you to manage large pools of dynamically allocated memory.

How It Works

Dynamically allocated memory is important to many long-running programs. It's essential for programs that allow users to generate their own content or load resources from files. It's usually very difficult if not impossible to provide enough memory for programs such as web browsers that are used to stream videos or social media content without the use of dynamically allocated memory, because you're unable to determine your memory requirements at the time of creating your program.

You can allocate dynamic memory in an address space commonly called the *heap* using the C++ new and delete operators. The new operator returns a pointer to dynamically allocated memory that is large enough to store the type of variable being created. Listing 10-6 shows how the new and delete operators are used.

Listing 10-6. Using new and delete

```
#include <iostream>

using namespace std;

int main(int argc, char* argv[])
{
    int* pInt{ new int };
    *pInt = 100;

    cout << hex << "The address at pInt is " << pInt << endl;
    cout << dec << "The value at pInt is " << *pInt << endl;

    delete pInt;
    pInt = nullptr;

    return 0;
}
```

This code uses the new operator to allocate enough memory to store a single int variable. A pointer is returned from new and stored in the variable pInt. The memory returned is uninitialized, and it's generally a good idea to initialize this memory at the point of creation. You can see this in main, where the pointer dereference operator is used to initialize the memory pointed to by pInt to 100.

Once you have allocated memory from the heap, it's your responsibility to ensure that it's returned correctly to the operating system. Failing to do so results in a memory leak. Memory leaks can cause problems for users and often result in poor computer performance, memory fragmentation, and, in severe cases, computer crashes due to insufficient memory.

You return heap memory to the operating system using the delete operator. This operator tells the system that you no longer need all the memory that was returned from the initial call to new. Your program should no longer attempt to use the memory returned by new after the call to delete has been made. Doing so causes undefined behavior that more often than not results in a program crash. Crashes caused by access to freed memory are usually very difficult to find, because they manifest themselves in places that you can't link to the offending code in any way. You can ensure that your program doesn't access deleted memory by setting any pointers to the memory to nullptr.

The output from Listing 10-6 is shown in Figure 10-5.

```
⊗ ⊖ ⊜    bruce@bruce-Virtual-Machine: ~/Projects/C-Recipes/Recipe10-3/Listing10-6
bruce@bruce-Virtual-Machine:~/Projects/C-Recipes/Recipe10-3/Listing10-6$ ./main
The address at pInt is 0x14d5010
The value at pInt is 100
bruce@bruce-Virtual-Machine:~/Projects/C-Recipes/Recipe10-3/Listing10-6$ ▮
```

Figure 10-5. *The output showing the address of and value stored in dynamically allocated memory from Listing 10-6*

The new and delete operators in Listing 10-6 are used to allocate single objects. There are also new and delete array operators for allocating multiples of the same object. Listing 10-7 shows the array new and delete operators in action.

Listing 10-7. The Array new and delete Operators

```cpp
#include <iostream>

using namespace std;

class MyClass
{
private:
    int m_Number{ 0 };

public:
    MyClass() = default;
    ~MyClass()
    {
        cout << "Destroying " << m_Number << endl;
    }

    void operator=(const int value)
    {
        m_Number = value;
    }
};

int main(int argc, char* argv[])
{
    const unsigned int NUM_ELEMENTS{ 5 };
    MyClass* pObjects{ new MyClass[NUM_ELEMENTS] };
    pObjects[0] = 100;
    pObjects[1] = 45;
    pObjects[2] = 31;
    pObjects[3] = 90;
```

```
    pObjects[4] = 58;

    delete[] pObjects;
    pObjects = nullptr;

    return 0;
}
```

The code in Listing 10-7 creates an array of objects. The MyClass class consists of an overloaded assignment operator to initialize the created objects and a destructor that shows the destruction order of the elements in the array. Using the standard delete operator on an array of objects can cause various problems for your program, because the standard delete operator only calls the class destructor on the first element of the array. If your class had allocated its own memory, then each of the subsequent objects in the array would leak their memory. Using the delete array operator ensures that each of the destructors in your array is called. You can see that each of the destructors for the elements in the array is called in Figure 10-6.

```
● ● ◎   bruce@bruce-Virtual-Machine: ~/Projects/C-Recipes/Recipe10-3/Listing10-7
bruce@bruce-Virtual-Machine:~/Projects/C-Recipes/Recipe10-3/Listing10-7$ ./main
Destroying 58
Destroying 90
Destroying 31
Destroying 45
Destroying 100
bruce@bruce-Virtual-Machine:~/Projects/C-Recipes/Recipe10-3/Listing10-7$ ▮
```

Figure 10-6. *The output showing that each of the destructors has been called when using the array* delete *operator*

10-4. Using Automated Shared Memory

Problem

You have an object that can be shared by multiple systems with different lifespans.

Solution

C++ provides the shared_ptr template that can automatically delete memory when it's no longer needed.

How It Works

Dynamically allocated memory in C++ must be deleted by a programmer. This means you're responsible for ensuring that your program behaves as a user expects at all times. C++ provides the shared_ptr template, which tracks how many places in your program are sharing access to the same memory and can delete that memory when it's no longer needed. Listing 10-8 shows how you can create a shared pointer.

Listing 10-8. Creating a Shared Pointer

```cpp
#include <iostream>
#include <memory>

using namespace std;

class MyClass
{
private:
    int m_Number{ 0 };

public:
    MyClass(int value)
        : m_Number{ value }
    {

    }

    ~MyClass()
    {
        cout << "Destroying " << m_Number << endl;
    }

    void operator=(const int value)
    {
        m_Number = value;
    }

    int GetNumber() const
    {
        return m_Number;
    }
};

using SharedMyClass = shared_ptr< MyClass >;

int main(int argc, char* argv[])
{
    SharedMyClass sharedMyClass{ new MyClass(10) };

    return 0;
}
```

This code contains a class, MyClass, that has a private integer member variable. There is also a type alias used to represent a shared_ptr to a MyClass object. This type alias is used to make writing your code easier and more maintainable in the long term. The shared_ptr template itself takes a parameter to the type of object that you would like to share around your program. In this case, you want to share dynamic objects of type MyClass.

An instance of SharedMyClass is created on the first line of the main function. This instance is initialized with a dynamically allocated MyClass object. The MyClass object itself is initialized with the value 10. The only other code in the body of main is the return statement. Despite this, Figure 10-7 shows that the destructor of MyClass has been called on the object stored in sharedMyClass.

```
bruce@bruce-Virtual-Machine: ~/Projects/C-Recipes/Recipe10-4/Listing10-8
bruce@bruce-Virtual-Machine:~/Projects/C-Recipes/Recipe10-4/Listing10-8$ ./main
Destroying 10
bruce@bruce-Virtual-Machine:~/Projects/C-Recipes/Recipe10-4/Listing10-8$ 
```

Figure 10-7. Output showing that the MyClass destructor has been called in Listing 10-8

The shared_ptr template automatically calls delete on the memory it wraps once the last instance of that shared_ptr goes out of scope. In this case, there is only a single shared_ptr in the main function; therefore the MyClass object is deleted, and its destructor is called after the function return statement is executed.

Listing 10-9 shows how you can use a shared_ptr to transfer ownership of shared memory from one function to another and still maintain this automated cleanup code.

Listing 10-9. Transferring Dynamic Memory between Functions

```cpp
#include <iostream>
#include <memory>

using namespace std;

class MyClass
{
private:
    int m_Number{ 0 };

public:
    MyClass(int value)
        : m_Number{ value }
    {

    }

    ~MyClass()
    {
        cout << "Destroying " << m_Number << endl;
    }

    void operator=(const int value)
    {
        m_Number = value;
    }
```

```
    int GetNumber() const
    {
        return m_Number;
    }
};

using SharedMyClass = shared_ptr< MyClass >;

void ChangeSharedValue(SharedMyClass sharedMyClass)
{
    if (sharedMyClass != nullptr)
    {
        *sharedMyClass = 100;
    }
}

int main(int argc, char* argv[])
{
    SharedMyClass sharedMyClass{ new MyClass(10) };

    ChangeSharedValue(sharedMyClass);

    return 0;
}
```

Listing 10-9 creates a SharedMyClass instance pointing to a MyClass object initialized with the value 10. The sharedMyClass instance is then passed by value into the ChangeSharedValue function. Passing a shared_ptr by value makes a copy of the pointer. You now have two instances of the SharedMyClass template, both pointing to the same MyClass instance. The destructor for MyClass isn't called until both of the shared_ptr instances of gone out of scope. Figure 10-8 shows that the initial value of the MyClass instance was changed and that the destructor was only called a single time.

```
⊗ ⊖ ⊡   bruce@bruce-Virtual-Machine: ~/Projects/C-Recipes/Recipe10-4/Listing10-9
bruce@bruce-Virtual-Machine:~/Projects/C-Recipes/Recipe10-4/Listing10-9$ ./main
Destroying 100
bruce@bruce-Virtual-Machine:~/Projects/C-Recipes/Recipe10-4/Listing10-9$ ▮
```

Figure 10-8. *Output showing that the shared object's stored value was changed and destroyed a single time*

10-5. Creating Single-Instance Dynamic Objects

Problem

You have an object that you would like to pass around, but you only wish to have a single instance of that object.

Solution

C++ provides the unique_ptr template, which allows a pointer instance to be transferred but not shared.

How It Works

unique_ptr is a template that can be used to store a pointer to dynamically allocated memory. It differs from shared_ptr in that there can only be a single reference to the dynamic memory at a time. Listing 10-10 shows how to create a unique_ptr.

Listing 10-10. Creating a unique_ptr

```cpp
#include <iostream>
#include <memory>

using namespace std;

class MyClass
{
private:
    int m_Number{ 0 };

public:
    MyClass(int value)
        : m_Number{ value }
    {

    }

    ~MyClass()
    {
        cout << "Destroying " << m_Number << endl;
    }

    void operator=(const int value)
    {
        m_Number = value;
    }

    int GetNumber() const
    {
        return m_Number;
    }
};
```

```
using UniqueMyClass = unique_ptr< MyClass >;

void CreateUniqueObject()
{
    UniqueMyClass uniqueMyClass{ make_unique<MyClass>(10) };
}

int main(int argc, char* argv[])
{
    cout << "Begin Main!" << endl;

    CreateUniqueObject();

    cout << "Back in Main!" << endl;

    return 0;
}
```

The unique_ptr in Listing 10-10 is created inside a function to demonstrate that the instance of the dynamically created object is destroyed when the unique_ptr goes out of scope. You can see this reflected in the output in Figure 10-9.

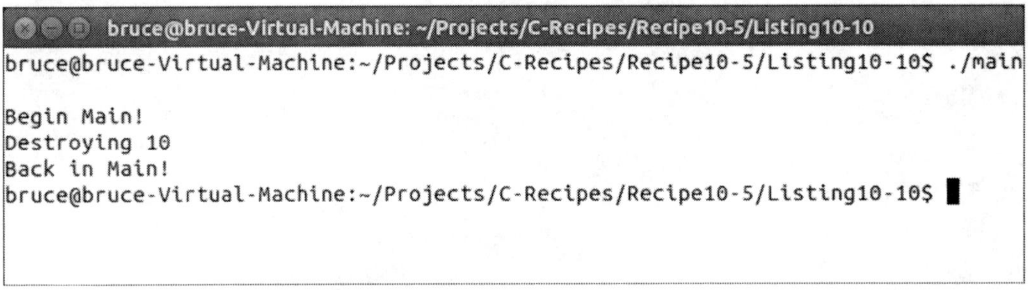

Figure 10-9. *Output showing the destruction of a dynamically allocated object stored in a unique_ptr*

Listing 10-10 showed that a unique_ptr can be used to automatically delete dynamically allocated memory when it's no longer needed. It didn't show that a unique_ptr can be used to transfer ownership of a single object between different scopes. This is shown in Listing 10-11.

Listing 10-11. Transferring Dynamically Allocated Memory Between unique_ptr instances

```
#include <iostream>
#include <memory>

using namespace std;

class MyClass
{
private:
    int m_Number{ 0 };
```

```
public:
    MyClass(int value)
        : m_Number{ value }
    {

    }

    ~MyClass()
    {
        cout << "Destroying " << m_Number << endl;
    }

    void operator=(const int value)
    {
        m_Number = value;
    }

    int GetNumber() const
    {
        return m_Number;
    }
};

using UniqueMyClass = unique_ptr< MyClass >;

void CreateUniqueObject(UniqueMyClass& referenceToUniquePtr)
{
    UniqueMyClass uniqueMyClass{ make_unique<MyClass>(10) };

    cout << hex << showbase;
    cout << "Address in uniqueMyClass " << uniqueMyClass.get() << endl;

    referenceToUniquePtr.swap(uniqueMyClass);

    cout << "Address in uniqueMyClass " << uniqueMyClass.get() << endl;
}

int main(int argc, char* argv[])
{
    cout << "Begin Main!" << endl;

    UniqueMyClass uniqueMyClass;
    CreateUniqueObject(uniqueMyClass);

    cout << "Address in main's uniqueMyClass " << uniqueMyClass.get() << endl;

    cout << dec << noshowbase << "Back in Main!" << endl;

    return 0;
}
```

227

The code in Listing 10-11 creates an instance of MyClass in the CreateUniqueObject function. That function also takes a reference to another unqiue_ptr<MyClass> that is used to transfer the dynamically allocated object out of the function. The transfer is achieved using the swap function supplied by the unique_ptr template. The MyClass destructor is called at the end of the main function when all the UniqueMyClass instances have gone out of scope. You can see the transfer of memory and the destruction order of the MyClass instance in Figure 10-10.

```
● ● ●   bruce@bruce-Virtual-Machine: ~/Projects/C-Recipes/Recipe10-5/Listing10-11
bruce@bruce-Virtual-Machine:~/Projects/C-Recipes/Recipe10-5/Listing10-11$ ./main

Begin Main!
Address in uniqueMyClass 0x12bb010
Address in uniqueMyClass 0
Address in main's uniqueMyClass 0x12bb010
Back in Main!
Destroying 10
bruce@bruce-Virtual-Machine:~/Projects/C-Recipes/Recipe10-5/Listing10-11$ ▊
```

Figure 10-10. *The output showing the transfer of a unique_ptr and the destruction of its dynamically allocated memory*

10-6. Creating Smart Pointers

Problem

You would like to use automated pointer management on systems that don't support shared_ptr and unique_ptr.

Solution

You can use member variables in a **class** to track how many references to the data are currently in use.

How It Works

The unique_ptr and shared_ptr templates were added to the STL in C++11. Some programs are written without access to C++11 or without access to the STL. In this situation, you can write your own smart pointer implementation. To begin, you need to create an object that can be used to reference-count. Reference counting works by increasing an integer every time you make a copy of the object you would like to count. Listing 10-12 shows the code for a reference-counting class.

Listing 10-12. The Code for a Reference-Counting Class

```
class ReferenceCount
{
private:
    int m_Count{ 0 };

public:
    void Increment()
    {
        ++m_Count;
    }

    int Decrement()
    {
        return --m_Count;
    }

    int GetCount() const
    {
        return m_Count;
    }
};
```

The ReferenceCount class is pretty basic. It simply consists of a member variable to keep track of a count and methods to increase and decrease that count. The GetCount method is there to provide access to the count, to allow for printing during debugging.

The ReferenceCount class is then used in a template class called SmartPointer. This class provides a template parameter you can use to specialize the template with the type of object you want to be automatically tracked. The class has a member variable that is a pointer to the object being tracked and another pointer to a ReferenceCount object. The ReferenceCount object is accessed through a pointer so that it can be shared among multiple SmartPointer objects that are all accessing the same dynamically allocated object. You can see the code for SmartPointer in Listing 10-13.

Listing 10-13. The SmartPointer Class

```
template <typename T>
class SmartPointer
{
private:
    T* m_Object{ nullptr };
    ReferenceCount* m_ReferenceCount{ nullptr };

public:
    SmartPointer()
    {

    }
```

```cpp
SmartPointer(T* object)
    : m_Object{ object }
    , m_ReferenceCount{ new ReferenceCount }
{
    m_ReferenceCount->Increment();

    cout << "Created smart pointer! Reference count is "
        << m_ReferenceCount->GetCount() << endl;
}

virtual ~SmartPointer()
{
    if (m_ReferenceCount)
    {
        int decrementedCount = m_ReferenceCount->Decrement();
        cout << "Destroyed smart pointer! Reference count is "
            << decrementedCount << endl;
        if (decrementedCount == 0)
        {
            delete m_ReferenceCount;
            delete m_Object;
        }
        m_ReferenceCount = nullptr;
        m_Object = nullptr;
    }
}

SmartPointer(const SmartPointer<T>& other)
    : m_Object{ other.m_Object }
    , m_ReferenceCount{ other.m_ReferenceCount }
{
    m_ReferenceCount->Increment();

    cout << "Copied smart pointer! Reference count is "
        << m_ReferenceCount->GetCount() << endl;
}

SmartPointer<T>& operator=(const SmartPointer<T>& other)
{
    if (this != &other)
    {
        if (m_ReferenceCount && m_ReferenceCount->Decrement() == 0)
        {
            delete m_ReferenceCount;
            delete m_Object;
        }

        m_Object = other.m_Object;
        m_ReferenceCount = other.m_ReferenceCount;
        m_ReferenceCount->Increment();
    }
```

```
        cout << "Assigning smart pointer! Reference count is "
            << m_ReferenceCount->GetCount() << endl;

        return *this;
    }

    SmartPointer(SmartPointer<T>&& other)
        : m_Object{ other.m_Object }
        , m_ReferenceCount{ other.m_ReferenceCount }
    {
        other.m_Object = nullptr;
        other.m_ReferenceCount = nullptr;
    }

    SmartPointer<T>& operator=(SmartPointer<T>&& other)
    {
        if (this != &other)
        {
            m_Object = other.m_Object;
            m_ReferenceCount = other.m_ReferenceCount;

            other.m_Object = nullptr;
            other.m_ReferenceCount = nullptr;
        }
    }

    T& operator*()
    {
        return *m_Object;
    }
};
```

You can see the member variables that are used to store the dynamically allocated object and the ReferenceCount object in the SmartPointer class in Listing 10-13. The m_Object pointer is a pointer to an abstract templatized type; this allows the use of any type to be tracked by the SmartPointer template.

The first public methods in SmartPointer are the constructors. A new SmartPointer can be created either as a null pointer or pointing to an already-existing object. A null SmartPointer has both m_Object and m_ReferenceCount set to nullptr. The other constructor takes a pointer to T that causes a SmartPointer to be initialized. In this case, a new ReferenceCount object is created to track the use of the object being passed to the constructor. The side effect of this is that a new SmartPointer can only be created when initialized with an object pointer; a null SmartPointer can only be assigned to from another SmartPointer object.

The SmartPointer destructor checks whether a ReferenceCount object is being held by the class (remember that it could be nullptr in a null SmartPointer). If a pointer to a ReferenceCount object is held, its count is decremented. If the count has reached 0, then you know this SmartPointer is the last to be referencing this dynamically allocated object. In this case, you're free to delete both the ReferenceCount object and the object being held by the SmartPointer.

The next method in the SmartPointer is the copy constructor. This method simply copies the m_Object and m_ReferenceCount pointers from the parameter passed to the method into the object being copy-constructed. It then makes sure the reference count is incremented. The call to Increment is essential because you now have two SmartPointer objects that are referencing the same dynamically allocated object. Missing the call to Increment here would cause delete to be called in the destructor of the first of these SmartPointers to go out of scope.

231

The assignment operator has a slightly different job than the copy constructor. In the copy constructor, you're free to assume that the existing object is new and therefore not already pointing to an existing object or ReferenceCount instance. This isn't true in the assignment operator; therefore it's necessary to account for this occurrence. You can see that the assignment operator first checks to ensure that the operator isn't assigning an object to itself; in this case, there would be no work to be done. If a new object is being assigned, then there is a check to see whether the ReferenceCount pointer is valid. If it is, then Decrement is called; and in the case where this returns 0, the existing m_ReferenceCount and m_Object pointers are deleted. The m_Object and m_ReferenceCount pointers are always copied from the parameter to the assignment operator method into the variables of this, and Increment is called on the new ReferenceCount object.

Next in the class are a move constructor and move assignment operator. These are present to conform with the C++ rule of five. This is a programming guideline that suggests that in any case where you overload the copy constructor or assignment operator, you should overload all five of the destructor, copy constructor, assignment operator, move constructor, and move assignment operator. Move operations are destructive in nature, so no calls to Increment or Decrement are made. These are unnecessary because the m_Object and m_ReferenceCount pointers are set to nullptr on the parameter in both cases, meaning delete will never be called in their destructors. Supporting the move constructor and move assignment operator provides a more efficient method to pass SmartPointer objects into and out of functions.

The final method provides access to the data stored by the SmartPointer object. This could result in crashes if this method is called on null SmartPointer objects. You should take care to only try to dereference valid SmartPointer instances.

■ **Note** Listing 10-14 contains debug code to allow the printing of object state for the purposes of illustration. This code can be removed from a working solution.

Listing 10-14 shows a complete working example of the SmartPointer class in use.

Listing 10-14. Using SmartPointer

```
#include <iostream>

using namespace std;

class ReferenceCount
{
private:
    int m_Count{ 0 };

public:
    void Increment()
    {
        ++m_Count;
    }

    int Decrement()
    {
        return --m_Count;
    }
```

```cpp
    int GetCount() const
    {
        return m_Count;
    }
};

template <typename T>
class SmartPointer
{
private:
    T* m_Object{ nullptr };
    ReferenceCount* m_ReferenceCount{ nullptr };

public:
    SmartPointer()
    {

    }

    SmartPointer(T* object)
        : m_Object{ object }
        , m_ReferenceCount{ new ReferenceCount }
    {
        m_ReferenceCount->Increment();

        cout << "Created smart pointer! Reference count is "
        << m_ReferenceCount->GetCount() << endl;
    }

    virtual ~SmartPointer()
    {
        if (m_ReferenceCount)
        {
            int decrementedCount = m_ReferenceCount->Decrement();
            cout << "Destroyed smart pointer! Reference count is "
            << decrementedCount << endl;
            if (decrementedCount <= 0)
            {
                delete m_ReferenceCount;
                delete m_Object;
            }
            m_ReferenceCount = nullptr;
            m_Object = nullptr;
        }
    }
```

```cpp
    SmartPointer(const SmartPointer<T>& other)
        : m_Object{ other.m_Object }
        , m_ReferenceCount{ other.m_ReferenceCount }
    {
        m_ReferenceCount->Increment();

        cout << "Copied smart pointer! Reference count is "
        << m_ReferenceCount->GetCount() << endl;
    }

    SmartPointer<T>& operator=(const SmartPointer<T>& other)
    {
        if (this != &other)
        {
            if (m_ReferenceCount && m_ReferenceCount->Decrement() == 0)
            {
                delete m_ReferenceCount;
                delete m_Object;
            }

            m_Object = other.m_Object;
            m_ReferenceCount = other.m_ReferenceCount;
            m_ReferenceCount->Increment();
        }

        cout << "Assigning smart pointer! Reference count is "
        << m_ReferenceCount->GetCount() << endl;

        return *this;
    }

    SmartPointer(SmartPointer<T>&& other)
        : m_Object{ other.m_Object }
        , m_ReferenceCount{ other.m_ReferenceCount }
    {
        other.m_Object = nullptr;
        other.m_ReferenceCount = nullptr;
    }

    SmartPointer<T>& operator=(SmartPointer<T>&& other)
    {
        if (this != &other)
        {
            m_Object = other.m_Object;
            m_ReferenceCount = other.m_ReferenceCount;

            other.m_Object = nullptr;
            other.m_ReferenceCount = nullptr;
        }
    }
```

```
    T& operator*()
    {
        return *m_Object;
    }
};

struct MyStruct
{
public:
    int m_Value{ 0 };

    ~MyStruct()
    {
        cout << "Destroying MyStruct object!" << endl;
    }
};

using SmartMyStructPointer = SmartPointer< MyStruct >;

SmartMyStructPointer PassValue(SmartMyStructPointer smartPointer)
{
    SmartMyStructPointer returnValue;
    returnValue = smartPointer;
    return returnValue;
}

int main(int argc, char* argv[])
{
    SmartMyStructPointer smartPointer{ new MyStruct };
    (*smartPointer).m_Value = 10;

    SmartMyStructPointer secondSmartPointer = PassValue(smartPointer);

    return 0;
}
```

Listing 10-14 shows a MyStruct instance being passed between the main and PassValue functions using the SmartPointer template. A type alias is created to ensure that the type of the SmartPointer for MyStruct is valid and easily maintainable throughout. The code uses the constructor, copy constructor, and assignment operators from the SmartPointer template. The MyStruct object is automatically deleted only when the last of the SmartPointer instances has gone out of scope at the end of the main function.

Figure 10-11 shows the output generated when running the code in Listing 10-14.

```
bruce@bruce-Virtual-Machine: ~/Projects/C-Recipes/Recipe10-6/Listing10-14
bruce@bruce-Virtual-Machine:~/Projects/C-Recipes/Recipe10-6/Listing10-14$ ./main

Created smart pointer! Reference count is 1
Copied smart pointer! Reference count is 2
Assigning smart pointer! Reference count is 3
Destroyed smart pointer! Reference count is 2
Destroyed smart pointer! Reference count is 1
Destroyed smart pointer! Reference count is 0
Destroying MyStruct object!
bruce@bruce-Virtual-Machine:~/Projects/C-Recipes/Recipe10-6/Listing10-14$
```

Figure 10-11. *A working example of SmartPointer in action*

10-7. Debugging Memory Problems by Overloading new and delete

Problem

You have some memory issues in your program and would like to add diagnostic code to the allocations and deallocations in the program.

Solution

C++ allows the replacement of the new and delete operators with custom written versions.

How It Works

The C++ new and delete operators boil down to being function calls. The signature for the global new function is

```
void* operator new(size_t size);
```

The signature for the global delete function is

```
void delete(void* ptr);
```

The new function takes the number of bytes to be allocated as a parameter, and the delete function takes a pointer to a memory address that has been returned from new. These functions can be replaced to provide added debugging information to your program. Listing 10-15 shows an example of adding a header to your memory allocations to help with program debugging.

Listing 10-15. Adding a Header to Memory Allocations

```cpp
#include <cstdlib>
#include <iostream>

using namespace std;

struct MemoryHeader
{
    const char* m_Filename{ nullptr };
    int m_Line{ -1 };
};

void* operator new(size_t size, const char* filename, int line) noexcept
{
    void* pMemory{ malloc(size + sizeof(MemoryHeader)) };

    MemoryHeader* pMemoryHeader{ reinterpret_cast<MemoryHeader*>(pMemory) };
    pMemoryHeader->m_Filename = filename;
    pMemoryHeader->m_Line = line;

    return static_cast<void*>(static_cast<char*>(pMemory)+sizeof(MemoryHeader));
}

void operator delete(void* pMemory) noexcept
{
    char* pMemoryHeaderStart{ reinterpret_cast<char*>(pMemory)-sizeof(MemoryHeader) };
    MemoryHeader* pMemoryHeader{ reinterpret_cast<MemoryHeader*>(pMemoryHeaderStart) };

    cout << "Deleting memory allocated from: "
        << pMemoryHeader->m_Filename << ":" << pMemoryHeader->m_Line << endl;

    free(pMemoryHeader);
}

#define new new(__FILE__, __LINE__)

class MyClass
{
private:
    int m_Value{ 1 };
};

int main(int argc, char* argv[])
{
    int* pInt{ new int };
    *pInt = 1;
    delete pInt;

    MyClass* pClass{ new MyClass };
    delete pClass;

    return 0;
}
```

This code replaces the new and delete function with custom versions. The custom version of new doesn't conform to the standard signature, so a macro was used to replace the standard version. This was done to allow the compiler to tell the custom new function the file name and line number where new is called. This allows you to track down individual allocations to their exact place in the program source code. This can be a very useful debugging tool when you're dealing with memory problems.

The custom new function adds the size of the MemoryHeader structure to the number of bytes being requested by the program. It then sets the m_Filename pointer in the MemoryHeader struct to the filename parameter supplied to new. The m_Line member is similarly set to the line parameter passed in. The address returned from new is the address of the beginning of the user area of memory, not including the MemoryHeader structure; this allows your debugging information to be added and addressed at the memory subsystem level and be completely transparent to the rest of your program.

The delete function shows a basic use for this debugging information. It simply prints out the line where the memory chunk being freed was allocated. It gets the address of the memory header by subtracting the size of the header from the address the function was passed.

The new macro is used to give a simple method for passing the __FILE__ and __LINE__ macros to the overloaded new function. These macros are known as *built-in macros* and are supplied by most modern C++ compilers. These macros are replaced by a pointer to the filename and the line number where they're used. Adding them to the new macro results in the filename and line number for every call to new in your program being passed to the custom new allocator.

The malloc and free functions used in the new and delete functions are the C-style memory-allocation functions. These are used to prevent conflicts with the many different types of C++ allocation functions. The functions shown in Listing 10-15 are suitable for allocating single objects. It's also possible to replace the C++ array new and delete functions. It's essential to replace these functions when you're trying to track down problems such as memory leaks. Listing 10-16 shows these functions in action.

Listing 10-16. Replacing the Array new and delete Operators

```cpp
#include <cstdlib>
#include <iostream>

using namespace std;

struct MemoryHeader
{
    const char* m_Filename{ nullptr };
    int m_Line{ -1 };
};

void* operator new(size_t size, const char* filename, int line) noexcept
{
    void* pMemory{ malloc(size + sizeof(MemoryHeader)) };

    MemoryHeader* pMemoryHeader{ reinterpret_cast<MemoryHeader*>(pMemory) };
    pMemoryHeader->m_Filename = filename;
    pMemoryHeader->m_Line = line;

    return static_cast<void*>(static_cast<char*>(pMemory)+sizeof(MemoryHeader));
}
```

```
void* operator new[](size_t size, const char* filename, int line) noexcept
{
    void* pMemory{ malloc(size + sizeof(MemoryHeader)) };

    MemoryHeader* pMemoryHeader{ reinterpret_cast<MemoryHeader*>(pMemory) };
    pMemoryHeader->m_Filename = filename;
    pMemoryHeader->m_Line = line;

    return static_cast<void*>(static_cast<char*>(pMemory)+sizeof(MemoryHeader));
}

void operator delete(void* pMemory) noexcept
{
    char* pMemoryHeaderStart{ reinterpret_cast<char*>(pMemory)-sizeof(MemoryHeader) };

    MemoryHeader* pMemoryHeader{ reinterpret_cast<MemoryHeader*>(pMemoryHeaderStart) };
    cout << "Deleting memory allocated from: "
        << pMemoryHeader->m_Filename << ":" << pMemoryHeader->m_Line << endl;

    free(pMemoryHeader);
}

void operator delete[](void* pMemory) noexcept
{
    char* pMemoryHeaderStart{ reinterpret_cast<char*>(pMemory)-sizeof(MemoryHeader) };

    MemoryHeader* pMemoryHeader{ reinterpret_cast<MemoryHeader*>(pMemoryHeaderStart) };
    cout << "Deleting memory allocated from: "
        << pMemoryHeader->m_Filename << ":" << pMemoryHeader->m_Line << endl;

    free(pMemoryHeader);
}

#define new new(__FILE__, __LINE__)

class MyClass
{
private:
    int m_Value{ 1 };
};

int main(int argc, char* argv[])
{
    int* pInt{ new int };
    *pInt = 1;
    delete pInt;

    MyClass* pClass{ new MyClass };
    delete pClass;
```

```
    const unsigned int NUM_ELEMENTS{ 5 };
    int* pArray{ new int[NUM_ELEMENTS] };
    delete[] pArray;

    return 0;
}
```

The array new and delete operators' signatures differ from the standard new and delete operators only by having the [ ] operator present in their signature, as you can see in Listing 10-16. Figure 10-12 shows the output generated by this code.

```
bruce@bruce-Virtual-Machine: ~/Projects/C-Recipes/Recipe10-7/Listing10-16
bruce@bruce-Virtual-Machine:~/Projects/C-Recipes/Recipe10-7/Listing10-16$ ./main

Deleting memory allocated from: main.cpp:66
Deleting memory allocated from: main.cpp:70
Deleting memory allocated from: main.cpp:74
bruce@bruce-Virtual-Machine:~/Projects/C-Recipes/Recipe10-7/Listing10-16$ 
```

Figure 10-12. *Output showing the use of the replaced new and delete operators*

The new and delete functions you have seen so far in this recipe have been global replacements for the new and delete operators. It's also possible to replace new and delete for specific classes. You can add these functions directly to a class definition, and those functions will be used when creating and destroying dynamic instances of that type of object. Listing 10-17 shows code that replaces the global new, new[ ], delete, and delete[ ] operators and also adds new and delete operators to the MyClass class definition.

Listing 10-17. Adding new and delete Operators to MyClass

```cpp
#include <cstdlib>
#include <iostream>

using namespace std;

struct MemoryHeader
{
    const char* m_Filename{ nullptr };
    int m_Line{ -1 };
};

void* operator new(size_t size, const char* filename, int line) noexcept
{
    void* pMemory{ malloc(size + sizeof(MemoryHeader)) };

    MemoryHeader* pMemoryHeader{ reinterpret_cast<MemoryHeader*>(pMemory) };
    pMemoryHeader->m_Filename = filename;
    pMemoryHeader->m_Line = line;

    return static_cast<void*>(static_cast<char*>(pMemory)+sizeof(MemoryHeader));
}
```

240

```
void* operator new[](size_t size, const char* filename, int line) noexcept
{
    void* pMemory{ malloc(size + sizeof(MemoryHeader)) };

    MemoryHeader* pMemoryHeader{ reinterpret_cast<MemoryHeader*>(pMemory) };
    pMemoryHeader->m_Filename = filename;
    pMemoryHeader->m_Line = line;

    return static_cast<void*>(static_cast<char*>(pMemory)+sizeof(MemoryHeader));
}

void operator delete(void* pMemory) noexcept
{
    char* pMemoryHeaderStart{ reinterpret_cast<char*>(pMemory)-sizeof(MemoryHeader) };

    MemoryHeader* pMemoryHeader{ reinterpret_cast<MemoryHeader*>(pMemoryHeaderStart) };

    cout << "Deleting memory allocated from: "
        << pMemoryHeader->m_Filename << ":" << pMemoryHeader->m_Line << endl;

    free(pMemoryHeader);
}

void operator delete[](void* pMemory) noexcept
{
    char* pMemoryHeaderStart{ reinterpret_cast<char*>(pMemory)-sizeof(MemoryHeader) };

    MemoryHeader* pMemoryHeader{ reinterpret_cast<MemoryHeader*>(pMemoryHeaderStart) };

    cout << "Deleting memory allocated from: "
        << pMemoryHeader->m_Filename << ":" << pMemoryHeader->m_Line << endl;

    free(pMemoryHeader);
}

class MyClass
{
private:
    int m_Value{ 1 };

public:
    void* operator new(size_t size, const char* filename, int line) noexcept
    {
        cout << "Allocating memory for MyClass!" << endl;
        return malloc(size);
    }

    void operator delete(void* pMemory) noexcept
    {
        cout << "Freeing memory for MyClass!" << endl;
        free(pMemory);
    }
};
```

241

```
#define new new(__FILE__, __LINE__)

int main(int argc, char* argv[])
{
    int* pInt{ new int };
    *pInt = 1;
    delete pInt;

    MyClass* pClass{ new MyClass };
    delete pClass;

    const unsigned int NUM_ELEMENTS{ 5 };
    MyClass* pArray{ new MyClass[NUM_ELEMENTS] };
    delete[] pArray;

    return 0;
}
```

The new and delete operators in the MyClass definition are called in the main function when creating a single instance of MyClass. You can see that this is the case in the output shown in Figure 10-13.

```
bruce@bruce-Virtual-Machine: ~/Projects/C-Recipes/Recipe10-7/Listing10-17
bruce@bruce-Virtual-Machine:~/Projects/C-Recipes/Recipe10-7/Listing10-17$ ./main

Deleting memory allocated from: main.cpp:81
Allocating memory for MyClass!
Freeing memory for MyClass!
Deleting memory allocated from: main.cpp:89
bruce@bruce-Virtual-Machine:~/Projects/C-Recipes/Recipe10-7/Listing10-17$
```

Figure 10-13. *Output showing the use of member new and delete operators in MyClass*

10-8. Calculating Performance Impacts of Code Changes

Problem

You would like to determine whether changes you're making to code are faster or slower than the existing code.

Solution

C++ provides access to a computer system's high-performance timers to carry out high-precision timing.

How It Works

The C++ programming language provides access to a high-resolution timer that allows you to make timing measurements around different parts of your code. This lets you record the time taken for your functions or algorithms and compare these across different versions to work out which are the most efficient and performant.

Listing 10-18 shows code that is used to time three different numbers of iterations around a loop.

Listing 10-18. Using `chrono::high_resolution_timer`

```cpp
#include <chrono>
#include <iostream>

using namespace std;

void RunTest(unsigned int numberIterations)
{
    auto start = chrono::high_resolution_clock::now();

    for (unsigned int i{ 0 }; i < numberIterations; ++i)
    {
        unsigned int squared{ i*i*I };
    }

    auto end = chrono::high_resolution_clock::now();
    auto difference = end - start;

    cout << "Time taken: "
        << chrono::duration_cast<chrono::microseconds>(difference).count()
        << " microseconds!" << endl;
}

int main(int argc, char* argv[])
{
    RunTest(10000000);
    RunTest(100000000);
    RunTest(1000000000);

    return 0;
}
```

This listing shows that the chrono namespace in the STL provides a struct named `high_resolution_clock` with a static function called now. This function returns an object that is of type time_point from the `chrono::system_clock` struct. Listing 10-18 uses the auto keyword to deduce this type for the start and end variables in the RunTest function. Both start and end are initialized using the high_resolution_timer::now function, start before the for loop, and end after the for loop. The value of start is subtracted from the value of end to give the duration of time elapsed while the function was executing the loop. The `chrono::duration_cast` template is then used to convert the time_point difference variable into a representation that can be expressed in a human-readable form, in this case microseconds.

The RunTest function is called three different times from the main function. Each call has a different number of loop iterations to be run, to show that the timing code can be used to tell which of the runs is the least time-efficient. Figure 10-14 shows the output generated when running the program on an Intel Core i7-3770.

```
bruce@bruce-Virtual-Machine: ~/Projects/C-Recipes/Recipe10-8/Listing10-18
bruce@bruce-Virtual-Machine:~/Projects/C-Recipes/Recipe10-8/Listing10-18$ ./main

Time taken: 21084 microseconds!
Time taken: 240873 microseconds!
Time taken: 2574822 microseconds!
bruce@bruce-Virtual-Machine:~/Projects/C-Recipes/Recipe10-8/Listing10-18$ ▮
```

Figure 10-14. Output showing that each subsequent call to RunTest in Listing 10-18 takes longer to execute

duration_cast can be used to convert system times into nanoseconds, milliseconds, seconds, minutes, and hours, as well as microseconds. Microsecond precision is what you're looking for when optimizing many computer-programming algorithms. The timing techniques used in this recipe will prove useful when comparing the impacts of memory storage types on program efficiency.

10-9. Understanding the Performance Impacts of Memory Choices

Problem

You have a program that is performing poorly, but you aren't sure why.

Solution

There is no silver bullet to solve performance problems in modern computer programs. However, a lack of understanding of how memory works on a modern computer can lead to poorly performing programs. Understanding the impacts of cache misses on program performance will help you write better-performing programs.

How It Works

The speed of modern processors has accelerated at a much faster rate than memory-access latencies. This had led to a situation where processing performance can be severely hampered by poor memory-access patterns in your programs. Understanding how to structure your C++ programs to take effective use of processor cache memory is essential to writing the most performant programs possible.

Reading and writing data from main memory can take several hundred cycles on modern computer systems. Processors implement caches to help alleviate this problem. A modern CPU cache works by reading large chunks of data simultaneously from main memory into much faster cache memory. These chunks are known as *cache lines*. An L1 cache line on an Intel Core i7-3770 processor is 32KB in size. The processor reads an entire 32KB chunk into the L1 cache in a single go. If the data you're reading or writing isn't present in the cache, the result is a cache miss, and the processor must retrieve the data from L2 cache, L3 cache, or system RAM. Cache misses can be very expensive, and seemingly innocuous mistakes or choices in your code can have massive performance implications. Listing 10-19 contains one loop to initialize some arrays and three different loops that have different memory-access patterns.

Listing 10-19. Exploring the Performance Impacts of Memory Access Patterns

```
#include <chrono>
#include <iostream>

using namespace std;

const int NUM_ROWS{ 10000 };
const int NUM_COLUMNS{ 1000 };
int elements[NUM_ROWS][NUM_COLUMNS];
int* pElements[NUM_ROWS][NUM_COLUMNS];

int main(int argc, char* argv[])
{
    for (int i{ 0 }; i < NUM_ROWS; ++i)
    {
        for (int j{ 0 }; j < NUM_COLUMNS; ++j)
        {
            elements[i][j] = i*j;
            pElements[i][j] = new int{ elements[i][j] };
        }
    }

    auto start = chrono::high_resolution_clock::now();

    for (int i{ 0 }; i < NUM_ROWS; ++i)
    {
        for (int j{ 0 }; j < NUM_COLUMNS; ++j)
        {
            const int result{ elements[j][i] };
        }
    }

    auto end = chrono::high_resolution_clock::now();
    auto difference = end - start;

    cout << "Time taken for j then i: "
        << chrono::duration_cast<chrono::microseconds>(difference).count()
        << " microseconds!" << endl;

    start = chrono::high_resolution_clock::now();

    for (int i{ 0 }; i < NUM_ROWS; ++i)
    {
        for (int j{ 0 }; j < NUM_COLUMNS; ++j)
        {
            const int result{ elements[i][j] };
        }
    }
}
```

245

```
end = chrono::high_resolution_clock::now();
difference = end - start;

cout << "Time taken for i then j: "
     << chrono::duration_cast<chrono::microseconds>(difference).count()
     << " microseconds!" << endl;

start = chrono::high_resolution_clock::now();

for (int i{ 0 }; i < NUM_ROWS; ++i)
{
    for (int j{ 0 }; j < NUM_COLUMNS; ++j)
    {
        const int result{ *(pElements[i][j]) };
    }
}

end = chrono::high_resolution_clock::now();
difference = end - start;

cout << "Time taken for pointers with i then j: "
     << chrono::duration_cast<chrono::microseconds>(difference).count()
     << " microseconds!" << endl;

return 0;
}
```

The first loop in Listing 10-19 is used to set up two arrays. The first array stores integer values directly, and the second array stores pointers to integers. Each of the arrays contains 10,000 × 1,000 unique elements.

It's important to understand how multidimensional arrays are laid out in memory, to understand why this test creates the results it does with respect to cache-miss performance problems. A 3 × 2 array can be thought of as laid out as shown in Table 10-1.

Table 10-1. *The Layout of a 3 × 2 Array*

	Column 1	Column 2	Column 3
Row 1	1	2	3
Row 2	4	5	6

But computer memory isn't two-dimensional in this manner. The elements of the array are laid out linearly in memory in the order of the numbers shown in Table 10-1. Given a 4-byte integer size, that means the value in Row 2 Column 1 can be found 12 bytes after the value in Row 1 Column 1. Extend the row size to 10,000, and you can see that there is no possibility for the element at the beginning of a following row residing in the same cache line as the previous row.

This fact allows the performance implications of cache misses to be tested with a simple loop. You can see this in the second loop in Listing 10-18, where the incremented j value is used to walk along the columns rather than the rows. The third loop walks along the array in the correct order. That is, it walks along the rows in linear order in memory. The fourth loop walks along the pElement array in linear order but has to dereference a pointer to reach the values stored in the array. The results show you the impacts of cache-unaware programming in the first loop, the ideal situation in the second, and the result of unnecessary memory indirection in the third. Figure 10-15 shows these results.

```
● ● ●   bruce@bruce-Virtual-Machine: ~/Projects/C-Recipes/Recipe10-9/Listing10-19
bruce@bruce-Virtual-Machine:~/Projects/C-Recipes/Recipe10-9/Listing10-19$ ./main

Time taken for j then i: 29957 microseconds!
Time taken for i then j: 21307 microseconds!
Time taken for pointers with i then j: 40526 microseconds!
bruce@bruce-Virtual-Machine:~/Projects/C-Recipes/Recipe10-9/Listing10-19$ ▊
```

Figure 10-15. The results from the loops in Listing 10-19

You can see that the processor in my computer has a ten-times increase in the length of time taken to complete a simple loop when walking an array out of order. Such problems can cause stutters and delays in programs that can leave users and customers feeling a sense of frustration with your software. The case with pointer dereferences is also around twice as slow as the case where the integers can be accessed directly. You should consider the implications of this before using dynamic memory liberally.

10-10. Reducing Memory Fragmentation

Problem

You have a program that requires you to create a lot of small memory allocations over a long period of time, which introduces memory-fragmentation problems.

Solution

You can create a small block allocator that can be used to pack small allocations into larger pages.

How It Works

The first step in bundling small allocations together is to create a class that contains a larger page of memory. This recipe shows you a straightforward way to wrap a 32KB memory page in a class and manage allocations from this pool. The memory is tracked using an array of Boolean values that knows whether a given memory block is free or is in use. New pages of memory are added when all current pages are full.

The downside to this approach is that all allocations have a minimum size of 32 bytes. Any request for memory that is smaller than 32 bytes is allocated an entire block from a currently active memory page. Pages are also freed when they're completely empty, to ensure that the program doesn't grow to a high water mark and never release unneeded memory. Listing 10-20 shows the class definition for Page.

Listing 10-20. The Page Class Definition

```cpp
class Page
{
private:
    char m_Memory[1024 * 32];
    bool m_Free[1024];
    Page* m_pNextPage;

public:
    Page();
    ~Page();

    void* Alloc();
    bool Free(void* pMem);

    bool IsEmpty() const;
};
```

The Page class definition contains two arrays. There is a char array that serves memory-allocation requests. This pool is an array of bytes and in this case is 32KB in size. There are 1,024 individual blocks in the pool, each 32 bytes in size. The 1,024 blocks are mirrored in the Boolean array m_Free. This array is used to track whether a given block is already allocated or is free for allocation. The m_pNextPage pointer stores the address of the next page. The next page is used to allocate a block if the current page is entirely in use.

The class consists of five methods: a constructor, a destructor, an Alloc method, a Free method, and the IsEmpty method to determine if the page is no longer in use. Listing 10-21 shows the function bodies for the Page class's constructor and destructor.

Listing 10-21. The Page Constructor and Destructor

```cpp
Page()
    : m_pNextPage{ nullptr }
{
    memset(m_Free, 1, 1024);
}

~Page()
{
    if (m_pNextPage)
    {
        delete m_pNextPage;
        m_pNextPage = nullptr;
    }
}
```

The Page constructor is responsible for initializing the m_pNextPage pointer to nullptr and for setting all the elements in the m_Free array to true. The destructor for Page is responsible for deleting the object pointer to m_pNextPage if it has been allocated.

Listing 10-22 shows the code for the Page::Alloc method.

Listing 10-22. The Page::Alloc Method

```cpp
void* Alloc()
{
    void* pMem{ nullptr };

    for (unsigned int i = 0; i < 1024; ++i)
    {
        if (m_Free[i] == true)
        {
            m_Free[i] = false;
            pMem = &m_Memory[i * 32];
            break;
        }
    }

    if (pMem == nullptr)
    {
        if (m_pNextPage == nullptr)
        {
            m_pNextPage = new Page();
        }

        pMem = m_pNextPage->Alloc();
    }

    return pMem;
}
```

The Alloc method is responsible for finding the first unused memory block in the page-linked list. The first step is to loop over the m_Free array and check each block to see whether it's currently in use. If a free block is found, the pMem return value is set to the address of the free block. The Boolean for that block is set to false to indicate that the block is now in use. If a free block is found, the loop is broken.

In the event that a free block isn't found, the memory must be allocated from another memory page. If another page has already been created, the pointer m_pNextPage already holds its address. If not, a new page is created. The Alloc method is then called on m_pNextPage. At this point, the Alloc method is recursive. It's called repeatedly until a memory page is found that contains a free memory block to return up the stack to the calling code. The memory returned from a page must also be returned to that page when it's no longer needed. The Free method in Listing 10-23 is responsible for carrying out this task.

Listing 10-23. The Page::Free Method

```cpp
bool Free(void* pMem)
{
    bool freed{ false };

    bool inPage{ pMem >= m_Memory && pMem <= &m_Memory[(NUM_PAGES * BLOCK_SIZE) - 1] };
    if (inPage)
    {
        unsigned int index{
            (reinterpret_cast<unsigned int>(pMem)-reinterpret_cast<unsigned int>(m_Memory))
            / BLOCK_SIZE };
```

```
        m_Free[index] = true;
        freed = true;
    }
    else if (m_pNextPage)
    {
        freed = m_pNextPage->Free(pMem);

        if (freed && m_pNextPage->IsEmpty())
        {
            Page* old = m_pNextPage;
            m_pNextPage = old->m_pNextPage;
            old->m_pNextPage = nullptr;
            delete m_pNextPage;
        }
    }

    return freed;
}
```

The Page::Free method begins by checking whether the memory address being released is contained within the current page. It does so by comparing the address against the address of the beginning of the memory page and the address of the last block in the page. If the memory being freed is greater than or equal to the page address and less than or equal to the last block in the page, then the memory was allocated from this page. In this case, the m_Free Boolean for this block can be set back to true. The memory itself doesn't need to be cleared, because new gives no guarantees of the values contained in the memory it returns—that is responsibility of the caller.

If the memory was not found in the current Page, then the Free method checks whether the Page has a pointer to another Page object. If it does, then the Free method is called on that Page. The Free method is recursive in nature in the same way as the Alloc method. If the call to Free on m_pNextPage returned a true value, the Page is checked to see if it's now empty. If it is, then the Page can be released. Because Page is using a simple linked list to track pages, you must make sure you don't orphan the tails of the list. You need to ensure that the m_pNextPage pointer of the current page is set to point to the m_pNextPage pointer of the Page being released. The IsEmpty method is called in the Free method; the body of this method is shown in Listing 10-24.

Listing 10-24. The Page::IsEmpty Method

```
bool IsEmpty() const
{
    bool isEmpty{ true };

    for (unsigned int i = 0; i < NUM_PAGES; ++i)
    {
        if (m_Free[i] == false)
        {
            isEmpty = false;
            break;
        }
    }

    return isEmpty;
}
```

The IsEmpty method checks the free list to determine whether the page is currently in use. If any of the blocks in the Page aren't free, than the Page isn't empty. The linked list of pages is accessed through another class called SmallBlockAllocator. This simplifies the management of the pages for the calling code. Listing 10-25 shows the SmallBlockAllocator class.

Listing 10-25. The SmallBlockAllocator Class

```cpp
class SmallBlockAllocator
{
public:
    static const unsigned int BLOCK_SIZE{ 32 };

private:
    static const unsigned int NUM_ BLOCKS { 1024 };
    static const unsigned int PAGE_SIZE{ NUM_ BLOCKS * BLOCK_SIZE };

    class Page
    {
    private:
        char m_Memory[PAGE_SIZE];
        bool m_Free[NUM_ BLOCKS];
        Page* m_pNextPage;

    public:
        Page()
            : m_pNextPage{ nullptr }
        {
            memset(m_Free, 1, NUM_ BLOCKS);
        }

        ~Page()
        {
            if (m_pNextPage)
            {
                delete m_pNextPage;
                m_pNextPage = nullptr;
            }
        }

        void* Alloc()
        {
            void* pMem{ nullptr };

            for (unsigned int i = 0; i < NUM_ BLOCKS; ++i)
            {
                if (m_Free[i] == true)
                {
                    m_Free[i] = false;
                    pMem = &m_Memory[i * BLOCK_SIZE];
                    break;
                }
            }
```

```
            if (pMem == nullptr)
            {
                if (m_pNextPage == nullptr)
                {
                    m_pNextPage = new Page();
                }

                pMem = m_pNextPage->Alloc();
            }

        return pMem;
    }

    bool Free(void* pMem)
    {
        bool freed{ false };

        bool inPage{ pMem >= m_Memory &&
            pMem <= &m_Memory[(NUM_ BLOCKS * BLOCK_SIZE) - 1] };
        if (inPage)
        {
            unsigned int index{
                (reinterpret_cast<unsigned int>(pMem)-
                reinterpret_cast<unsigned int>(m_Memory)) / BLOCK_SIZE };
            m_Free[index] = true;
            freed = true;
        }
        else if (m_pNextPage)
        {
            freed = m_pNextPage->Free(pMem);

            if (freed && m_pNextPage->IsEmpty())
            {
                Page* old = m_pNextPage;
                m_pNextPage = old->m_pNextPage;
                old->m_pNextPage = nullptr;
                delete m_pNextPage;
            }
        }

        return freed;
    }

    bool IsEmpty() const
    {
        bool isEmpty{ true };
```

```
                for (unsigned int i = 0; i < NUM_BLOCKS; ++i)
                {
                    if (m_Free[i] == false)
                    {
                        isEmpty = false;
                        break;
                    }
                }

                return isEmpty;
            }
        };

        Page m_FirstPage;

public:
        SmallBlockAllocator() = default;

        void* Alloc()
        {
            return m_FirstPage.Alloc();
        }

        bool Free(void* pMem)
        {
            return m_FirstPage.Free(pMem);
        }
    };
```

The Page class can be seen as an internal class to SmallBlockAllocator in Listing 10-25. This helps ensure that only the SmallBlockAllocator itself can be used as an interface to the Page objects. SmallBlockAllocator begins by creating static constants to control the size of the blocks and number of blocks each Page contains. The only public methods exposed from SmallBlockAllocator are an Alloc method and a Free method. These simply wrap calls to Page::Alloc and Page::Free and are called on the member m_FirstPage. This means the SmallBlockAllocator class always has at least one page of memory allocated for small allocations, and this page will be resident in your program for as long as SmallBlockAllocator is active.

Listing 10-26 shows the overloaded new and delete operators that are needed to route small allocations to SmallBlockAllocator.

Listing 10-26. Routing Small Allocations to SmallBlockAllocator

```
static SmallBlockAllocator sba;

void* operator new(unsigned int numBytes)
{
    void* pMem{ nullptr };

    if (numBytes <= SmallBlockAllocator::BLOCK_SIZE)
    {
        pMem = sba.Alloc();
    }
```

```
    else
    {
        pMem = malloc(numBytes);
    }

    return pMem;
}

void* operator new[](unsigned int numBytes)
{
    void* pMem{ nullptr };

    if (numBytes <= SmallBlockAllocator::BLOCK_SIZE)
    {
        pMem = sba.Alloc();
    }
    else
    {
        pMem = malloc(numBytes);
    }

    return pMem;
}

void operator delete(void* pMemory)
{
    if (!sba.Free(pMemory))
    {
        free(pMemory);
    }
}

void operator delete[](void* pMemory)
{
    if (!sba.Free(pMemory))
    {
        free(pMemory);
    }
}
```

The new and new[] operators in Listing 10-26 check the number of bytes being allocated against the supported block size of the SmallBlockAllocator class. If the size of memory being requested is smaller or equal to the block size of the SBA, the Alloc method is called on the static sba object. If it was larger, then malloc is used. The two delete functions both call Free on sba. If Free returns false, then the memory being released wasn't present in any of the small block pages and is released using the free function.

That covers all the code needed to implement a simple small-block allocator. Listing 10-27 shows the entire listing for a working example program that uses this class.

Listing 10-27. A Working Small-Block Allocator Example

```cpp
#include <cstdlib>
#include <iostream>

using namespace std;

class SmallBlockAllocator
{
public:
    static const unsigned int BLOCK_SIZE{ 32 };

private:
    static const unsigned int NUM_BLOCKS{ 1024 };
    static const unsigned int PAGE_SIZE{ NUM_BLOCKS * BLOCK_SIZE };

    class Page
    {
    private:
        char m_Memory[PAGE_SIZE];
        bool m_Free[NUM_BLOCKS];
        Page* m_pNextPage;

    public:
        Page()
            : m_pNextPage{ nullptr }
        {
            memset(m_Free, 1, NUM_BLOCKS);
        }

        ~Page()
        {
            if (m_pNextPage)
            {
                delete m_pNextPage;
                m_pNextPage = nullptr;
            }
        }

        void* Alloc()
        {
            void* pMem{ nullptr };

            for (unsigned int i{ 0 }; i < NUM_BLOCKS; ++i)
            {
                if (m_Free[i] == true)
                {
                    m_Free[i] = false;
                    pMem = &m_Memory[i * BLOCK_SIZE];
                    break;
                }
            }
```

```cpp
        if (pMem == nullptr)
        {
            if (m_pNextPage == nullptr)
            {
                m_pNextPage = new Page();
            }

            pMem = m_pNextPage->Alloc();
        }

        return pMem;
    }

    bool Free(void* pMem)
    {
        bool freed{ false };

        bool inPage{ pMem >= m_Memory &&
            pMem <= &m_Memory[(NUM_BLOCKS * BLOCK_SIZE) - 1] };
        if (inPage)
        {
            unsigned int index{
                (reinterpret_cast<unsigned int>(pMem)-
                 reinterpret_cast<unsigned int>(m_Memory)) / BLOCK_SIZE };
            m_Free[index] = true;
            freed = true;
        }
        else if (m_pNextPage)
        {
            freed = m_pNextPage->Free(pMem);

            if (freed && m_pNextPage->IsEmpty())
            {
                Page* old = m_pNextPage;
                m_pNextPage = old->m_pNextPage;
                old->m_pNextPage = nullptr;
                delete m_pNextPage;
            }
        }

        return freed;
    }

    bool IsEmpty() const
    {
        bool isEmpty{ true };
```

```
                for (unsigned int i{ 0 }; i < NUM_BLOCKS; ++i)
                {
                    if (m_Free[i] == false)
                    {
                        isEmpty = false;
                        break;
                    }
                }

                return isEmpty;
            }
        };

        Page m_FirstPage;

    public:
        SmallBlockAllocator() = default;

        void* Alloc()
        {
            return m_FirstPage.Alloc();
        }

        bool Free(void* pMem)
        {
            return m_FirstPage.Free(pMem);
        }
    };

    static SmallBlockAllocator sba;

    void* operator new(size_t numBytes, const std::nothrow_t& tag) noexcept
    {
        void* pMem{ nullptr };

        if (numBytes <= SmallBlockAllocator::BLOCK_SIZE)
        {
            pMem = sba.Alloc();
        }
        else
        {
            pMem = malloc(numBytes);
        }

        return pMem;
    }
```

```cpp
void* operator new[](size_t numBytes, const std::nothrow_t& tag) noexcept
{
    void* pMem{ nullptr };

    if (numBytes <= SmallBlockAllocator::BLOCK_SIZE)
    {
        pMem = sba.Alloc();
    }
    else
    {
        pMem = malloc(numBytes);
    }

    return pMem;
}

void operator delete(void* pMemory)
{
    if (!sba.Free(pMemory))
    {
        free(pMemory);
    }
}

void operator delete[](void* pMemory)
{
    if (!sba.Free(pMemory))
    {
        free(pMemory);
    }
}

int main(int argc, char* argv[])
{
    const unsigned int NUM_ALLOCS{ 2148 };
    int* pInts[NUM_ALLOCS];

    for (unsigned int i{ 0 }; i < NUM_ALLOCS; ++i)
    {
        pInts[i] = new int;
        *pInts[i] = i;
    }

    for (unsigned int i{ 0 }; i < NUM_ALLOCS; ++i)
    {
        delete pInts[i];
        pInts[i] = nullptr;
    }

    return 0;
}
```

CHAPTER 11

■ ■ ■

Concurrency

CPU manufacturers have recently struggled to improve CPU frequencies at the same rate of progress as was possible in the 1990s. CPU performance improvements over time have been maintained by clever CPU design and multiple processors being included on a single chip. This means programmers today must embrace concurrent programming or multithreaded programming if they wish their programs to perform quickly on modern computer chips.

Concurrent programming can be a challenge for programmers to get right. Many pitfalls await concurrent programs, including data that gets out of sync and therefore is wrong as well as deadlocks once your tasks require the use of locks to manage access. The recipes in this chapter introduce you to some practical applications of the STL features supplied by C++ to help you write concurrent programs.

11-1. Using Threads to Execute Concurrent Tasks

Problem

You're writing a program that is performing poorly, and you'd like to speed up execution by using multiple processors in a system.

Solution

C++ provides the thread type, which can be used to create a native operating system thread. Program threads can be run on more than a single processor and therefore allow you to write programs that can use multiple CPUs and CPU cores.

How It Works

Detecting the Number of Logical CPU Cores

The C++ thread library provides a feature set that lets programs use all the cores and CPUs available in a given computer system. The first important function supplied by the C++ threading capabilities that you should be aware of allows you to query the number of execution units the computer contains. Listing 11-1 shows the C++ thread::hardware_concurrency method.

Listing 11-1. The thread::hardware_concurrency Method

```
#include <iostream>
#include <thread>

using namespace std;

int main(int argc, char* argv[])
{
    const unsigned int numberOfProcessors{ thread::hardware_concurrency() };

    cout << "This system can run " << numberOfProcessors << " concurrent tasks" << endl;

    return 0;
}
```

This code uses the thread::hardware_concurrency method to query the number of simultaneous threads that can be run on the computer executing the program. Figure 11-1 shows the output generated by this program on my desktop computer.

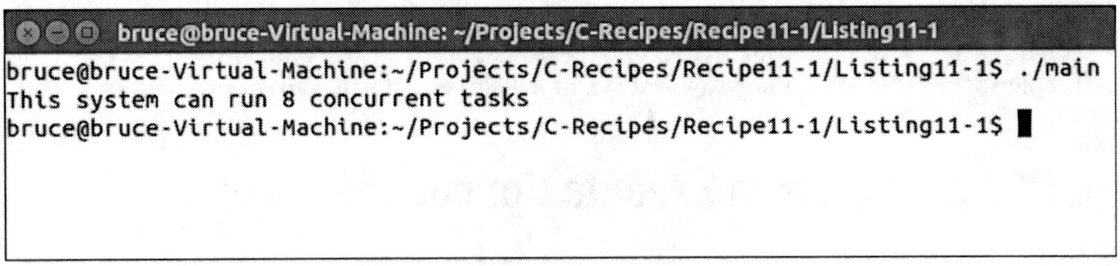

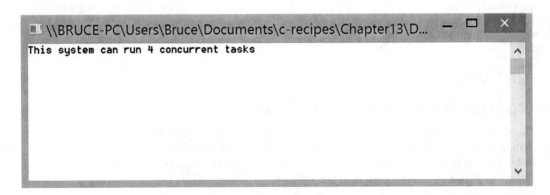

Figure 11-1. The result of calling thread::hardware_concurrency on an Intel Core i7 3770

Running the same code on a Surface Pro 2 with an Intel Core i5 4200U processor results in a value of 4 being returned, as opposed to the 8 returned by the Core i7 3770. You can see the results given by the Surface Pro 2 in Figure 11-2.

Figure 11-2. The result of running Listing 11-1 on a Surface Pro 2

Running too many threads on a computer that has too few logical cores can cause the computer to become unresponsive, so it's important to keep this in mind when you're creating programs.

Creating Threads

Once you know the system you're running on might benefit from the use of concurrent execution, you can use the C++ thread class to create tasks to be run on multiple processor cores. The thread class is a portable, built-in type that allows you to write multithreaded code for any operating system.

■ **Note**   The thread class is a recent addition to the C++ programming language. It was added in the C++11 language spec, so you may need to check the documentation for the STL library you're using to ensure that it supports this feature.

The **thread** constructor is simple to use and takes a function to execute on another CPU core. Listing 11-2 shows a simple thread that outputs to the console.

Listing 11-2. Creating a thread

```cpp
#include <iostream>
#include <thread>

using namespace std;

void ThreadTask()
{
    for (unsigned int i{ 0 }; i < 20; ++i)
    {
        cout << "Output from thread" << endl;
    }
}

int main(int argc, char* argv[])
{
    const unsigned int numberOfProcessors{ thread::hardware_concurrency() };

    cout << "This system can run " << numberOfProcessors << " concurrent tasks" << endl;

    if (numberOfProcessors > 1)
    {
        thread myThread{ ThreadTask };

        cout << "Output from main" << endl;

        myThread.join();
    }
    else
    {
        cout << "CPU does not have multiple cores." << endl;
    }

    return 0;
}
```

Listing 11-2 determines whether to create a **thread** based on the number of logical cores on the computer executing the program.

■ **Note** Most operating systems allow you to run more threads than there are processors, but you might find that doing so slows your program due to the overhead of managing multiple threads.

If the CPU has more than one logical core, the program creates a thread object called myThread. The myThread variable is initialized with a pointer to a function. This function will be executed in the **thread** context and, more likely than not, on a different CPU thread than the main function.

The ThreadTask function consists of a for loop that simply outputs to the console multiple times. The main function also outputs to the console. The intent is to show that both functions are running concurrently. You can see that this is true in Figure 11-3, where the output from main occurs in the middle of the output from ThreadTask.

```
● ● ●    bruce@bruce-Virtual-Machine: ~/Projects/C-Recipes/Recipe11-1/Listing11-2
bruce@bruce-Virtual-Machine:~/Projects/C-Recipes/Recipe11-1/Listing11-2$ ./main
This system can run 8 concurrent tasks
Output from main
Output from thread
Output from thread
Output from thread
Output from thread
Output from thread
Output from thread
Output from thread
Output from thread
Output from thread
Output from thread
Output from thread
Output from thread
Output from thread
Output from thread
Output from thread
Output from thread
Output from thread
Output from thread
Output from thread
Output from thread
bruce@bruce-Virtual-Machine:~/Projects/C-Recipes/Recipe11-1/Listing11-2$ █
```

Figure 11-3. *The output showing that both* main *and* ThreadTask, *from Listing 11-2, are running concurrently*

Cleaning Up After Threads

The main function in Listing 11-2 immediately calls the join method on the thread. The join method is used to tell the current **thread** to wait for the additional **thread** to end execution before continuing. This is important because C++ programs are required to destroy their own threads to prevent leaks from occurring. Calling the destructor on a thread object doesn't destroy the currently executing thread context. Listing 11-3 shows code that has been modified to not call join on myThread.

Listing 11-3. Forgetting to Call join on a thread

```
#include <iostream>
#include <thread>

using namespace std;

void ThreadTask()
{
    for (unsigned int i{ 0 }; i < 20; ++i)
    {
        cout << "Output from thread" << endl;
    }
}

int main(int argc, char* argv[])
{
    const unsigned int numberOfProcessors{ thread::hardware_concurrency() };

    cout << "This system can run " << numberOfProcessors << " concurrent tasks" << endl;

    if (numberOfProcessors > 1)
    {
        thread myThread{ ThreadTask };

        cout << "Output from main" << endl;
    }
    else
    {
        cout << "CPU does not have multiple cores." << endl;
    }

    return 0;
}
```

This code causes the myThread object to go out of scope before the ThreadTask function has completed execution. This can cause a **thread** leak in your program that may eventually cause the program or the operating system to become unstable. A program running on the Linux command line will fail with the error shown in Figure 11-4.

```
bruce@bruce-Virtual-Machine: ~/Projects/C-Recipes/Recipe11-1/Listing11-3
bruce@bruce-Virtual-Machine:~/Projects/C-Recipes/Recipe11-1/Listing11-3$ ./main
This system can run 8 concurrent tasks
Output from main
terminate called without an active exception
Aborted (core dumped)
bruce@bruce-Virtual-Machine:~/Projects/C-Recipes/Recipe11-1/Listing11-3$ ▊
```

Figure 11-4. *The Linux error when a thread destructor is called before completion*

As you can see, this warning isn't particularly descriptive, and there's no guarantee that you'll get any warning when using other operating systems and libraries. It's therefore important to be aware of your **threads'** lifetimes and ensure that you're dealing with them appropriately.

One approach is to use the `join` method to make the program wait for **threads** to finish before closing them down. C++ also provides a second option: the `detach` method. Listing 11-4 shows the `detach` method in use.

Listing 11-4. Using the `detach` Method

```cpp
#include <iostream>
#include <thread>

using namespace std;

void ThreadTask()
{
    for (unsigned int i = 0; i < 20; ++i)
    {
        cout << "Output from thread" << endl;
    }
}

int main(int argc, char* argv[])
{
    const unsigned int numberOfProcessors{ thread::hardware_concurrency() };

    cout << "This system can run " << numberOfProcessors << " concurrent tasks" << endl;

    if (numberOfProcessors > 1)
    {
        thread myThread{ ThreadTask };

        cout << "Output from main" << endl;

        myThread.detach();
    }
    else
    {
        cout << "CPU does not have multiple cores." << endl;
    }

    return 0;
}
```

Listing 11-4 shows that the `detach` method can be used in place of `join`. The `join` method causes the program to wait for a running **thread** to complete before continuing, but the `detach` method doesn't. The `detach` method allows you to create **threads** that outlive the execution of your program. These may be useful for system tasks that need to track time over long periods; however, I'm skeptical about whether many day-to-day programs will find a use for this method. There's also a risk that your program will leak **threads** that have been detached and have no way to get those tasks back. Once an execution context in a **thread** has been detached, you can never reattach it.

11-2. Creating thread Scope Variables

Problem

You have classes of objects that use static data in their implementations, and you'd like to use them with **threads**.

Solution

C++ provides the thread_local specifier to allow the computer to create an instance of the static data on a per-thread basis.

How It Works

Before I cover how to use thread_local, let's step through a scenario where this problem can occur so you can clearly see the issue and the problem the solution itself can cause. Listing 11-5 contains a class that uses a static vector of objects to prevent many calls to new and delete.

Listing 11-5. Creating a Class that Uses Static Data to Track State#include <cstdlib>

```cpp
#include <iostream>
#include <stack>
#include <thread>
#include <vector>

using namespace std;

class MyManagedObject
{
private:
    static const unsigned int MAX_OBJECTS{ 4 };

    using MyManagedObjectCollection = vector < MyManagedObject > ;
    static MyManagedObjectCollection s_ManagedObjects;

    static stack<unsigned int> s_FreeList;

    unsigned int m_Value{ 0xFFFFFFFF };

public:
    MyManagedObject() = default;
    MyManagedObject(unsigned int value)
        : m_Value{ value }
    {

    }

    void* operator new(size_t numBytes)
    {
        void* objectMemory{};
```

```
        if (s_ManagedObjects.capacity() < MAX_OBJECTS)
        {
            s_ManagedObjects.reserve(MAX_OBJECTS);
        }

        if (numBytes == sizeof(MyManagedObject) &&
            s_ManagedObjects.size() < s_ManagedObjects.capacity())
        {
            unsigned int index{ 0xFFFFFFFF };
            if (s_FreeList.size() > 0)
            {
                index = s_FreeList.top();
                s_FreeList.pop();
            }

            if (index == 0xFFFFFFFF)
            {
                s_ManagedObjects.push_back({});
                index = s_ManagedObjects.size() - 1;
            }

            objectMemory = s_ManagedObjects.data() + index;
        }
        else
        {
            objectMemory = malloc(numBytes);
        }

        return objectMemory;
    }

    void operator delete(void* pMem)
    {
        const intptr_t index{
            (static_cast<MyManagedObject*>(pMem) - s_ManagedObjects.data()) /
            static_cast<intptr_t>(sizeof(MyManagedObject)) };
        if (0 <= index && index < static_cast<intptr_t>(s_ManagedObjects.size()))
        {
            s_FreeList.emplace(static_cast<unsigned int>(index));
        }
        else
        {
            free(pMem);
        }
    }
};

MyManagedObject::MyManagedObjectCollection MyManagedObject::s_ManagedObjects{};
stack<unsigned int> MyManagedObject::s_FreeList{};
```

```cpp
    int main(int argc, char* argv[])
{
    cout << hex << showbase;

    MyManagedObject* pObject1{ new MyManagedObject(1) };

    cout << "pObject1: " << pObject1 << endl;

    MyManagedObject* pObject2{ new MyManagedObject(2) };

    cout << "pObject2: " << pObject2 << endl;

    delete pObject1;
    pObject1 = nullptr;

    MyManagedObject* pObject3{ new MyManagedObject(3) };

    cout << "pObject3: " << pObject3 << endl;

    pObject1 = new MyManagedObject(4);

    cout << "pObject1: " << pObject1 << endl;

    delete pObject2;
    pObject2 = nullptr;

    delete pObject3;
    pObject3 = nullptr;

    delete pObject1;
    pObject1 = nullptr;

    return 0;
}
```

The code in Listing 11-5 overloads the new and delete methods on the MyManagedObject class. These overloads are used to return newly created objects from an initial pool of preallocated memory. Doing this would allow you to restrict the number of a given type of object to a prearranged limit but still let you use the familiar new and delete syntax.

■ **Note**   The code in Listing 11-5 doesn't actually enforce the limit; it simply falls back to dynamic allocation when the limit has been reached.

The managed class works by using a constant to determine the number of preallocated objects that should exist. This number is used to initialize a vector on the first allocation. Each subsequent allocation is fulfilled from this vector until it's exhausted. A free list of indices is maintained. If an object from the pool is released, its index is added to the top of the free stack. Objects on the free list are then reissued in the order that they were added to this stack. Figure 11-5 shows that pObject3 ends up with the same address that was used by pObject1 before it was deleted.

```
⊗ ⊜ ⊕   bruce@bruce-Virtual-Machine: ~/Projects/C-Recipes/Recipe11-2/Listing11-5
bruce@bruce-Virtual-Machine:~/Projects/C-Recipes/Recipe11-2/Listing11-5$ ./main
pObject1: 0x1f4b2c0
pObject2: 0x1f4b2c4
pObject3: 0x1f4b2c0
pObject1: 0x1f4b2c8
bruce@bruce-Virtual-Machine:~/Projects/C-Recipes/Recipe11-2/Listing11-5$ ▊
```

Figure 11-5. *Output showing the correct operation of the MyManagedObject pool*

The operation of this managed pool uses a static vector and a static stack to maintain the pool across all MyManagedObject instances. This causes problems when coupled with **threads**, because you can't be sure that different **threads** won't try to access these objects at the same time.

Listing 11-6 updates the code from Listing 11-5 to use a thread to also create MyManagedObject instances.

Listing 11-6. Using a thread to Create MyManagedObject Instances

```cpp
#include <cstdlib>
#include <iostream>
#include <stack>
#include <thread>
#include <vector>

using namespace std;

class MyManagedObject
{
private:
    static const unsigned int MAX_OBJECTS{ 8 };

    using MyManagedObjectCollection = vector < MyManagedObject >;
    static MyManagedObjectCollection s_ManagedObjects;

    static stack<unsigned int> s_FreeList;

    unsigned int m_Value{ 0xFFFFFFFF };

public:
    MyManagedObject() = default;
    MyManagedObject(unsigned int value)
        : m_Value{ value }
    {

    }
```

```
    void* operator new(size_t numBytes)
    {
        void* objectMemory{};

        if (s_ManagedObjects.capacity() < MAX_OBJECTS)
        {
            s_ManagedObjects.reserve(MAX_OBJECTS);
        }

        if (numBytes == sizeof(MyManagedObject) &&
            s_ManagedObjects.size() < s_ManagedObjects.capacity())
        {
            unsigned int index{ 0xFFFFFFFF };
            if (s_FreeList.size() > 0)
            {
                index = s_FreeList.top();
                s_FreeList.pop();
            }

            if (index == 0xFFFFFFFF)
            {
                s_ManagedObjects.push_back({});
                index = s_ManagedObjects.size() - 1;
            }

            objectMemory = s_ManagedObjects.data() + index;
        }
        else
        {
            objectMemory = malloc(numBytes);
        }

        return objectMemory;
    }

    void operator delete(void* pMem)
    {
        const intptr_t index{
            (static_cast<MyManagedObject*>(pMem)-s_ManagedObjects.data()) /
            static_cast< intptr_t >(sizeof(MyManagedObject)) };
        if (0 <= index && index < static_cast< intptr_t >(s_ManagedObjects.size()))
        {
            s_FreeList.emplace(static_cast<unsigned int>(index));
        }
        else
        {
            free(pMem);
        }
    }
};
```

```cpp
MyManagedObject::MyManagedObjectCollection MyManagedObject::s_ManagedObjects{};
stack<unsigned int> MyManagedObject::s_FreeList{};

void ThreadTask()
{
    MyManagedObject* pObject4{ new MyManagedObject(5) };

    cout << "pObject4: " << pObject4 << endl;

    MyManagedObject* pObject5{ new MyManagedObject(6) };

    cout << "pObject5: " << pObject5 << endl;

    delete pObject4;
    pObject4 = nullptr;

    MyManagedObject* pObject6{ new MyManagedObject(7) };

    cout << "pObject6: " << pObject6 << endl;

    pObject4 = new MyManagedObject(8);

    cout << "pObject4: " << pObject4 << endl;

    delete pObject5;
    pObject5 = nullptr;

    delete pObject6;
    pObject6 = nullptr;

    delete pObject4;
    pObject4 = nullptr;
}

int main(int argc, char* argv[])
{
    cout << hex << showbase;

    thread myThread{ ThreadTask };

    MyManagedObject* pObject1{ new MyManagedObject(1) };

    cout << "pObject1: " << pObject1 << endl;

    MyManagedObject* pObject2{ new MyManagedObject(2) };

    cout << "pObject2: " << pObject2 << endl;

    delete pObject1;
    pObject1 = nullptr;
```

```
MyManagedObject* pObject3{ new MyManagedObject(3) };

cout << "pObject3: " << pObject3 << endl;

pObject1 = new MyManagedObject(4);

cout << "pObject1: " << pObject1 << endl;

delete pObject2;
pObject2 = nullptr;

delete pObject3;
pObject3 = nullptr;

delete pObject1;
pObject1 = nullptr;

myThread.join();

return 0;
}
```

The code in Listing 11-6 uses a thread to allocate objects from the pool concurrently with the main function. This means the static pool can be accessed simultaneously from two locations, and your program can run into problems. Two common issues are unexpected program crashes and data races.

A data race is a more subtle problem and results in unexpected memory corruption. Figure 11-6 illustrates the problem.

```
bruce@bruce-Virtual-Machine: ~/Projects/C-Recipes/Recipe11-2/Listing11-6
bruce@bruce-Virtual-Machine:~/Projects/C-Recipes/Recipe11-2/Listing11-6$ ./main
pObject1: 0x1d65550
pObject2: 0x1d65558
pObject3: 0x1d65550
pObject1: 0x1d6555c
pObject4: 0x1d65554
pObject5: 0x1d65550
pObject6: 0x1d65550
pObject4: 0x1d65550
bruce@bruce-Virtual-Machine:~/Projects/C-Recipes/Recipe11-2/Listing11-6$
```

Figure 11-6. The problem caused by running into data races between threads

The problem presented by allocating objects from the same pool may be subtle and difficult to spot at first. If you look closely, you see that pObject6 and pObject3 are pointing to the same memory address. These pointers are created and initialized on different threads, and at no point do you expect them to point at the same memory address, even with object reuse in your pools. This again is a difficulty in working with **threads**. The associated problems are very time-sensitive and their manifestations can be altered by the conditions of the computer at the time of execution. Other programs may create threads that cause your own to be delayed slightly, so that a problem in your thread logic can manifest itself in many different ways despite having the same root cause.

C++ provides a solution to this problem: the thread_local keyword. The thread_local keyword works by telling the compiler that the static objects you're creating should be unique for every thread you create that uses these objects. The side effect is that you don't have a single shared instance of the static object across all classes. This is a significant departure from the normal usage of static, where there is a single shared object for all instances of the type. Listing 11-7 shows the memory-pool functions and the associated static variables updated to use thread_local.

Listing 11-7. Using thread_local

```cpp
#include <cstdlib>
#include <iostream>
#include <stack>
#include <thread>
#include <vector>

using namespace std;

class MyManagedObject
{
private:
    static thread_local const unsigned int MAX_OBJECTS;

    using MyManagedObjectCollection = vector < MyManagedObject >;
    static thread_local MyManagedObjectCollection s_ManagedObjects;

    static thread_local stack<unsigned int> s_FreeList;

    unsigned int m_Value{ 0xFFFFFFFF };

public:
    MyManagedObject() = default;
    MyManagedObject(unsigned int value)
        : m_Value{ value }
    {

    }

    void* operator new(size_t numBytes)
    {
        void* objectMemory{};

        if (s_ManagedObjects.capacity() < MAX_OBJECTS)
        {
            s_ManagedObjects.reserve(MAX_OBJECTS);
        }
```

```
        if (numBytes == sizeof(MyManagedObject) &&
            s_ManagedObjects.size() < s_ManagedObjects.capacity())
        {
            unsigned int index{ 0xFFFFFFFF };
            if (s_FreeList.size() > 0)
            {
                index = s_FreeList.top();
                s_FreeList.pop();
            }

            if (index == 0xFFFFFFFF)
            {
                s_ManagedObjects.push_back({});
                index = s_ManagedObjects.size() - 1;
            }

            objectMemory = s_ManagedObjects.data() + index;
        }
        else
        {
            objectMemory = malloc(numBytes);
        }

        return objectMemory;
    }

    void operator delete(void* pMem)
    {
        const intptr_t index{
            (static_cast<MyManagedObject*>(pMem)-s_ManagedObjects.data()) /
            static_cast<intptr_t>(sizeof(MyManagedObject)) };
        if (0 <= index && index < static_cast< intptr_t >(s_ManagedObjects.size()))
        {
            s_FreeList.emplace(static_cast<unsigned int>(index));
        }
        else
        {
            free(pMem);
        }
    }
};

thread_local const unsigned int MyManagedObject::MAX_OBJECTS{ 8 };
thread_local MyManagedObject::MyManagedObjectCollection MyManagedObject::s_ManagedObjects{};
thread_local stack<unsigned int> MyManagedObject::s_FreeList{};

void ThreadTask()
{
    MyManagedObject* pObject4{ new MyManagedObject(5) };

    cout << "pObject4: " << pObject4 << endl;
```

```
    MyManagedObject* pObject5{ new MyManagedObject(6) };

    cout << "pObject5: " << pObject5 << endl;

    delete pObject4;
    pObject4 = nullptr;

    MyManagedObject* pObject6{ new MyManagedObject(7) };

    cout << "pObject6: " << pObject6 << endl;

    pObject4 = new MyManagedObject(8);

    cout << "pObject4: " << pObject4 << endl;

    delete pObject5;
    pObject5 = nullptr;

    delete pObject6;
    pObject6 = nullptr;

    delete pObject4;
    pObject4 = nullptr;
}

int main(int argc, char* argv[])
{
    cout << hex << showbase;

    thread myThread{ ThreadTask };

    MyManagedObject* pObject1{ new MyManagedObject(1) };

    cout << "pObject1: " << pObject1 << endl;

    MyManagedObject* pObject2{ new MyManagedObject(2) };

    cout << "pObject2: " << pObject2 << endl;

    delete pObject1;
    pObject1 = nullptr;

    MyManagedObject* pObject3{ new MyManagedObject(3) };

    cout << "pObject3: " << pObject3 << endl;

    pObject1 = new MyManagedObject(4);

    cout << "pObject1: " << pObject1 << endl;

    delete pObject2;
```

```
    pObject2 = nullptr;

    delete pObject3;
    pObject3 = nullptr;

    delete pObject1;
    pObject1 = nullptr;

    myThread.join();

    return 0;
}
```

Listing 11-7 shows that you can specify static variables as having thread_local storage by adding the thread_local identifier to their declaration and definitions. The impact of this change is that the main function and the ThreadTask function have separate s_ManagedObjects, s_FreeList, and MAX_OBJECT variables in their own execution context. Now that there are two copies of each, you have twice the number of potential objects, because as the pools have been duplicated. This may or may not be a problem for your program, but you should be careful when using thread_local and consider any unintended consequences. Figure 11-7 shows the result of running the code in Listing 11-7.

```
bruce@bruce-Virtual-Machine: ~/Projects/C-Recipes/Recipe11-2/Listing11-7
bruce@bruce-Virtual-Machine:~/Projects/C-Recipes/Recipe11-2/Listing11-7$ ./main
pObject1: 0x23195c0
pObject2: 0x23195c4
pObject3: 0x23195c0
pObject1: 0x23195c8
pObject4: 0x7f6388000bd0
pObject5: 0x7f6388000bd4
pObject6: 0x7f6388000bd0
pObject4: 0x7f6388000bd8
bruce@bruce-Virtual-Machine:~/Projects/C-Recipes/Recipe11-2/Listing11-7$
```

Figure 11-7. Output when using thread_local

You can see the problems when using **threads**. The first line of output is split between the two **threads**, but it should be very apparent that the two **threads** are being assigned values from completely separate places in memory. This proves that the compiler has made sure the static variables are unique for each thread in the program. You could take this further by adding even more threads to the program and seeing that they're allocating objects from different places in memory and that at no point can two pointers on different **threads** be pointing to the same memory address.

11-3. Accessing Shared Objects Using Mutual Exclusion

Problem

You have an object that you would like to be able to access on more than one **thread** at a time.

Solution

C++ provides mutex objects that allow you to provide mutually exclusive access to sections of code.

How It Works

A mutex can be used to synchronize **threads**. This is achieved by the mutex class and the methods it provides to acquire and release the **mutex**. A **thread** can be sure that no other **thread** is currently accessing a shared resource by waiting until it can acquire the **mutex** before continuing execution. The program in Listing 11-8 contains a *data race*: a situation in which two **threads** can access a shared resource at the same time and cause unstable and unexpected program behavior.

Listing 11-8. A Program Containing a Data Race

```
#include <cstdlib>
#include <iostream>
#include <stack>
#include <thread>
#include <vector>

using namespace std;

class MyManagedObject
{
private:
    static const unsigned int MAX_OBJECTS{ 8 };

    using MyManagedObjectCollection = vector < MyManagedObject >;
    static MyManagedObjectCollection s_ManagedObjects;

    static stack<unsigned int> s_FreeList;

    unsigned int m_Value{ 0xFFFFFFFF };

public:
    MyManagedObject() = default;
    MyManagedObject(unsigned int value)
        : m_Value{ value }
    {

    }

    void* operator new(size_t numBytes)
    {
        void* objectMemory{};
```

```
        if (s_ManagedObjects.capacity() < MAX_OBJECTS)
        {
            s_ManagedObjects.reserve(MAX_OBJECTS);
        }

        if (numBytes == sizeof(MyManagedObject) &&
            s_ManagedObjects.size() < s_ManagedObjects.capacity())
        {
            unsigned int index{ 0xFFFFFFFF };
            if (s_FreeList.size() > 0)
            {
                index = s_FreeList.top();
                s_FreeList.pop();
            }

            if (index == 0xFFFFFFFF)
            {
                s_ManagedObjects.push_back({});
                index = s_ManagedObjects.size() - 1;
            }

            objectMemory = s_ManagedObjects.data() + index;
        }
        else
        {
            objectMemory = malloc(numBytes);
        }

        return objectMemory;
    }

    void operator delete(void* pMem)
    {
        const intptr_t index{
            (static_cast<MyManagedObject*>(pMem)-s_ManagedObjects.data()) /
            static_cast<intptr_t>(sizeof(MyManagedObject)) };
        if (0 <= index && index < static_cast< intptr_t >(s_ManagedObjects.size()))
        {
            s_FreeList.emplace(static_cast<unsigned int>(index));
        }
        else
        {
            free(pMem);
        }
    }
};

MyManagedObject::MyManagedObjectCollection MyManagedObject::s_ManagedObjects{};
stack<unsigned int> MyManagedObject::s_FreeList{};
```

```cpp
void ThreadTask()
{
    MyManagedObject* pObject4{ new MyManagedObject(5) };

    cout << "pObject4: " << pObject4 << endl;

    MyManagedObject* pObject5{ new MyManagedObject(6) };

    cout << "pObject5: " << pObject5 << endl;

    delete pObject4;
    pObject4 = nullptr;

    MyManagedObject* pObject6{ new MyManagedObject(7) };

    cout << "pObject6: " << pObject6 << endl;

    pObject4 = new MyManagedObject(8);

    cout << "pObject4: " << pObject4 << endl;

    delete pObject5;
    pObject5 = nullptr;

    delete pObject6;
    pObject6 = nullptr;

    delete pObject4;
    pObject4 = nullptr;
}

int main(int argc, char* argv[])
{
    cout << hex << showbase;

    thread myThread{ ThreadTask };

    MyManagedObject* pObject1{ new MyManagedObject(1) };

    cout << "pObject1: " << pObject1 << endl;

    MyManagedObject* pObject2{ new MyManagedObject(2) };

    cout << "pObject2: " << pObject2 << endl;

    delete pObject1;
    pObject1 = nullptr;

    MyManagedObject* pObject3{ new MyManagedObject(3) };

    cout << "pObject3: " << pObject3 << endl;
```

```
    pObject1 = new MyManagedObject(4);

    cout << "pObject1: " << pObject1 << endl;

    delete pObject2;
    pObject2 = nullptr;

    delete pObject3;
    pObject3 = nullptr;

    delete pObject1;
    pObject1 = nullptr;

    myThread.join();

    return 0;
}
```

This program can't prevent the code in ThreadTask and the main function from accessing the s_ManagedObjects and s_FreeList pools in the MyManagedObject class. Access to these objects can be protected by a **mutex**, as you can see in Listing 11-9.

Listing 11-9. Adding a Mutex to Protect Access to Shared Objects

```
#include <cstdlib>
#include <iostream>
#include <mutex>
#include <stack>
#include <thread>
#include <vector>

using namespace std;

class MyManagedObject
{
private:
    static const unsigned int MAX_OBJECTS{ 8 };

    using MyManagedObjectCollection = vector < MyManagedObject >;
    static MyManagedObjectCollection s_ManagedObjects;

    static stack<unsigned int> s_FreeList;

    static mutex s_Mutex;

    unsigned int m_Value{ 0xFFFFFFFF };

public:
    MyManagedObject() = default;
    MyManagedObject(unsigned int value)
        : m_Value{ value }
    {

    }
```

```cpp
void* operator new(size_t numBytes)
{
    void* objectMemory{};

    s_Mutex.lock();

    if (s_ManagedObjects.capacity() < MAX_OBJECTS)
    {
        s_ManagedObjects.reserve(MAX_OBJECTS);
    }

    if (numBytes == sizeof(MyManagedObject) &&
        s_ManagedObjects.size() < s_ManagedObjects.capacity())
    {
        unsigned int index{ 0xFFFFFFFF };
        if (s_FreeList.size() > 0)
        {
            index = s_FreeList.top();
            s_FreeList.pop();
        }

        if (index == 0xFFFFFFFF)
        {
            s_ManagedObjects.push_back({});
            index = s_ManagedObjects.size() - 1;
        }

        objectMemory = s_ManagedObjects.data() + index;
    }
    else
    {
        objectMemory = malloc(numBytes);
    }

    s_Mutex.unlock();

    return objectMemory;
}

void operator delete(void* pMem)
{
    s_Mutex.lock();

    const intptr_t index{
        (static_cast<MyManagedObject*>(pMem)-s_ManagedObjects.data()) /
        static_cast<intptr_t>(sizeof(MyManagedObject)) };
    if (0 <= index && index < static_cast< intptr_t >(s_ManagedObjects.size()))
    {
        s_FreeList.emplace(static_cast<unsigned int>(index));
    }
    else
```

```
        {
            free(pMem);
        }

        s_Mutex.unlock();
    }
};

MyManagedObject::MyManagedObjectCollection MyManagedObject::s_ManagedObjects{};
stack<unsigned int> MyManagedObject::s_FreeList{};
mutex MyManagedObject::s_Mutex;

void ThreadTask()
{
    MyManagedObject* pObject4{ new MyManagedObject(5) };

    cout << "pObject4: " << pObject4 << endl;

    MyManagedObject* pObject5{ new MyManagedObject(6) };

    cout << "pObject5: " << pObject5 << endl;

    delete pObject4;
    pObject4 = nullptr;

    MyManagedObject* pObject6{ new MyManagedObject(7) };

    cout << "pObject6: " << pObject6 << endl;

    pObject4 = new MyManagedObject(8);

    cout << "pObject4: " << pObject4 << endl;

    delete pObject5;
    pObject5 = nullptr;

    delete pObject6;
    pObject6 = nullptr;

    delete pObject4;
    pObject4 = nullptr;
}

int main(int argc, char* argv[])
{
    cout << hex << showbase;

    thread myThread{ ThreadTask };

    MyManagedObject* pObject1{ new MyManagedObject(1) };
```

```
    cout << "pObject1: " << pObject1 << endl;

    MyManagedObject* pObject2{ new MyManagedObject(2) };

    cout << "pObject2: " << pObject2 << endl;

    delete pObject1;
    pObject1 = nullptr;

    MyManagedObject* pObject3{ new MyManagedObject(3) };

    cout << "pObject3: " << pObject3 << endl;

    pObject1 = new MyManagedObject(4);

    cout << "pObject1: " << pObject1 << endl;

    delete pObject2;
    pObject2 = nullptr;

    delete pObject3;
    pObject3 = nullptr;

    delete pObject1;
    pObject1 = nullptr;

    myThread.join();

    return 0;
}
```

This code uses a **mutex** to ensure that the new and delete functions in the MyManagedObject class are only executing on a single **thread** at any given time. This ensures that the object pool being maintained for this **class** is always in a valid state and that the same addresses aren't being given to different **threads**. The code requires that the lock be held for the entire execution of the functions it's protecting. C++ provides a helper class named lock_guard that automatically locks a **mutex** on construction and frees the **mutex** on destruction. Listing 11-10 shows a lock_guard in use.

Listing 11-10. Using a lock_guard

```
#include <cstdlib>
#include <iostream>
#include <mutex>
#include <stack>
#include <thread>
#include <vector>

using namespace std;
```

```cpp
class MyManagedObject
{
private:
    static const unsigned int MAX_OBJECTS{ 8 };

    using MyManagedObjectCollection = vector < MyManagedObject >;
    static MyManagedObjectCollection s_ManagedObjects;

    static stack<unsigned int> s_FreeList;

    static mutex s_Mutex;

    unsigned int m_Value{ 0xFFFFFFFF };

public:
    MyManagedObject() = default;
    MyManagedObject(unsigned int value)
        : m_Value{ value }
    {

    }

    void* operator new(size_t numBytes)
    {
        lock_guard<mutex> lock{ s_Mutex };

        void* objectMemory{};

        if (s_ManagedObjects.capacity() < MAX_OBJECTS)
        {
            s_ManagedObjects.reserve(MAX_OBJECTS);
        }

        if (numBytes == sizeof(MyManagedObject) &&
            s_ManagedObjects.size() < s_ManagedObjects.capacity())
        {
            unsigned int index{ 0xFFFFFFFF };
            if (s_FreeList.size() > 0)
            {
                index = s_FreeList.top();
                s_FreeList.pop();
            }

            if (index == 0xFFFFFFFF)
            {
                s_ManagedObjects.push_back({});
                index = s_ManagedObjects.size() - 1;
            }
```

```
                objectMemory = s_ManagedObjects.data() + index;
        }
        else
        {
            objectMemory = malloc(numBytes);
        }

        return objectMemory;
    }

    void operator delete(void* pMem)
    {
        lock_guard<mutex> lock{ s_Mutex };

        const intptr_t index{
            (static_cast<MyManagedObject*>(pMem)-s_ManagedObjects.data()) /
            static_cast<intptr_t>(sizeof(MyManagedObject)) };
        if (0 <= index && index < static_cast<intptr_t>(s_ManagedObjects.size()))
        {
            s_FreeList.emplace(static_cast<unsigned int>(index));
        }
        else
        {
            free(pMem);
        }
    }
};

MyManagedObject::MyManagedObjectCollection MyManagedObject::s_ManagedObjects{};
stack<unsigned int> MyManagedObject::s_FreeList{};
mutex MyManagedObject::s_Mutex;

void ThreadTask()
{
    MyManagedObject* pObject4{ new MyManagedObject(5) };

    cout << "pObject4: " << pObject4 << endl;

    MyManagedObject* pObject5{ new MyManagedObject(6) };

    cout << "pObject5: " << pObject5 << endl;

    delete pObject4;
    pObject4 = nullptr;

    MyManagedObject* pObject6{ new MyManagedObject(7) };

    cout << "pObject6: " << pObject6 << endl;

    pObject4 = new MyManagedObject(8);
```

```
        cout << "pObject4: " << pObject4 << endl;

        delete pObject5;
        pObject5 = nullptr;

        delete pObject6;
        pObject6 = nullptr;

        delete pObject4;
        pObject4 = nullptr;
    }

    int main(int argc, char* argv[])
    {
        cout << hex << showbase;

        thread myThread{ ThreadTask };

        MyManagedObject* pObject1{ new MyManagedObject(1) };

        cout << "pObject1: " << pObject1 << endl;

        MyManagedObject* pObject2{ new MyManagedObject(2) };

        cout << "pObject2: " << pObject2 << endl;

        delete pObject1;
        pObject1 = nullptr;

        MyManagedObject* pObject3{ new MyManagedObject(3) };

        cout << "pObject3: " << pObject3 << endl;

        pObject1 = new MyManagedObject(4);

        cout << "pObject1: " << pObject1 << endl;

        delete pObject2;
        pObject2 = nullptr;

        delete pObject3;
        pObject3 = nullptr;

        delete pObject1;
        pObject1 = nullptr;

        myThread.join();

        return 0;
    }
```

Using a lock_guard means you don't have to worry about calling unlock on the **mutex** for yourself. It also conforms to the Resource Allocation Is Initialization (RAII) pattern that many C++ developers try to follow.

11-4. Creating Threads that Wait for Events

Problem

You would like to create a **thread** that waits for another event in your program.

Solution

C++ provides the condition_variable class that can be used to signal that an event has occurred to a waiting **thread**.

How It Works

A condition_variable is another C++ construct that wraps a complex behavior into a simple object interface. It's common in multithreaded programming to create **threads** that you would like to have wait for some event to occur in another **thread**. This is common in a producer/consumer situation, where one **thread** may be creating tasks and another **thread** is auctioning or carrying out those tasks. A condition variable is perfect in these scenarios.

A condition_variable requires a **mutex** to be effective. It works by waiting for some condition to become **true** and then attempting to acquire a lock on the **mutex** protecting a shared resource. Listing 11-11 uses a **mutex**, a unique_lock, and a condition_variable to communicate between **threads** when a producer **thread** has queued work for two consumer threads.

Listing 11-11. Using a condition_variable to Wake a Thread

```
#include <condition_variable>
#include <cstdlib>
#include <functional>
#include <iostream>
#include <mutex>
#include <thread>
#include <stack>
#include <vector>

using namespace std;

class MyManagedObject
{
private:
    static const unsigned int MAX_OBJECTS{ 8 };

    using MyManagedObjectCollection = vector < MyManagedObject >;
    static MyManagedObjectCollection s_ManagedObjects;

    static stack<unsigned int> s_FreeList;
```

```
    static mutex s_Mutex;

    unsigned int m_Value{ 0xFFFFFFFF };

public:
    MyManagedObject() = default;
    MyManagedObject(unsigned int value)
        : m_Value{ value }
    {

    }

    unsigned int GetValue() const { return m_Value; }

    void* operator new(size_t numBytes)
    {
        lock_guard<mutex> lock{ s_Mutex };

        void* objectMemory{};

        if (s_ManagedObjects.capacity() < MAX_OBJECTS)
        {
            s_ManagedObjects.reserve(MAX_OBJECTS);
        }

        if (numBytes == sizeof(MyManagedObject) &&
            s_ManagedObjects.size() < s_ManagedObjects.capacity())
        {
            unsigned int index{ 0xFFFFFFFF };
            if (s_FreeList.size() > 0)
            {
                index = s_FreeList.top();
                s_FreeList.pop();
            }

            if (index == 0xFFFFFFFF)
            {
                s_ManagedObjects.push_back({});
                index = s_ManagedObjects.size() - 1;
            }

            objectMemory = s_ManagedObjects.data() + index;
        }
        else
        {
            objectMemory = malloc(numBytes);
        }

        return objectMemory;
    }
```

```cpp
        void operator delete(void* pMem)
    {
        lock_guard<mutex> lock{ s_Mutex };

        const intptr_t index{
            (static_cast<MyManagedObject*>(pMem)-s_ManagedObjects.data()) /
            static_cast<intptr_t>(sizeof(MyManagedObject)) };
        if (0 <= index && index < static_cast<intptr_t>(s_ManagedObjects.size()))
        {
            s_FreeList.emplace(static_cast<unsigned int>(index));
        }
        else
        {
            free(pMem);
        }
    }
};

MyManagedObject::MyManagedObjectCollection MyManagedObject::s_ManagedObjects{};
stack<unsigned int> MyManagedObject::s_FreeList{};
mutex MyManagedObject::s_Mutex;

using ProducerQueue = vector < unsigned int > ;

void ThreadTask(
    reference_wrapper<condition_variable> condition,
    reference_wrapper<mutex> queueMutex,
    reference_wrapper<ProducerQueue> queueRef,
    reference_wrapper<bool> die)
{
    ProducerQueue& queue{ queueRef.get() };

    while (!die.get() || queue.size())
    {
        unique_lock<mutex> lock{ queueMutex.get() };

        function<bool()> predicate{
            [&queue]()
            {
                return !queue.empty();
            }
        };
        condition.get().wait(lock, predicate);

        unsigned int numberToCreate{ queue.back() };
        queue.pop_back();

        cout << "Creating " <<
            numberToCreate <<
            " objects on thread " <<
            this_thread::get_id() << endl;
```

```cpp
        for (unsigned int i = 0; i < numberToCreate; ++i)
        {
            MyManagedObject* pObject{ new MyManagedObject(i) };
        }
    }
}

int main(int argc, char* argv[])
{
    condition_variable condition;
    mutex queueMutex;
    ProducerQueue queue;
    bool die{ false };

    thread myThread1{ ThreadTask, ref(condition), ref(queueMutex), ref(queue), ref(die) };
    thread myThread2{ ThreadTask, ref(condition), ref(queueMutex), ref(queue), ref(die) };

    queueMutex.lock();
    queue.emplace_back(300000);
    queue.emplace_back(400000);
    queueMutex.unlock();

    condition.notify_all();

    this_thread::sleep_for( 10ms );
    while (!queueMutex.try_lock())
    {
        cout << "Main waiting for queue access!" << endl;
        this_thread::sleep_for( 100ms );
    }

    queue.emplace_back(100000);
    queue.emplace_back(200000);

    this_thread::sleep_for( 1000ms );

    condition.notify_one();

    this_thread::sleep_for( 1000ms );

    condition.notify_one();

    this_thread::sleep_for( 1000ms );

    queueMutex.unlock();

    die = true;

    cout << "main waiting for join!" << endl;

    myThread1.join();
    myThread2.join();

    return 0;
}
```

This code contains a complex scenario using the C++ language's multithreading capabilities. The first aspect of this example that you need to understand is the method used to pass variables from main into the **threads**. When the **thread** object is created, you can think of the values you pass to it as being passed into a function by value. In effect, this causes your **threads** to receive copies of variables and not the variables themselves. This causes difficulty when you're trying to share objects between **threads**, because changes in one aren't reflected in the other. You can overcome this limitation by using the reference_wrapper template. A reference_wrapper essentially stores a pointer to the object you're trying to share between **threads**, but it helps overcome the problem where you would normally have to account for a null pointer by ensuring that the value can't be null. When you pass the variable into the thread constructor, you actually pass the variable into the ref function, which in turn passes a reference_wrapper containing your object to thread. When the **thread** constructor makes a copy of the values you passed to it, you receive a copy of the reference_wrapper and not a copy of the object itself. You could achieve the same result by using pointers to objects, but this built-in C++ method is much simpler and provides more safety. The ThreadTask function retrieves the shared objects from their reference_wrapper instances using the get method supplied by the reference_wrapper template.

The ThreadTask function is used by two different **threads** in the program, and therefore the use of reference_wrapper is essential to ensure that the two instances share the same **mutex** and condition_ variable along with main. Each instance uses a unique_lock to wrap the behavior of the **mutex**. Curiously, a unique_lock automatically locks a **mutex** when it's constructed, but the code in Listing 11-11 never calls unlock on the **mutex**. The unlock call is carried out by the wait method in the first instance. The condition_variable::wait method unlocks the **mutex** and waits for a signal from another thread that it should continue. Unfortunately, this waiting isn't completely reliable, because some operating systems can decide to unblock **threads** without the appropriate signal being sent. For this reason, it's a good idea to have a backup plan—and the wait method provides this by taking a predicate parameter. The predicate takes a variable that can be called like a function. The code in Listing 11-11 provides a closure that determines whether the queue is empty. When the **thread** wakes, because it has been signaled to wake either by the program or by the operating system, it first checks to see if the predicate is **true** before attempting to reacquire the lock on the supplied **mutex**. If the predicate is **true**, the wait function calls lock and returns; doing so allows the **thread's** function to continue execution. The ThreadTask function creates the appropriate number of objects before starting over due to the while loop. At the end of each iteration of the while loop, the unique_lock wrapper for the **mutex** goes out of scope; its destructor calls unlock on the **mutex**, allowing other **threads** to be unblocked.

■ **Note**   The use of unique_lock in Listing 11-11 is technically inefficient. Holding the lock for longer than it takes to retrieve the number of objects to be created from the **queue** essentially serializes the creation of the objects by causing all **threads** to synchronize while one **thread** is creating objects. This example is poorly designed on purpose to show how these objects can be used in practice.

Whereas the ThreadTask function is used in two **threads** to consume jobs from queue, the main function is a producer **thread** that adds jobs to queue. It begins by creating the two consumer **threads** that will carry out its tasks. Once the **threads** are created, the main function carries on with the task of adding jobs to queue. It lock the **mutex**, adds two jobs—one to create 300,000 objects and another to create 400,000 objects—and unlocks the **mutex**. It then calls notify_all on the condition_variable. The condition_variable object stores a list of **threads** that are waiting for a signal to continue; the notify_all method wakes all of these threads so they can carry out work. The main function then uses try_lock to show that it can't add tasks while the **threads** are busy. In normal code, you could call lock; but this is an example of how to make a **thread** wait for a certain amount of time and how the try_lock method can be used to conditionally execute code if the **mutex** can't be locked. More tasks are added to queue once try_lock returns **true** and before the

mutex is unlocked again. The notify_one function is then used to wake a single **thread** at a time to show that it's possible to write code with finer control over **threads**. The second **thread** must also be awakened, or the program will stall on the join calls indefinitely.

Figure 11-8 shows the output generated by running this code. You see that main can be blocked while waiting for access to the **mutex** and that both **threads** are used to consume tasks from queue.

```
bruce@bruce-Virtual-Machine: ~/Projects/C-Recipes/Recipe11-4/Listing11-11
bruce@bruce-Virtual-Machine:~/Projects/C-Recipes/Recipe11-4/Listing11-11$ ./main

Creating 400000 objects on thread 140300638865152
Main waiting for queue access!
Creating 300000 objects on thread 140300638865152
main waiting for join!
Creating 200000 objects on thread 140300638865152
Creating 100000 objects on thread 140300630472448
bruce@bruce-Virtual-Machine:~/Projects/C-Recipes/Recipe11-4/Listing11-11$
```

Figure 11-8. *Output showing multiple threads being awakened by a condition variable*

11-5. Retrieving Results from a Thread

Problem

You would like to create a **thread** that is capable of returning a result.

Solution

C++ provides promise and future objects that can be used to transfer data between **threads**.

How It Works

Using the promise and future Classes

Transferring data from a worker **thread** back to the **thread** that begins a task can be a complicated process. You must ensure mutually exclusive access to the memory set aside to store the result as well as handle all the signaling between **threads**. These signals include having the working **thread** specifying when the result of the **thread** operation is available as well as having the scheduling **thread** wait for that result to be available. Modern C++ solves this problem using the promise template.

A promise template can be specialized with a thread task return type. This creates a contract between **threads** that allows the transfer of this type of object from one to another. A promise contains a future. This means a promise can fulfil its name: it essentially promises to provide a value of its specialized type to the holder of its future at some point in the future. There is no requirement for a promise to be used on more than a single **thread**, but promises are thread-safe and perfect for this job. Alternate uses for promise/future pairs could be to retrieve results from asynchronous operations such as HTTP requests. Listing 11-12 shows the use of a promise on a single thread.

Listing 11-12. Using a promise on One Thread

```
#include <future>
#include <iostream>

using namespace std;

using FactorialPromise = promise< long long >;

long long Factorial(unsigned int value)
{
    return value == 1
        ? 1
        : value * Factorial(value - 1);
}

int main(int argc, char* argv[])
{
    using namespace chrono;

    FactorialPromise promise;
    future<long long> taskFuture{ promise.get_future() };

    promise.set_value(Factorial(3));
    cout << "Factorial result was " << taskFuture.get() << endl;

    return 0;
}
```

Listing 11-12 shows the use of a promise to provide storage for a value that can be calculated later and retrieved in the future. You could use this for long-running tasks such as loading data from a file or retrieving information from a server. A program can continue rendering a UI or a progress bar while the promise hasn't been fulfilled.

The promise is initialized with a default constructor, and you can use the get_future method to get the future into which the promise places its value. The set_value method on the promise sets the value on the future, and the get method on the future provides access to the value.

It can be a little difficult to see the separation of concerns between the promise and the future when they're used close together as in Listing 11-12. Listing 11-13 overcomes this issue by moving the promise to another **thread**.

Listing 11-13. Moving a promise to a Second Thread

```
#include <future>
#include <iostream>

using namespace std;

using FactorialPromise = promise< long long > ;

long long Factorial(unsigned int value)
{
    this_thread::sleep_for(chrono::seconds(2));
```

```
    return value == 1
        ? 1
        : value * Factorial(value - 1);
}

void ThreadTask(FactorialPromise& threadPromise, unsigned int value)
{
    threadPromise.set_value(Factorial(value));
}

int main(int argc, char* argv[])
{
    using namespace chrono;

    FactorialPromise promise;
    future<long long> taskFuture{ promise.get_future() };

    thread taskThread{ ThreadTask, std::move(promise), 3 };

    while (taskFuture.wait_until(system_clock::now() + seconds(1)) != future_status::ready)
    {
        cout << "Still Waiting!" << endl;
    }

    cout << "Factorial result was " << taskFuture.get() << endl;

    taskThread.join();

    return 0;
}
```

In Listing 11-13, the promise and future objects are initialized the same way as in Listing 11-12; however, the Factorial function is called from a **thread** using the ThreadTask function. Some additional lines show how you can use a future to wait for completion without necessarily blocking a **thread**. The Factorial method has a sleep_for call that causes the calculation of the Factorial to take much longer than usual. This allows for the example of the future::wait_until method. This method waits either until the supplied absolute time or until the promise has been fulfilled and the future's value can be retrieved. The wait_until method takes an absolute system time to wait; this can be supplied easily using the system_clock::now method with a suitable duration, in this case one second. If the loop that prints "Still Waiting!" wasn't present, then the call to get on the future would be a blocking call. This would cause your **thread** to stall until the set_value method had been called on the promise. Sometimes this behavior is suitable, and other times it isn't. It depends on the requirements of the software you're writing.

The use of a promise and a future directly relies on you managing your own thread function. Sometimes this can be overkill, as is the case in Listing 11-13. The ThreadTask function has only one job: to call set_value on the promise. C++ provides the packaged_task template, which removes the need for you to create your own thread function. A packaged_task constructor takes the function to call as a parameter; a corresponding thread constructor that can take a packaged_task. A **thread** constructed in this way can automatically call the method in the supplied packaged_task and call set_value on its internal promise. Listing 11-14 shows the use of a packaged_task.

Listing 11-14. Using a packaged_task

```
#include <future>
#include <iostream>

using namespace std;

long long Factorial(unsigned int value)
{
    this_thread::sleep_for(chrono::seconds(2));
    return value == 1
        ? 1
        : value * Factorial(value - 1);
}

int main(int argc, char* argv[])
{
    using namespace chrono;

    packaged_task<long long(unsigned int)> task{ Factorial };
    future<long long> taskFuture{ task.get_future() };

    thread taskThread{ std::move(task), 3 };

    while (taskFuture.wait_until(system_clock::now() + seconds(1)) != future_status::ready)
    {
        cout << "Still Waiting!" << endl;
    }

    cout << "Factorial result was " << taskFuture.get() << endl;

    taskThread.join();

    return 0;
}
```

Listing 11-14 shows that the ThreadTask function is no longer needed when using a packaged_task. The packaged_task constructor takes a function pointer as a parameter. The packaged_task template also supplies a get_future method and is passed to a thread using move semantics.

Although a packaged task removes the need for a thread function, you must still create your own **thread** manually. C++ supplies a fourth level of abstraction that prevents you from having to worry about **threads**. Listing 11-15 uses the async function to call a function asynchronously.

Listing 11-15. Using async to Call Functions

```cpp
#include <future>
#include <iostream>

using namespace std;

long long Factorial(unsigned int value)
{
    cout << "ThreadTask thread: " << this_thread::get_id() << endl;
    return value == 1
        ? 1
        : value * Factorial(value - 1);
}

int main(int argc, char* argv[])
{
    using namespace chrono;

    cout << "main thread: " << this_thread::get_id() << endl;

    auto taskFuture1 = async(Factorial, 3);
    cout << "Factorial result was " << taskFuture1.get() << endl;

    auto taskFuture2 = async(launch::async, Factorial, 3);
    cout << "Factorial result was " << taskFuture2.get() << endl;

    auto taskFuture3 = async(launch::deferred, Factorial, 3);
    cout << "Factorial result was " << taskFuture3.get() << endl;

    auto taskFuture4 = async(launch::async | launch::deferred, Factorial, 3);
    cout << "Factorial result was " << taskFuture4.get() << endl;

    return 0;
}
```

Listing 11-15 shows the different possible combinations of the async function and its overloaded version, which takes the launch enum as a parameter. The first call to async is the simplest: you call async and pass it a function and the parameters for that function. The async function returns a future that can be used to get the value returned from the function supplied to async. There is no guarantee, however, that the function will be called on another **thread**. All async guarantees is that the function will be called sometime between where you create the object and when you call get on the future.

The overloaded version of async gives you more control. Passing launch::async guarantees that the function will be called on another **thread** as soon as possible. This may not necessarily be a brand-new thread. The implementer of async is free to use any **thread** they choose. This may mean having a pool of **threads** that can be reused if they're available. The deferred option, on the other hand, tells the returned future to evaluate the supplied function when get is called. This isn't a concurrent process and causes the **thread** calling get to block, but again this is implementation specific and not the same across all C++ libraries. You have to check the documentation for your library or test your code by running and checking execution times and thread IDs.

The final call to async passes both async and deferred using an or. This is the same as calling async without specifying an execution policy and lets the implementation decide whether async or deferred should be used. Figure 11-9 shows the result of each call to async.

```
bruce@bruce-Virtual-Machine: ~/Projects/C-Recipes/Recipe11-5/Listing11-15
bruce@bruce-Virtual-Machine:~/Projects/C-Recipes/Recipe11-5/Listing11-15$ ./main

main thread: 140443965425536
Factorial result was ThreadTask thread: 140443965425536
ThreadTask thread: 140443965425536
ThreadTask thread: 140443965425536
6
Factorial result was ThreadTask thread: 140443948570368
ThreadTask thread: 140443948570368
ThreadTask thread: 140443948570368
6
Factorial result was ThreadTask thread: 140443965425536
ThreadTask thread: 140443965425536
ThreadTask thread: 140443965425536
6
Factorial result was ThreadTask thread: 140443965425536
ThreadTask thread: 140443965425536
ThreadTask thread: 140443965425536
6
bruce@bruce-Virtual-Machine:~/Projects/C-Recipes/Recipe11-5/Listing11-15$ ▌
```

Figure 11-9. *The thread IDs used when calling async*

As you can see, the library uses the main thread for every call except the one explicitly marked as async. Be sure to test your programs on all platforms and libraries in use to ensure that you're seeing the behavior you expect.

11-6. Synchronizing Queued Messages between Threads

Problem

You have a **thread** that you would like to live for the entire duration of your program and respond to messages it's sent.

Solution

You can use a combination of function, bind, condition_variable, mutex, and unique_lock to create a double-buffered message queue to transfer work from one **thread** to another.

How It Works

Many programs benefit from separating their display logic from their business logic (or, in video games, separating simulation from rendering) and running them on different CPU cores. Ultimately, these tasks can usually be carried out independently of each other as long as you can define a well-structured boundary between the systems and develop a method for transferring data from one **thread** to the other. One such approach is to create a double buffer of messages or commands. The business-logic **thread** can add commands to the queue while the display logic **thread** is reading commands from the queue. Double-buffering the queue allows you to reduce the number of sync points that exist between the threads in an effort to increase throughput on both. The producer **thread** carries out work and queues a lot of tasks into one side of the buffer while the consumer **thread** is busy working through the last set of tasks to be queued. The only time delays occur on either **thread** is when one is finished and waiting for the other. Listing 11-16 shows the class definition for a double-buffered message queue.

Listing 11-16. Creating a Double-Buffered Message Queue

```cpp
#include <future>
#include <iostream>

using namespace std;

template <typename T>
class MessageQueue
{
private:
    using Queue = vector < T > ;
    using QueueIterator = typename Queue::iterator;

    Queue m_A;
    Queue m_B;

    Queue* m_Producer{ &m_A };
    Queue* m_Consumer{ &m_B };

    QueueIterator m_ConsumerIterator{ m_B.end() };

    condition_variable& m_MessageCondition;
    condition_variable m_ConsumptionFinished;

    mutex m_MutexProducer;
    mutex m_MutexConsumer;

    unsigned int m_SwapCount{ 0 };

public:
    MessageQueue(condition_variable& messageCondition)
        : m_MessageCondition{ messageCondition }
    {

    }
```

```cpp
unsigned int GetCount() const
{
    return m_SwapCount;
}

void Add(T&& operation)
{
    unique_lock<mutex> lock{ m_MutexProducer };
    m_Producer->insert(m_Producer->end(), std::move(operation));
}

void BeginConsumption()
{
    m_MutexConsumer.lock();
}

T Consume()
{
    T operation;

    if (m_Consumer->size() > 0)
    {
        operation = *m_ConsumerIterator;
        m_ConsumerIterator = m_Consumer->erase(m_ConsumerIterator);
        assert(m_ConsumerIterator == m_Consumer->begin());
    }

    return operation;
}

void EndConsumption()
{
    assert(m_Consumer->size() == 0);
    m_MutexConsumer.unlock();
    m_ConsumptionFinished.notify_all();
}

unsigned int Swap()
{
    unique_lock<mutex> lockB{ m_MutexConsumer };
    m_ConsumptionFinished.wait(
        lockB,
        [this]()
        {
            return m_Consumer->size() == 0;
        }
    );

    unique_lock<mutex> lockA{ m_MutexProducer };

    Queue* temp{ m_Producer };
```

```
        m_Producer = m_Consumer;
        m_Consumer = temp;

        m_ConsumerIterator = m_Consumer->begin();

        m_MessageCondition.notify_all();

        return m_SwapCount++;
    }
};
```

The class template shown in Listing 11-16 is a functional message queue containing a double buffer for passing objects from one **thread** to another. It consists of two vectors, m_A and m_B, that are accessed through the pointers m_Producer and m_Consumer. The class, when used properly, allows for nonblocking access across the Add and Consume methods. If you were simply adding from one **thread** and consuming from another, you could buffer a lot of work without ever having to synchronize the **threads**. The only time the two **threads** require synchronization is when the producer **thread** would like to synchronize work into the consumer **thread**. This is handled in the Swap method. The Swap method uses the m_ConsumptionFinished condition_variable to wait for the m_Consumer queue to be empty. The condition_variable here is notified by the EndConsumption method. This implementation relies on the consumer **thread** exhausting the queued objects before informing the queue that it has finished. Not doing so would result in a deadlock.

The Add method works by taking an rvalue reference to an object to be moved to the other **thread**. An rvalue reference is used to ensure that the object being sent to the other thread is invalidated in the current **thread** after being moved to the queue. This helps to prevent data races where the producer **thread** could be left a valid reference to data being sent to another **thread**. Every object added goes at the end of the queue so that objects can be consumed in order by the consumer. The Consume method pulls objects from the beginning of the queue using a copy operation and then removes the original object from the queue. The Swap method simply switches the m_Producer and m_Consumer pointers; it does this under the protection of both **mutexes** and therefore can be confident that the switch is occurring when all producer and consumer **threads** should be able to handle it. Swap also sets m_ConsumerIterator to the correct queue and issues a notify to all **threads** waiting for the swap operation to be complete.

To show this queue in action, the example in Listing 11-17 uses an object to maintain a running total of some arithmetic operations. The main function acts as a producer that adds operations to be completed to the queue, and a **thread** is created that receives these operations and carries them out.

Listing 11-17. A Working MessageQueue Example

```
#include <cassert>
#include <future>
#include <iostream>
#include <vector>

using namespace std;

class RunningTotal
{
private:
    int m_Value{ 0 };
    bool m_Finished{ false };
```

```cpp
public:
    RunningTotal& operator+=(int value)
    {
        m_Value += value;
        return *this;
    }

    RunningTotal& operator-=(int value)
    {
        m_Value -= value;
        return *this;
    }

    RunningTotal& Finish()
    {
        m_Finished = true;
        return *this;
    }

    int operator *() const throw(int)
    {
        if (!m_Finished)
        {
            throw m_Value;
        }
        return m_Value;
    }
};

template <typename T>
class MessageQueue
{
private:
    using Queue = vector < T > ;
    using QueueIterator = typename Queue::iterator;

    Queue m_A;
    Queue m_B;

    Queue* m_Producer{ &m_A };
    Queue* m_Consumer{ &m_B };

    QueueIterator m_ConsumerIterator{ m_B.end() };

    condition_variable& m_MessageCondition;
    condition_variable m_ConsumptionFinished;

    mutex m_MutexProducer;
    mutex m_MutexConsumer;
```

```
        unsigned int m_SwapCount{ 0 };

public:
    MessageQueue(condition_variable& messageCondition)
        : m_MessageCondition{ messageCondition }
    {

    }

    unsigned int GetCount() const
    {
        return m_SwapCount;
    }

    void Add(T&& operation)
    {
        unique_lock<mutex> lock{ m_MutexProducer };
        m_Producer->insert(m_Producer->end(), std::move(operation));
    }

    void BeginConsumption()
    {
        m_MutexConsumer.lock();
    }

    T Consume()
    {
        T operation;

        if (m_Consumer->size() > 0)
        {
            operation = *m_ConsumerIterator;
            m_ConsumerIterator = m_Consumer->erase(m_ConsumerIterator);
            assert(m_ConsumerIterator == m_Consumer->begin());
        }

        return operation;
    }

    void EndConsumption()
    {
        assert(m_Consumer->size() == 0);
        m_MutexConsumer.unlock();
        m_ConsumptionFinished.notify_all();
    }

    unsigned int Swap()
    {
        unique_lock<mutex> lockB{ m_MutexConsumer };
        m_ConsumptionFinished.wait(
            lockB,
```

```
            [this]()
            {
                return m_Consumer->size() == 0;
            }
        );

        unique_lock<mutex> lockA{ m_MutexProducer };

        Queue* temp{ m_Producer };
        m_Producer = m_Consumer;
        m_Consumer = temp;

        m_ConsumerIterator = m_Consumer->begin();

        m_MessageCondition.notify_all();

        return m_SwapCount++;
    }
};

using RunningTotalOperation = function < RunningTotal&() > ;
using RunningTotalMessageQueue = MessageQueue < RunningTotalOperation > ;

int Task(reference_wrapper<mutex> messageQueueMutex,
        reference_wrapper<condition_variable> messageCondition,
        reference_wrapper<RunningTotalMessageQueue> messageQueueRef)
{
    int result{ 0 };

    RunningTotalMessageQueue& messageQueue = messageQueueRef.get();
    unsigned int currentSwapCount{ 0 };

    bool finished{ false };
    while (!finished)
    {
        unique_lock<mutex> lock{ messageQueueMutex.get() };
        messageCondition.get().wait(
            lock,
            [&messageQueue, &currentSwapCount]()
            {
                return currentSwapCount != messageQueue.GetCount();
            }
        );

        messageQueue.BeginConsumption();
        currentSwapCount = messageQueue.GetCount();

        while (RunningTotalOperation operation{ messageQueue.Consume() })
        {
            RunningTotal& runningTotal = operation();
```

```
            try
            {
                result = *runningTotal;
                finished = true;
                break;
            }
            catch (int param)
            {
                // nothing to do, not finished yet!
                cout << "Total not yet finished, current is: " << param << endl;
            }
        }
        messageQueue.EndConsumption();
    }

    return result;
}

int main(int argc, char* argv[])
{
    RunningTotal runningTotal;

    mutex messageQueueMutex;
    condition_variable messageQueueCondition;
    RunningTotalMessageQueue messageQueue(messageQueueCondition);

    auto myFuture = async(launch::async,
        Task,
        ref(messageQueueMutex),
        ref(messageQueueCondition),
        ref(messageQueue));

    messageQueue.Add(bind(&RunningTotal::operator+=, &runningTotal, 3));
    messageQueue.Swap();

    messageQueue.Add(bind(&RunningTotal::operator-=, &runningTotal, 100));
    messageQueue.Add(bind(&RunningTotal::operator+=, &runningTotal, 100000));
    messageQueue.Add(bind(&RunningTotal::operator-=, &runningTotal, 256));
    messageQueue.Swap();

    messageQueue.Add(bind(&RunningTotal::operator-=, &runningTotal, 100));
    messageQueue.Add(bind(&RunningTotal::operator+=, &runningTotal, 100000));
    messageQueue.Add(bind(&RunningTotal::operator-=, &runningTotal, 256));
    messageQueue.Swap();

    messageQueue.Add(bind(&RunningTotal::Finish, &runningTotal));
    messageQueue.Swap();

    cout << "The final total is: " << myFuture.get() << endl;

    return 0;
}
```

This code represents a complex use of many modern C++ language features. Let's break the source into smaller examples to show how individual tasks are executed on a long-running helper thread. Listing 11-18 covers the RunningTotal class.

Listing 11-18. The RunningTotal Class

```
class RunningTotal
{
private:
    int m_Value{ 0 };
    bool m_Finished{ false };

public:
    RunningTotal& operator+=(int value)
    {
        m_Value += value;
        return *this;
    }

    RunningTotal& operator-=(int value)
    {
        m_Value -= value;
        return *this;
    }

    RunningTotal& Finish()
    {
        m_Finished = true;
        return *this;
    }

    int operator *() const throw(int)
    {
        if (!m_Finished)
        {
            throw m_Value;
        }
        return m_Value;
    }
};
```

The RunningTotal class in Listing 11-18 is a simple object that represents a long-running store of data. In a proper program, this class could be an interface to a web server, database, or rendering engine that exposes methods to update its state. For the purposes of this example, the class simply wraps an int that keeps track of the results of the operations and a bool that determines when the calculations are complete. These values are manipulated using an overridden += operator, -= operator, and * operator. There is also a Finished method that sets the m_Finished Boolean to true.

The main function is responsible for instantiating the RunningTotal object as well as the message queue and the consumer **thread**. It can be seen in Listing 11-19.

Listing 11-19. The main Function

```
#include <future>
#include <iostream>

using namespace std;

using RunningTotalOperation = function < RunningTotal&() >;
using RunningTotalMessageQueue = MessageQueue < RunningTotalOperation > ;

int main(int argc, char* argv[])
{
    RunningTotal runningTotal;

    mutex messageQueueMutex;
    condition_variable messageQueueCondition;
    RunningTotalMessageQueue messageQueue(messageQueueCondition);

    auto myFuture = async(launch::async,
        Task,
        ref(messageQueueMutex),
        ref(messageQueueCondition),
        ref(messageQueue));

    messageQueue.Add(bind(&RunningTotal::operator+=, &runningTotal, 3));
    messageQueue.Swap();

    messageQueue.Add(bind(&RunningTotal::operator-=, &runningTotal, 100));
    messageQueue.Add(bind(&RunningTotal::operator+=, &runningTotal, 100000));
    messageQueue.Add(bind(&RunningTotal::operator-=, &runningTotal, 256));
    messageQueue.Swap();

    messageQueue.Add(bind(&RunningTotal::operator-=, &runningTotal, 100));
    messageQueue.Add(bind(&RunningTotal::operator+=, &runningTotal, 100000));
    messageQueue.Add(bind(&RunningTotal::operator-=, &runningTotal, 256));
    messageQueue.Swap();

    messageQueue.Add(bind(&RunningTotal::Finish, &runningTotal));
    messageQueue.Swap();

    cout << "The final total is: " << myFuture.get() << endl;

    return 0;
}
```

The first piece of important code in Listing 11-19 is the type aliases before main. These are used to create types that represent the message queue you'll be using and the type of objects the message queue contains. In this case, I have created a type that you ca n use to carry out operations on the RunningTotal class. This type alias is created using the C++ function object, which allows you to create a representation of a function to be called later. This type requires that you specify the signature type of the function in the template—and you may be surprised to see that the signature is described without parameters. This means the functors stored in the queue won't have parameters passed to them directly. This would normally cause issues for operations such as += and -= that need parameters; but the bind function comes to the rescue. You can see several uses of bind in the main function. All of these examples of bind are used to bind a method pointer to a method instance of that type. The second parameter passed to bind when using a method pointer should always be the instance of the object on which the method will be called. Any subsequent parameters are automatically passed to the function when the functor is executed. This automatic passing of bound parameters is why you don't need to specify any parameter types in the type alias and why you can use a single queue to represent functions that have different signatures.

main creates a thread using the async function and queues several operations to be carried out on the **thread** along with multiple swaps. The last piece of the example is the Task function, which is executed on the second **thread;** see Listing 11-20.

Listing 11-20. The Task Function

```cpp
#include <future>
#include <iostream>

using namespace std;

int Task(reference_wrapper<mutex> messageQueueMutex,
        reference_wrapper<condition_variable> messageCondition,
        reference_wrapper<RunningTotalMessageQueue> messageQueueRef)
{
    int result{ 0 };

    RunningTotalMessageQueue& messageQueue = messageQueueRef.get();
    unsigned int currentSwapCount{ 0 };

    bool finished{ false };
    while (!finished)
    {
        unique_lock<mutex> lock{ messageQueueMutex.get() };
        messageCondition.get().wait(
            lock,
            [&messageQueue, &currentSwapCount]()
            {
                return currentSwapCount != messageQueue.GetCount();
            }
        );

        messageQueue.BeginConsumption();
        currentSwapCount = messageQueue.GetCount();

        while (RunningTotalOperation operation{ messageQueue.Consume() })
        {
            RunningTotal& runningTotal = operation();

            try
            {
                result = *runningTotal;
                finished = true;
                break;
            }
```

```
        catch (int param)
        {
            // nothing to do, not finished yet!
            cout << "Total not yet finished, current is: " << param << endl;
        }
    }
    messageQueue.EndConsumption();
}

    return result;
}
```

The Task function loops until the finished bool has been set to true. It waits for the messageCondition condition_variable to be signaled before continuing work, and it uses the lambda to ensure that a swap has actually occurred in case the **thread** was awakened by the operating system rather than by a notify call.

Once the **thread** has been kicked and there is work to be carried out, it calls the BeginConsumption method on the queue. This has the effect of locking the queue's Swap method until all the current jobs in the **thread** have been completed. The currentSwapCount variable is updated to ensure that the condition_variable can guarantee safety the next time the loop is entered. A second while loop is responsible for pulling each of the functors from the queue until the queue is empty. This is where the bound function objects created by main are executed. The **thread** itself doesn't know the substance of the work it's carrying out; it simply responds to the requests that have been queued in the main function.

The * operator is used after every operation to test whether the Finished command has been sent. The RunningTotal::operator* method will throw an **int** exception containing the current value stored if the Finished method hasn't been called. You can see how this is used in the Task function with the try... catch block. The result variable, finished bool, and break statements are executed only in the event that the operator* returns a value rather than throwing the value. The current total is printed to the console each time an operation completes that doesn't mark the operations as finished. You can see the result of this code in Figure 11-10.

```
bruce@bruce-Virtual-Machine: ~/Projects/C-Recipes/Recipe11-6/Listing11-17
bruce@bruce-Virtual-Machine:~/Projects/C-Recipes/Recipe11-6/Listing11-17$ ./main
Total not yet finished, current is: 3
Total not yet finished, current is: -97
Total not yet finished, current is: 99903
Total not yet finished, current is: 99647
Total not yet finished, current is: 99547
Total not yet finished, current is: 199547
Total not yet finished, current is: 199291
The final total is: 199291
bruce@bruce-Virtual-Machine:~/Projects/C-Recipes/Recipe11-6/Listing11-17$
```

Figure 11-10. The output showing a working message queue in actions

CHAPTER 12

■ ■ ■

Networking

Communicating over the Internet is becoming an increasingly integral part of many modern computer programs. It's hard to find any programs that don't connect to another instance of the same program or to a web server that provides essential functionality to some part of the program or an app. This creates opportunities for developers to specialize in the field of network programming. You can take several different approaches when writing connected programs, and using a high-level library is a valid technique; however, this chapter looks at the Berkeley Sockets library that can be used on OS X, Linux, and Windows.

Berkeley Sockets first appeared in 1983 in the Unix operating system. That OS became unencumbered by copyright issues in the late 1980s, allowing the Berkeley Sockets API to become the standard implementation used on most OSs today. Even though Windows doesn't support Berkeley directly, its network API is almost entirely the same as the Berkeley standard API.

This chapter covers how to create and use sockets to produce programs that can communicate with each other over a network such as the Internet. Recipes 14-1, 14-2, and 14-3 cover the same material for each of the major OSs in use today. You should read the Recipe relevant to the system you're using for development then move on to Recipe 12-4.

12-1. Setting Up a Berkeley Sockets Application on OS X

Problem

You would like to create a network socket program that can be used on OS X.

Solution

OS X supplies the Berkeley Sockets API as part of the OS and can be used without having to resort to external libraries.

How It Works

Apple provides the Xcode IDE, which you can use to build OS X applications from an Apple computer. Xcode is freely available from the App Store. Once installed, you can use Xcode to create programs to be run on computers of your choosing. This recipe creates a command-line program that connects to the Internet and opens a socket to a server.

To begin, you have to create a valid project for your application. Open Xcode, and select the Create a New Xcode Project option shown in Figure 12-1.

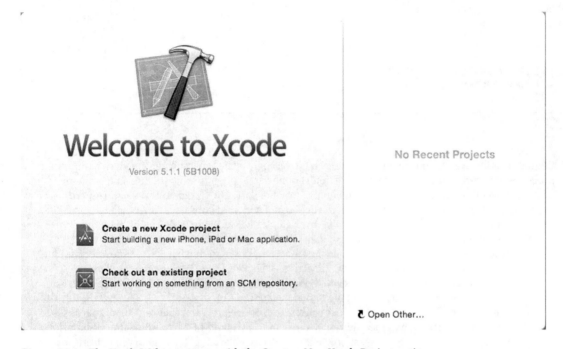

Figure 12-1. *The Xcode Welcome screen with the Create a New Xcode Project option*

You're asked to select the type of application you wish to create. Select the Command Line Tool option under the OS X Application category; Figure 12-2 shows this window.

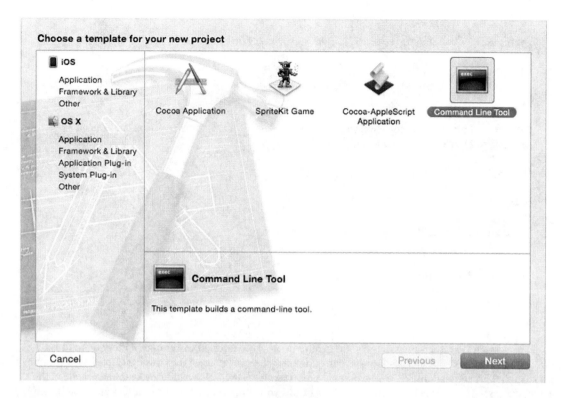

Figure 12-2. *The OS X Application Command Line Tool option*

Next, you're asked to nominate a folder in which to store your projects files. After you do, the main Xcode window opens, and you can select your source files from the Project View on the left. Replace the code in the new CPP file with the code from Listing 12-1 to create an application that opens a socket to the Google HTTP web server.

Listing 12-1. Opening a Berkeley Socket

```cpp
#include <iostream>
#include <netdb.h>
#include <sys/types.h>
#include <sys/socket.h>

using SOCKET = int;

using namespace std;

int main(int argc, const char * argv[])
{
    addrinfo hints{};
    hints.ai_family = AF_UNSPEC;
    hints.ai_socktype = SOCK_STREAM;
```

```cpp
    addrinfo *servinfo{};
    getaddrinfo("www.google.com", "80", &hints, &servinfo);

    SOCKET sockfd{
        socket(servinfo->ai_family, servinfo->ai_socktype, servinfo->ai_protocol)
    };

    int connectionResult{ connect(sockfd, servinfo->ai_addr, servinfo->ai_addrlen) };
    if (connectionResult == -1)
    {
        cout << "Connection failed!" << endl;
    }
    else
    {
        cout << "Connection successful!" << endl;
    }

    freeaddrinfo(servinfo);

    return 0;
}
```

The code in Listing 12-1 requires a short primer on how the Internet works in order for you to fully understand what is happening. Before you can connect to a server, you need to know the address at which it's located. This is best found using the domain name service (DNS). DNS works by keeping a cache of the server addresses for a given host name. In this example, you're asking DNS for the address associated with www.google.com. If you're creating a program to run on your own network, you can specify the IP addresses of the servers manually, but this usually isn't possible for programs that access information using the Internet. Servers can be moved, and IP addresses can be changed or reused for different systems at different times. The getaddrinfo function asks DNS for the address associated with www.google.com on port 80.

Server addresses for specific services usually consist of two parts: the IP address of the computer to connect to and the port of the specific service on that server that you wish to communicate with. The World Wide Web communicates using the HTTP protocol, which is commonly configured to serve data using port 80. You can see in Listing 12-1 that this is the port with which you try to establish a connection on the remote computer.

The getaddrinfo function takes the web address, the port, and two addrinfo structs as parameters. These first of these structs provides the DNS service with some hints as to the type of connection you want to establish with the remote computer. The two most important at this point are the ai_family and ai_socktype fields.

The ai_family field specifies the type of address you would like to retrieve for your program. This allows you to specify whether you want an IPv4, IPv6, NetBIOS, Infrared, or Bluetooth address. The option supplied in Listing 12-1 is unspecified, which allows the getaddrinfo function to return all the valid IP addresses for the requested web address. These valid IP addresses are represented by the same addrinfo struct and are passed back to the program through the pointer supplied to getaddrinfo's fourth parameter.

The ai_socktype field lets you specify the type of transmission mechanism to be used with the socket in question. The SOCK_STREAM option in Listing 12-1 creates a socket that uses TCP/IP as the transport mechanism. This type of socket allows you to send packets of information that are guaranteed to arrive in order at the destination. The only other type of transmission mechanism used in this chapter is the SOCK_DGRAM type. This transport mechanism doesn't guarantee that packets will arrive or that they will arrive in the order expected; however, they don't have the same overheads that come with the TCP/IP mechanism and therefore can result in packets being sent with much lower latency between computers.

The `servinfo` returned by the `getaddrinfo` function can be used to create a socket. A socket file descriptor is obtained from the `socket` function, which is passed the info from the `servinfo` structure. The `servinfo` structure could be a linked list in this instance, because Google supports both the IPv4 and IPv6 address formats. You could write code here that chooses the address to use and acts appropriately. The `ai_next` field stores a pointer to the next element in the list for as long as the list has more elements. The `ai_family`, `ai_socktype`, and `ai_protocol` variables are all passed into the `socket` function to create a valid socket to use. You can call the `connect` function once you have a valid socket. The `connect` function takes the socket ID, the `ai_addr` field from the `servinfo` object containing the address, and `ai_addrlen` to determine the length of the address. If the connection wasn't obtained successfully, you receive a return value of -1 from `connect`. Listing 12-1 demonstrates this by printing whether the connection was successful.

12-2. Setting Up a Berkeley Sockets Application in Eclipse on Ubuntu

Problem

You would like to create a network socket program that can be used on Ubuntu using Eclipse.

Solution

Ubuntu supplies the Berkeley Sockets API as part of the OS and can be used without having to resort to external libraries.

How It Works

The Eclipse IDE can be used to build applications on a computer running Linux. Eclipse is freely available from the Ubuntu Software Center. Once installed, you can use Eclipse to create programs to be run on computers of your choosing. This recipe creates a command-line program that connects to the Internet and opens a socket to a server.

To begin, you have to create a valid project for your application. Open Eclipse, and select the Project ➤ New option from the menu bar. The New Project Wizard opens, as shown in Figure 12-3.

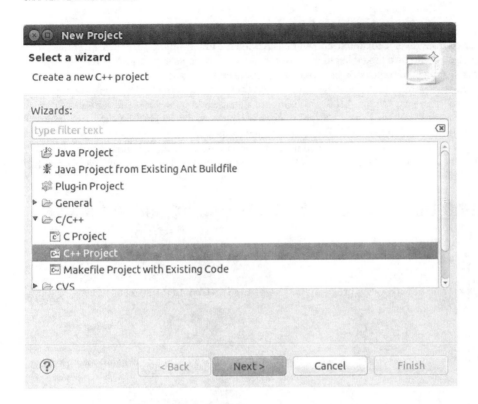

Figure 12-3. *The Eclipse New Project Wizard*

The New Project Wizard allows you to select C++ Project as an option. Then, click Next, and you're presented with the C++ Project settings window shown in Figure 12-4.

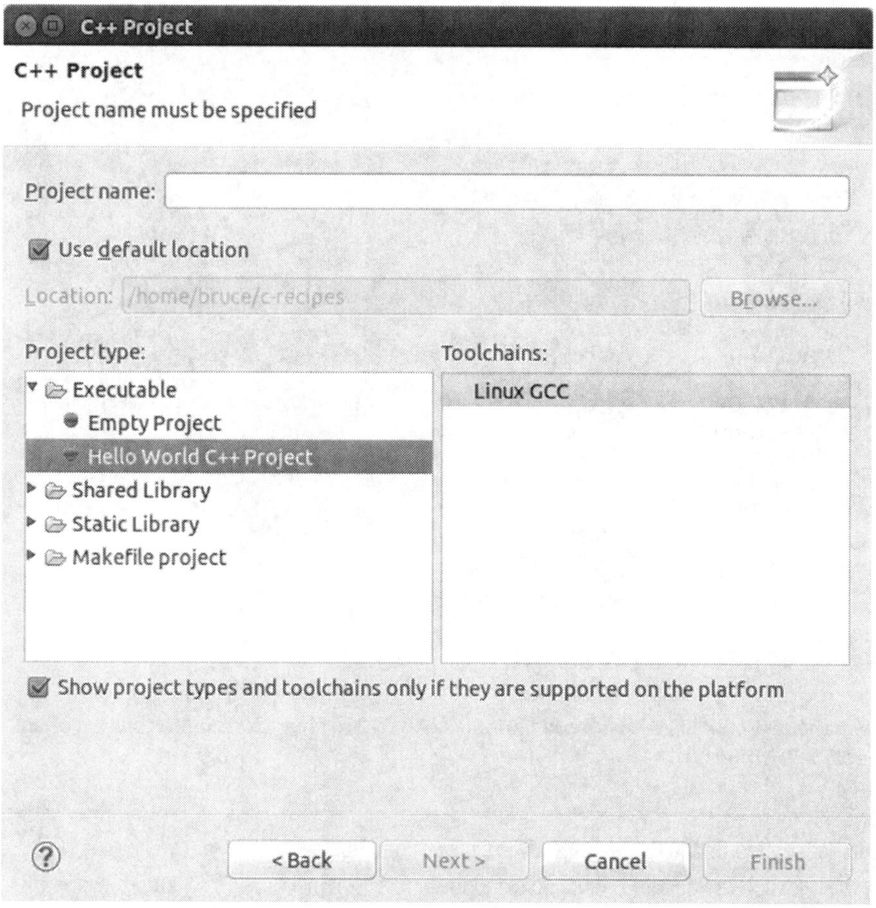

Figure 12-4. *The Eclipse C++ Project settings window*

In this window, you can name your project and decide which folder it should be created in. Under Project Type, select Executable ➤ Hello World C++ Project. Doing so creates a project that's configured to be built as an executable and that contains a source file for adding your own code.

The sample code in this chapter uses features from the C++11 language specification. A default Eclipse project doesn't have this enabled. You can turn it on by right-clicking your project and selecting Properties. You should see the Settings window shown in Figure 12-5, with categories on the left side. To enable C++11 support, select Settings under C/C++ Build, adding –std=c++11 to the All Options field, and click OK.

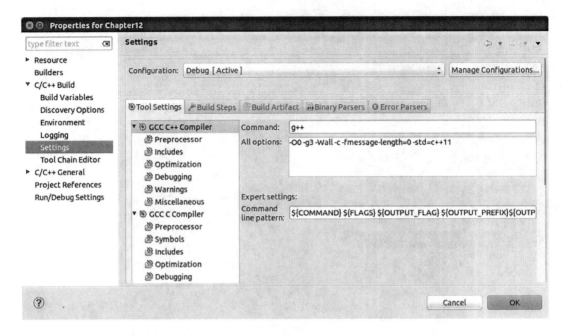

Figure 12-5. *Adding C++11 support to your Eclipse project*

Replace the code in the new CPP file with the code from Listing 12-2 to create an application that opens a socket to the Google HTTP web server.

■ **Note**   The code and description that follow are exactly the same as in Recipe 12-1. If you've already read this material, you may wish to skip to Recipe 12-4. If you skipped Recipe 12-1 because OS X isn't relevant to you, then read on.

Listing 12-2. Opening a Berkeley Socket

```
#include <iostream>
#include <netdb.h>
#include <sys/types.h>
#include <sys/socket.h>

using SOCKET = int;

using namespace std;

int main(int argc, const char * argv[])
{
    addrinfo hints{};
    hints.ai_family = AF_UNSPEC;
    hints.ai_socktype = SOCK_STREAM;
```

```
addrinfo *servinfo{};
getaddrinfo("www.google.com", "80", &hints, &servinfo);

SOCKET sockfd{
    socket(servinfo->ai_family, servinfo->ai_socktype, servinfo->ai_protocol)
};

int connectionResult{ connect(sockfd, servinfo->ai_addr, servinfo->ai_addrlen) };
if (connectionResult == -1)
{
    cout << "Connection failed!" << endl;
}
else
{
    cout << "Connection successful!" << endl;
}

freeaddrinfo(servinfo);

return 0;
}
```

The code in Listing 12-2 requires a short primer on how the Internet works in order for you to fully understand what is happening. Before you can connect to a server, you need to know the address at which it's located. This is best found using the domain name service (DNS). DNS works by keeping a cache of the server addresses for a given host name. In this example, you're asking DNS for the address associated with www.google.com. If you're creating a program to run on your own network, you can specify the IP addresses of the servers manually, but this usually isn't possible for programs that access information using the Internet. Servers can be moved, and IP addresses can be changed or reused for different systems at different times. The getaddrinfo function asks DNS for the address associated with www.google.com on port 80.

Server addresses for specific services usually consist of two parts: the IP address of the computer to connect to and the port of the specific service on that server that you wish to communicate with. The World Wide Web communicates using the HTTP protocol, which is commonly configured to serve data using port 80. You can see in Listing 12-2 that this is the port with which you try to establish a connection on the remote computer.

The getaddrinfo function takes the web address, the port, and two addrinfo structs as parameters. These first of these structs provides the DNS service with some hints as to the type of connection you want to establish with the remote computer. The two most important at this point are the ai_family and ai_socktype fields.

The ai_family field specifies the type of address you would like to retrieve for your program. This allows you to specify whether you want an IPv4, IPv6, NetBIOS, Infrared, or Bluetooth address. The option supplied in Listing 12-2 is unspecified, which allows the getaddrinfo function to return all the valid IP addresses for the requested web address. These valid IP addresses are represented by the same addrinfo struct and are passed back to the program through the pointer supplied to getaddrinfo's fourth parameter.

The ai_socktype field lets you specify the type of transmission mechanism to be used with the socket in question. The SOCK_STREAM option in Listing 12-2 creates a socket that uses TCP/IP as the transport mechanism. This type of socket allows you to send packets of information that are guaranteed to arrive in order at the destination. The only other type of transmission mechanism used in this chapter is the SOCK_DGRAM type. This transport mechanism doesn't guarantee that packets will arrive or that they will arrive in the order expected; however, they don't have the same overheads that come with the TCP/IP mechanism and therefore can result in packets being sent with much lower latency between computers.

The servinfo returned by the getaddrinfo function can be used to create a socket. A socket file descriptor is obtained from the socket function, which is passed the info from the servinfo structure. The servinfo structure could be a linked list in this instance, because Google supports both the IPv4 and IPv6 address formats. You could write code here that chooses the address to use and acts appropriately. The ai_next field stores a pointer to the next element in the list for as long as the list has more elements. The ai_family, ai_socktype, and ai_protocol variables are all passed into the socket function to create a valid socket to use. You can call the connect function once you have a valid socket. The connect function takes the socket ID, the ai_addr field from the servinfo object containing the address, and ai_addrlen to determine the length of the address. If the connection wasn't obtained successfully, you receive a return value of -1 from connect. Listing 12-2 demonstrates this by printing whether the connection was successful.

12-3. Setting Up a Winsock 2 Application in Visual Studio on Windows

Problem

You would like to create a network socket program that can be used on Windows machines.

Solution

Microsoft supplies the Winsock library, which enable socket-based communication between computers.

How It Works

The Windows OS doesn't come with a native Berkeley Sockets implementation like OS X or Ubuntu. Instead, Microsoft supplies the Winsock library. This library is fortunately very similar to the Berkeley Sockets library, to the extent that most of the code is interchangeable between the three platforms. You can create a new C++ application that uses Winsock by opening Visual Studio and selecting the File ➤ New ➤ Project option. Doing so opens the New Project Wizard shown in Figure 12-6.

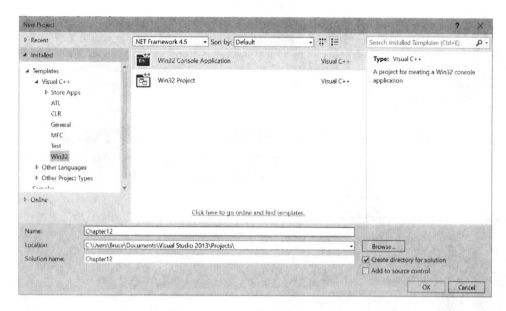

Figure 12-6. *The Visual Studio New Project Wizard*

You want to create a Win32 Console Application to run the sample code from this chapter. Select this type of application, enter a name, and choose a folder in which to store the data; then click OK.

You're taken to the Win32 Application Wizard. Click Next to go to the dialog shown in Figure 12-7.

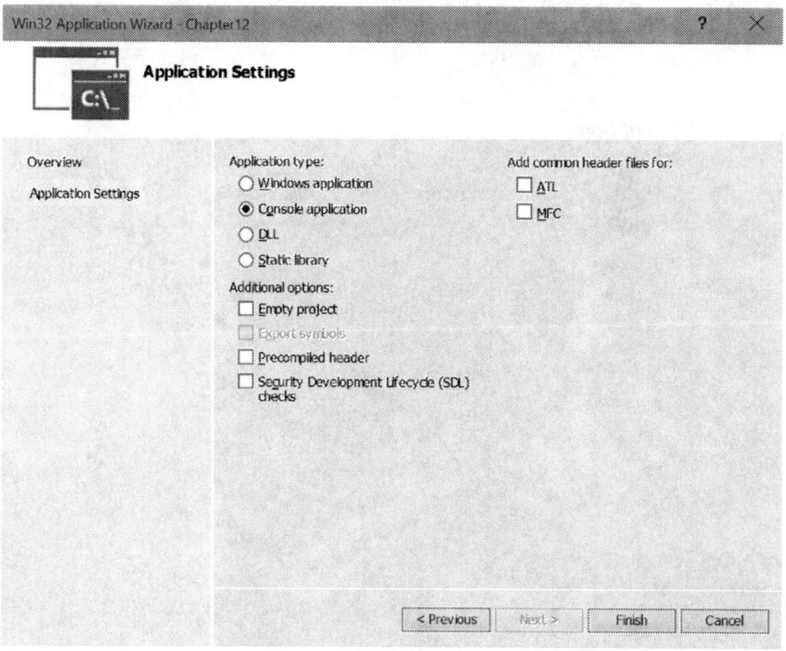

Figure 12-7. *The Win32 Application Wizard*

Deselect the Precompiled Header and Security Development Lifecycle (SDL) Checks options, and click Finish. When you do, you're presented with a working project. The project doesn't support sockets, though, because Windows requires that you link against a library to provide socket support. You can do this by right-clicking the project from the Solution Explorer window and selecting Properties. Specify the libraries to be linked against in the Configuration Properties ➤ Linker ➤ Input section. Figure 12-8 shows this window with specific option selected.

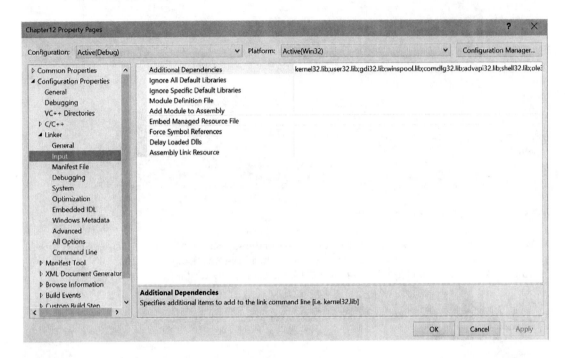

Figure 12-8. *The Visual Studio linker input options*

You want to add a new library to the Additional Dependencies section. Select this option, and click the down arrow to open the dialog shown in Figure 12-9.

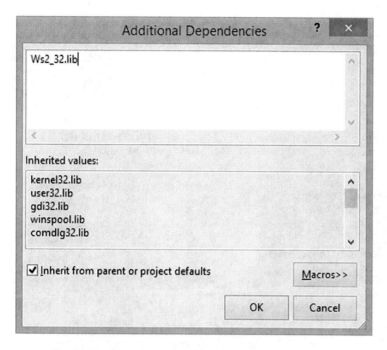

Figure 12-9. *The Additional Dependencies dialog*

The Winsock API is provided by the `Ws2_32.lib` static library. Enter this value in the text box, and click OK. This allows you to use the Winsock 2 API in your program without issue.

Replace the code in the new CPP file with the code from Listing 12-3 to create an application that opens a socket to the Google HTTP web server.

■ **Note** The code and description that follow are mostly the same as in Recipe 12-1. However, some parts are unique to Windows. If you've already read this material, you may wish to cover the Windows-unique aspects and then skip to Recipe 12-4. If you skipped Recipe 12-1 and Recipe 12-2, read on.

Listing 12-3. Opening a Winsock Socket

```
#include <iostream>
#include <winsock2.h>
#include <WS2tcpip.h>

using namespace std;

int main(int argc, char* argv[])
{
    WSADATA wsaData;
    if (WSAStartup(MAKEWORD(2, 2), &wsaData) != 0)
    {
        return 1;
    }
```

```
addrinfo hints{};
hints.ai_family = AF_UNSPEC;      // don't care IPv4 or IPv6
hints.ai_socktype = SOCK_STREAM; // TCP stream sockets

// get ready to connect
addrinfo* servinfo{};  // will point to the results
getaddrinfo("www.google.com", "80", &hints, &servinfo);

SOCKET sockfd{ socket(servinfo->ai_family, servinfo->ai_socktype, servinfo->ai_protocol) };
int connectionResult{ connect(sockfd, servinfo->ai_addr, servinfo->ai_addrlen) };
if (connectionResult == -1)
{
    cout << "Connection failed!" << endl;
}
else
{
    cout << "Connection successful!" << endl;
}

freeaddrinfo(servinfo);

WSACleanup();

return 0;
}
```

The code sections in bold in Listing 12-3 are unique to the Windows socket library and aren't transferable to the Unix and OS X implementations of Berkeley Sockets. Windows requires that your program start and shut down the Winsock library. This is achieved using the WSAStartup and WSACleanup functions. Another subtle difference is that the Winsock API specifies the SOCKET type to be an unsigned int. The Berkeley implementations found in OS X and Ubuntu both return a standard int from the socket function. The code in Listing 12-1 and Listing 12-2 uses a type alias to specify the SOCKET type to make the code appear more portable; however, the types still differ between the platforms.

This code requires a short primer on how the Internet works in order for you to fully understand what is happening. Before you can connect to a server, you need to know the address at which it's located. This is best found using the domain name service (DNS). DNS works by keeping a cache of the server addresses for a given host name. In this example, you're asking DNS for the address associated with www.google.com. If you're creating a program to run on your own network, you can specify the IP addresses of the servers manually, but this usually isn't possible for programs that access information using the Internet. Servers can be moved, and IP addresses can be changed or reused for different systems at different times. The getaddrinfo function asks DNS for the address associated with www.google.com on port 80.

Server addresses for specific services usually consist of two parts: the IP address of the computer to connect to and the port of the specific service on that server that you wish to communicate with. The World Wide Web communicates using the HTTP protocol, which is commonly configured to serve data using port 80. You can see in Listing 12-3 that this is the port with which you try to establish a connection on the remote computer.

The getaddrinfo function takes the web address, the port, and two addrinfo structs as parameters. These first of these structs provides the DNS service with some hints as to the type of connection you want to establish with the remote computer. The two most important at this point are the ai_family and ai_socktype fields.

The ai_family field specifies the type of address you would like to retrieve for your program. This allows you to specify whether you want an IPv4, IPv6, NetBIOS, Infrared, or Bluetooth address. The option supplied in Listing 12-3 is unspecified, which allows the getaddrinfo function to return all the valid IP addresses for the requested web address. These valid IP addresses are represented by the same addrinfo struct and are passed back to the program through the pointer supplied to getaddrinfo's fourth parameter.

The ai_socktype field lets you specify the type of transmission mechanism to be used with the socket in question. The SOCK_STREAM option in Listing 12-3 creates a socket that uses TCP/IP as the transport mechanism. This type of socket allows you to send packets of information that are guaranteed to arrive in order at the destination. The only other type of transmission mechanism used in this chapter is the SOCK_DGRAM type. This transport mechanism doesn't guarantee that packets will arrive or that they will arrive in the order expected; however, they don't have the same overheads that come with the TCP/IP mechanism and therefore can result in packets being sent with much lower latency between computers.

The servinfo returned by the getaddrinfo function can be used to create a socket. A socket file descriptor is obtained from the socket function, which is passed the info from the servinfo structure. The servinfo structure could be a linked list in this instance, because Google supports both the IPv4 and IPv6 address formats. You could write code here that chooses the address to use and acts appropriately. The ai_next field stores a pointer to the next element in the list for as long as the list has more elements. The ai_family, ai_socktype, and ai_protocol variables are all passed into the socket function to create a valid socket to use. You can call the connect function once you have a valid socket. The connect function takes the socket ID, the ai_addr field from the servinfo object containing the address, and ai_addrlen to determine the length of the address. If the connection wasn't obtained successfully, you receive a return value of -1 from connect. Listing 12-3 demonstrates this by printing whether the connection was successful.

12-4. Creating a Socket Connection between Two Programs

Problem

You would like to write a network client program and a server program that can communicate across a network.

Solution

You can use the Berkeley Sockets API to send and receive data across a socket.

How It Works

Berkeley sockets are designed to send and receive information across a network. The API provides send and recv functions to achieve this goal. The difficulty in getting this to work is that you have to ensure that your sockets are configured properly for data transfer. The operations required to receive data are very different than the operations required to send data when setting up your sockets. This recipe also creates code that can run on multiple platforms and compiles using Microsoft Visual Studio, using Xcode, or on a Linux machine using Clang as the compiler.

■ **Note** The Socket class won't compile when using GCC because that compiler doesn't yet support move constructors for the stringstream class. You can alter the sample code to prevent the need to call move with stringstream if you're using GCC.

The first class to look at starts and stops Winsock when the program is built to run on Windows machines. This class shouldn't have any effect when you're building and running on OS X or Linux computers. Listing 12-4 shows how this can be achieved.

Listing 12-4. Wrapping Winsock

```
#include <iostream>

using namespace std;

#ifdef _MSC_VER

#pragma comment(lib, "Ws2_32.lib")

#include <WinSock2.h>
#include <WS2tcpip.h>

#define UsingWinsock 1

using ssize_t = SSIZE_T;

#else

#define UsingWinsock 0

#endif

class WinsockWrapper
{
public:
    WinsockWrapper()
    {
#if UsingWinsock
        WSADATA wsaData;
        if (WSAStartup(MAKEWORD(2, 2), &wsaData) != 0)
        {
            exit(1);
        }

#ifndef NDEBUG
        cout << "Winsock started!" << endl;
#endif
#endif
    }

    ~WinsockWrapper()
    {
#if UsingWinsock
        WSACleanup();
```

```
#ifndef NDEBUG
        cout << "Winsock shut down!" << endl;
#endif
#endif
    }
};

int main(int argc, char* argv[])
{
    WinsockWrapper myWinsockWrapper;

    return 0;
}
```

The code in Listing 12-4 detects the presence of Microsoft Visual Studio using the preprocessor. Visual Studio defines the symbol **_MSC_VER** when building. You can use this when building a Windows program with Visual Studio to include Windows-specific files as I have done here. The Winsock 2 library is included using a pragma in this program only when Visual Studio is being used to build; the necessary Winsock header files are also included. A define is set up that's used specifically for this program. When the code is building in Visual Studio, the UsingWinsock macro is defined as 1; when the code isn't building using Visual Studio, it's set to 0. Windows builds also require that you create a type alias to map SSIZE_T to ssize_t, because this type uses the lowercase spelling when not building on Windows computers.

The WinsockWrapper class detects the value of UsingWinsock in its constructor and destructor. If this value is 1, then the functions to start and stop the Winsock API are compiled in. This code isn't compiled in when not building with Visual Studio; therefore it's safe to include in this manner.

The main function creates a WinsockWrapper object on its first line. This causes the constructor to be called and Winsock to be initialized on Windows machines; it has no effect on non-Windows builds. The Winsock API is also shut down when this object goes out of scope, because the destructor is called. You now have a convenient method for starting and stopping Winsock in a manner that is portable across multiple platforms.

The Socket class is integral to communicating from one program to another. It's responsible for providing an object-oriented wrapper for the C-based Berkeley Sockets API. The socket itself is represented by a descriptor that is essentially an int. A method creates a class that associates the data needed for creating Berkeley sockets with the code necessary to work with sockets. The entire source for the Socket class is shown in Listing 12-5.

Listing 12-5. Creating an Object-Oriented Socket Class

```
class Socket
{
private:
#if !UsingWinsock
    using SOCKET = int;
#endif

    addrinfo* m_ServerInfo{ nullptr };
    SOCKET m_Socket{ static_cast<SOCKET>(0xFFFFFFFF) };
    sockaddr_storage m_AcceptedSocketStorage{};
    socklen_t m_AcceptedSocketSize{ sizeof(m_AcceptedSocketStorage) };
```

```
    void CreateSocket(string& webAddress, string& port, addrinfo& hints)
    {
        getaddrinfo(webAddress.c_str(), port.c_str(), &hints, &m_ServerInfo);

        m_Socket = socket(
            m_ServerInfo->ai_family,
            m_ServerInfo->ai_socktype,
            m_ServerInfo->ai_protocol);
    }

    Socket(int newSocket, sockaddr_storage&& socketStorage)
        : m_Socket{ newSocket }
        , m_AcceptedSocketStorage(move(socketStorage))
    {

    }

public:
    Socket(string& port)
    {
#ifndef NDEBUG
        stringstream portStream{ port };
        int portValue{};
        portStream >> portValue;
        assert(portValue > 1024); // Ports under 1024 are reserved for certain
        applications and protocols!
#endif

        addrinfo hints{};
        hints.ai_family = AF_UNSPEC;
        hints.ai_socktype = SOCK_STREAM;
        hints.ai_flags = AI_PASSIVE;

        string address{ "" };
        CreateSocket(address, port, hints);
    }

    Socket(string& webAddress, string& port)
    {
        addrinfo hints{};
        hints.ai_family = AF_UNSPEC;
        hints.ai_socktype = SOCK_STREAM;

        CreateSocket(webAddress, port, hints);
    }

    Socket(string& webAddress, string& port, addrinfo& hints)
    {
        CreateSocket(webAddress, port, hints);
    }
```

```
    ~Socket()
    {
        Close();
    }

    bool IsValid()
    {
        return m_Socket != -1;
    }

    int Connect()
    {
        int connectionResult{
            connect(m_Socket, m_ServerInfo->ai_addr, m_ServerInfo->ai_addrlen)
        };

#ifndef NDEBUG
        if (connectionResult == -1)
        {
            cout << "Connection failed!" << endl;
        }
        else
        {
            cout << "Connection successful!" << endl;
        }
#endif

        return connectionResult;
    }

    int Bind()
    {
        int bindResult{ ::bind(m_Socket, m_ServerInfo->ai_addr, m_ServerInfo->ai_addrlen) };

#ifndef NDEBUG
        if (bindResult == -1)
        {
            cout << "Bind Failed!" << endl;
        }
        else
        {
            cout << "Bind Successful" << endl;
        }
#endif

        return bindResult;
    }
```

```
    int Listen(int queueSize)
    {
        int listenResult{ listen(m_Socket, queueSize) };

#ifndef NDEBUG
        if (listenResult == -1)
        {
            cout << "Listen Failed" << endl;
        }
        else
        {
            cout << "Listen Succeeded" << endl;
        }
#endif

        return listenResult;
    }

    Socket Accept()
    {
        SOCKET newSocket{
            accept(m_Socket,
            reinterpret_cast<sockaddr*>(&m_AcceptedSocketStorage),
            &m_AcceptedSocketSize)
        };

#ifndef NDEBUG
        if (newSocket == -1)
        {
            cout << "Accept Failed" << endl;
        }
        else
        {
            cout << "Accept Succeeded" << endl;
        }
#endif

        m_AcceptedSocketSize = sizeof(m_AcceptedSocketStorage);
        return Socket(newSocket, move(m_AcceptedSocketStorage));
    }

    void Close()
    {
#ifdef _MSC_VER
        closesocket(m_Socket);
#else
        close(m_Socket);
#endif

        m_Socket = -1;
        freeaddrinfo(m_ServerInfo);
    }
```

```
    ssize_t Send(stringstream data)
    {
        string packetData{ data.str() };
        ssize_t sendResult{ send(m_Socket, packetData.c_str(), packetData.length(), 0) };

#ifndef NDEBUG
        if (sendResult == -1)
        {
            cout << "Send Failed" << endl;
        }
        else
        {
            cout << "Send Succeeded" << endl;
        }
#endif

        return sendResult;
    }

    stringstream Receive()
    {
        const int size{ 1024 };
        char dataReceived[size];

        ssize_t receiveResult{ recv(m_Socket, dataReceived, size, 0) };

#ifndef NDEBUG
        if (receiveResult == -1)
        {
            cout << "Receive Failed" << endl;
        }
        else if (receiveResult == 0)
        {
            cout << "Receive Detected Closed Connection!" << endl;
            Close();
        }
        else
        {
            dataReceived[receiveResult] = '\0';
            cout << "Receive Succeeded" << endl;
        }
#endif
        stringstream data{ dataReceived };
        return move(data);
    }
};
```

The Socket class comes with three different constructors, allowing you to create sockets for different purposes. The first public constructor only takes a port as a parameter. This method of construction is suitable for Socket objects used to listen for incoming connections. The hints addrinfo struct in the constructor sets the ai_flags parameter to the AI_PASSIVE value and passes an empty string for the address. This tells the getaddrinfo function to fill in the local computer's IP address as the address to use for the socket.

329

Using the local address this way lets you open sockets for listening on a computer—this is an essential task when you wish to receive data in a program from an external source.

The second public constructor takes an address and a port. This lets you create a Socket that automatically uses IPv6 or IPv4 and TCP/IP to create a socket that can be used for sending data. Both the first and second constructors are for convenience—both could be deleted in favor of the third public constructor, which takes an address, a port, and an addrinfo struct and allows the user to configure a Socket as they wish.

The final constructor is a private constructor. This type of constructor is used when an external program connects to a socket listening for connections. You can see how this is used in the Accept method.

The IsValid method determines whether the Socket has been initialized with a proper descriptor. The socket function in CreateSocket returns -1 in the result of a failure; the default value of m_Socket is also -1.

The Connect method is used when you wish to establish a connection to a remote computer and you aren't interested in receiving connections from other programs. It's primarily used on the client side of a client-server relationship; however, it's not inconceivable that you could write peer-to-peer programs that use different sockets for listening and connecting to others. Connect calls the Berkeley connect function but is able to use the m_Socket and m_ServerInfo objects from the object rather than your having to pass them manually from an external location.

The Bind method is used when you wish to receive incoming connections. The Berkeley bind function is responsible for negotiating for access to the port you wish to use with the OS. The OS is responsible for sending and receiving the network traffic, and ports are used for the computer to know which program is waiting for data on which port. The scope operator on the bind function is necessary with this code when the using namespace std; statement is present. This tells the compiler to use the bind method from the global namespace and not from the std namespace. The bind method from the std namespace is used to create functors and has nothing to do with sockets.

The Listen method comes after the call to Bind and tells the socket to begin queuing connections from remote machines. The queueSize parameter specifies the size of the queue; once the queue is full, connections will be dropped from by OS. The number of connections that your OS can support will vary. Desktop OSs generally support many fewer queued connections than server-specific OSs. A number such as 5 is fine for most uses.

The Accept method pulls connections from the queue created when Listen is called. Accept calls the Berkeley accept function, which takes the m_Socket variable as its first parameter. The second and third parameters are the m_AcceptedSocketStorage and m_AcceptedSocketSize variables. The m_AcceptedSocketStorage member variable is of type sockaddr_storage and not the sockaddr type that the accept method expects. The sockaddr_storage type is large enough to handle both IPv4 and IPv6 addresses, but the accept method still expects a pointer to the sockaddr type. This isn't ideal; however, it can be addressed using a reinterpret_cast, because accept also takes into account the size of the object being passed. The size is altered if the object returned is smaller than the size being passed in; therefore, the size is reset before the function returns. The m_AcceptedSocketStorage object is moved into the new Socket object being returned from the function to ensure that the copy in the initial Socket is invalidated.

The Close method is responsible for shutting down the Socket when it's no longer needed. The closesocket function is called on Windows, and the close function is used on non-Windows platforms. The freeaddrinfo object is also released in the destructor for the class.

The next method is Send. Unsurprisingly, this method sends data to the machine on the other end of the connection. Send is set up to send a stringstream object for now, because properly serializing binary data is a little outside the scope of this book. You can see that the send Berkeley function is called with the m_Socket descriptor along with the string data and size pulled from the stringstream object passed in.

The Receive method is responsible for bringing data in from the remote connection. This call blocks until data is ready to be read from the socket connection. The Receive function can return three types of values: -1 when an error has been encountered, 0 when the connection has been closed by the remote computer, or a positive value indicating the number of bytes received. The received data is read into a char array, which is in turn passed into a stringstream object to be returned from the function using a move constructor.

Now that you have a fully functioning Socket class, you can create programs to send and receive data. The code in Listing 12-6 can be used to create a program that waits for a remote connection and a single received message.

Listing 12-6. Creating a Program That Can Receive Data

```
#include <cassert>
#include <iostream>
#include <type_traits>
#include <vector>

#ifndef NDEBUG
#include <sstream>
#endif

using namespace std;

#ifdef _MSC_VER

#pragma comment(lib, "Ws2_32.lib")

#include <WinSock2.h>
#include <WS2tcpip.h>

#define UsingWinsock 1

using ssize_t = SSIZE_T;

#else

#include <netdb.h>
#include <sys/types.h>
#include <sys/socket.h>
#include <unistd.h>

#define UsingWinsock 0

#endif

class WinsockWrapper
{
public:
    WinsockWrapper()
    {
#if UsingWinsock
        WSADATA wsaData;
        if (WSAStartup(MAKEWORD(2, 2), &wsaData) != 0)
        {
            exit(1);
        }

        cout << "Winsock started!" << endl;
#endif
    }
```

```cpp
    ~WinsockWrapper()
    {
#if UsingWinsock
        WSACleanup();

        cout << "Winsock shut down!" << endl;
#endif
    }
};

class Socket
{
private:
#if !UsingWinsock
    using SOCKET = int;
#endif

    addrinfo* m_ServerInfo{ nullptr };
    SOCKET m_Socket{ static_cast<SOCKET>(0xFFFFFFFF) };
    sockaddr_storage m_AcceptedSocketStorage{};
    socklen_t m_AcceptedSocketSize{ sizeof(m_AcceptedSocketStorage) };

    void CreateSocket(string& webAddress, string& port, addrinfo& hints)
    {
        getaddrinfo(webAddress.c_str(), port.c_str(), &hints, &m_ServerInfo);

        m_Socket = socket(
            m_ServerInfo->ai_family,
            m_ServerInfo->ai_socktype,
            m_ServerInfo->ai_protocol);
    }

    Socket(int newSocket, sockaddr_storage&& socketStorage)
        : m_Socket{ newSocket }
        , m_AcceptedSocketStorage(move(socketStorage))
    {

    }

public:
    Socket(string& port)
    {
#ifndef NDEBUG
        stringstream portStream{ port };
        int portValue{};
        portStream >> portValue;
        assert(portValue > 1024);
        // Ports under 1024 are reserved for certain applications and protocols!
#endif
```

```
        addrinfo hints{};
        hints.ai_family = AF_UNSPEC;
        hints.ai_socktype = SOCK_STREAM;
        hints.ai_flags = AI_PASSIVE;

        string address{ "" };
        CreateSocket(address, port, hints);
    }

    Socket(string& webAddress, string& port)
    {
        addrinfo hints{};
        hints.ai_family = AF_UNSPEC;
        hints.ai_socktype = SOCK_STREAM;

        CreateSocket(webAddress, port, hints);
    }

    Socket(string& webAddress, string& port, addrinfo& hints)
    {
        CreateSocket(webAddress, port, hints);
    }

    ~Socket()
    {
        Close();
    }

    bool IsValid()
    {
        return m_Socket != -1;
    }

    int Connect()
    {
        int connectionResult{
            connect(m_Socket, m_ServerInfo->ai_addr, m_ServerInfo->ai_addrlen)
        };

#ifndef NDEBUG
        if (connectionResult == -1)
        {
            cout << "Connection failed!" << endl;
        }
        else
        {
            cout << "Connection successful!" << endl;
        }
#endif

        return connectionResult;
    }
```

```
    int Bind()
    {
        int bindResult{ ::bind(m_Socket, m_ServerInfo->ai_addr, m_ServerInfo->ai_addrlen) };

#ifndef NDEBUG
        if (bindResult == -1)
        {
            cout << "Bind Failed!" << endl;
        }
        else
        {
            cout << "Bind Successful" << endl;
        }
#endif

        return bindResult;
    }

    int Listen(int queueSize)
    {
        int listenResult{ listen(m_Socket, queueSize) };

#ifndef NDEBUG
        if (listenResult == -1)
        {
            cout << "Listen Failed" << endl;
        }
        else
        {
            cout << "Listen Succeeded" << endl;
        }
#endif

        return listenResult;
    }

    Socket Accept()
    {
        SOCKET newSocket{
            accept(m_Socket,
                reinterpret_cast<sockaddr*>(&m_AcceptedSocketStorage),
                &m_AcceptedSocketSize)
        };

#ifndef NDEBUG
        if (newSocket == -1)
        {
            cout << "Accept Failed" << endl;
        }
```

```
        else
        {
            cout << "Accept Succeeded" << endl;
        }
#endif

        m_AcceptedSocketSize = sizeof(m_AcceptedSocketStorage);
        return Socket(newSocket, move(m_AcceptedSocketStorage));
    }

    void Close()
    {
#ifdef _MSC_VER
        closesocket(m_Socket);
#else
        close(m_Socket);
#endif

        m_Socket = -1;
        freeaddrinfo(m_ServerInfo);
    }

    ssize_t Send(stringstream data)
    {
        string packetData{ data.str() };
        ssize_t sendResult{ send(m_Socket, packetData.c_str(), packetData.length(), 0) };

#ifndef NDEBUG
        if (sendResult == -1)
        {
            cout << "Send Failed" << endl;
        }
        else
        {
            cout << "Send Succeeded" << endl;
        }
#endif

        return sendResult;
    }

    stringstream Receive()
    {
        const int size{ 1024 };
        char dataReceived[size];

        ssize_t receiveResult{ recv(m_Socket, dataReceived, size, 0) };
```

```
#ifndef NDEBUG
        if (receiveResult == -1)
        {
            cout << "Receive Failed" << endl;
        }
        else if (receiveResult == 0)
        {
            cout << "Receive Detected Closed Connection!" << endl;
            Close();
        }
        else
        {
            dataReceived[receiveResult] = '\0';
            cout << "Receive Succeeded" << endl;
        }
#endif
        stringstream data{ dataReceived };
        return move(data);
    }
};

int main(int argc, char* argv[])
{
    WinsockWrapper myWinsockWrapper;

    string port{ "3000" };
    Socket myBindingSocket(port);
    myBindingSocket.Bind();

    int listenResult{ myBindingSocket.Listen(5) };
    assert(listenResult != -1);

    Socket acceptResult{ myBindingSocket.Accept() };
    assert(acceptResult.IsValid());

    stringstream data{ acceptResult.Receive() };

    string message;
    getline(data, message, '\0');

    cout << "Received Message: " << message << endl;

    return 0;
}
```

The code in Listing 12-6 creates a program that has a socket that waits for a single message to be received from a remote connection. The main function ends up consisting of only a handful of lines of code, thanks to the difficult work wrapped up in the WinsockWrapper and Socket classes. The main function begins by creating a WinsockWrapper to initialize Winsock if running on a server built by Visual Studio for Windows computers. A Socket is then initialized to port 3000 with an empty address. This port will be used to listen for connections on the local computer. You can see that this is the case, because the main function goes on to call Bind and then Listen with a queue size of 5 before finally calling Accept. The Accept call blocks until a remote connection is present in the queue. Accept returns a separate Socket object that should be used to receive data. The Receive call on that Socket is also a blocking call, and the program waits there until data is available. The program ends by printing out the received message before returning.

Once you have the server program built and running, you need a client program to connect to it and send a message. This is shown in Listing 12-7.

Listing 12-7. The Client Program

```
#include <cassert>
#include <iostream>
#include <type_traits>

#ifndef NDEBUG
#include <sstream>
#endif

using namespace std;

#ifdef _MSC_VER

#pragma comment(lib, "Ws2_32.lib")

#include <WinSock2.h>
#include <WS2tcpip.h>

#define UsingWinsock 1

using ssize_t = SSIZE_T;

#else

#include <netdb.h>
#include <sys/types.h>
#include <sys/socket.h>

#define UsingWinsock 0

#endif

class WinsockWrapper
{
public:
    WinsockWrapper()
    {
#if UsingWinsock
        WSADATA wsaData;
        if (WSAStartup(MAKEWORD(2, 2), &wsaData) != 0)
        {
            exit(1);
        }
```

```
#ifndef NDEBUG
        cout << "Winsock started!" << endl;
#endif
#endif
    }

    ~WinsockWrapper()
    {
#if UsingWinsock
        WSACleanup();

#ifndef NDEBUG
        cout << "Winsock shut down!" << endl;
#endif
#endif
    }
};

class Socket
{
private:
#if !UsingWinsock
    using SOCKET = int;
#endif

    addrinfo* m_ServerInfo{ nullptr };
    SOCKET m_Socket{ static_cast<SOCKET>(0xFFFFFFFF) };
    sockaddr_storage m_AcceptedSocketStorage{};
    socklen_t m_AcceptedSocketSize{ sizeof(m_AcceptedSocketStorage) };

    void CreateSocket(string& webAddress, string& port, addrinfo& hints)
    {
        getaddrinfo(webAddress.c_str(), port.c_str(), &hints, &m_ServerInfo);

        m_Socket = socket(m_ServerInfo->ai_family,
            m_ServerInfo->ai_socktype,
            m_ServerInfo->ai_protocol);
    }

    Socket(int newSocket, sockaddr_storage&& socketStorage)
        : m_Socket{ newSocket }
        , m_AcceptedSocketStorage(move(socketStorage))
    {

    }
```

```cpp
public:
    Socket(string& port)
    {
#ifndef NDEBUG
        stringstream portStream{ port };
        int portValue{};
        portStream >> portValue;
        assert(portValue > 1024);
        // Ports under 1024 are reserved for certain applications and protocols!
#endif

        addrinfo hints{};
        hints.ai_family = AF_UNSPEC;
        hints.ai_socktype = SOCK_STREAM;
        hints.ai_flags = AI_PASSIVE;

        string address{ "" };
        CreateSocket(address, port, hints);
    }

    Socket(string& webAddress, string& port)
    {
        addrinfo hints{};
        hints.ai_family = AF_UNSPEC;
        hints.ai_socktype = SOCK_STREAM;

        CreateSocket(webAddress, port, hints);
    }

    Socket(string& webAddress, string& port, addrinfo& hints)
    {
        CreateSocket(webAddress, port, hints);
    }

    ~Socket()
    {
        Close();
    }

    bool IsValid()
    {
        return m_Socket != -1;
    }

    int Connect()
    {
        int connectionResult{ connect(
            m_Socket,
            m_ServerInfo->ai_addr,
            m_ServerInfo->ai_addrlen)
        };
```

```
#ifndef NDEBUG
        if (connectionResult == -1)
        {
            cout << "Connection failed!" << endl;
        }
        else
        {
            cout << "Connection successful!" << endl;
        }
#endif

        return connectionResult;
    }

    int Bind()
    {
        int bindResult{ ::bind(m_Socket, m_ServerInfo->ai_addr, m_ServerInfo->ai_addrlen) };

#ifndef NDEBUG
        if (bindResult == -1)
        {
            cout << "Bind Failed!" << endl;
        }
        else
        {
            cout << "Bind Successful" << endl;
        }
#endif

        return bindResult;
    }

    int Listen(int queueSize)
    {
        int listenResult{ listen(m_Socket, queueSize) };

#ifndef NDEBUG
        if (listenResult == -1)
        {
            cout << "Listen Failed" << endl;
        }
        else
        {
            cout << "Listen Succeeded" << endl;
        }
#endif

        return listenResult;
    }
```

```
    Socket Accept()
    {
        SOCKET newSocket{ accept(m_Socket, reinterpret_cast<sockaddr*>
        (&m_AcceptedSocketStorage), &m_AcceptedSocketSize) };

#ifndef NDEBUG
        if (newSocket == -1)
        {
            cout << "Accept Failed" << endl;
        }
        else
        {
            cout << "Accept Succeeded" << endl;
        }
#endif

        m_AcceptedSocketSize = sizeof(m_AcceptedSocketStorage);
        return Socket(newSocket, move(m_AcceptedSocketStorage));
    }

    void Close()
    {
#ifdef _MSC_VER
        closesocket(m_Socket);
#else
        close(m_Socket);
#endif

        m_Socket = -1;
        freeaddrinfo(m_ServerInfo);
    }

    ssize_t Send(stringstream data)
    {
        string packetData{ data.str() };
        ssize_t sendResult{ send(m_Socket, packetData.c_str(), packetData.length(), 0) };

#ifndef NDEBUG
        if (sendResult == -1)
        {
            cout << "Send Failed" << endl;
        }
        else
        {
            cout << "Send Succeeded" << endl;
        }
#endif

        return sendResult;
    }
```

```
    stringstream Receive()
    {
        const int size{ 1024 };
        char dataReceived[size];

        ssize_t receiveResult{ recv(m_Socket, dataReceived, size, 0) };

#ifndef NDEBUG
        if (receiveResult == -1)
        {
            cout << "Receive Failed" << endl;
        }
        else if (receiveResult == 0)
        {
            cout << "Receive Detected Closed Connection!" << endl;
            Close();
        }
        else
        {
            dataReceived[receiveResult] = '\0';
            cout << "Receive Succeeded" << endl;
        }
#endif
        stringstream data{ dataReceived };
        return move(data);
    }
};

int main(int argc, char* argv[])
{
    WinsockWrapper myWinsockWrapper;

    string address("192.168.178.44");
    string port("3000");
    Socket myConnectingSocket(address, port);
    myConnectingSocket.Connect();

    string message("Sending Data Over a Network!");
    stringstream data;
    data << message;

    myConnectingSocket.Send(move(data));

    return 0;
}
```

Listing 12-7 shows that the same Socket class can be used on the server and the client. The client's main function also uses the WinsockWrapper object to handle starting and closing the Winsock library. A Socket is then created that connects to IP address 192.168.178.44. (This is the address of the computer I used to host the server program.) The Connect method is called after the Socket is created to establish a connection between the two programs running on different computers. The Send method is the last function call and sends the string "Sending Data Over a Network!" Figure 12-10 shows the output obtained by running the server on a MacBook Pro and the client on a Windows 8.1 desktop PC.

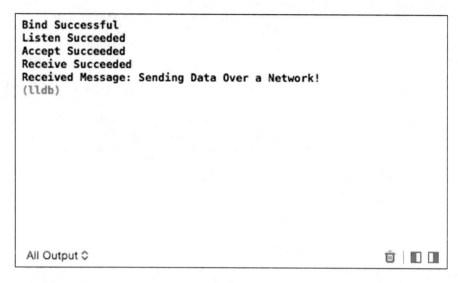

```
Bind Successful
Listen Succeeded
Accept Succeeded
Receive Succeeded
Received Message: Sending Data Over a Network!
(lldb)




All Output ◇                                          🗑 | ▯▯ ▯
```

Figure 12-10. *The output generated by running the server on OS X*

12-5. Creating a Networking Protocol between Two Programs

Problem

You would like to create two programs that are able to communicate with each other following standard patterns.

Solution

You can create an agreed-on protocol that both programs can follow so that each knows how to respond to a given request.

How It Works

A socket connection that is established between two programs can be used to send data both ways: from the program that initiated the connection to the receiver, and also back from the receiver to the initiator. This feature allows you to write networked applications that can respond to requests and even build more complicated protocols that require several messages to be sent back and forth in a single application.

The most common example of a protocol in use today that you may be familiar with is HTTP. HTTP is the network protocol that powers the World Wide Web. It's a request and response protocol that lets a client program request data from a server. Common applications can be seen when a browser requests a web page from a server, but it's also not uncommon for mobile apps to use HTTP to transfer data between their app and their server back end. Other common protocols are FTP for facilitating file transfers between computers and the POP and SMTP e-mail protocols.

This recipe shows a very simple network protocol that asks a server for a question, has a client respond with an answer, and has the server tell the client whether the answer was correct. This protocol is trivial compared to a complicated example such as HTTP, but it's an excellent place to start.

The protocol consists of four messages: QUESTION, ANSWER, QUIT, and FINISHED. The QUESTION message is sent from the client to the server when the user should be asked a question. The server responds to this message by sending a question to the client. The client responds to the question by sending ANSWER followed by the user's answer to the server. The client could instead send QUIT to the server at any time to terminate the socket connection. Once the server has sent all the questions to the server, a subsequent QUESTION request from the client will result in FINISHED being sent to the client; then the connection will be terminated.

The server program in this recipe can handle multiple client connections at a time. It does this by accepting a single connection using the Socket::Accept method and then handing the Socket connected to the client to a thread using the async function. You can see the source for the server program in Listing 12-8.

Listing 12-8. The Protocol Server Program

```
#include <array>
#include <cassert>
#include <future>
#include <iostream>
#include <thread>
#include <type_traits>
#include <vector>

#ifndef NDEBUG
#include <sstream>
#endif

using namespace std;

#ifdef _MSC_VER

#pragma comment(lib, "Ws2_32.lib")

#include <WinSock2.h>
#include <WS2tcpip.h>

#define UsingWinsock 1

using ssize_t = SSIZE_T;

#else

#include <netdb.h>
#include <sys/types.h>
#include <sys/socket.h>
#include <unistd.h>
```

```cpp
#define UsingWinsock 0

#endif

class WinsockWrapper
{
public:
    WinsockWrapper()
    {
#if UsingWinsock
        WSADATA wsaData;
        if (WSAStartup(MAKEWORD(2, 2), &wsaData) != 0)
        {
            exit(1);
        }

        cout << "Winsock started!" << endl;
#endif
    }

    ~WinsockWrapper()
    {
#if UsingWinsock
        WSACleanup();

        cout << "Winsock shut down!" << endl;
#endif
    }
};

class Socket
{
private:
#if !UsingWinsock
    using SOCKET = int;
#endif

    addrinfo* m_ServerInfo{ nullptr };
    SOCKET m_Socket{ static_cast<SOCKET>(0xFFFFFFFF) };
    sockaddr_storage m_AcceptedSocketStorage{};
    socklen_t m_AcceptedSocketSize{ sizeof(m_AcceptedSocketStorage) };

    void CreateSocket(string& webAddress, string& port, addrinfo& hints)
    {
        getaddrinfo(webAddress.c_str(), port.c_str(), &hints, &m_ServerInfo);

        m_Socket = socket(m_ServerInfo->ai_family,
            m_ServerInfo->ai_socktype,
            m_ServerInfo->ai_protocol);
    }
```

```cpp
    Socket(int newSocket, sockaddr_storage&& socketStorage)
        : m_Socket{ newSocket }
        , m_AcceptedSocketStorage(move(socketStorage))
    {

    }

public:
    Socket(string& port)
    {
#ifndef NDEBUG
        stringstream portStream{ port };
        int portValue{};
        portStream >> portValue;
        assert(portValue > 1024);
        // Ports under 1024 are reserved for certain applications and protocols!
#endif

        addrinfo hints{};
        hints.ai_family = AF_UNSPEC;
        hints.ai_socktype = SOCK_STREAM;
        hints.ai_flags = AI_PASSIVE;

        string address{ "" };
        CreateSocket(address, port, hints);
    }

    Socket(string& webAddress, string& port)
    {
        addrinfo hints{};
        hints.ai_family = AF_UNSPEC;
        hints.ai_socktype = SOCK_STREAM;

        CreateSocket(webAddress, port, hints);
    }

    Socket(string& webAddress, string& port, addrinfo& hints)
    {
        CreateSocket(webAddress, port, hints);
    }

    ~Socket()
    {
        Close();
    }

    Socket(const Socket& other) = delete;

    Socket(Socket&& other)
        : m_ServerInfo( other.m_ServerInfo )
        , m_Socket( other.m_Socket )
```

```
        , m_AcceptedSocketStorage( other.m_AcceptedSocketStorage )
        , m_AcceptedSocketSize( other.m_AcceptedSocketSize )
    {
        if (this != &other)
        {
            other.m_ServerInfo = nullptr;
            other.m_Socket = -1;
            other.m_AcceptedSocketStorage = sockaddr_storage{};
            other.m_AcceptedSocketSize = sizeof(other.m_AcceptedSocketStorage);
        }
    }

    bool IsValid()
    {
        return m_Socket != -1;
    }

    int Connect()
    {
        int connectionResult{
            connect(m_Socket,
                m_ServerInfo->ai_addr,
                m_ServerInfo->ai_addrlen)
        };

#ifndef NDEBUG
        if (connectionResult == -1)
        {
            cout << "Connection failed!" << endl;
        }
        else
        {
            cout << "Connection successful!" << endl;
        }
#endif

        return connectionResult;
    }

    int Bind()
    {
        int bindResult{ ::bind(m_Socket, m_ServerInfo->ai_addr, m_ServerInfo->ai_addrlen) };

#ifndef NDEBUG
        if (bindResult == -1)
        {
            cout << "Bind Failed!" << endl;
        }
```

```
        else
        {
            cout << "Bind Successful" << endl;
        }
#endif

        return bindResult;
    }

    int Listen(int queueSize)
    {
        int listenResult{ listen(m_Socket, queueSize) };

#ifndef NDEBUG
        if (listenResult == -1)
        {
            cout << "Listen Failed" << endl;
        }
        else
        {
            cout << "Listen Succeeded" << endl;
        }
#endif

        return listenResult;
    }

    Socket Accept()
    {
        SOCKET newSocket{
            accept(m_Socket,
                reinterpret_cast<sockaddr*>(&m_AcceptedSocketStorage),
                &m_AcceptedSocketSize)
        };

#ifndef NDEBUG
        if (newSocket == -1)
        {
            cout << "Accept Failed" << endl;
        }
        else
        {
            cout << "Accept Succeeded" << endl;
        }
#endif

        m_AcceptedSocketSize = sizeof(m_AcceptedSocketStorage);
        return Socket(newSocket, move(m_AcceptedSocketStorage));
    }
```

```
    void Close()
    {
#ifdef _MSC_VER
        closesocket(m_Socket);
#else
        close(m_Socket);
#endif

        m_Socket = -1;
        freeaddrinfo(m_ServerInfo);
    }

    ssize_t Send(stringstream data)
    {
        string packetData{ data.str() };
        ssize_t sendResult{ send(m_Socket, packetData.c_str(), packetData.length(), 0) };

#ifndef NDEBUG
        if (sendResult == -1)
        {
            cout << "Send Failed" << endl;
        }
        else
        {
            cout << "Send Succeeded" << endl;
        }
#endif

        return sendResult;
    }

    stringstream Receive()
    {
        const int size{ 1024 };
        char dataReceived[size];

        ssize_t receiveResult{ recv(m_Socket, dataReceived, size, 0) };

#ifndef NDEBUG
        if (receiveResult == -1)
        {
            cout << "Receive Failed" << endl;
        }
        else if (receiveResult == 0)
        {
            cout << "Receive Detected Closed Connection!" << endl;
            Close();
        }
```

```
        else
        {
            dataReceived[receiveResult] = '\0';
            cout << "Receive Succeeded" << endl;
        }
#endif
        stringstream data{ dataReceived };
        return move(data);
    }
};

namespace
{
    const int NUM_QUESTIONS{ 2 };
    const array<string, NUM_QUESTIONS> QUESTIONS
    {
        "What is the capital of Australia?",
        "What is the capital of the USA?"
    };
    const array<string, NUM_QUESTIONS> ANSWERS{ "Canberra", "Washington DC" };
}

bool ProtocolThread(reference_wrapper<Socket> connectionSocketRef)
{
    Socket socket{ move(connectionSocketRef.get()) };

    int currentQuestion{ 0 };

    string message;
    while (message != "QUIT")
    {
        stringstream sstream{ socket.Receive() };
        if (sstream.rdbuf()->in_avail() == 0)
        {
            break;
        }

        sstream >> message;

        stringstream output;
        if (message == "QUESTION")
        {
            if (currentQuestion >= NUM_QUESTIONS)
            {
                output << "FINISHED";
                socket.Send(move(output));

                cout << "Quiz Complete!" << endl;
                break;
            }

            output << QUESTIONS[currentQuestion];
        }
```

```
        else if (message == "ANSWER")
        {
            string answer;
            sstream >> answer;

            if (answer == ANSWERS[currentQuestion])
            {
                output << "You are correct!";
            }
            else
            {
                output << "Sorry the correct answer is " << ANSWERS[currentQuestion];
            }
            ++currentQuestion;
        }
        socket.Send(move(output));
    }

    return true;
}

int main(int argc, char* argv[])
{
    WinsockWrapper myWinsockWrapper;

    string port("3000");
    Socket myListeningSocket(port);

    int bindResult{ myListeningSocket.Bind() };
    assert(bindResult != -1);
    if (bindResult != -1)
    {
        int listenResult{ myListeningSocket.Listen(5) };
        assert(listenResult != -1);
        if (listenResult != -1)
        {
            while (true)
            {
                Socket acceptedSocket{ myListeningSocket.Accept() };
                async(launch::async, ProtocolThread, ref(acceptedSocket));
            }
        }
    }

    return 0;
}
```

The server program in Listing 12-8 uses the same Socket class that is described in detail in Recipe 12-4. The main function is responsible for handling multiple clients simultaneously. It does this by creating a Socket and binding it to port 3000. The bound Socket is then asked to listen for incoming connections; it does so with a queue length of 5. The final part of main uses a while loop to accept any incoming connections and hands them off to the async function. The async function creates a thread to handle each Socket retrieved from Socket::Accept; the first parameter is launch::async.

The ProtocolThread function responds to the requests of the connected client and upholds the server side of the simple quiz network protocol. Data is transferred between the client and the server by packing a string into each packet. The message variable holds individual messages from a stringstream. This protocol can be handled with a basic if...else if block. When the QUESTION message is received, the server packs the current question into the output stringstream. If the message is ANSWER, then the server checks whether the user is correct and packs the appropriate response into output. The output stringstream is sent to the client using the same Socket that received the data initially, showing that a Socket connection need not necessarily be a one-way communication channel. If the QUESTION message is received and all the questions that the server has available have been sent, then the server sends the client the FINISHED message and breaks out of the loop; this causes the Socket to fall out of scope and in turn closes the connection.

All of this activity requires a client to be connected to communicate with the server program. You can see a basic client implementation in Listing 12-9.

Listing 12-9. A Simple Quiz Protocol Client

```
#include <cassert>
#include <iostream>
#include <type_traits>

#ifndef NDEBUG
#include <sstream>
#endif

using namespace std;

#ifdef _MSC_VER

#pragma comment(lib, "Ws2_32.lib")

#include <WinSock2.h>
#include <WS2tcpip.h>

#define UsingWinsock 1

using ssize_t = SSIZE_T;

#else

#include <netdb.h>
#include <sys/types.h>
#include <sys/socket.h>
#include <unistd.h>

#define UsingWinsock 0

#endif
```

```cpp
class WinsockWrapper
{
public:
    WinsockWrapper()
    {
#if UsingWinsock
        WSADATA wsaData;
        if (WSAStartup(MAKEWORD(2, 2), &wsaData) != 0)
        {
            exit(1);
        }

        cout << "Winsock started!" << endl;
#endif
    }

    ~WinsockWrapper()
    {
#if UsingWinsock
        WSACleanup();

        cout << "Winsock shut down!" << endl;
#endif
    }
};

class Socket
{
private:
#if !UsingWinsock
    using SOCKET = int;
#endif

    addrinfo* m_ServerInfo{ nullptr };
    SOCKET m_Socket{ static_cast<SOCKET>(0xFFFFFFFF) };
    sockaddr_storage m_AcceptedSocketStorage{};
    socklen_t m_AcceptedSocketSize{ sizeof(m_AcceptedSocketStorage) };

    void CreateSocket(string& webAddress, string& port, addrinfo& hints)
    {
        getaddrinfo(webAddress.c_str(), port.c_str(), &hints, &m_ServerInfo);

        m_Socket = socket(
            m_ServerInfo->ai_family,
            m_ServerInfo->ai_socktype,
            m_ServerInfo->ai_protocol);
    }
```

```
    Socket(int newSocket, sockaddr_storage&& socketStorage)
        : m_Socket{ newSocket }
        , m_AcceptedSocketStorage(move(socketStorage))
    {

    }

public:
    Socket(string& port)
    {
#ifndef NDEBUG
        stringstream portStream{ port };
        int portValue{};
        portStream >> portValue;
        assert(portValue > 1024);
        // Ports under 1024 are reserved for certain applications and protocols!
#endif

        addrinfo hints{};
        hints.ai_family = AF_UNSPEC;
        hints.ai_socktype = SOCK_STREAM;
        hints.ai_flags = AI_PASSIVE;

        string address{ "" };
        CreateSocket(address, port, hints);
    }

    Socket(string& webAddress, string& port)
    {
        addrinfo hints{};
        hints.ai_family = AF_UNSPEC;
        hints.ai_socktype = SOCK_STREAM;

        CreateSocket(webAddress, port, hints);
    }

    Socket(string& webAddress, string& port, addrinfo& hints)
    {
        CreateSocket(webAddress, port, hints);
    }

    ~Socket()
    {
        Close();
    }

    Socket(const Socket& other) = delete;

    Socket(Socket&& other)
        : m_ServerInfo(other.m_ServerInfo)
        , m_Socket(other.m_Socket)
```

```
        , m_AcceptedSocketStorage(other.m_AcceptedSocketStorage)
        , m_AcceptedSocketSize(other.m_AcceptedSocketSize)
    {
        if (this != &other)
        {
            other.m_ServerInfo = nullptr;
            other.m_Socket = -1;
            other.m_AcceptedSocketStorage = sockaddr_storage{};
            other.m_AcceptedSocketSize = sizeof(other.m_AcceptedSocketStorage);
        }
    }

    bool IsValid()
    {
        return m_Socket != -1;
    }

    int Connect()
    {
        int connectionResult{ connect(
            m_Socket,
            m_ServerInfo->ai_addr,
            m_ServerInfo->ai_addrlen)
        };

#ifndef NDEBUG
        if (connectionResult == -1)
        {
            cout << "Connection failed!" << endl;
        }
        else
        {
            cout << "Connection successful!" << endl;
        }
#endif

        return connectionResult;
    }

    int Bind()
    {
        int bindResult{ ::bind(m_Socket, m_ServerInfo->ai_addr, m_ServerInfo->ai_addrlen) };

#ifndef NDEBUG
        if (bindResult == -1)
        {
            cout << "Bind Failed!" << endl;
        }
```

```
            else
            {
                cout << "Bind Successful" << endl;
            }
#endif

            return bindResult;
    }

    int Listen(int queueSize)
    {
        int listenResult{ listen(m_Socket, queueSize) };

#ifndef NDEBUG
        if (listenResult == -1)
        {
            cout << "Listen Failed" << endl;
        }
        else
        {
            cout << "Listen Succeeded" << endl;
        }
#endif

        return listenResult;
    }

    Socket Accept()
    {
        SOCKET newSocket{ accept(
            m_Socket,
            reinterpret_cast<sockaddr*>(&m_AcceptedSocketStorage),
            &m_AcceptedSocketSize)
        };

#ifndef NDEBUG
        if (newSocket == -1)
        {
            cout << "Accept Failed" << endl;
        }
        else
        {
            cout << "Accept Succeeded" << endl;
        }
#endif

        m_AcceptedSocketSize = sizeof(m_AcceptedSocketStorage);
        return Socket(newSocket, move(m_AcceptedSocketStorage));
    }
```

```cpp
    void Close()
    {
#ifdef _MSC_VER
        closesocket(m_Socket);
#else
        close(m_Socket);
#endif

        m_Socket = -1;
        freeaddrinfo(m_ServerInfo);
    }

    ssize_t Send(stringstream data)
    {
        string packetData{ data.str() };
        ssize_t sendResult{ send(m_Socket, packetData.c_str(), packetData.length(), 0) };

#ifndef NDEBUG
        if (sendResult == -1)
        {
            cout << "Send Failed" << endl;
        }
        else
        {
            cout << "Send Succeeded" << endl;
        }
#endif

        return sendResult;
    }

    stringstream Receive()
    {
        const int size{ 1024 };
        char dataReceived[size];

        ssize_t receiveResult{ recv(m_Socket, dataReceived, size, 0) };

#ifndef NDEBUG
        if (receiveResult == -1)
        {
            cout << "Receive Failed" << endl;
        }
        else if (receiveResult == 0)
        {
            cout << "Receive Detected Closed Connection!" << endl;
            Close();
        }
```

```
        else
        {
            dataReceived[receiveResult] = '\0';
            cout << "Receive Succeeded" << endl;
        }
#endif
        stringstream data{ dataReceived };
        return move(data);
    }
};

int main(int argc, char* argv[])
{
    WinsockWrapper myWinsockWrapper;

    string address("192.168.178.44");
    string port("3000");
    Socket mySocket(address, port);
    int connectionResult{ mySocket.Connect() };
    if (connectionResult != -1)
    {
        stringstream output{ "QUESTION" };
        mySocket.Send(move(output));

        stringstream input{ mySocket.Receive() };
        if (input.rdbuf()->in_avail() > 0)
        {
            string question;
            getline(input, question, '\0');
            input.clear();

            while (question != "FINISHED")
            {
                cout << question << endl;

                string answer;
                cin >> answer;

                output << "ANSWER ";
                output << answer;
                mySocket.Send(move(output));

                input = mySocket.Receive();
                if (input.rdbuf()->in_avail() == 0)
                {
                    break;
                }

                string result;
                getline(input, result, '\0');
                cout << result << endl;
```

```
            output << "QUESTION";
            mySocket.Send(move(output));

            input = mySocket.Receive();
            getline(input, question, '\0');
            input.clear();
        }
    }
}

    return 0;
}
```

The client program in Listing 12-9 can connect to the server in Listing 12-8 and present the server quiz to the player. The client code is simpler than the server because it only has to consider a single connection and therefore has no need for threads or handling multiple sockets. The client does need to know the address of the server to connect to; the IP address is the IP for the MacBook Pro I have running the server on my home network. The client sends QUESTION to the server and then waits for a response in the Receive call. Receive is a blocking call; therefore, the client sits and waits until the data is available. It then gets input from the player to send back to the server and waits for the response regarding whether the user is correct. This process is repeated in a loop until the server notifies the client that the quiz has ended.

The beauty of network protocols implemented in this manner is that they can be reused in different programs. If you wanted to extend this example, you could easily create a GUI version using a framework such as Qt, make all the calls to Receive occur in a thread, and have the UI animate a spinning logo to indicate to the user that the program is waiting for data to come across a remote connection. You could also extend the server application to store results and add to the protocol to let users restart quizzes that were in progress. In the end, the protocol simply specifies how two programs should communicate with each other to facilitate providing a service from one computer to another.

CHAPTER 13

Scripting

C++ is a powerful programming language that can be used in a number of ways and supports several different programming paradigms. It allows for high-level object-oriented abstractions and generic programming, but it also allows you to code at a very low level that takes into consideration CPU characteristics such as the length of cache lines. This power comes at the expense of the need to compile the language into machine code. Compiling, building, and linking C++ is a task that programmers need to take on and not something that is simple for non-programmers to understand.

Scripting languages can help lower the barrier to making code-related changes to your program and enable art and design teams to take control over high-level tasks. It's not uncommon for things such as screen layouts and UI flows to be written in a scripting language so they can easily be changed by non-programming members of a team. Several popular scripting languages are available, one of which is Lua. This chapter looks at how the Lua programming language differs from C++ and how the Lua interpreter and engine can be incorporated into your C++ programs.

13-1. Creating a Lua Library Project in Visual Studio

Problem

You wish to make a program using Visual Studio that incorporates the Lua scripting language.

Solution

The Lua programming language is supplied with all the source files you need to make a working Lua program. You can include these files into a separate Visual Studio project that can be used to build a static library.

How It Works

Visual Studio programs can be built from several constituent parts. Visual Studio supports this by creating a solution file for your application that contains multiple projects. A project in Visual Studio can be configured to create an EXE, a static library, or a dynamic library. For this recipe, you create a solution that consists of two projects: one to build a static library containing the Lua library and another to create an application that links statically to the Lua project and uses Lua in its code. Follow these steps to create a project that builds an application linked to the Lua C Library:

1. Open Visual Studio, and select the option to create a new project from the start screen or the File menu.

2. Click the Visual C++ category under Installed Templates, and select the Win32 Project template for your new application.

3. Give your project a name, choose a location to store its files, and click OK to proceed. Figure 13-1 shows the New Project Wizard.

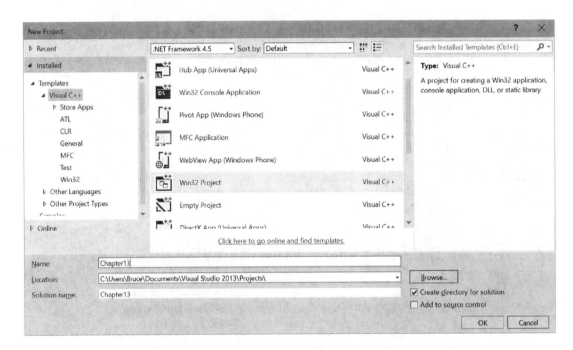

Figure 13-1. The Visual Studio New Project Wizard at step 3

4. In the Application Wizard, select Console Application, and uncheck the Precompiled Header and Security Development Lifecycle (SDL) options.

5. Click Finish.

6. Right-click the newly created solution in the Solution Explorer window, and select Add ➤ New Project.

7. Select Win32 Project again, name the project Lua, and click OK.

8. Click Next in the Application Wizard, and then select the Static Library option.

9. Uncheck the Precompiled Header option and the SDL option, and click finish.

10. Download the Lua source code from `www.lua.org`.

11. Unpack the `tar.gz` file you downloaded, using an application such as 7-Zip, and copy the `src` folder to the folder you used to create your Lua project.

12. Right-click the Source Files folder in your Lua project in the Visual Studio Solution Explorer window, and select Add ➤ Existing Item.

13. Add the following files from the `src` Lua folder you copied into the project directory:

- `lapi.c`
- `lauxlib.c`
- `lbaselib.c`
- `lbitlib.c`
- `lcode.c`
- `lcorolib.c`
- `lctype.c`
- `ldblib.c`
- `ldebug.c`
- `ldo.c`
- `ldump.c`
- `lfunc.c`
- `lgc.c`
- `linit.c`
- `liolib.c`
- `llex.c`
- `lmathlib.c`
- `lmem.c`
- `loadlib.c`
- `lobject.c`
- `lopcodes.c`
- `loslib.c`
- `lparser.c`
- `lstate.c`
- `lstring.c`
- `lstrlib.c`
- `ltable.c`
- `ltablib.c`

- ltm.c

- lundump.c

- lutf8lib.c

- lvm.c

- lzio.c

14. Right-click your Lua project, and click Build to see that the Lua.lib file is generated without error.

15. Right-click the Chapter 13 project, and select Properties.

16. Expand the Common Properties section, and click References.

17. Click Add New Reference.

18. Check the Lua project, and select OK.

19. Expand the C/C++ section under Configuration Properties, and click General.

20. Ensure that the Configuration option is set to All Configurations.

21. Edit the Additional Include Directories option so it has the path to the Lua source folder you copied into the Lua project folder.

22. Replace your main function source in the project CPP file with the code from Listing 13-1.

Listing 13-1. A Simple Lua Program

```
#include "lua.hpp"

int main(int argc, char* argv[])
{
    lua_State* pLuaState{ luaL_newstate() };
    if (pLuaState)
    {
        luaL_openlibs(pLuaState);

        lua_close(pLuaState);
    }

    return 0;
}
```

23. Build and execute your program to see that the Lua static library is successfully included in your project.

Following these steps allows you to create a Lua static library project that you can use throughout the remainder of the recipes in this chapter.

13-2. Creating a Lua Library Project in Eclipse

Problem

You wish to create a C++ program using Lua as a scripting language, and you're developing on a Linux computer with Eclipse installed.

Solution

Lua is supplied as source code, and you can create an Eclipse project that can be built into a static library for inclusion in other programs.

How It Works

The Eclipse IDE allows you to create new static library projects that can be linked into application projects. Follow these steps to create an Eclipse project that builds a Linux-compatible static library for your Lua projects:

1. Open your Eclipse IDE, and navigate to the C/C++ perspective.

2. Right-click in the Project Explorer window, and select New ➤ C++ Project.

3. Expand the Static Library category, and select Empty Project.

4. Give the project a name, and choose a folder to store the project.

5. Click Finish.

6. Right-click your new project in the Project Explorer window, and select New ➤ Source Folder. Give it a name.

7. Download the Lua source from www.lua.org.

8. Unpack the tar.gz file you obtained, and copy the .c and .h files from the src folder to your newly created project source folder.

9. Right-click your project in the Project Explorer window, and select Refresh.

10. Observe that the Lua source and header files appear in the Project Explorer window.

11. Right-click the project, and select Build to ensure that the source compiles correctly.

12. Right-click empty space in the Project Explorer window, and select New ➤ C++ Project.

13. Select Executable ➤ Hello World C++ Project.

14. Set the Project Name field.

15. Select a location.

16. Click Finish.

17. Right-click your new executable project in the Project Explorer window, and select Properties.

18. Click the C/C++ Build category, and ensure that Configuration is set to Debug.

19. Expand the C/C++ Build category, and click Settings.

20. Select the Libraries option under the GCC C++ Linker category.

21. Click the Add option in the Libraries section, and type **Lua** (you don't need to type **libLua.a**—the lib and .a parts are added automatically).

22. Click the Add option on the Library search path option.

23. Click Workspace.

24. Select the Debug folder in the Lua project.

25. Repeat steps 18–24 for the Release configuration (you need to build the Lua project in the Release configuration before the Release folder and library are generated).

26. Select the GCC C++ Compiler ➤ Includes section in the C/C++ Build ➤ Settings dialog.

27. Set Configuration to All Configurations.

28. Click the Add option in the Include paths section.

29. Click the Workspace button.

30. Select the source folder that you added to the Lua project in step 6.

31. Select the Miscellaneous section under the GCC C++ Compiler settings in the C/C++ Build ➤ Settings section.

32. Add –std=c++11 to the Other Flags field.

33. Replace your main function with the source code in Listing 13-2.

Listing 13-2. A Simple Lua Program

```
#include "lua.hpp"

int main()
{
    luaState* pLuaState{ luaL_newstate() };
    if (pLuaState)
    {
        luaL_openlibs(pLuaState);

        lua_close(pLuaState);
    }

    return 0;
}
```

34. Debug your application, and step through to ensure that the pLuaState variable in Listing 13-2 is valid and everything completes as expected.

The steps in this recipe allow you to create a Lua static library project in Eclipse that you can now use throughout the rest of this chapter.

13-3. Creating a Lua Project in Xcode

Problem

You would like to create a C++ program in Xcode that uses the Lua programming language for scripting.

Solution

You can create projects in Xcode that allow you to generate static libraries to be linked into C++ applications.

How It Works

The Xcode IDE lets you create projects that can build executables or libraries. This recipe shows you how to configure a project to build the Lua source as a static library and link this into another project that generates an executable. Follow these steps to set up your projects:

1. Open Xcode.

2. Select Create a New Xcode Project.

3. Select the Library option in the OS X Framework & Library section.

4. Click Next.

5. Set Product Name to Lua.

6. Change Framework to None.

7. Change Type to Static.

8. Select a folder to store the Xcode library project.

9. Download the Lua source from www.lua.org.

10. Unpack the tar,gz file obtained from the web page.

11. Copy the source files from the src folder to the Lua project folder created in step 8.

12. Right-click the project in Xcode, and select Add Files to Lua.

13. Close Xcode.

14. Open Xcode.

15. Select Create a New Xcode Project.

16. Select the Command Line Tool option from the OS X Application section.

17. Set the Product Name field.

18. Uncheck the Use Storyboards option.

19. Click Next.

20. Select a folder to store the project.

21. Open Finder, and browse to the folder containing your Lua project.

23. Drag the xcodeproj file into the app project in the Xcode window. You should now have the Lua project under the app project.

24. Click the app project, and then click the Build Phases option.

25. Expand the Link Binary with Libraries option.

26. Click the plus sign.

27. Select libLua.a from the Workspace section.

28. Click Build Settings.

29. Double-click the Header Search Paths option.

30. Click the plus sign, and enter the path to the Lua source in your Lua project.

31. Replace the code in AppDelegate.m with the code in Listing 13-3.

Listing 13-3. A Simple Lua Program

```
#import "AppDelegate.h"
#include "lua.hpp"

@property (weak) IBOutlet NSWindow *window;
@end

@implementation AppDelegate

- (void)applicationDidFinishLaunching:(NSNotofication *)aNotification {
    lua_State* pLuaState{ luaL_newstate() };
    if (pLuaState)
    {
        luaL_openlibs(pLuaState);

        lua_close(pLuaState);
    }
}

- (void)applicationWillTerminate:(NSNotification *)aNotification {
}

@end
```

32. Build and debug your program, using breakpoints to ensure that the Lua state is initialized properly.

The steps and code provided in this chapter were generated using Xcode 6.1.1. You may have to alter the remaining examples in the chapter to replace the main function with the applicationDidFinishLaunching Objective-C method. If your programs won't compile, try changing Type of Source File from Objective-C to Objective-C++ in the Identity and Type settings.

13-4. Using the Lua Programming Language

Problem

You're a C++ programmer and would like to learn the Lua programming language before you add it to your own applications.

Solution

The Lua programming language documentation is available at /www.lua.org/manual/5.3, and a live demo for testing code is available at www.lua.org/demo.html.

How It Works

The Lua programming language differs from C++ almost entirely. C++ is a compiled language that executes directly on a CPU. Lua, on the other hand, is an interpreted language that is executed by a virtual machine that in turn is running on a CPU. The Lua language comes with a virtual machine that is written in C, and the source is supplied. This means you can embed the virtual machine in any C or C++ program you write, and use the scripting language to write and control high-level features of your application.

It's a good idea to learn some of the features of the Lua programming language before taking on such a task.

Working with Variables

C++ variables are statically typed. That means their type is specified when the variable is declared, and it can't be changed at any point in the future. An int remains an int for the entirety of its lifetime. This helps make C++ programs predictable and highly performant when running on a CPU, because the correct instructions can be used on the correct types of variables. Lua code, on the other hand, runs in a virtual machine; therefore there are fewer restrictions on the types a variable can represent. This leads to Lua being known as a *dynamically typed language*. Listing 13-4 shows the effect dynamic types have on an executing program.

Listing 13-4. Working with Lua Variables

```
variable = 1
print(variable)
print(type(variable))

variable = "1"
print(variable)
print(type(variable))
```

You can copy the code in Listing 13-4 and paste it directly into the Lua Live Demo available at www.lua.org/demo.html. The demo has controls to Run, Clear, Restore, and Restart the Lua virtual machine. Click Run after pasting or typing the code from Listing 13-4, and the following output is generated by the web page:

```
1
number
1
string
```

This output lets you see dynamic types in action. Listing 13-4 initially assigns an integer value to variable. This is output by the print function as the number 1 in the log. The type function returns a string that represents the type of the variable when it's called. The first call to type returns number as the type of variable. A string representation of the value "1" is then assigned to variable. The print function represents the string value of 1 the same way as the integer value. There's no way to tell from that which type is currently stored in the variable. The second call to the type function makes it clear that the value is actually a string and is no longer a number.

Dynamically typed languages can make interesting things happen to your program if you aren't careful. In C++, there is no way to add a number to a string unless you overload the assignment operator to handle this special case. Lua can handle such an operation with ease. Listing 13-5 shows this in action.

Listing 13-5. Adding a Number to a String

```
variable = 1
print(variable)
print(type(variable))

variable = "1"
print(variable)
print(type(variable))

variable = variable + 1
print(variable)
print(type(variable))
```

Listing 13-5 adds an extra operation to the code originally shown in Listing 13-4. This operation adds the value 1 to variable. Recall from the earlier output that the value in variable was last represented by a string. The following output shows what has happened after executing Listing 13-5:

```
1
number
1
string
2.0
number
```

The variable now holds a number that is represented by the floating-point value 2.0. Not all strings are created equal, however. If you try to add a number to a string that can't be converted to a numeric, then you'll receive an error. Listing 13-6 shows code that attempts this.

Listing 13-6. Adding a Number to a Non-Numeric String

```
variable = "name"
variable = variable + 1
```

This code causes the Lua virtual machine to produce the following error:

```
input:2: attempt to perform arithmetic on a string value (global 'variable')
```

All the Lua arithmetic operators can convert types. If both variables are integers, then the resulting value is also an integer. If one or both of the values is a floating-point number, then the result is a floating-point number. And finally, if one or both of the values is a string that can be converted to a number, then the resulting value is a floating-point number. You saw this in the output from Listing 13-4, where the value shown by print was 2.0 with the .0 representing a floating-point number. Some operators, such as the division operator and the exponent operator, always return values that are represented by floating-point numbers.

These examples show one of the features of the Lua programming language that makes it easier for non-programmers to work with. You don't need to have as firm a grasp on the underlying types of variables as you do when using C++. There is no concern about having an adequate number of bytes to represent the value 512 and having to choose between a char, a short, or an int. You also don't need to be concerned with working with C-style strings or C++ STL strings. Any variable can store any type supported by Lua just by assigning a value to a variable at any time in the code.

Working with Functions

The previous section showed that Lua has some built-in functions you can call. It's also possible to create your own functions using the function keyword. Listing 13-7 creates a Lua function.

Listing 13-7. Creating and Calling a Function

```
variable = "name"

function ChangeName()
    variable = "age"
end

print(variable)
ChangeName()
print(variable)
```

Listing 13-7 begins by defining a variable that stores the value "name". This is followed by a function definition that changes the value of variable to "age". The code in the function isn't called at the time of the function definition. This can be seen in the output generated by the print calls. The first call to print generates the output name, and the second call generates the output age.

This is a useful example because it shows that by default, Lua variables are global in nature. The value stored by variable is printed twice: once before the call to ChangeName and once after. If variable wasn't global, you would expect the value to be the same both times. Lua does support the creation of local variables, but you must be careful with their usage. Listing 13-8 shows what happens when you make variable local.

Listing 13-8. Making variable Local

```
local variable = "name"

function ChangeName()
    variable = "age"
end

print(variable)
ChangeName()
print(variable)
```

Adding the local specifier to variable in Listing 13-8 doesn't achieve anything for the code shown. Making this local essentially tells the Lua virtual machine that the variable can be accessed anywhere in the current scope—which means anywhere in the current file. If you're using the Lua demo, you can imagine that the text box for entering your code is a single Lua file. To prevent the ChangeName function from accessing the same instance of variable, you have to use the local keyword on this variable as well, as shown in Listing 13-9.

Listing 13-9. Making the ChangeName variable Local

```
local variable = "name"

function ChangeName()
    local variable = "age"
end

print(variable)
ChangeName()
print(variable)
```

Both calls to print in Listing 13-9 result in the value "name" being printed to the output window. I recommend making all of your variables local to ensure that your code is less likely to introduce bugs that are hard to track down, caused by inadvertently using the same variable name in more than one place at a time.

Functions in Lua always return values. The ChangeName function in Listing 13-9 doesn't specify a return value, so it implicitly returns nil. This can be seen in Listing 13-10.

Listing 13-10. Function Returning nil

```
function GetValue()
    local variable = "age"
end

local value = GetValue()
print(value)
```

This code returns nil to the variable value, and this is printed by the print function. The nil value is the Lua equivalent of nullptr in C++. It means the absence of a value rather than representing 0. Trying to manipulate nil values results in a Lua error such as the following:

```
input:8: attempt to perform arithmetic on a nil value (local 'value')
```

This error was generated by trying to add 1 to value when it stores nil. You can avoid the error by properly returning a value from the GetValue function, as shown in Listing 13-11.

Listing 13-11. Returning Properly from a Function

```
function GetValue()
    return "age"
end

local value = GetValue()
print(value)
```

This listing shows that the return function can be used the same as it is in C++. Lua's return statement isn't the same as return in C++, though. You can use it to return multiple values from a function using the comma operator (,). Listing 13-12 shows this in action.

Listing 13-12. Multiple Return Values

```lua
function GetValues()
    return "name", "age"
end

local name, age = GetValues()
print(name)
print(age)
```

Listing 13-12 shows that to return and store multiple values from a function, you must use the comma operator on the return statement and the assignment statement when defining the function and calling the function.

Working with Tables

Lua provides tables as a means of storing collections of information. A table can be used as either a standard array with an integer-based index or an associative array with key-value pairs. You create a table using curly braces, as shown in Listing 13-13.

Listing 13-13. Creating a Tables

```lua
newTable = {}
```

This code simply creates a table that can now be used to store values. An associative table can use any type of variable as a key. This is true for strings, floats, integers, and even other tables. Listing 13-14 shows how to use a Lua table as an associative array.

Listing 13-14. Adding Values to an Associative Array

```lua
newTable = {}

newTable["value"] = 3.14

newTable[3.14] = "value"

keyTable = {}
newTable[keyTable] = "VALID"

print(newTable["value"])
print(newTable[3.14])
print(newTable[keyTable])
```

Listing 13-14 adds values to a Lua table using keys. There are examples of using strings, floats, and other tables as keys in this listing, and you can see how to use the array operator to assign values to a key in a table as well as read values from a table. Trying to read the value at newTable[3.14] would result in nil being returned before any value was assigned to that key. This is also how you can remove values from a table: assign nil to the key you wish to remove. Listing 13-15 shows the removal of objects from a table.

Listing 13-15. Removing Objects from a Table

```
newTable = {}

newTable["nilValue1"] = 1
newTable["nilValue2"] = 2

print(newTable["nilValue1"])
print(newTable["nilValue2"])

newTable["nilValue1"] = nil
print(newTable["nilValue1"])

print(newTable["nilValue2"])
```

Lua tables can also be used as C-style arrays, and the Lua language provides helper functions to aid in the management of these types of arrays. Listing 13-16 shows the creation of an array table and the modification of its elements.

Listing 13-16. Creating a Lua Array

```
newTable = {}

table.insert(newTable, "first")
table.insert(newTable, "second")
table.insert(newTable, "third")
print(newTable[2])

print(newTable[2])

table.insert(newTable, 2, "fourth")

print(newTable[2])

table.remove(newTable, 1)

print(newTable[1])
print(newTable[2])
print(newTable[3])
print(newTable[4])
```

Listing 13-16 uses the `table.insert` and `table.remove` Lua functions. You can use the `insert` function two ways: without an index, to add elements to the end of the array; or with an index as the second parameter, to insert elements into the array and shift everything from that point on up a place. This shows you that Lua arrays behave more like a C++ `vector`. The `remove` function takes the index that you would like to see removed from the array.

Lua also provides a # operator that can be used with array-style tables. Listing 13-17 shows it in action.

Listing 13-17. Using the # Operator

```
newTable = {}

table.insert(newTable, "first")
table.insert(newTable, "second")
table.insert(newTable, "third")

print(#newTable)

newTable[9] = "fourth"
print(newTable[9])

print(#newTable)
```

The # operator in Listing 13-17 returns the last continuous index that it can find. The first three elements are added without issue, using the insert method; therefore they have continuous indices. However, the element added manually at 9 doesn't. This prevents you from being able to use the # operator to count the number of elements in the array unless you can be certain that all the indices in the array are contiguous.

Using Flow Control

Lua provides an if statement, a for loop, and a while loop to help you structure your programs. These can be used to make decisions and to loop over all the elements in a table. Listing 13-18 shows the Lua if statement.

Listing 13-18. Using the Lua if Statement

```
value1 = 1
value2 = 2

if value1 == value2 then
    print("Are equal")
elseif value1 ~= value2 then
    print("Not equal")
else
    print("Shouldn't be here!")
end
```

Lua's if statement is formed by creating an expression that evaluates to not nil and not false wrapped in the if...then statement. The code in the if block creates its own scope and can consist of its own local variables. The elseif statement is supplied to allow multiple expressions to be evaluated in a sequential order, and the else statement can provide a default behavior of required. Both the elseif and else statements are optional and not required. The entire if statement block is terminated using the end keyword.

There are a couple of things to consider when coming from C++ to Lua and using flow-control statements such as if. Assigning a 0 value to a variable would result in a positive test when working with if statements. The if statement evaluates for not nil and not false, so a value of 0 is given as true. Listing 13-18 also shows the not-equal operator, which in Lua uses the ~ character in place of the C++ language's use of !.

These cases are also true of the while statement, as shown in Listing 13-19.

Listing 13-19. Using a Lua while Loop

```
value1 = 2

while value1 do
    print("We got here! " .. value1)
    value1 = value1 - 1
    if value1 == -1 then
        value1 = nil
    end
end
```

This code uses a while loop to show that a value of 0 evaluates to true in a Lua control statement. The output is as follows:

```
We got here! 2
We got here! 1
We got here! 0
```

The loop is finally terminated after the if statement has triggered and set the value of value1 to nil. A better method for controlling the termination of the while loop is shown in Listing 13-20.

Listing 13-20. Better while Termination

```
value1 = 2

while value1 do
    print("We got here! " .. value1)
    value1 = value1 - 1
    if value1 == -1 then
        break
    end
end
```

Listing 13-20 uses a break statement to exit the execution of the while loop. The break statement works exactly as you would expect when coming from C++. Yet another option for leaving the loop is shown in Listing 13-21.

Listing 13-21. Using Comparison Operators to Leave a Loop

```
value1 = 2

while value1 >= 0 do
    print("We got here! " .. value1)
    value1 = value1 - 1
end
```

Despite the value 0 resulting in a true result in the while loop test, a comparison for 0 or any other valid comparison eventually returns false under normal operating circumstances. Here the value of value1 is compared with 0, and the loop stops executing once the value falls below 0.

You can use the Lua for loop to iterate in an algorithm. Listing 13-22 shows a simple for loop.

Listing 13-22. A Lua for Loop

```
for i=0, 10, 2 do
    print(i)
end
```

This for loop prints the numbers 0, 2, 4, 6, 8, and 10. The statement to generate a for loop takes a start position (in this case, a variable and its value), a limit, and finally a step. This example creates a variable and assigns it 0, loops until the variable is greater than the limit, and adds the step to the variable at each iteration. The loop starts at 0, adds 2 with each iteration, and ends once the variable holds a number greater than 10. It the step was negative, it would loop until the variable held a value less than the limit.

You can also use a for loop to iterate over tables using the pairs or ipairs functions. Listing 13-23 shows these in action.

Listing 13-23. Using pairs and ipairs

```
newTable = {}
newTable["first"] = 1
newTable["second"] = 2
newTable["third"] = 3

for key, value in pairs(newTable) do
    print(key .. ": " .. value)
end

newTable = {}
table.insert(newTable, "first")
table.insert(newTable, "second")
table.insert(newTable, "third")

for index, value in ipairs(newTable) do
    print(index .. ": " .. value)
end
```

The pairs function returns the key and value from each element in an associative array table, and the ipairs function returns the numeric indices of an array-style table. This code shows the benefit of Lua's ability to return multiple values from a function.

13-5. Calling Lua Functions from C++

Problem

You have a task in your program that would benefit from the fast iteration capabilities afforded by scripting in Lua.

Solution

The Lua programming language comes with source code that allows you to compile and execute scripts while your program is running.

How It Works

The Lua C++ API provides a programming interface to the Lua state's stack. The C++ API can manipulate this stack to pass parameters to Lua code and receive values from Lua in return. This capability lets you create Lua source files that can then act as Lua functions. These Lua functions can be updated while your program is running, allowing you to iterate on your program logic much more quickly than would be possible with C++ alone.

The Lua APIs are supplied using the C programming language. This means you have to create proxy objects if you wish to take a more C++-style approach to using Lua. Listing 13-24 shows how you can create a program that loads and executes a Lua script as a function from C++.

Listing 13-24. Calling a Simple Lua Script as a Function

```
#include <iostream>
#include "lua.hpp"

using namespace std;

class Lua
{
private:
    lua_State* m_pLuaState{ nullptr };

public:
    Lua()
        : m_pLuaState{ luaL_newstate() }
    {
        if (m_pLuaState)
        {
            luaL_openlibs(m_pLuaState);
        }
    }

    ~Lua()
    {
        lua_close(m_pLuaState);
    }

    Lua(const Lua& other) = delete;
    Lua& operator=(const Lua& other) = delete;

    Lua(Lua&& rvalue) = delete;
    Lua& operator=(Lua&& rvalue) = delete;
```

```cpp
    bool IsValid() const
    {
        return m_pLuaState != nullptr;
    }

    int LoadFile(const string& filename)
    {
        int status{ luaL_loadfile(m_pLuaState, filename.c_str()) };
        if (status == 0)
        {
            lua_setglobal(m_pLuaState, filename.c_str());
        }
        return status;
    }

    int PCall()
    {
        return lua_pcall(m_pLuaState, 0, LUA_MULTRET, 0);
    }
};

class LuaFunction
{
private:
    Lua& m_Lua;
    string m_Filename;

    int PCall()
    {
        return m_Lua.PCall();
    }

public:
    LuaFunction(Lua& lua, const string& filename)
        : m_Lua{ lua }
        , m_Filename(filename)
    {
        m_Lua.LoadFile(m_Filename);
    }

    ~LuaFunction() = default;

    LuaFunction(const LuaFunction& other) = delete;
    LuaFunction& operator=(const LuaFunction& other) = delete;

    LuaFunction(LuaFunction&& rvalue) = delete;
    LuaFunction& operator=(LuaFunction&& rvalue) = delete;
```

```
    int Call()
    {
        m_Lua.GetGlobal(m_Filename);
        return m_Lua.PCall();
    }
};

int main(int argc, char* argv[])
{
    Lua lua;
    if (lua.IsValid())
    {
        const string filename{ "LuaCode1.lua" };
        LuaFunction function(lua, filename);
        function.Call();
    }

    return 0;
}
```

Listing 13-24 shows a method of containing all the Lua C functions in a single class implementation. This lets you put the definitions for all of these methods in a single C++ file and limit the dependencies on Lua throughout your program. The Lua class is therefore responsible for maintaining the lua_State pointer that manages the Lua context for the program. This example creates a class that limits the ability to copy or move the Lua object; you may need this to be possible, but it isn't necessary for these examples.

The constructor for the Lua class calls the luaL_newstate function. This function calls the lua_newstate function and passes default parameters. You could call lua_newstate directly if you wanted to supply your own memory allocator to the Lua state machine. A successful call to luaL_newstate results in the m_pLuaState field storing a valid address for the state. If that's true, then the luaL_openlibs function is called. This function automatically loads the Lua-provided libraries into the state you created. You can avoid calling this function if you have no need for the Lua built-in library functionality.

The Lua class destructor is responsible for calling lua_close to destroy the Lua context created by luaL_newstate in the constructor. The IsValid function provides a simple method for your calling code to determine whether the Lua context was initialized correctly in the constructor.

The LuaFunction class stores a reference to the Lua class that it uses for the context. This class once again prevents copying and moving. The constructor takes a reference to the Lua object that provides it with functionality and a string containing the name of the file to load that contains the Lua source code. The constructor uses the m_Lua object to call the LoadFile method and passes the m_Filename field. The LoadFile method calls luaL_loadfile, which reads the file, compiles the Lua source, and pushes a Lua function object onto the top of the Lua stack using the compiled code. If the luaL_loadfile call was successful, the lua_setglobal function is called. This function gets the top object from the stack and assigns it to a global object with the name supplied. In this case, the function object created by luaL_loadfile is assigned to a global variable named with the name of the source file.

The main function creates a LuaFunction object with a file named LuaCode1.lua. The source of this file is shown in Listing 13-25.

Listing 13-25. The Code from LuaCode1.lua

```
print("Printing From Lua!")
```

This Lua code results in a simple message being printed to the console. This occurs when the main function calls the LuaFunction::Call method. This method uses the Lua::GetGlobal function to move the global object with a given name to the top of the stack. In this case, the m_Filename variable moves the function object created in the LoadFile method onto the stack. The Lua::PCall method then calls the function that is closest to the top of the stack. The output generated by this program is shown in Figure 13-2.

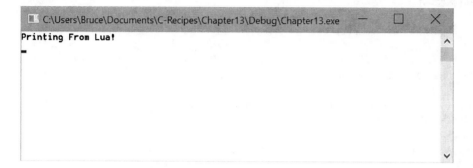

Figure 13-2. *The output generated by running the code in Listing 13-24 and Listing 13-25*

Listing 13-24 doesn't initialize any data to be consumed by the Lua script. You can handle this by creating classes to represent Lua types. Listing 13-26 creates a LuaTable class to create Lua tables in C++ that can then be accessed by Lua.

Listing 13-26. Creating a Lua Table in C++

```cpp
#include <iostream>
#include "lua.hpp"
#include <vector>

using namespace std;

class Lua
{
private:
    lua_State* m_pLuaState{ nullptr };

public:
    Lua()
        : m_pLuaState{ luaL_newstate() }
    {
        if (m_pLuaState)
        {
            luaL_openlibs(m_pLuaState);
        }
    }

    ~Lua()
    {
        lua_close(m_pLuaState);
    }
```

```cpp
    Lua(const Lua& other) = delete;
    Lua& operator=(const Lua& other) = delete;

    Lua(Lua&& rvalue) = delete;
    Lua& operator=(Lua&& rvalue) = delete;

    bool IsValid() const
    {
        return m_pLuaState != nullptr;
    }

    int LoadFile(const string& filename)
    {
        int status{ luaL_loadfile(m_pLuaState, filename.c_str()) };
        if (status == 0)
        {
            lua_setglobal(m_pLuaState, filename.c_str());
            Pop(1);
        }
        return status;
    }

    int PCall()
    {
        return lua_pcall(m_pLuaState, 0, LUA_MULTRET, 0);
    }

    void NewTable(const string& name)
    {
        lua_newtable(m_pLuaState);
        lua_setglobal(m_pLuaState, name.c_str());
    }

    void GetGlobal(const string& name)
    {
        lua_getglobal(m_pLuaState, name.c_str());
    }

    void PushNumber(double number)
    {
        lua_pushnumber(m_pLuaState, number);
    }

    void SetTableValue(double index, double value)
    {
        PushNumber(index);
        PushNumber(value);
        lua_rawset(m_pLuaState, -3);
    }
```

382

```
    double GetNumber()
    {
        return lua_tonumber(m_pLuaState, -1);
    }

    void Pop(int number)
    {
        lua_pop(m_pLuaState, number);
    }
};

class LuaTable
{
private:
    Lua& m_Lua;
    string m_Name;

public:
    LuaTable(Lua& lua, const string& name)
        : m_Lua{ lua }
        , m_Name(name)
    {
        m_Lua.NewTable(m_Name);
    }

    void Set(const vector<int>& values)
    {
        Push();

        for (unsigned int i = 0; i < values.size(); ++i)
        {
            m_Lua.SetTableValue(i +  1, values[i]);
        }

        m_Lua.Pop(1);
    }

    void Push()
    {
        m_Lua.GetGlobal(m_Name);
    }
};

class LuaFunction
{
private:
    Lua& m_Lua;
    string m_Filename;
```

```
    int PCall()
    {
        return m_Lua.PCall();
    }

protected:
    int Call()
    {
        m_Lua.GetGlobal(m_Filename);
        return m_Lua.PCall();
    }

    double GetReturnValue()
    {
        double result{ m_Lua.GetNumber() };
        m_Lua.Pop(1);
        return result;
    }

public:
    LuaFunction(Lua& lua, const string& filename)
        : m_Lua{ lua }
        , m_Filename( filename )
    {
        int status{ m_Lua.LoadFile(m_Filename) };
    }
};

class PrintTable
    : public LuaFunction
{
public:
    PrintTable(Lua& lua, const string& filename)
        : LuaFunction(lua, filename)
    {

    }

    double Call(LuaTable& table)
    {
        double sum{};

        int status{ LuaFunction::Call() };
        if (status)
        {
            throw(status);
        }
        else
        {
            sum = LuaFunction::GetReturnValue();
        }
```

```
            return sum;
        }
    };

    int main(int argc, char* argv[])
    {
        Lua lua;
        if (lua.IsValid())
        {
            int loop = 2;
            while (loop > 0)
            {
                const string tableName("cTable");
                LuaTable table(lua, tableName);

                vector<int> values{ 1, 2, 3, 4, 5 };
                table.Set(values);

                const string filename{ "LuaCode.lua" };
                PrintTable printTableFunction(lua, filename);

                try
                {
                    double result{ printTableFunction.Call(table) };
                    cout << "Result: " << result << endl;
                }
                catch (int error)
                {
                    cout << "Call error: " << error << endl;
                }

                cout << "Waiting" << endl;

                int input;
                cin >> input;

                --loop;
            }
        }

        return 0;
    }
```

Listing 13-26 adds a LuaTable class along with the relevant methods to the Lua class to manage the table. The lua_newtable function creates a new table and pushes it onto the stack. Then element is then assigned to a global variable with the supplied name in the LuaTable constructor. Values are added to the table using the Lua::SetTableValue method. This method only supports number indices for the tables and works by pushing two numbers onto the stack: the index to be assigned in the table and the value to assign to that index. The lua_rawset function assigns a value to an index on a table, with the table in question existing at the supplied index. The first element on the stack is referenced by -1, and this will be the value; the second element on the stack at this point is the index; and the third element is the table, so the value -3 is passed to the lua_rawset function. Both the index and the value are popped from the stack by this call, and therefore the table is once again found at position -1.

The LuaFunction class is inherited into a new class named PrintTable. This class provides a new call method that knows how to retrieve the value returned from the Lua script supplied. The Lua code in Listing 13-27 shows why this is necessary.

Listing 13-27. The LuaCode2.lua Source

```
local x = 0
for i = 1, #cTable do
  print(i, cTable[i])
  x = x + cTable[i]
end
return x
```

This code loops over the cTable table set up in C++ and prints out the values. It also calculates the total of all the values in the table and returns them to the calling code using the stack.

The C++ main function creates a table and assigns five integers to it using a vector. The PrintTable class creates a C++ Lua function with the LuaCode2.lua file. This function is called, and the value returned is retrieved from the stack using the Lua::GetReturnValue function.

The big thing to notice in main is the ability to reload Lua scripts and update the code executed at runtime. The main function stalls using cin. While it's waiting, you can alter the Lua script and see the changes reflected once you unblock execution. Figure 13-3 shows output proving that this can occur.

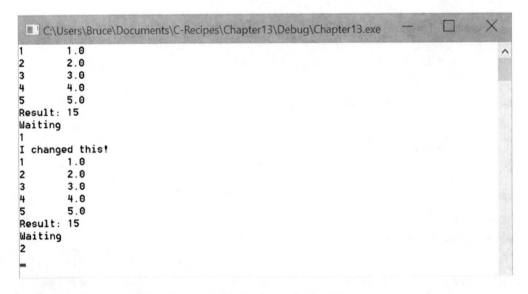

Figure 13-3. Output showing that scripts can be changed at runtime

This output shows that changing the Lua code and reloading the function replaces the code at the given global variable. I added a single line of output to the script: you can see this in the figure where the line "I changed this!" is printed.

CHAPTER 13 ■ SCRIPTING

13-6. Calling C Functions from Lua

Problem

You have some highly complex code that would benefit from the high performance afforded by C/C++ code, but you would like to be able to call these functions from Lua.

Solution

Lua provides the `lua_CFunction` type that lets you create C functions that can be referenced by Lua code.

How It Works

The Lua API provides a type `lua_CFunction` that essentially determines the signature that can be used with a C function to allow it to be called from Lua. Listing 13-28 shows an example that creates a function that can add all the parameters supplied to it by Lua.

Listing 13-28. Calling a C Function from Lua

```
#include <iostream>
#include "lua.hpp"
#include <vector>

using namespace std;

namespace
{
    int Sum(lua_State *L)
    {
        unsigned int numArguments{ static_cast<unsigned int>(lua_gettop(L)) };
        lua_Number sum{ 0 };
        for (unsigned int i = 1; i <= numArguments; ++i)
        {
            if (!lua_isnumber(L, i))
            {
                lua_pushstring(L, "incorrect argument");
                lua_error(L);
            }
            sum += lua_tonumber(L, i);
        }
        lua_pushnumber(L, sum / numArguments);
        lua_pushnumber(L, sum);
        return 2;
    }
}

class Lua
{
private:
    lua_State* m_pLuaState{ nullptr };
```

```cpp
public:
    Lua()
        : m_pLuaState{ luaL_newstate() }
    {
        if (m_pLuaState)
        {
            luaL_openlibs(m_pLuaState);
        }
    }

    ~Lua()
    {
        lua_close(m_pLuaState);
    }

    Lua(const Lua& other) = delete;
    Lua& operator=(const Lua& other) = delete;

    Lua(Lua&& rvalue) = delete;
    Lua& operator=(Lua&& rvalue) = delete;

    bool IsValid() const
    {
        return m_pLuaState != nullptr;
    }

    int LoadFile(const string& filename)
    {
        int status{ luaL_loadfile(m_pLuaState, filename.c_str()) };
        if (status == 0)
        {
            lua_setglobal(m_pLuaState, filename.c_str());
        }
        return status;
    }

    int PCall()
    {
        return lua_pcall(m_pLuaState, 0, LUA_MULTRET, 0);
    }

    void NewTable(const string& name)
    {
        lua_newtable(m_pLuaState);
        lua_setglobal(m_pLuaState, name.c_str());
    }

    void GetGlobal(const string& name)
    {
        lua_getglobal(m_pLuaState, name.c_str());
    }
```

```cpp
    void PushNumber(double number)
    {
        lua_pushnumber(m_pLuaState, number);
    }

    void SetTableValue(double index, double value)
    {
        PushNumber(index);
        PushNumber(value);
        lua_rawset(m_pLuaState, -3);
    }

    double GetNumber()
    {
        return lua_tonumber(m_pLuaState, -1);
    }

    void Pop(int number)
    {
        lua_pop(m_pLuaState, number);
    }

    void CreateCFunction(const string& name, lua_CFunction function)
    {
        lua_pushcfunction(m_pLuaState, function);
        lua_setglobal(m_pLuaState, name.c_str());
    }
};

class LuaTable
{
private:
    Lua& m_Lua;
    string m_Name;

public:
    LuaTable(Lua& lua, const string& name)
        : m_Lua{ lua }
        , m_Name(name)
    {
        m_Lua.NewTable(m_Name);
    }

    void Set(const vector<int>& values)
    {
        Push();

        for (unsigned int i = 0; i < values.size(); ++i)
        {
            m_Lua.SetTableValue(i + 1, values[i]);
        }
```

```cpp
        m_Lua.Pop(1);
    }

    void Push()
    {
        m_Lua.GetGlobal(m_Name);
    }
};

class LuaFunction
{
private:
    Lua& m_Lua;
    string m_Filename;

protected:
    int PCall()
    {
        m_Lua.GetGlobal(m_Filename);
        return m_Lua.PCall();
    }

    double GetReturnValue()
    {
        double result{ m_Lua.GetNumber() };
        m_Lua.Pop(1);
        return result;
    }

public:
    LuaFunction(Lua& lua, const string& filename)
        : m_Lua{ lua }
        , m_Filename(filename)
    {
        int status{ m_Lua.LoadFile(m_Filename) };
    }
};

class PrintTable
    : public LuaFunction
{
public:
    PrintTable(Lua& lua, const string& filename)
        : LuaFunction(lua, filename)
    {

    }

    double Call(LuaTable& table)
    {
        double sum{};
```

```
        int status{ LuaFunction::PCall() };
        if (status)
        {
            throw(status);
        }
        else
        {
            sum = LuaFunction::GetReturnValue();
        }

        return sum;
    }
};

int main(int argc, char* argv[])
{
    Lua lua;
    if (lua.IsValid())
    {
        const string functionName("Sum");
        lua.CreateCFunction(functionName, Sum);

        const string tableName("cTable");
        LuaTable table(lua, tableName);

        vector<int> values{ 1, 2, 3, 4, 5 };
        table.Set(values);

        const string filename{ "LuaCode3.lua" };
        PrintTable printTableFunction(lua, filename);

        try
        {
            double result{ printTableFunction.Call(table) };
            cout << "Result: " << result << endl;
        }
        catch (int error)
        {
            cout << "Call error: " << error << endl;
        }

        cout << "Waiting" << endl;

        int input;
        cin >> input;
    }

    return 0;
}
```

The Sum function in Listing 13-28 shows how a C function must interface with Lua. The signature is simple: a C function that can be called from Lua returns an integer and receives a pointer to a lua_State object as a parameter. When Lua calls a C function, it pushes the number of arguments passed onto the top of the Lua stack. This value is read by the function called, which can then loop and pull the appropriate number of elements from the stack. A C function then pushes the appropriate number of results onto the stack and returns the number of elements that the calling code must pop from the stack.

The Lua::CreateCFunction method uses the lua_pushcfunction method to push a lua_CFunction object onto the stack and then uses lua_setglobal to assign it to a named object in the global context. The main function simply calls CreateCFunction and supplies the name to use in Lua along with the function pointer to be used. The Lua code to call this function is shown in Listing 13-29.

Listing 13-29. Lua Code Calling a C Function

```
local x = 0
for i = 1, #cTable do
  print(i, cTable[i])
  x = x + cTable[i]
end
local average, sum = Sum(cTable[1], cTable[2], cTable[3])
print("Average: " .. average)
print("Sum: " .. sum)
return sum
```

This Lua code shows the call to Sum and retrieves the average and sum values.

13-7. Creating Asynchronous Lua Functions

Problem

You have a long-running Lua operation that you would like to prevent from blocking your program's execution.

Solution

Lua allows you to create *coroutines*. These can be yielded from to let your program execution continue and allow for the creation of well-behaved, long-running Lua tasks. Each coroutine receives its own unique Lua context.

How It Works

The Lua programming language allows for the creation of coroutines. Coroutines differ from normal functions in that they can call the coroutine.yield function from Lua to inform the state machine that their execution is suspended. The C API provides a resume function that you can call to wake up the coroutine after some time to allow the thread to check whether the situation it was waiting for has occurred. This could be because you want to wait for an animation to complete or the Lua script is waiting for information to be obtained from an I/O process, such as reading from a file or accessing data on a server.

You create a Lua coroutine using the lua_newthread function. Despite the name, a Lua coroutine is executed in the thread where the lua_resume call is made. The lua_resume call is passed a pointer to a lua_State object that contains a stack for the coroutine. The code executed on the stack is the Lua function object that exists closest to the top at the time of the lua_resume call. Listing 13-30 shows the C++ code required to set up a Lua thread and execute its code.

Listing 13-30. Creating a Lua Coroutine

```cpp
#include <iostream>
#include <lua.hpp>

using namespace std;

class Lua
{
private:
    lua_State* m_pLuaState{ nullptr };
    bool m_IsThread{ false };

public:
    Lua()
        : m_pLuaState{ luaL_newstate() }
    {
        if (m_pLuaState)
        {
            luaL_openlibs(m_pLuaState);
        }
    }

    Lua(lua_State* pLuaState)
        : m_pLuaState{ pLuaState }
    {
        if (m_pLuaState)
        {
            luaL_openlibs(m_pLuaState);
        }
    }
    ~Lua()
    {
        if (!m_IsThread && m_pLuaState)
        {
            lua_close(m_pLuaState);
        }
    }

    Lua(const Lua& other) = delete;
    Lua& operator=(const Lua& other) = delete;

    Lua(Lua&& rvalue)
        : m_pLuaState( rvalue.m_pLuaState )
        , m_IsThread( rvalue.m_IsThread )
    {
        rvalue.m_pLuaState = nullptr;
    }
```

```cpp
    Lua& operator=(Lua&& rvalue)
    {
        if (this != &rvalue)
        {
            m_pLuaState = rvalue.m_pLuaState;
            m_IsThread = rvalue.m_IsThread;
            rvalue.m_pLuaState = nullptr;
        }
    }

    bool IsValid() const
    {
        return m_pLuaState != nullptr;
    }

    int LoadFile(const string& filename)
    {
        int status{ luaL_loadfile(m_pLuaState, filename.c_str()) };
        if (status == 0)
        {
            lua_setglobal(m_pLuaState, filename.c_str());
        }
        return status;
    }

    void GetGlobal(const string& name)
    {
        lua_getglobal(m_pLuaState, name.c_str());
    }

    Lua CreateThread()
    {
        Lua threadContext(lua_newthread(m_pLuaState));
        threadContext.m_IsThread = true;
        return move(threadContext);
    }

    int ResumeThread()
    {
        return lua_resume(m_pLuaState, m_pLuaState, 0);
    }
};

class LuaFunction
{
private:
    Lua& m_Lua;
    string m_Filename;
```

```cpp
public:
    LuaFunction(Lua& lua, const string& filename)
        : m_Lua{ lua }
        , m_Filename(filename)
    {
        int status{ m_Lua.LoadFile(m_Filename) };
    }

    void Push()
    {
        m_Lua.GetGlobal(m_Filename);
    }
};

class LuaThread
{
private:
    Lua m_Lua;
    LuaFunction m_LuaFunction;
    int m_Status{ -1 };

public:
    LuaThread(Lua&& lua, const string& functionFilename)
        : m_Lua(move(lua))
        , m_LuaFunction(m_Lua, functionFilename)
    {

    }

    ~LuaThread() = default;

    LuaThread(const LuaThread& other) = delete;
    LuaThread& operator=(const LuaThread& other) = delete;

    LuaThread(LuaThread&& rvalue) = delete;
    LuaThread& operator=(LuaThread&& rvalue) = delete;

    void Resume()
    {
        if (!IsFinished())
        {
            if (m_Status == -1)
            {
                m_LuaFunction.Push();
            }

            m_Status = m_Lua.ResumeThread();
        }
    }
```

```
        bool IsFinished() const
        {
            return m_Status == LUA_OK;
        }
};

int main(int argc, char* argv[])
{
    Lua lua;
    if (lua.IsValid())
    {
        const string functionName("LuaCode4.lua");
        LuaThread myThread(lua.CreateThread(), functionName);

        while (!myThread.IsFinished())
        {
            myThread.Resume();
            cout << "myThread yielded or finished!" << endl;
        }
        cout << "myThread finished!" << endl;
    }

    return 0;
}
```

The Lua class in Listing 13-30 contains a pointer to a lua_State object and a bool variable indicating whether a specific object has been created to handle a Lua thread. This is necessary to ensure that only a single Lua object is responsible for calling lua_close in its destructor. You can see that this bool value is checked in the ~Lua method.

The m_IsThread bool is set to true in the Lua::CreateThread method. This method calls the lua_newthread function and passes the new lua_State pointer to a newly constructed Lua object. This object then has the m_IsThread bool set to true and is returned from the function. The Lua object is returned using move semantics. This ensures that there can't be any duplicates of a single Lua object at any time, and this is enforced by the delete keyword being specified in the copy constructor and copy assignment operator. Only the move constructor and move assignment operator are defined.

The Lua::Resume method is also shown in Listing 13-30. This method is responsible for starting or resuming the execution of a Lua coroutine.

The LuaThread class is responsible for managing a Lua coroutine. The constructor takes an rvalue reference to a Lua object and a string containing the name of the file to be loaded. The class has fields to store the Lua object and a LuaFunction object that will be used to Push the function onto the coroutine's stack. The m_Status field determines when the coroutine has finished execution. It's initialized to -1 because this value isn't used by Lua to represent a state. The LUA_OK value is returned from lua_resume when the coroutine execution has been completed, and the LUA_YIELD value is returned when the coroutine has yielded. The LuaThread::Resume function first checks whether the status has been set to LUA_OK; if it has, then nothing is done. If the m_Status variable contains -1, then the m_LuaFunction object is pushed onto the stack. The m_Status variable is updated with the value returned by Lua::ResumeThread.

The main function uses all of this functionality by creating a LuaThread object and calling LuaThread::Resume in a while loop that executes until IsFinished returns true on the myThread object. The LuaCode4.lua file contains the Lua code from Listing 13-31, which contains several yields in a loop.

Listing 13-31. The LuaCode4.lua Source

```lua
for i=1, 10, 1 do
        print("Going for yield " .. i .. "!")
        coroutine.yield()
end
```

This is a simple example of how to use the coroutine.yield function from within Lua code. The lua_resume C function returns LUA_YIELD when this Lua function is executed in the running Lua script. Figure 13-4 shows the result of running the combination containing the C++ code in Listing 13-30 and the Lua code in Listing 13-31.

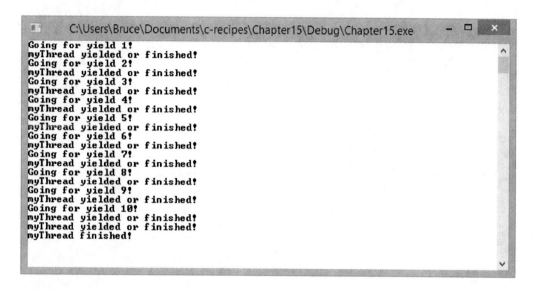

Figure 13-4. *The output generated by executing Listing 13-30 in combination with Listing 13-31*

CHAPTER 14

■ ■ ■

3D Graphics Programming

C++ is the programming language of choice for developers of high-performance applications. This often includes applications that are required to display 3D graphics to a user. 3D graphics are common in medical applications, design applications, and video games. All of these types of applications demand responsiveness as a key usability feature. This makes the C++ language a perfect choice for this type of program, because programmers can target and optimize for specific hardware platforms.

Microsoft supplies the proprietary DirectX API for building 3D applications for the Windows operating system. This chapter, however, looks at writing a simple 3D program using the OpenGL API. OpenGL is supported on Windows, OS X, and most Linux distributions; it's a perfect choice in this case, because you might be using any of these operating systems.

One of the more tedious aspects of OpenGL programming is the requirement to set up and manage windows in multiple operating systems if you're targeting more than one. This job is made much easier by the GLFW package, which abstracts this task away behind an API so you don't have to worry about the details.

14-1. An Introduction to GLFW

Problem

You're writing a cross platform application containing 3D graphics, and you want a fast way to get up and running.

Solution

GLFW abstracts out the task of creating and managing a window for many popular operating systems.

How It Works

The GLFW API is written in the C programming language and can therefore be used in C++ applications without issue. The API is available to download from www.glfw.org. You can also read the documentation for the API at the same web site. The instructions to configure and build a GLFW library change frequently and so aren't included with this chapter. At the time of this writing, the most up-to-date instructions for building GLFW can be found at www.glfw.org/docs/latest/compile.html.

The instructions for GLFW currently involve using CMake to build a project that can then be used to compile a library that you can link into your own project. Once you have this up and running, you can use the code in Listing 14-1 to run a program that initializes OpenGL and creates a window for your program.

Listing 14-1. A Simple GLFW Program

```
#include "GLFW\glfw3.h"

intmain()
{
    GLFWwindow* window;

    /* Initialize the library */
    if (!glfwInit())
        return -1;

    /* Create a windowed mode window and its OpenGL context */
    window = glfwCreateWindow(640, 480, "Hello World", NULL, NULL);
    if (!window)
    {
        glfwTerminate();
        return -1;
    }

    /* Make the window's context current */
    glfwMakeContextCurrent(window);

    /* Loop until the user closes the window */
    while (!glfwWindowShouldClose(window))
    {
        /* Render here */

        /* Swap front and back buffers */
        glfwSwapBuffers(window);

        /* Poll for and process events */
        glfwPollEvents();
    }

    glfwTerminate();
    return 0;
}
```

The code in Listing 14-1 is the sample program supplied on the GLFW web site to ensure that your build is working properly. It initializes the glfw library with a call to glfwInit. A window is created using the glfwCreateWindow function. The sample creates a window with 640 × 480 resolution and the title "Hello World". If the window creation fails, then the glfwTerminate function is called. If it's successful, the program calls glfwMakeContextCurrent. The OpenGL API supports multiple rendering contexts, and you have to ensure that yours is the current context when you want to render. The main loop of the program continues until the glfwWindowShouldClose function returns true. The glfwSwapBuffers function is responsible for swapping the front buffer with the back buffer. Double-buffered rendering is useful to prevent the user from seeing unfinished frames of animation. The graphics card can display one buffer while the program is rendering into a second. These buffers are swapped at the end of each frame. The glfwPollEvents function is responsible for communicating with the operating system and receiving any messages. The program ends with a call to glfwTerminate to shut everything down.

The OpenGL API provides a lot of its functionality through extensions, and this means the functions you're using may not be supported directly by the platform you're working on. Fortunately, the GLEW library is available to help with using OpenGL extensions on multiple platforms. Again, the instructions for obtaining, building, and linking this library change from time to time. The latest information can be obtained from the GLEW web site at http://glew.sourceforge.net.

Once you have GLEW up and running, you can initialize the library using the glewInit function call shown in Listing 14-2.

Listing 14-2. Initializing GLEW

```
#include <GL/glew.h>
#include "GLFW/glfw3.h"

int main(void)
{
    GLFWwindow* window;

    // Initialize the library
    if (!glfwInit())
    {
        return -1;
    }

    // Create a windowed mode window and its OpenGL context
    window = glfwCreateWindow(640, 480, "Hello World", NULL, NULL);
    if (!window)
    {
        glfwTerminate();
        return -1;
    }

    // Make the window's context current
    glfwMakeContextCurrent(window);

    GLenum glewError{ glewInit() };
    if (glewError != GLEW_OK)
    {
        return -1;
    }

    // Loop until the user closes the window
    while (!glfwWindowShouldClose(window))
    {
        // Swap front and back buffers
        glfwSwapBuffers(window);

        // Poll for and process events
        glfwPollEvents();
    }

    glfwTerminate();
    return 0;
}
```

It's important that this step occurs after you have a valid and current OpenGL context, because the GLEW library relies on this in order to load the most common extensions you may be using from the OpenGL API.

There are sample applications accompanying this book that have both GLEW and GLFW included and configured. You should download these if you would like to see a project that has been configured to work with these libraries. In addition, excellent documentation is available at the libraries' web sites (http://glew.sourceforge.net/install.html and www.glfw.org/download.html).

14-2. Rendering a Triangle

Problem

You would like to render a 3D object in your application.

Solution

OpenGL provides APIs to configure the rendering pipeline on a graphics card and display 3D objects onscreen.

How It Works

OpenGL is a graphics library that allows an application to send data to a GPU in a computer to render images to a window. This recipe introduces you to three concepts that are necessary for rendering graphics to a window when using OpenGL on a modern computer system. The first is the concept of *geometry*.

The geometry of an object is made up of a collection of vertices and indices. A vertex specifies the point in space where the vertex should be rendered onto the screen. A vertex passes through the GPU, and different operations are applied to it at different points. This recipe bypasses most of the processing of the vertices and instead specifies vertices in what is known as normalized device coordinates. A GPU transforms vertices using a vertex shader to generate vertices that sit inside a normalized cube. These vertices are then passed to a fragment shader, and the fragments are used to determine the output color to be written to the frame buffer at a given point. You learn more about these operations as you move through this chapter's recipes.

The code in Listing 14-3 shows the Geometry class and how it can be used to specify storage for vertices and indices.

Listing 14-3. The Geometry Class

```
using namespace std;

class Geometry
{
public:
    using Vertices = vector < float >;
    using Indices = vector < unsigned short >;

private:
    Vertices m_Vertices;
    Indices m_Indices;
```

```cpp
public:
    Geometry() = default;
    ~Geometry() = default;

    void SetVertices(const Vertices& vertices)
    {
        m_Vertices = vertices;
    }

    Vertices::size_type GetNumVertices() const
    {
        return m_Vertices.size();
    }

    Vertices::const_pointer GetVertices() const
    {
        return m_Vertices.data();
    }

    void SetIndices(const Indices& indices)
    {
        m_Indices = indices;
    }

    Indices::size_type GetNumIndices() const
    {
        return m_Indices.size();
    }

    Indices::const_pointer GetIndices() const
    {
        return m_Indices.data();
    }
};
```

The Geometry class contains two vector aliases. The first alias is used to define a type that represents a vector of floats. This type is used to store vertices in the Geometry class. The second type alias defines a vector of unsigned shorts. This type alias is used to create the m_Indices vector that is used to store indices.

Indices are a useful tool when working with OpenGL because they allow you to reduce duplicate vertices in your vertex data. A mesh is typically made up of a collection of triangles, each of which shares edges with other triangles to create a complete shape that doesn't have any holes. This means a s ingle vertex that isn't at the edge of an object is shared between multiple triangles. Indices let you create all the vertices for a mesh and then use the indices to represent the order in which OpenGL reads the vertices to create the individual triangles of the mesh. You see vertex and index definitions later in this recipe.

A typical OpenGL program consists of multiple shader programs. Shaders allow you control the behavior of multiple stages of the OpenGL rendering pipeline. At this point, you need to be able to create a vertex shader and a fragment shader that can act as a single pipeline for the GPU. OpenGL enforces this by having you create a vertex shader and a fragment shader independently and link them into a single shader program. You typically have more than one of these, so the Shader base class in Listing 14-4 shows how to create a base class to be shared among multiple derived shader programs.

Listing 14-4. The Shader Class

```cpp
class Shader
{
private:
    void LoadShader(GLuint id, const std::string& shaderCode)
    {
        const unsigned int NUM_SHADERS{ 1 };

        const char* pCode{ shaderCode.c_str() };
        GLint length{ static_cast<GLint>(shaderCode.length()) };

        glShaderSource(id, NUM_SHADERS, &pCode, &length);

        glCompileShader(id);

        glAttachShader(m_ProgramId, id);
    }

protected:
    GLuint m_VertexShaderId{ GL_INVALID_VALUE };
    GLuint m_FragmentShaderId{ GL_INVALID_VALUE };
    GLint m_ProgramId{ GL_INVALID_VALUE };

    std::string m_VertexShaderCode;
    std::string m_FragmentShaderCode;

public:
    Shader() = default;
    virtual ~Shader() = default;

    virtual void Link()
    {
        m_ProgramId = glCreateProgram();

        m_VertexShaderId = glCreateShader(GL_VERTEX_SHADER);
        LoadShader(m_VertexShaderId, m_VertexShaderCode);

        m_FragmentShaderId = glCreateShader(GL_FRAGMENT_SHADER);
        LoadShader(m_FragmentShaderId, m_FragmentShaderCode);

        glLinkProgram(m_ProgramId);
    }

    virtual void Setup(const Geometry& geometry)
    {
        glUseProgram(m_ProgramId);
    }
};
```

The Shader class is the first time you see the use of the OpenGL API. This class contains variables for storing the IDs that OpenGL provides to act as handles to the vertex and fragment shaders as well as the shader program. The m_ProgramId field is initialized in the Link method when it's assigned the result of the glCreateProgram method. m_VertexShaderId is assigned the value of the glCreateShader program, which is passed the GL_VERTEX_SHADER variable. The m_FragmentShaderId variable is initialized using the same variable, but it's passed the GL_FRAGMENT_SHADER variable. You can use the LoadShader method to load shader code for either a vertex shader of a fragment shader. You can see this when the LoadShader method is called twice in the Link method: first with the m_VertexShaderId and m_VertexShaderCode variables as parameters and the second time with the m_FragmentShaderId and m_FragentShaderCode variables. The Link method ends with a call to glLinkProgram.

The LoadShader method is responsible for attaching the shader source code to the shader ID, compiling the shader, and attaching it to the relevant OpenGL shader program. The Setup method is used while rendering objects and tells OpenGL that you would like to make this shader program the active shader in use. This recipe needs a single shader program to render a triangle to the screen. This shader program is created by deriving a class named BasicShader from the Shader class in Listing 14-4, as shown in Listing 14-5.

Listing 14-5. The BasicShader Class

```
class BasicShader
    : public Shader
{
private:
    GLint           m_PositionAttributeHandle;

public:
    BasicShader()
    {
        m_VertexShaderCode =
            "attribute vec4 a_vPosition;                     \n"
            "void main(){                                    \n"
            "        gl_Position = a_vPosition;              \n"
            "}                                               \n";

        m_FragmentShaderCode =
            "#version 150                                    \n"
            "precision mediump float;                        \n"
            "void main(){                                    \n"
            "    gl_FragColor = vec4(0.2, 0.2, 0.2, 1.0);   \n"
            "}                                               \n";
    }

    ~BasicShader() override = default;

    void Link() override
    {
        Shader::Link();

        GLint success;
        glGetProgramiv(m_ProgramId, GL_ACTIVE_ATTRIBUTES, &success);

        m_PositionAttributeHandle = glGetAttribLocation(m_ProgramId, "a_vPosition");
    }
```

```
    void Setup(const Geometry& geometry) override
    {
        Shader::Setup(geometry);

        glVertexAttribPointer(
            m_PositionAttributeHandle,
            3,
            GL_FLOAT,
            GL_FALSE,
            0,
            geometry.GetVertices());
        glEnableVertexAttribArray(m_PositionAttributeHandle);
    }
};
```

The BasicShader class begins by initializing the protected m_VertexShaderCode and m_FragmentShaderCode variables from the Shader class in its constructor. The Link method is responsible for calling the base class Link method and then retrieving handles to the attributes in the shader code. The Setup method also calls the Setup method in the base class. It then sets up the attribute in the shader program. An *attribute* is a variable that receives data from a data stream or fields set using the OpenGL API functions from the application code. In this case, the attribute is a vec4 field in the GL Shading Language (GLSL) code. GLSL is used to write OpenGL shader code; this language is based on C and is therefore familiar, but it contains its own types and keywords necessary for communication with the application-side OpenGL calls. The a_vPosition vec4 attribute in the vertex shader code is responsible for receiving every position in a stream of vertices sent to OpenGL for rendering. A handle to the attribute is retrieved using the glGetAttribLocation OpenGL API function that takes the program ID and the name of the attribute to be retrieved. The attribute handle for a vertex position can then be used with the glVertexAttribPointer function in the Setup method. This method takes the attribute handle as a parameter followed by the number of elements per vertex. In this case, the vertices are supplied with an x, y, z component; therefore the number 3 is passed to the size parameter. The GL_FLOAT value specifies that the vertices are floating-point. GL_FALSE tells OpenGL that the vertices should not be normalized by the API when it receives them. The 0 value tells OpenGL the size of the gap between positions of the vertex data; in this case there are no gaps, so you can pass 0. Finally, a pointer to the vertex data is supplied. After this function call, the glEnableVertexAttribArray function is called to tell OpenGL that the attribute should be enabled using the data supplied to it in the previous call, to supply position data to the vertex-shader execution system on the GPU.

The next step is to use these classes in the main function to render a triangle to your window. Listing 14-6 contains the complete listing for a program that achieves this.

Listing 14-6. A Program that Renders a Triangle

```
#include "GL/glew.h"
#include "GLFW/glfw3.h"
#include <string>
#include <vector>

using namespace std;

class Geometry
{
public:
    using Vertices = vector < float >;
    using Indices = vector < unsigned short >;
```

```cpp
private:
    Vertices m_Vertices;
    Indices m_Indices;

public:
    Geometry() = default;
    ~Geometry() = default;

    void SetVertices(const Vertices& vertices)
    {
        m_Vertices = vertices;
    }

    Vertices::size_type GetNumVertices() const
    {
        return m_Vertices.size();
    }

    Vertices::const_pointer GetVertices() const
    {
        return m_Vertices.data();
    }

    void SetIndices(const Indices& indices)
    {
        m_Indices = indices;
    }

    Indices::size_type GetNumIndices() const
    {
        return m_Indices.size();
    }

    Indices::const_pointer GetIndices() const
    {
        return m_Indices.data();
    }
};

class Shader
{
private:
    void LoadShader(GLuint id, const std::string& shaderCode)
    {
        const unsigned int NUM_SHADERS{ 1 };

        const char* pCode{ shaderCode.c_str() };
        GLint length{ static_cast<GLint>(shaderCode.length()) };
```

```cpp
        glShaderSource(id, NUM_SHADERS, &pCode, &length);

        glCompileShader(id);

        glAttachShader(m_ProgramId, id);
    }

protected:
    GLuint m_VertexShaderId{ GL_INVALID_VALUE };
    GLuint m_FragmentShaderId{ GL_INVALID_VALUE };
    GLint m_ProgramId{ GL_INVALID_VALUE };

    std::string m_VertexShaderCode;
    std::string m_FragmentShaderCode;

public:
    Shader() = default;
    virtual ~Shader() = default;

    virtual void Link()
    {
        m_ProgramId = glCreateProgram();

        m_VertexShaderId = glCreateShader(GL_VERTEX_SHADER);
        LoadShader(m_VertexShaderId, m_VertexShaderCode);

        m_FragmentShaderId = glCreateShader(GL_FRAGMENT_SHADER);
        LoadShader(m_FragmentShaderId, m_FragmentShaderCode);

        glLinkProgram(m_ProgramId);
    }

    virtual void Setup(const Geometry& geometry)
    {
        glUseProgram(m_ProgramId);
    }
};

class BasicShader
    : public Shader
{
private:
    GLint        m_PositionAttributeHandle;

public:
    BasicShader()
    {
        m_VertexShaderCode =
            "attribute vec4 a_vPosition;              \n"
            "void main(){                             \n"
            "    gl_Position = a_vPosition;           \n"
            "}                                        \n";
```

```
        m_FragmentShaderCode =
            "#version 150                                      \n"
            "precision mediump float;                          \n"
            "void main(){                                      \n"
            "    gl_FragColor = vec4(0.2, 0.2, 0.2, 1.0);      \n"
            "}                                                 \n";
    }

    ~BasicShader() override = default;

    void Link() override
    {
        Shader::Link();

        m_PositionAttributeHandle = glGetAttribLocation(m_ProgramId, "a_vPosition");
    }

    void Setup(const Geometry& geometry) override
    {
        Shader::Setup(geometry);

        glVertexAttribPointer(
            m_PositionAttributeHandle,
            3,
            GL_FLOAT,
            GL_FALSE,
            0,
            geometry.GetVertices());
        glEnableVertexAttribArray(m_PositionAttributeHandle);
    }
};

int CALLBACK WinMain(
    _In_ HINSTANCE hInstance,
    _In_ HINSTANCE hPrevInstance,
    _In_ LPSTR lpCmdLine,
    _In_ int nCmdShow
    )
{
    GLFWwindow* window;

    // Initialize the library
    if (!glfwInit())
    {
        return -1;
    }
```

```
// Create a windowed mode window and its OpenGL context
window = glfwCreateWindow(640, 480, "Hello World", NULL, NULL);
if (!window)
{
    glfwTerminate();
    return -1;
}

// Make the window's context current
glfwMakeContextCurrent(window);

GLenum glewError{ glewInit() };
if (glewError != GLEW_OK)
{
    return -1;
}

BasicShader basicShader;
basicShader.Link();

Geometry triangle;

Geometry::Vertices vertices{
    0.0f, 0.5f, 0.0f,
    0.5f, -0.5f, 0.0f,
    -0.5f, -0.5f, 0.0f
};

Geometry::Indices indices{ 0, 1, 2 };

triangle.SetVertices(vertices);
triangle.SetIndices(indices);

glClearColor(0.25f, 0.25f, 0.95f, 1.0f);

// Loop until the user closes the window
while (!glfwWindowShouldClose(window))
{
    glClear(GL_COLOR_BUFFER_BIT);

    basicShader.Setup(triangle);

    glDrawElements(GL_TRIANGLES,
        triangle.GetNumIndices(),
        GL_UNSIGNED_SHORT,
        triangle.GetIndices());

    // Swap front and back buffers
    glfwSwapBuffers(window);
```

```
      // Poll for and process events
      glfwPollEvents();
   }

   glfwTerminate();
   return 0;
}
```

The main function in Listing 14-6 shows how and where to use the Geometry and BasicShader classes to render a triangle to your window. The OpenGL API is available to use immediately after the call to glewInit has completed successfully. The main function follows this call by initializing a BasicShader object and calling BasicShader::Link then a Geometry object to represent the vertices of a triangle. The vertices are supplied in a post-transformed state because the vertex shader in BasicShader isn't carrying out any operations on the data passed through. The vertices are specified in normalized device coordinates; in OpenGL, these coordinates must fit inside a cube that ranges from -1, -1, -1 to 1, 1, 1 for the x, y, and z coordinates. The indices tell OpenGL the order in which to pass the vertices to the vertex shader; in this case, you're passing the vertices in the order they're defined.

The glClearColor function tells OpenGL the color to use to represent the background color when no other pixels have been rendered to that position. Here the color is set to light blue so it's easy to tell when a pixel has been rendered to. Colors are represented in OpenGL using four components: red, green, blue, and alpha. The red, green, and blue components combine to generate a color for a pixel. When all the component values are 1, the color is white; and when all the values are 0, the color is black. The alpha component is used to determine how transparent a pixel is. There's little reason to set a transparency value of less than 1 on the background color.

You can find a call to glClear in the render loop. This call uses the values set by glClearColor to fill the framebuffer and overwrite anything rendered the last time this buffer was used. Remember that when you're using double buffering, the buffer you're rendering to is two frames old, not one. The BasicShader::Setup function sets up the shader with the current geometry for rendering. This could have been a one-time operation in this program, but it's more common for programs to render more than one object with a given shader.

Finally, the glDrawElements function is responsible for asking OpenGL to render the triangle. The glDrawElements call specifies that you want to render triangle primitives, the number of indices to render, the type of the indices, and a pointer to the index data stream.

Figure 14-1 shows the output generated by this program.

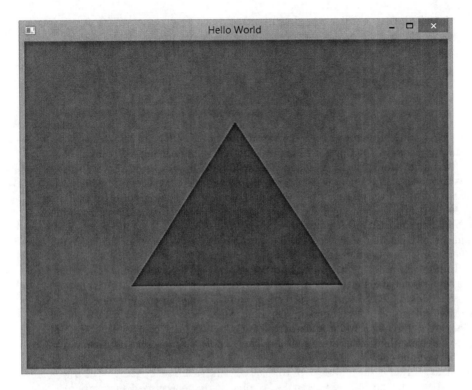

Figure 14-1. The triangle rendered by the code in Listing 14-6

14-3. Creating a Textured Quad

Problem

GPU power is limited, and you would like to give your objects a more highly detailed appearance.

Solution

Texture mapping allows you to create 2D images that you can map over the surface of a mesh to give the appearance of increased geometric complexity.

How It Works

GLSL provides support for samplers that you can use to read texels from an assigned texture. A *texel* is a single color element from a texture; the term is short for *texture element* in the same way that *pixel* is short for *picture element*. The term *pixel* is usually used when referring to individual colors that make up the image on your display, whereas *texel* is used when referring to individual colors in a texture image.

A texture is mapped to a mesh using texture coordinates. Each vertex in a mesh is given an associated texture coordinate that you can use to look up the color to be applied to the fragment in a fragment shader. The texture coordinate from each vertex is interpolated across the surface of a polygon using an interpolator unit on the GPU. Interpolated values to be passed from a vertex shader to a fragment shader are represented in OpenGL using the varying keyword. This keyword makes logical sense because varyings are used to represent variables that vary across the surface of the polygon. Varyings are initialized in the vertex shader by being either assigned from an attribute or by generated by code.

You need a way to represent mesh data that contains texture coordinates before you can worry about having textures in your applications. Listing 14-7 shows a definition of the Geometry class that supports texture coordinates in the vertex data.

Listing 14-7. A Geometry Class that Supports Texture Coordinates

```cpp
class Geometry
{
public:
    using Vertices = vector < float >;
    using Indices = vector < unsigned short >;

private:
    Vertices m_Vertices;
    Indices m_Indices;

    unsigned int m_NumVertexPositionElements{};
    unsigned int m_NumTextureCoordElements{};
    unsigned int m_VertexStride{};

public:
    Geometry() = default;
    ~Geometry() = default;

    void SetVertices(const Vertices& vertices)
    {
        m_Vertices = vertices;
    }

    Vertices::size_type GetNumVertices() const
    {
        return m_Vertices.size();
    }

    Vertices::const_pointer GetVertices() const
    {
        return m_Vertices.data();
    }

    void SetIndices(const Indices& indices)
    {
        m_Indices = indices;
    }

    Indices::size_type GetNumIndices() const
    {
        return m_Indices.size();
    }
```

```cpp
    Indices::const_pointer GetIndices() const
    {
        return m_Indices.data();
    }

    Vertices::const_pointer GetTexCoords() const
    {
        return static_cast<Vertices::const_pointer>(&m_Vertices
        [m_NumVertexPositionElements]);
    }

    void SetNumVertexPositionElements(unsigned int numVertexPositionElements)
    {
        m_NumVertexPositionElements = numVertexPositionElements;
    }

    unsigned int GetNumVertexPositionElements() const
    {
        return m_NumVertexPositionElements;
    }

    void SetNumTexCoordElements(unsigned int numTexCoordElements)
    {
        m_NumTextureCoordElements = numTexCoordElements;
    }

    unsigned int GetNumTexCoordElements() const
    {
        return m_NumTextureCoordElements;
    }

    void SetVertexStride(unsigned int vertexStride)
    {
        m_VertexStride = vertexStride;
    }

    unsigned int GetVertexStride() const
    {
        return m_VertexStride;
    }
};
```

This code shows the definition for a Geometry class that stores vertices and indices in separate vectors. There are also fields that store the number of vertex position elements and the number of texture coordinate elements. A single vertex can consist of a variable number of vertex elements and a variable number of texture coordinates. The m_VertexStride field stores the number of bytes from the beginning of one vertex to the beginning of the next vertex. The GetTexCoords method is one of the more important methods in this class because it shows that the vertex data this class supports is in an array of structures format. There are two main ways to read in vertex data: you can set up separate streams for the vertices and the texture coordinates in separate arrays, or you can set up a single stream that interleaves the vertex position and texture-coordinate data per vertex. This class supports the latter style, because it's the most optimal data format for modern GPUs. The GetTexCoords method returns the address of the first texture coordinate using the m_NumVertexPositionElements as an index to find that data. This relies on your mesh data being tightly packed and your first texture coordinate coming immediately after the vertex position elements.

The next important element when rendering textured object with OpenGL is a class that can load texture data from a file. The TGA file format is simple and easy to use and can store image data. Its simplicity means it's a common choice of file format for uncompressed textures when working with OpenGL. The TGAFile class in Listing 14-8 shows how a TGA file is loaded.

Listing 14-8. The TGAFile Class

```
class TGAFile
{
private:
#ifdef _MSC_VER
#pragma pack(push, 1)
#endif
    struct TGAHeader
    {
        unsigned char m_IdSize{};
        unsigned char m_ColorMapType{};
        unsigned char m_ImageType{};

        unsigned short m_PaletteStart{};
        unsigned short m_PaletteLength{};
        unsigned char m_PaletteBits{};

        unsigned short m_XOrigin{};
        unsigned short m_YOrigin{};
        unsigned short m_Width{};
        unsigned short m_Height{};

        unsigned char m_BytesPerPixel{};
        unsigned char m_Descriptor{};
    }
#ifndef _MSC_VER
    __attribute__ ((packed))
#endif // _MSC_VER
        ;

#ifdef _MSC_VER
#pragma pack(pop)
#endif

    std::vector<char> m_FileData;

    TGAHeader* m_pHeader{};
    void* m_pImageData{};
```

```cpp
public:
    TGAFile(const std::string& filename)
    {
        std::ifstream fileStream{ filename, std::ios_base::binary };
        if (fileStream.is_open())
        {
            fileStream.seekg(0, std::ios::end);
            m_FileData.resize(static_cast<unsigned int>(fileStream.tellg()));

            fileStream.seekg(0, std::ios::beg);
            fileStream.read(m_FileData.data(), m_FileData.size());

            fileStream.close();

            m_pHeader = reinterpret_cast<TGAHeader*>(m_FileData.data());
            m_pImageData = static_cast<void*>(m_FileData.data() + sizeof(TGAHeader));
        }
    }

    unsigned short GetWidth() const
    {
        return m_pHeader->m_Width;
    }

    unsigned short GetHeight() const
    {
        return m_pHeader->m_Height;
    }

    unsigned char GetBytesPerPixel() const
    {
        return m_pHeader->m_BytesPerPixel;
    }

    unsigned int GetDataSize() const
    {
        return m_FileData.size() - sizeof(TGAHeader);
    }

    void* GetImageData() const
    {
        return m_pImageData;
    }
};
```

The TGAFile class contains a header structure that represents the header data included in a TGA file when saved by an image-editing program such as Adobe Photoshop. This structure has some interesting compiler metadata associated with it. A modern C++ compiler is aware of the memory layout of the data structures in applications. A given CPU architecture may operate more efficiently with variables that lie on certain memory boundaries. This is fine for structures that are non-portable and used in a single program on a single-CPU architecture, but it may cause problems for data that is saved and loaded by different programs on different computers. To counteract this, you can specify the amount of padding a compiler can add to your programs to optimize access to individual variables. The TGAHeader struct requires that no padding be added, because the TGA file format doesn't contain any padding when the file is saved. This is achieved when using Visual Studio by using the pragma preprocessor directive along with the pack command to push and pop a packing value of 1. This disables the automatic spacing of variables for speed efficiency. On most other compilers, you can use the __attribute__ ((packed)) compiler directive to achieve the same result.

The TGAHeader fields store metadata that represents the type of image data stored in the file. This recipe only deals with RGBA data in a TGA, so the only relevant fields are the width, height, and bytes per pixel. These are found in the file in the exact byte positions represented in the TGAHeader structure. The data from the file is mapped into the TGAHeader object by using a pointer. The filename is passed to the constructor for the class, and this file is opened and read using an ifstream object. The ifstream object is the STL class provided for reading data in from a file. The ifstream is constructed by passing it the filename to be opened and the binary data mode, because you want to read binary data from the file. The entire file is read into a vector of char variables by seeking to the end of the file, reading the position of the end of file to determine the size of the data in the file, and then seeking back to the beginning and using the size to resize the vector. The data is then read into the vector by using the ifstream read method that takes a pointer to the buffer where the data should be read and the size of the buffer to read into. You can then use reinterpret_cast to map the data read from the file onto a TGAHeader struct, and a static_cast can be used to store a pointer to the beginning of the image data.

Loading the TGA data is separated from the OpenGL texture setup by using separate classes. The data loaded from the TGA can be passed to the texture class shown in Listing 14-9 to create an OpenGL texture object.

Listing 14-9. The Texture Class

```
class Texture
{
private:
    unsigned int m_Width{};
    unsigned int m_Height{};
    unsigned int m_BytesPerPixel{};
    unsigned int m_DataSize{};

    GLuint m_Id{};

    void* m_pImageData;

public:
    Texture(const TGAFile& tgaFile)
        : Texture(tgaFile.GetWidth(),
            tgaFile.GetHeight(),
            tgaFile.GetBytesPerPixel(),
            tgaFile.GetDataSize(),
            tgaFile.GetImageData())
    {

    }
```

```cpp
    Texture(unsigned int width,
            unsigned int height,
            unsigned int bytesPerPixel,
            unsigned int dataSize,
            void* pImageData)
        : m_Width(width)
        , m_Height(height)
        , m_BytesPerPixel(bytesPerPixel)
        , m_DataSize(dataSize)
        , m_pImageData(pImageData)
    {

    }

    ~Texture() = default;

    GLuint GetId() const
    {
        return m_Id;
    }

    void Init()
    {
        GLint packBits{ 4 };
        GLint internalFormat{ GL_RGBA };
        GLint format{ GL_BGRA };

        glGenTextures(1, &m_Id);
        glBindTexture(GL_TEXTURE_2D, m_Id);
        glPixelStorei(GL_UNPACK_ALIGNMENT, packBits);
        glTexImage2D(GL_TEXTURE_2D,
            0,
            internalFormat,
            m_Width,
            m_Height,
            0,
            format,
            GL_UNSIGNED_BYTE,
            m_pImageData);
    }
};
```

The Texture class initializes an OpenGL texture for use when rendering objects. The two class constructors are provided to simplify initializing the class from a TGA file or from in-memory data. The constructor that takes a TGAFile reference uses the C++11 concept of delegating constructors to call the in-memory constructor. The Init method is responsible for creating an OpenGL texture object. This method can create RGBA textures from a BGRA source using the width and height supplied in the constructor. You might notice here that the source pixels in a TGA file are back to front; this method is responsible for transposing the red and green channels into the correct position for the GPU. The image data is copied onto the GPU by the glTextImage2D function so that draw calls can use this texture data in your fragment shaders.

The next step in being able to render with textures is to look at the TextureShader class, which includes a vertex shader that can read in texture coordinates and pass them to the fragment shader through a varying object. You can see this class in Listing 14-10.

Listing 14-10. The TextureShader Class

```
class Shader
{
private:
    void LoadShader(GLuint id, const std::string& shaderCode)
    {
        const unsigned int NUM_SHADERS{ 1 };

        const char* pCode{ shaderCode.c_str() };
        GLint length{ static_cast<GLint>(shaderCode.length()) };

        glShaderSource(id, NUM_SHADERS, &pCode, &length);

        glCompileShader(id);

        glAttachShader(m_ProgramId, id);
    }

protected:
    GLuint m_VertexShaderId{ GL_INVALID_VALUE };
    GLuint m_FragmentShaderId{ GL_INVALID_VALUE };
    GLint m_ProgramId{ GL_INVALID_VALUE };

    std::string m_VertexShaderCode;
    std::string m_FragmentShaderCode;

public:
    Shader() = default;
    virtual ~Shader() = default;

    virtual void Link()
    {
        m_ProgramId = glCreateProgram();

        m_VertexShaderId = glCreateShader(GL_VERTEX_SHADER);
        LoadShader(m_VertexShaderId, m_VertexShaderCode);

        m_FragmentShaderId = glCreateShader(GL_FRAGMENT_SHADER);
        LoadShader(m_FragmentShaderId, m_FragmentShaderCode);

        glLinkProgram(m_ProgramId);
    }

    virtual void Setup(const Geometry& geometry)
    {
        glUseProgram(m_ProgramId);
    }
};
```

```cpp
class TextureShader
    : public Shader
{
private:
    const Texture& m_Texture;

    GLint m_PositionAttributeHandle;
    GLint m_TextureCoordinateAttributeHandle;
    GLint m_SamplerHandle;

public:
    TextureShader(const Texture& texture)
        : m_Texture(texture)
    {
        m_VertexShaderCode =
            "attribute  vec4 a_vPosition;              \n"
            "attribute  vec2 a_vTexCoord;              \n"
            "varying    vec2 v_vTexCoord;              \n"
            "                                          \n"
            "void main() {                             \n"
            "   gl_Position = a_vPosition;             \n"
            "   v_vTexCoord = a_vTexCoord;             \n"
            "}                                         \n";

        m_FragmentShaderCode =
            "#version 150                              \n"
            "                                          \n"
            "precision highp float;                    \n"
            "varying vec2 v_vTexCoord;                 \n"
            "uniform sampler2D s_2dTexture;            \n"
            "                                          \n"
            "void main() {                             \n"
            "   gl_FragColor =                         \n"
            "       texture2D(s_2dTexture, v_vTexCoord); \n"
            "}                                         \n";
    }

    ~TextureShader() override = default;

    void Link() override
    {
        Shader::Link();

        m_PositionAttributeHandle = glGetAttribLocation(m_ProgramId, "a_vPosition");
        m_TextureCoordinateAttributeHandle = glGetAttribLocation(m_ProgramId, "a_vTexCoord");

        m_SamplerHandle = glGetUniformLocation(m_ProgramId, "s_2dTexture");
    }
```

```
void Setup(const Geometry& geometry) override
{
    Shader::Setup(geometry);

    glActiveTexture(GL_TEXTURE0);
    glBindTexture(GL_TEXTURE_2D, m_Texture.GetId());
    glUniform1i(m_SamplerHandle, 0);

    glTexParameteri(GL_TEXTURE_2D, GL_TEXTURE_WRAP_S, GL_CLAMP_TO_EDGE);
    glTexParameteri(GL_TEXTURE_2D, GL_TEXTURE_WRAP_T, GL_CLAMP_TO_EDGE);

    glTexParameteri(GL_TEXTURE_2D, GL_TEXTURE_MIN_FILTER, GL_LINEAR);
    glTexParameteri(GL_TEXTURE_2D, GL_TEXTURE_MAG_FILTER, GL_LINEAR);

    glVertexAttribPointer(
        m_PositionAttributeHandle,
        geometry.GetNumVertexPositionElements(),
        GL_FLOAT,
        GL_FALSE,
        geometry.GetVertexStride(),
        geometry.GetVertices());
    glEnableVertexAttribArray(m_PositionAttributeHandle);

    glVertexAttribPointer(
        m_TextureCoordinateAttributeHandle,
        geometry.GetNumTexCoordElements(),
        GL_FLOAT,
        GL_FALSE,
        geometry.GetVertexStride(),
        geometry.GetTexCoords());
    glEnableVertexAttribArray(m_TextureCoordinateAttributeHandle);
}
};
```

The TextureShader class inherits from the Shader class. The vertex shader code in the TextureShader class constructor contains two attributes and a varying. The position element of the vertex is passed straight through without modification to the built-in gl_Position variable, which receives the final transformed position of a vertex. The a_vTexCoord attribute is passed to the v_vTexCoord varying. Varyings are used to transfer interpolated data from vertex shaders to fragment shaders, so it's important that both your vertex shader and your fragment shader contain a varying with the same type and name. OpenGL works out the plumbing behind the scenes to make sure the varying output from the vertex shader is passed to the same varying in the fragment shader.

The fragment shader contains a *uniform*. Uniforms are more like shader constants in that they're set by a single call for each draw call, and every instance of the shader receives the same value. In this case, every instance of the fragment shader receives the same sampler ID to retrieve data from the same texture. This data is read using the texture2D function, which takes a sampler2D uniform and the v_vTexCoord varying. The texture-coordinate varying has been interpolated across the surface of a polygon, so the polygon is mapped using different texels from the texture data.

The TextureShader::Setup function is responsible for initializing the sampler state before each draw call. The texture unit you want to use is initialized using the glActiveTexture function. A texture is bound to this texture unit using glBindTexture, which is passed the ID of the OpenGL texture. The uniform binding is somewhat unintuitive. glActiveTexture receives the constant value GL_TEXTURE0 as the value and not 0. This allows the glActiveTexture call to associate the texture with the texture-image unit binding, but the fragment shader doesn't use the same value; instead, it uses an index to the texture-image units. In this case, GL_TEXTURE0 can be found at index 0, so the value 0 is bound to the m_SamplerHandle uniform in the fragment shader.

The sampler parameters are then initialized for the bound texture. They're set to clamp the texture in both directions. This would be useful for cases where you want to use values outside the normal range of 0 to 1 for texture coordinates. It's also possible to set up textures to wrap, repeat, or mirror in these cases. The next two options configure the settings for sampling textures when they're minified or magnified on the screen. Minification happens when the texture is being applied to an object that takes up less screen space than the texture would at a 1-to-1 mapping. This could occur with a 512 × 512 texture that was being rendered onscreen at 256 × 256. Magnification occurs in the opposite case, where the texture is being rendered to an object that is taking up more screen space than the texture provides texels for. The linear mapping uses the four texels nearest to the sampling point to work out an average of the color to be applied to the fragment. This gives textures a less blocky appearance at the expense of blurring the texture slightly. The effect is more pronounced depending on how much minification or magnification is applied to the texture.

The TextureShader::Setup function then initializes the data streams for the vertex shader's attribute fields. The vertex-position elements are bound to the m_PositionAttributeHandle location using the number of position elements from the geometry object as well as the stride from that location. After the attribute is initialized, it's enabled with a call to glEnableVertexAttribArray. The m_TextureCoordinateAttributeHandle attribute is initialized using the same functions but with different data. The number of texture elements per vertex is retrieved from the geometry object, as is the texture coordinate stream. The stride of the data remains the same for both the vertex data and the texture data because they're packed into the same stream in the array-of-structures format.

The code in Listing 14-11 brings all of this together and adds a main function to show how a texture and geometry can be initialized to render a quad to the screen that has a texture image applied.

Listing 14-11. The Textured Quad Program

```
#include "GL/glew.h"
#include "GLFW/glfw3.h"
#include <string>
#include <vector>

using namespace std;

class Geometry
{
public:
    using Vertices = vector < float >;
    using Indices = vector < unsigned short >;

private:
    Vertices m_Vertices;
    Indices m_Indices;

    unsigned int m_NumVertexPositionElements{};
    unsigned int m_NumTextureCoordElements{};
    unsigned int m_VertexStride{};
```

```cpp
public:
    Geometry() = default;
    ~Geometry() = default;

    void SetVertices(const Vertices& vertices)
    {
        m_Vertices = vertices;
    }

    Vertices::size_type GetNumVertices() const
    {
        return m_Vertices.size();
    }

    Vertices::const_pointer GetVertices() const
    {
        return m_Vertices.data();
    }

    void SetIndices(const Indices& indices)
    {
        m_Indices = indices;
    }

    Indices::size_type GetNumIndices() const
    {
        return m_Indices.size();
    }

    Indices::const_pointer GetIndices() const
    {
        return m_Indices.data();
    }

    Vertices::const_pointer GetTexCoords() const
    {
        return static_cast<Vertices::const_pointer>(&m_Vertices
        [m_NumVertexPositionElements]);
    }

    void SetNumVertexPositionElements(unsigned int numVertexPositionElements)
    {
        m_NumVertexPositionElements = numVertexPositionElements;
    }

    unsigned int GetNumVertexPositionElements() const
    {
        return m_NumVertexPositionElements;
    }
```

```cpp
    void SetNumTexCoordElements(unsigned int numTexCoordElements)
    {
        m_NumTextureCoordElements = numTexCoordElements;
    }

    unsigned int GetNumTexCoordElements() const
    {
        return m_NumTextureCoordElements;
    }

    void SetVertexStride(unsigned int vertexStride)
    {
        m_VertexStride = vertexStride;
    }

    unsigned int GetVertexStride() const
    {
        return m_VertexStride;
    }
};

class TGAFile
{
private:
#ifdef _MSC_VER
#pragma pack(push, 1)
#endif
    struct TGAHeader
    {
        unsigned char m_IdSize{};
        unsigned char m_ColorMapType{};
        unsigned char m_ImageType{};

        unsigned short m_PaletteStart{};
        unsigned short m_PaletteLength{};
        unsigned char m_PaletteBits{};

        unsigned short m_XOrigin{};
        unsigned short m_YOrigin{};
        unsigned short m_Width{};
        unsigned short m_Height{};

        unsigned char m_BytesPerPixel{};
        unsigned char m_Descriptor{};
    }
#ifndef _MSC_VER
    __attribute__ ((packed))
#endif // _MSC_VER
        ;
```

```cpp
#ifdef _MSC_VER
#pragma pack(pop)
#endif

    std::vector<char> m_FileData;

    TGAHeader* m_pHeader{};
    void* m_pImageData{};

public:
    TGAFile(const std::string& filename)
    {
        std::ifstream fileStream{ filename, std::ios_base::binary };
        if (fileStream.is_open())
        {
            fileStream.seekg(0, std::ios::end);
            m_FileData.resize(static_cast<unsigned int>(fileStream.tellg()));

            fileStream.seekg(0, std::ios::beg);
            fileStream.read(m_FileData.data(), m_FileData.size());

            fileStream.close();

            m_pHeader = reinterpret_cast<TGAHeader*>(m_FileData.data());
            m_pImageData = static_cast<void*>(m_FileData.data() + sizeof(TGAHeader));
        }
    }

    unsigned short GetWidth() const
    {
        return m_pHeader->m_Width;
    }

    unsigned short GetHeight() const
    {
        return m_pHeader->m_Height;
    }

    unsigned char GetBytesPerPixel() const
    {
        return m_pHeader->m_BytesPerPixel;
    }

    unsigned int GetDataSize() const
    {
        return m_FileData.size() - sizeof(TGAHeader);
    }
```

```cpp
    void* GetImageData() const
    {
        return m_pImageData;
    }
};

class Texture
{
private:
    unsigned int m_Width{};
    unsigned int m_Height{};
    unsigned int m_BytesPerPixel{};
    unsigned int m_DataSize{};

    GLuint m_Id{};

    void* m_pImageData;

public:
    Texture(const TGAFile& tgaFile)
        : Texture(tgaFile.GetWidth(),
            tgaFile.GetHeight(),
            tgaFile.GetBytesPerPixel(),
            tgaFile.GetDataSize(),
            tgaFile.GetImageData())
    {

    }

    Texture(unsigned int width,
            unsigned int height,
            unsigned int bytesPerPixel,
            unsigned int dataSize,
            void* pImageData)
        : m_Width(width)
        , m_Height(height)
        , m_BytesPerPixel(bytesPerPixel)
        , m_DataSize(dataSize)
        , m_pImageData(pImageData)
    {

    }

    ~Texture() = default;

    GLuint GetId() const
    {
        return m_Id;
    }
```

```cpp
    void Init()
    {
        GLint packBits{ 4 };
        GLint internalFormat{ GL_RGBA };
        GLint format{ GL_BGRA };

        glGenTextures(1, &m_Id);
        glBindTexture(GL_TEXTURE_2D, m_Id);
        glPixelStorei(GL_UNPACK_ALIGNMENT, packBits);
        glTexImage2D(GL_TEXTURE_2D,
            0,
            internalFormat,
            m_Width,
            m_Height,
            0,
            format,
            GL_UNSIGNED_BYTE,
            m_pImageData);
    }
};

class Shader
{
private:
    void LoadShader(GLuint id, const std::string& shaderCode)
    {
        const unsigned int NUM_SHADERS{ 1 };

        const char* pCode{ shaderCode.c_str() };
        GLint length{ static_cast<GLint>(shaderCode.length()) };

        glShaderSource(id, NUM_SHADERS, &pCode, &length);

        glCompileShader(id);

        glAttachShader(m_ProgramId, id);
    }

protected:
    GLuint m_VertexShaderId{ GL_INVALID_VALUE };
    GLuint m_FragmentShaderId{ GL_INVALID_VALUE };
    GLint m_ProgramId{ GL_INVALID_VALUE };

    std::string m_VertexShaderCode;
    std::string m_FragmentShaderCode;

public:
    Shader() = default;
    virtual ~Shader() = default;
```

```
    virtual void Link()
    {
        m_ProgramId = glCreateProgram();

        m_VertexShaderId = glCreateShader(GL_VERTEX_SHADER);
        LoadShader(m_VertexShaderId, m_VertexShaderCode);

        m_FragmentShaderId = glCreateShader(GL_FRAGMENT_SHADER);
        LoadShader(m_FragmentShaderId, m_FragmentShaderCode);

        glLinkProgram(m_ProgramId);
    }

    virtual void Setup(const Geometry& geometry)
    {
        glUseProgram(m_ProgramId);
    }
};

class TextureShader
    : public Shader
{
private:
    const Texture& m_Texture;

    GLint m_PositionAttributeHandle;
    GLint m_TextureCoordinateAttributeHandle;
    GLint m_SamplerHandle;

public:
    TextureShader(const Texture& texture)
        : m_Texture(texture)
    {
        m_VertexShaderCode =
            "attribute  vec4 a_vPosition;              \n"
            "attribute  vec2 a_vTexCoord;              \n"
            "varying    vec2 v_vTexCoord;              \n"
            "                                          \n"
            "void main() {                             \n"
            "   gl_Position = a_vPosition;             \n"
            "   v_vTexCoord = a_vTexCoord;             \n"
            "}                                         \n";

        m_FragmentShaderCode =
            "#version 150                              \n"
            "                                          \n"
            "precision highp float;                    \n"
            "varying vec2 v_vTexCoord;                 \n"
            "uniform sampler2D s_2dTexture;            \n"
            "                                          \n"
```

```cpp
            "void main() {                                    \n"
            "   gl_FragColor =                                 \n"
            "       texture2D(s_2dTexture, v_vTexCoord);       \n"
            "}                                                 \n";
    }

    ~TextureShader() override = default;

    void Link() override
    {
        Shader::Link();

        m_PositionAttributeHandle = glGetAttribLocation(m_ProgramId, "a_vPosition");
        m_TextureCoordinateAttributeHandle = glGetAttribLocation(m_ProgramId, "a_vTexCoord");

        m_SamplerHandle = glGetUniformLocation(m_ProgramId, "s_2dTexture");
    }

    void Setup(const Geometry& geometry) override
    {
        Shader::Setup(geometry);

        glActiveTexture(GL_TEXTURE0);
        glBindTexture(GL_TEXTURE_2D, m_Texture.GetId());
        glUniform1i(m_SamplerHandle, 0);

        glTexParameteri(GL_TEXTURE_2D, GL_TEXTURE_WRAP_S, GL_CLAMP_TO_EDGE);
        glTexParameteri(GL_TEXTURE_2D, GL_TEXTURE_WRAP_T, GL_CLAMP_TO_EDGE);

        glTexParameteri(GL_TEXTURE_2D, GL_TEXTURE_MIN_FILTER, GL_LINEAR);
        glTexParameteri(GL_TEXTURE_2D, GL_TEXTURE_MAG_FILTER, GL_LINEAR);

        glVertexAttribPointer(
            m_PositionAttributeHandle,
            geometry.GetNumVertexPositionElements(),
            GL_FLOAT,
            GL_FALSE,
            geometry.GetVertexStride(),
            geometry.GetVertices());
        glEnableVertexAttribArray(m_PositionAttributeHandle);

        glVertexAttribPointer(
            m_TextureCoordinateAttributeHandle,
            geometry.GetNumTexCoordElements(),
            GL_FLOAT,
            GL_FALSE,
            geometry.GetVertexStride(),
            geometry.GetTexCoords());
        glEnableVertexAttribArray(m_TextureCoordinateAttributeHandle);
    }
};
```

```cpp
int CALLBACK WinMain(
    _In_ HINSTANCE hInstance,
    _In_ HINSTANCE hPrevInstance,
    _In_ LPSTR lpCmdLine,
    _In_ int nCmdShow
    )
{
    GLFWwindow* window;

    // Initialize the library
    if (!glfwInit())
    {
        return -1;
    }

    // Create a windowed mode window and its OpenGL context
    window = glfwCreateWindow(640, 480, "Hello World", NULL, NULL);
    if (!window)
    {
        glfwTerminate();
        return -1;
    }

    // Make the window's context current
    glfwMakeContextCurrent(window);

    GLenum glewError{ glewInit() };
    if (glewError != GLEW_OK)
    {
        return -1;
    }

    TGAFile myTextureFile("MyTexture.tga");
    Texture myTexture(myTextureFile);
    myTexture.Init();

    TextureShader textureShader(myTexture);
    textureShader.Link();

    Geometry quad;

    Geometry::Vertices vertices{
        -0.5f, 0.5f, 0.0f,
        0.0f, 1.0f,
        0.5f, 0.5f, 0.0f,
        1.0f, 1.0f,
        -0.5f, -0.5f, 0.0f,
        0.0f, 0.0f,
        0.5f, -0.5f, 0.0f,
        1.0f, 0.0f
    };
```

```
Geometry::Indices indices{ 0, 2, 1, 2, 3, 1 };

quad.SetVertices(vertices);
quad.SetIndices(indices);
quad.SetNumVertexPositionElements(3);
quad.SetNumTexCoordElements(2);
quad.SetVertexStride(sizeof(float) * 5);

glClearColor(0.25f, 0.25f, 0.95f, 1.0f);

// Loop until the user closes the window
while (!glfwWindowShouldClose(window))
{
    glClear(GL_COLOR_BUFFER_BIT);

    textureShader.Setup(quad);

    glDrawElements(GL_TRIANGLES,
        quad.GetNumIndices(),
        GL_UNSIGNED_SHORT,
        quad.GetIndices());

    // Swap front and back buffers
    glfwSwapBuffers(window);

    // Poll for and process events
    glfwPollEvents();
}

glfwTerminate();
return 0;
}
```

The full source for the program in Listing 14-11 shows how all the classes introduced in this recipe can be brought together to render a single textured quad. The TGAFile class is initialized to load the MyTexture.tga file. This is passed to the myTexture object, which is of type Texture. The Texture::Init function is called to initialize the OpenGL texture object. The initialized texture is in turn passed to an instance of the TextureShader class, which creates, initializes, and links an OpenGL shader program that can be used to render 2D textured geometry. The geometry is then created; the vertices specified include three position elements and two texture-coordinate elements for each vertex. OpenGL uses four vertices and six indices to render a quad made from two triangles. The vertices at indices 1 and 2 are shared by both triangles; you can see how indices can be used to reduce the required geometry definitions for the mesh. There's another optimization advantage here: many modern CPUs cache the results from already-processed vertices, so you can read reused vertex data from a cache rather than have the GPU reprocess it.

The actual rendering is trivial after all the setup work is done. There are calls to clear the frame buffer, set up the shader, draw the elements, swap the buffers, and poll for operating system events. Figure 14-2 shows what the output from this program looks like when everything is complete and working properly.

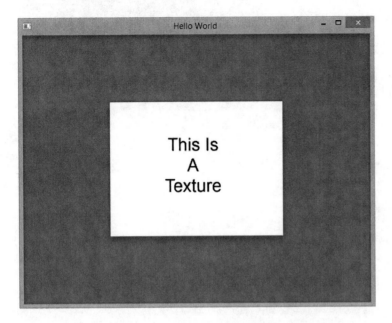

Figure 14-2. Output showing a textured quad rendered using OpenGL

14-4. Loading Geometry from a File

Problem

You would like to be able to load mesh data from files created by artists on your team.

Solution

C++ allows you to write code that can load many different file formats. This recipe shows you how to load Wavefront `.obj` files.

How It Works

The `.obj` file format was initially developed by Wavefront Technologies. It can be exported from many 3D modelling programs and is a simple text-based format, making it an ideal intermediary for learning how to import 3D data. The OBJFile class in Listing 14-12 shows how to load an `.obj` file from a source file.

Listing 14-12. Loading an `.obj` File

```
class OBJFile
{
public:
    using Vertices = vector < float > ;
    using TextureCoordinates = vector < float > ;
    using Normals = vector < float > ;
    using Indices = vector < unsigned short > ;
```

```cpp
private:
    Vertices m_VertexPositions;
    TextureCoordinates m_TextureCoordinates;
    Normals m_Normals;

    Indices m_Indices;

public:
    OBJFile(const std::string& filename)
    {
        std::ifstream fileStream{ filename, std::ios_base::in };
        if (fileStream.is_open())
        {
            while (!fileStream.eof())
            {
                std::string line;
                getline(fileStream, line);

                stringstream lineStream{ line };

                std::string firstSymbol;
                lineStream >> firstSymbol;

                if (firstSymbol == "v")
                {
                    float vertexPosition{};

                    for (unsigned int i = 0; i < 3; ++i)
                    {
                        lineStream >> vertexPosition;
                        m_VertexPositions.emplace_back(vertexPosition);
                    }
                }
                else if (firstSymbol == "vt")
                {
                    float textureCoordinate{};

                    for (unsigned int i = 0; i < 2; ++i)
                    {
                        lineStream >> textureCoordinate;
                        m_TextureCoordinates.emplace_back(textureCoordinate);
                    }
                }
                else if (firstSymbol == "vn")
                {
                    float normal{};

                    for (unsigned int i = 0; i < 3; ++i)
                    {
                        lineStream >> normal;
                        m_Normals.emplace_back(normal);
                    }
                }
```

433

```
            else if (firstSymbol == "f")
            {
                char separator;
                unsigned short index{};

                for (unsigned int i = 0; i < 3; ++i)
                {
                    for (unsigned int j = 0; j < 3; ++j)
                    {
                        lineStream >> index;
                        m_Indices.emplace_back(index);

                        if (j < 2)
                        {
                            lineStream >> separator;
                        }
                    }
                }
            }
        }
    }

    const Vertices& GetVertices() const
    {
        return m_VertexPositions;
    }

    const TextureCoordinates& GetTextureCoordinates() const
    {
        return m_TextureCoordinates;
    }

    const Normals& GetNormals() const
    {
        return m_Normals;
    }

    const Indices& GetIndices() const
    {
        return m_Indices;
    }
};
```

This code shows how to read data from an .obj file. The .obj data is stored in lines. A line that represents a vertex position starts with the letter *v* and contains three floating-point numbers representing the x, y, and z displacement of a vertex. A line beginning with *vt* contains a texture coordinate and the two floating-point numbers represent the *u* and *v* components of the texture coordinate. The *vn* lines represent vertex normals and contains the x, y, and z components of the vertex normal. The last type of line you're interested in begins with an *n* and represents the indices for a triangle. Each vertex is represented in the face using three numbers: an index into the list of vertex positions, an index into the texture coordinates, and an index into the vertex normals. All of this data is loaded into the four vectors in the class; there are accessors to retrieve the data from the class. The Geometry class in Listing 14-13 has a constructor that can take a reference to an OBJFile object and create a mesh that OpenGL can render.

Listing 14-13. The Geometry Class

```cpp
class Geometry
{
public:
    using Vertices = vector < float >;
    using Indices = vector < unsigned short >;

private:
    Vertices m_Vertices;
    Indices m_Indices;

    unsigned int m_NumVertexPositionElements{};
    unsigned int m_NumTextureCoordElements{};
    unsigned int m_VertexStride{};

public:
    Geometry() = default;
    Geometry(const OBJFile& objFile)
    {
        const OBJFile::Indices& objIndices{ objFile.GetIndices() };

        const OBJFile::Vertices& objVertexPositions{ objFile.GetVertices() };
        const OBJFile::TextureCoordinates& objTextureCoordinates{
            objFile.GetTextureCoordinates() };

        for (unsigned int i = 0; i < objIndices.size(); i += 3U)
        {
            m_Indices.emplace_back(i / 3);

            const Indices::value_type index{ objIndices[i] - 1U };
            const unsigned int vertexPositionIndex{ index * 3U };

            m_Vertices.emplace_back(objVertexPositions[vertexPositionIndex]);
            m_Vertices.emplace_back(objVertexPositions[vertexPositionIndex+1]);
            m_Vertices.emplace_back(objVertexPositions[vertexPositionIndex+2]);

            const OBJFile::TextureCoordinates::size_type texCoordObjIndex{
                objIndices[i + 1] - 1U };
            const unsigned int textureCoodsIndex{ texCoordObjIndex * 2U };

            m_Vertices.emplace_back(objTextureCoordinates[textureCoodsIndex]);
            m_Vertices.emplace_back(objTextureCoordinates[textureCoodsIndex+1]);
        }
    }
```

```cpp
~Geometry() = default;

void SetVertices(const Vertices& vertices)
{
    m_Vertices = vertices;
}

Vertices::size_type GetNumVertices() const
{
    return m_Vertices.size();
}

Vertices::const_pointer GetVertices() const
{
    return m_Vertices.data();
}

void SetIndices(const Indices& indices)
{
    m_Indices = indices;
}

Indices::size_type GetNumIndices() const
{
    return m_Indices.size();
}

Indices::const_pointer GetIndices() const
{
    return m_Indices.data();
}

Vertices::const_pointer GetTexCoords() const
{
    return static_cast<Vertices::const_pointer>(&m_Vertices[m_NumVertexPositionElements]);
}

void SetNumVertexPositionElements(unsigned int numVertexPositionElements)
{
    m_NumVertexPositionElements = numVertexPositionElements;
}

unsigned int GetNumVertexPositionElements() const
{
    return m_NumVertexPositionElements;
}

void SetNumTexCoordElements(unsigned int numTexCoordElements)
{
    m_NumTextureCoordElements = numTexCoordElements;
}
```

```
unsigned int GetNumTexCoordElements() const
{
    return m_NumTextureCoordElements;
}

void SetVertexStride(unsigned int vertexStride)
{
    m_VertexStride = vertexStride;
}

unsigned int GetVertexStride() const
{
    return m_VertexStride;
}
};
```

Listing 14-13 contains a constructor for the Geometry class that can build the geometry for OpenGL from an OBJFile instance. The OBJFile::m_Indices vector contains three indices per OpenGL vertex. The Geometry class for this recipe is only concerned with the vertex-position index and the texture-coordinate index, but the for loop is still configured to skip ahead three indices for each iteration. The vertex index for the Geometry object is the obj index divided by 3; the current vertex is constructed from the data obtained by looking up the obj vertex positions and texture coordinates for the given obj index obtained in each iteration of the for loop. The vertex indices and texture-coordinate indices in the .obj file start at 1 and not 0, so 1 is subtracted from each index to get the correct vector index. This index is then multiplied by 3 for vertex -position indices or 2 for texture-coordinate indices, because there are three elements per vertex position and two elements per texture coordinate read in from the original .obj file. By the end of the loop, you have a Geometry object with the vertex and texture-coordinate data loaded from the file. The code in Listing 14-14 shows how you can use these classes in a program to render a textured sphere that has been created and exported using the Blender 3D modelling package.

■ **Note** Most of the recipes in this book are self-contained, but the OpenGL API covers a lot of code that is necessary to carry out seemingly simple tasks. Listing 14-14 contains the Texture, Shader, and TextureShader classes covered in Recipe 14-3.

Listing 14-14. Rendering a Textured Sphere

```
#include <cassert>
#include <fstream>
#include "GL/glew.h"
#include "GLFW/glfw3.h"
#include <memory>
#include <sstream>
#include <string>
#include <vector>
```

```cpp
using namespace std;

class OBJFile
{
public:
    using Vertices = vector < float > ;
    using TextureCoordinates = vector < float > ;
    using Normals = vector < float > ;
    using Indices = vector < unsigned short > ;

private:
    Vertices m_VertexPositions;
    TextureCoordinates m_TextureCoordinates;
    Normals m_Normals;

    Indices m_Indices;

public:
    OBJFile(const std::string& filename)
    {
        std::ifstream fileStream{ filename, std::ios_base::in };
        if (fileStream.is_open())
        {
            while (!fileStream.eof())
            {
                std::string line;
                getline(fileStream, line);

                stringstream lineStream{ line };

                std::string firstSymbol;
                lineStream >> firstSymbol;

                if (firstSymbol == "v")
                {
                    float vertexPosition{};

                    for (unsigned int i = 0; i < 3; ++i)
                    {
                        lineStream >> vertexPosition;
                        m_VertexPositions.emplace_back(vertexPosition);
                    }
                }
                else if (firstSymbol == "vt")
                {
                    float textureCoordinate{};

                    for (unsigned int i = 0; i < 2; ++i)
                    {
                        lineStream >> textureCoordinate;
                        m_TextureCoordinates.emplace_back(textureCoordinate);
                    }
                }
```

```cpp
                    else if (firstSymbol == "vn")
                    {
                        float normal{};

                        for (unsigned int i = 0; i < 3; ++i)
                        {
                            lineStream >> normal;
                            m_Normals.emplace_back(normal);
                        }
                    }
                    else if (firstSymbol == "f")
                    {
                        char separator;
                        unsigned short index{};

                        for (unsigned int i = 0; i < 3; ++i)
                        {
                            for (unsigned int j = 0; j < 3; ++j)
                            {
                                lineStream >> index;
                                m_Indices.emplace_back(index);

                                if (j < 2)
                                {
                                    lineStream >> separator;
                                }
                            }
                        }
                    }
                }
            }
        }
    }
}

const Vertices& GetVertices() const
{
    return m_VertexPositions;
}

const TextureCoordinates& GetTextureCoordinates() const
{
    return m_TextureCoordinates;
}

const Normals& GetNormals() const
{
    return m_Normals;
}
```

```cpp
        const Indices& GetIndices() const
        {
            return m_Indices;
        }
};

class Geometry
{
public:
    using Vertices = vector < float >;
    using Indices = vector < unsigned short >;

private:
    Vertices m_Vertices;
    Indices m_Indices;

    unsigned int m_NumVertexPositionElements{};
    unsigned int m_NumTextureCoordElements{};
    unsigned int m_VertexStride{};

public:
    Geometry() = default;
    Geometry(const OBJFile& objFile)
    {
        const OBJFile::Indices& objIndices{ objFile.GetIndices() };

        const OBJFile::Vertices& objVertexPositions{ objFile.GetVertices() };
        const OBJFile::TextureCoordinates& objTextureCoordinates{
            objFile.GetTextureCoordinates() };

        for (unsigned int i = 0; i < objIndices.size(); i += 3U)
        {
            m_Indices.emplace_back(i / 3);

            const Indices::value_type index{ objIndices[i] - 1U };
            const unsigned int vertexPositionIndex{ index * 3U };

            m_Vertices.emplace_back(objVertexPositions[vertexPositionIndex]);
            m_Vertices.emplace_back(objVertexPositions[vertexPositionIndex+1]);
            m_Vertices.emplace_back(objVertexPositions[vertexPositionIndex+2]);

            const OBJFile::TextureCoordinates::size_type texCoordObjIndex{
                objIndices[i + 1] - 1U };
            const unsigned int textureCoodsIndex{ texCoordObjIndex * 2U };

            m_Vertices.emplace_back(objTextureCoordinates[textureCoodsIndex]);
            m_Vertices.emplace_back(objTextureCoordinates[textureCoodsIndex+1]);
        }
    }
```

```cpp
~Geometry() = default;

void SetVertices(const Vertices& vertices)
{
    m_Vertices = vertices;
}

Vertices::size_type GetNumVertices() const
{
    return m_Vertices.size();
}

Vertices::const_pointer GetVertices() const
{
    return m_Vertices.data();
}

void SetIndices(const Indices& indices)
{
    m_Indices = indices;
}

Indices::size_type GetNumIndices() const
{
    return m_Indices.size();
}

Indices::const_pointer GetIndices() const
{
    return m_Indices.data();
}

Vertices::const_pointer GetTexCoords() const
{
    return static_cast<Vertices::const_pointer>(&m_Vertices
    [m_NumVertexPositionElements]);
}

void SetNumVertexPositionElements(unsigned int numVertexPositionElements)
{
    m_NumVertexPositionElements = numVertexPositionElements;
}

unsigned int GetNumVertexPositionElements() const
{
    return m_NumVertexPositionElements;
}
```

```cpp
    void SetNumTexCoordElements(unsigned int numTexCoordElements)
    {
        m_NumTextureCoordElements = numTexCoordElements;
    }

    unsigned int GetNumTexCoordElements() const
    {
        return m_NumTextureCoordElements;
    }

    void SetVertexStride(unsigned int vertexStride)
    {
        m_VertexStride = vertexStride;
    }

    unsigned int GetVertexStride() const
    {
        return m_VertexStride;
    }
};

class TGAFile
{
private:
#ifdef _MSC_VER
#pragma pack(push, 1)
#endif
    struct TGAHeader
    {
        unsigned char m_IdSize{};
        unsigned char m_ColorMapType{};
        unsigned char m_ImageType{};

        unsigned short m_PaletteStart{};
        unsigned short m_PaletteLength{};
        unsigned char m_PaletteBits{};

        unsigned short m_XOrigin{};
        unsigned short m_YOrigin{};
        unsigned short m_Width{};
        unsigned short m_Height{};

        unsigned char m_BytesPerPixel{};
        unsigned char m_Descriptor{};
    }
#ifndef _MSC_VER
    __attribute__ ((packed))
#endif // _MSC_VER
        ;
```

```
#ifdef _MSC_VER
#pragma pack(pop)
#endif

    std::vector<char> m_FileData;

    TGAHeader* m_pHeader{};
    void* m_pImageData{};

public:
    TGAFile(const std::string& filename)
    {
        std::ifstream fileStream{ filename, std::ios_base::binary };
        if (fileStream.is_open())
        {
            fileStream.seekg(0, std::ios::end);
            m_FileData.resize(static_cast<unsigned int>(fileStream.tellg()));

            fileStream.seekg(0, std::ios::beg);
            fileStream.read(m_FileData.data(), m_FileData.size());

            fileStream.close();

            m_pHeader = reinterpret_cast<TGAHeader*>(m_FileData.data());
            m_pImageData = static_cast<void*>(m_FileData.data() + sizeof(TGAHeader));
        }
    }

    unsigned short GetWidth() const
    {
        return m_pHeader->m_Width;
    }

    unsigned short GetHeight() const
    {
        return m_pHeader->m_Height;
    }

    unsigned char GetBytesPerPixel() const
    {
        return m_pHeader->m_BytesPerPixel;
    }

    unsigned int GetDataSize() const
    {
        return m_FileData.size() - sizeof(TGAHeader);
    }
```

```cpp
    void* GetImageData() const
    {
        return m_pImageData;
    }
};

class Texture
{
private:
    unsigned int m_Width{};
    unsigned int m_Height{};
    unsigned int m_BytesPerPixel{};
    unsigned int m_DataSize{};

    GLuint m_Id{};

    void* m_pImageData;

public:
    Texture(const TGAFile& tgaFile)
        : Texture(tgaFile.GetWidth(),
            tgaFile.GetHeight(),
            tgaFile.GetBytesPerPixel(),
            tgaFile.GetDataSize(),
            tgaFile.GetImageData())
    {

    }

    Texture(unsigned int width,
            unsigned int height,
            unsigned int bytesPerPixel,
            unsigned int dataSize,
            void* pImageData)
        : m_Width(width)
        , m_Height(height)
        , m_BytesPerPixel(bytesPerPixel)
        , m_DataSize(dataSize)
        , m_pImageData(pImageData)
    {

    }

    ~Texture() = default;

    GLuint GetId() const
    {
        return m_Id;
    }
```

```cpp
    void Init()
    {
        GLint packBits{ 4 };
        GLint internalFormat{ GL_RGBA };
        GLint format{ GL_BGRA };

        glGenTextures(1, &m_Id);
        glBindTexture(GL_TEXTURE_2D, m_Id);
        glPixelStorei(GL_UNPACK_ALIGNMENT, packBits);
        glTexImage2D(GL_TEXTURE_2D,
            0,
            internalFormat,
            m_Width,
            m_Height,
            0,
            format,
            GL_UNSIGNED_BYTE,
            m_pImageData);
    }
};

class Shader
{
private:
    void LoadShader(GLuint id, const std::string& shaderCode)
    {
        const unsigned int NUM_SHADERS{ 1 };

        const char* pCode{ shaderCode.c_str() };
        GLint length{ static_cast<GLint>(shaderCode.length()) };

        glShaderSource(id, NUM_SHADERS, &pCode, &length);

        glCompileShader(id);

        glAttachShader(m_ProgramId, id);
    }

protected:
    GLuint m_VertexShaderId{ GL_INVALID_VALUE };
    GLuint m_FragmentShaderId{ GL_INVALID_VALUE };
    GLint m_ProgramId{ GL_INVALID_VALUE };

    std::string m_VertexShaderCode;
    std::string m_FragmentShaderCode;

public:
    Shader() = default;
    virtual ~Shader() = default;
```

```cpp
    virtual void Link()
    {
        m_ProgramId = glCreateProgram();

        m_VertexShaderId = glCreateShader(GL_VERTEX_SHADER);
        LoadShader(m_VertexShaderId, m_VertexShaderCode);

        m_FragmentShaderId = glCreateShader(GL_FRAGMENT_SHADER);
        LoadShader(m_FragmentShaderId, m_FragmentShaderCode);

        glLinkProgram(m_ProgramId);
    }

    virtual void Setup(const Geometry& geometry)
    {
        glUseProgram(m_ProgramId);
    }
};

class TextureShader
    : public Shader
{
private:
    const Texture& m_Texture;

    GLint m_PositionAttributeHandle;
    GLint m_TextureCoordinateAttributeHandle;
    GLint m_SamplerHandle;

public:
    TextureShader(const Texture& texture)
        : m_Texture(texture)
    {
        m_VertexShaderCode =
            "attribute  vec4 a_vPosition;                \n"
            "attribute  vec2 a_vTexCoord;                \n"
            "varying    vec2 v_vTexCoord;                \n"
            "                                            \n"
            "void main() {                               \n"
            "   gl_Position = a_vPosition;               \n"
            "   v_vTexCoord = a_vTexCoord;               \n"
            "}                                           \n";

        m_FragmentShaderCode =
            "#version 150                                \n"
            "                                            \n"
            "varying vec2 v_vTexCoord;                   \n"
            "uniform sampler2D s_2dTexture;              \n"
            "                                            \n"
```

```cpp
            "void main() {                              \n"
            "   gl_FragColor =                          \n"
            "       texture2D(s_2dTexture, v_vTexCoord); \n"
            "}                                          \n";
    }

    ~TextureShader() override = default;

    void Link() override
    {
        Shader::Link();

        m_PositionAttributeHandle = glGetAttribLocation(m_ProgramId, "a_vPosition");
        m_TextureCoordinateAttributeHandle = glGetAttribLocation(m_ProgramId,
        "a_vTexCoord");

        m_SamplerHandle = glGetUniformLocation(m_ProgramId, "s_2dTexture");
    }

    void Setup(const Geometry& geometry) override
    {
        Shader::Setup(geometry);

        glActiveTexture(GL_TEXTURE0);
        glBindTexture(GL_TEXTURE_2D, m_Texture.GetId());
        glUniform1i(m_SamplerHandle, 0);

        glTexParameteri(GL_TEXTURE_2D, GL_TEXTURE_WRAP_S, GL_REPEAT);
        glTexParameteri(GL_TEXTURE_2D, GL_TEXTURE_WRAP_T, GL_REPEAT);

        glTexParameteri(GL_TEXTURE_2D, GL_TEXTURE_MIN_FILTER, GL_LINEAR);
        glTexParameteri(GL_TEXTURE_2D, GL_TEXTURE_MAG_FILTER, GL_LINEAR);

        glVertexAttribPointer(
            m_PositionAttributeHandle,
            geometry.GetNumVertexPositionElements(),
            GL_FLOAT,
            GL_FALSE,
            geometry.GetVertexStride(),
            geometry.GetVertices());
        glEnableVertexAttribArray(m_PositionAttributeHandle);

        glVertexAttribPointer(
            m_TextureCoordinateAttributeHandle,
            geometry.GetNumTexCoordElements(),
            GL_FLOAT,
            GL_FALSE,
            geometry.GetVertexStride(),
            geometry.GetTexCoords());
        glEnableVertexAttribArray(m_TextureCoordinateAttributeHandle);
    }
};
```

```cpp
int main(void)
{
    GLFWwindow* window;

    // Initialize the library
    if (!glfwInit())
    {
        return -1;
    }

    glfwWindowHint(GLFW_RED_BITS, 8);
    glfwWindowHint(GLFW_GREEN_BITS, 8);
    glfwWindowHint(GLFW_BLUE_BITS, 8);
    glfwWindowHint(GLFW_DEPTH_BITS, 8);
    glfwWindowHint(GLFW_DOUBLEBUFFER, true);

    // Create a windowed mode window and its OpenGL context
    window = glfwCreateWindow(480, 480, "Hello World", NULL, NULL);
    if (!window)
    {
        glfwTerminate();
        return -1;
    }

    // Make the window's context current
    glfwMakeContextCurrent(window);

    GLenum glewError{ glewInit() };
    if (glewError != GLEW_OK)
    {
        return -1;
    }

    TGAFile myTextureFile("earthmap.tga");
    Texture myTexture(myTextureFile);
    myTexture.Init();

    TextureShader textureShader(myTexture);
    textureShader.Link();

    OBJFile objSphere("sphere.obj");
    Geometry sphere(objSphere);

    sphere.SetNumVertexPositionElements(3);
    sphere.SetNumTexCoordElements(2);
    sphere.SetVertexStride(sizeof(float) * 5);

    glClearColor(0.0f, 0.0f, 0.0f, 1.0f);

    glEnable(GL_CULL_FACE);
    glCullFace(GL_BACK);

    glEnable(GL_DEPTH_TEST);
```

```
// Loop until the user closes the window
while (!glfwWindowShouldClose(window))
{
    glClear(GL_COLOR_BUFFER_BIT | GL_DEPTH_BUFFER_BIT);

    textureShader.Setup(sphere);

    glDrawElements(GL_TRIANGLES,
        sphere.GetNumIndices(),
        GL_UNSIGNED_SHORT,
        sphere.GetIndices());

    // Swap front and back buffers
    glfwSwapBuffers(window);

    // Poll for and process events
    glfwPollEvents();
}

glfwTerminate();
return 0;
}
```

Listing 14-14 shows how to load and render an .obj file using the classes covered in this recipe and in Recipe 14-3. There are some differences in how the window is created in this recipe. The glfwWindowHint function specifies some of the parameters that you wish the frame buffer for the application to possess. The most important here is the depth buffer. A depth buffer works on modern GPUs by storing the normalized device coordinate of the z component from a polygon at each fragment position during rendering. You can then use a depth test to allow or disallow new color writes to the frame buffer during rendering. This is useful when rendering your sphere to ensure that the pixels rendered at the rear of the sphere don't overwrite the colors for the fragments at the front of the sphere.

Face culling is also enabled to ensure that you see only the front faces of each polygon. Polygons can have two sides: front and back. OpenGL determines whether a polygon is front facing or back facing depending on the winding order of the vertices. By default, OpenGL determines that polygons whose vertices are specified in counterclockwise order are facing the front and polygons whose vertices are specified in clockwise order are facing the back. This can change when an object is rotating, so OpenGL can drop polygons early when they aren't facing toward the camera. You can change the winding order of a front-facing polygon using the glFrontFace function if you wish.

The earthmap.tga texture obtained from http://planetpixelemporium.com/earth.html is loaded to give the sphere the appearance of the planet Earth; the sphere itself is loaded from a file named sphere.obj. You enable front-face culling by calling glEnable and passing the GL_CULL_FACE constant; the face to be culled is specified by calling glCullFace. The depth test is enabled by calling glEnable and passing GL_DEPTH_TEST; and the glClear call is passed GL_COLOR_BUFFER_BIT | GL_DEPTH_BUFFER_BIT to ensure that the color buffer and the depth buffer are both cleared at the beginning of each rendered frame.

Compiling and running the code supplied along with the data from this book's accompanying web site result in a program that renders the planet Earth as shown in Figure 14-3.

Figure 14-3. *The rendered planet Earth generated by the code in Listing 14-14*

Index

■ D, E

Get the eBook for only $5!

Why limit yourself?

Now you can take the weightless companion with you wherever you go and access your content on your PC, phone, tablet, or reader.

Since you've purchased this print book, we're happy to offer you the eBook in all 3 formats for just $5.

Convenient and fully searchable, the PDF version enables you to easily find and copy code—or perform examples by quickly toggling between instructions and applications. The MOBI format is ideal for your Kindle, while the ePUB can be utilized on a variety of mobile devices.

To learn more, go to https://www.apress.com/index.php/companion or contact support@apress.com.

CPSIA information can be obtained at www.ICGtesting.com
Printed in the USA

9 781484 201589